Watching TV with a Linguist

Television and Popular Culture
Robert J. Thompson, *Series Editor*

Other titles in Television and Popular Culture

Bigger than Ben-Hur: The Book, Its Adaptations, and Their Audiences
Barbara Ryan and Milette Shamir, eds.

Black Male Frames: African Americans in a Century of Hollywood Cinema, 1903–2003
Roland Leander Williams Jr.

Captain America, Masculinity, and Violence: The Evolution of a National Icon
J. Richard Stevens

Inside the TV Writer's Room: Practical Advice for Succeeding in Television
Lawrence Meyers, ed.

Interrogating "The Shield"
Nicholas Ray, ed.

Reading Joss Whedon
Rhonda V. Wilcox, Tanya R. Cochran, Cynthea Masson,
and David Lavery, eds.

Screwball Television: Critical Perspectives on "Gilmore Girls"
David Scott Diffrient and David Lavery, eds.

Watching TV: Eight Decades of American Television, Third Edition
Harry Castleman and Walter J. Podrazik

WATCHING TV with a LINGUIST

Edited by
Kristy Beers Fägersten

Syracuse University Press

First Edition 2016
16 17 18 19 20 21 6 5 4 3 2 1

∞ The paper used in this publication meets the minimum requirements of the American National Standard for Information Sciences—Permanence of Paper for Printed Library Materials, ANSI Z39.48-1992.

For a listing of books published and distributed by Syracuse University Press, visit www.SyracuseUniversityPress.syr.edu.

ISBN: 978-0-8156-3493-5 (hardcover) 978-0-8156-1081-6 (paperback)
978-0-8156-5395-0 (e-book)

Library of Congress Cataloging-in-Publication Data
Available from publisher upon request.

Manufactured in the United States of America

To my parents, Leroy Beers (1935–2004) and Sheila Kelly,
for subscribing to cable throughout my childhood;
to Falko and Tintin, who show promising signs
of becoming television enthusiasts; and
to King, who is in acute need of
more television in his life.

Contents

Illustrations

Figures

Tables

Acknowledgments

The Internet has become intrinsically linked with television viewing. I am grateful for the commercial streaming services currently available that have allowed the authors and me to revisit many of the featured series in this volume and to re-view and listen carefully to featured episodes. I am also grateful to fan-managed Internet websites for their full-episode transcripts, which can serve to complement the author-transcribed extracts of this volume. In particular, I would like to thank the following websites for promoting meaningful television viewing and for granting permission to use partial transcriptions: kacl.780.net, seinfeldscripts.com, and ariane devere.livejournal.com.

Each of the authors in this book deserves a special acknowledgment for their unwavering enthusiasm, collaborative spirit, patience, and lively correspondence during the many stages of publication. I am also very grateful to Philip Carr and Ben Ambridge for their sustained interest in and contributions to the volume.

I am grateful to Södertörn University's Publications Committee and English Department for supporting this volume in its final stages. I am also indebted to the anonymous reviewers, who greatly helped to improve the volume through insightful comments and targeted suggestions.

Thank you, Kimb, for listening to my editing updates, frustrations, indignations, and victories. Thank you, Karl, King, Falko, and Tintin for tolerating years of high-volume, recursive television viewing while I sought out and transcribed examples.

Finally, I have to accept that any attempt at an eloquent expression of gratitude will be inadequate at best when it comes to Deborah Manion.

For your guidance, expertise, wisdom, patience, humor, ability to recognize absurdity, and steadfast championing of this volume, I thank you, Deb, so very, very much.

Abbreviations

AAVE	African American Vernacular English
AdjP	Adjective Phrase
AdvP	Adverbial Phrase
ANC	American National Corpus
Art	Article
Aux	Auxiliary Verb
BNC	British National Corpus
CA	Conversational Analysis
COCA	Corpus of Contemporary American English
DO	Direct Object
EFL	English as a Foreign Language
ESL	English as a Second Language
GA	General American
GerP	Gerundive Phrase
InfP	Infinitival Phrase
HIMYM	*How I Met Your Mother*
IPA	International Phonetic Alphabet
KWIC	Key Word in Context
NP	Noun Phrase
NSE	Nonstandard English
P	Predicate
PartP	Participial Phrase

POS	Parts of Speech
PP	Prepositional Phrase
Prep	Preposition
RP	Received Pronunciation
S	Sentence
SATC	*Sex and the City*
SE	Standard English
SM	Speech Meaning
SV	Subject-Verb
UM	Utterance Meaning
VP	Verb Phrase
VS	Verb-Subject

Watching TV with a Linguist

Introduction

The Linguist's View of Television

KRISTY BEERS FÄGERSTEN

Why TV?

Should anyone ever dare to make the claim "I don't read books!" it would, in many social circles, be met with disbelief and disdain. Reading books is the most widely recognized sign of accomplished erudition, intellectual accountability, and, of course, basic literacy. Indeed, this volume wouldn't exist if books were not the de facto medium of academic exchange. Isn't it curious, though, that each of the glowing qualities associated with bibliophiles can just as effectively be implied by substituting the predicative proposition 'read books' with 'watch television'? In other words, to announce, "I don't watch television!" is to assert, albeit not explicitly, that one is pursuing or has already achieved sublime sophistication, having excised the basest form of entertainment from one's cultural repertoire and devoted oneself entirely to higher forms of intellectual activity. The message is clear: television is lowbrow with no cultural or educational value.

Disparaging comments about television also tend to subject it to discriminating qualifications that serve to establish a hierarchy among television genres and series. Those who claim to eschew television can thus probably be expected to qualify their position by specifying either that they do not watch 'lowbrow' television or that they watch exclusively 'quality' television. Exactly which kinds of television programming or specific series count as one or the other is, however, somewhat open to debate (see for example Claessens and Dhoest 2010). Scholars themselves grapple with both popular and academic evaluations of television as, for example, significant, worthy, quality, serious, or highbrow (Attallah 1984; Claessens and Dhoest 2010, 50–51; Thompson 1997, 11–12; Tulloch 2002, 3–5).

The authors of *Watching TV with a Linguist* reject the belief that television is devoid of value, and in their chapters they refrain from engaging in the discourse of quality. First, when television is summarily dismissed, not only does it go unrecognized for its social, political, and cultural influence, but it is also denied its value as a legitimate field of academic study. Second, although the quality and seriousness of television content can be critically evaluated and measured, they should not serve to exclude any content from academic study. This volume, based on the authors' shared belief that all television content has value and is thus a potential target of scholarly research, thus joins the growing number of scholarly publications devoted to championing the value of television and to advancing critical approaches to television content. By including linguistics in television scholarship and, simultaneously, incorporating television into linguistic scholarship, the volume aims to raise awareness about how language is used, represented, and mediated in the television context. The focus throughout the volume is on what many of the authors refer to as linguistic identities, the speech patterns of particular characters or the typical language use of a particular series.

Watching TV with a Linguist is thereby not proposed as an example of theoretical television research. As the title indicates, the authors are not television scholars but linguists, who wish to acknowledge the considerable progress of the relatively young field of television scholarship and to contribute to further advances by highlighting linguistic approaches to television language. The volume's authors understand television series as media artifacts that potentially serve as mirrors of society, forums for social and political commentary, and influential vehicles for change, but also, significantly, as multilayered examples of language in action. Each chapter thus aims to provide both television scholars and viewers with the tools required to characterize and (de)construct television language.

The choices of fictional television series featured in the chapters have not been informed by critical acclaim, nor do the contributing authors attempt to offer evaluative critique with regard to the place of the various series in the larger television landscape or within television scholarship. Instead, the series were specifically selected because the language used by one or more characters deftly illustrates certain linguistic concepts and phenomena. However, it is also the case that all of the featured series were or currently are popular, long-running, award-winning programs. While such indicators of commercial or cultural success were not criteria for being selected, it may be that successful series have a distinct linguistic fingerprint.

Watching TV with a Linguist is an educational product, and it capitalizes on television as an educational resource. However, the authors do not focus on educational television content, news broadcasting, or other forms of topic-specific programming, but explore exclusively fictional television series. Fictional television programming offers the general public an ever-increasing number of comedies and dramas (of varying degrees of quality and entertainment value) featuring a range of characters both simple and complex, irritating and irresistible, familiar and foreign. The dialogue these characters engage in is by turns sophisticated, edgy, heavy-handed, tedious, and witty, reflecting scriptwriting that can aspire to raw authenticity, aim for catch-phrase immortality, or simply capture the essence of quotidian communication. It is television characters' interpersonal interactions in the form of dialogue or narration delivered in coherent social contexts that are explored and analyzed in *Watching TV with a Linguist*.

Talking on TV

The interactions depicted on fictional television drama and comedy series are deliberately scripted and designed, or "constructed" and "prefabricated" (Chovanec 2011, 246; Dynel 2011a, 43), as a result of the premeditated, planned, and even rehearsed circumstances of television production. As such, television dialogue could be thought of as representing a communicative ideal: all participants have, potentially, equal opportunity to speak; conversational contributions are well formed, smoothly delivered, and (usually) impeccably timed; there are rarely any pauses, hesitations, interruptions, or even external disruptions; and instances of misspeaking, mishearing, or misunderstanding are unusual (Kozloff 2000; Richardson

2010). In other words, television dialogue seems to be stripped of all of the meaningless imperfections of spontaneous speech and face-to-face interaction, and instead consists of features that are at once essential and aesthetic, rendering it "polished material" (Dose 2013).

Jill Marshall and Angela Werndly (2002) argue that scripted dialogue (which they call "represented talk") "can never be a faithful or accurate reflection of actual conversation" (78). Nor, as the authors claim, do writers or directors intend for it to be so. Instead, the sole purpose of interaction or conversation between television characters is for narrative purpose and for the sake of the viewer. In other words, actors inhabit characters, who speak to each other in order to develop a story line and as a way of communicating to the audience (Bubel 2005; Short 1989)—not because they have genuine communicative goals. For this reason, television dialogue may resemble authentic conversation, but it is nevertheless regarded by some, in line with Marshall and Werndly's terminology, as merely a representation of talk, not to be confused with the real thing and thus no viable substitute for empirical data (see for example Emmison 1993; Schegloff 1988).

Conversely, others have favorably compared scripted dialogue to authentic conversation and spontaneous speech, noting the similarities and thereby highlighting realistic aspects of television dialogue. For example, two of the authors in this volume have prominently championed the comparison of television dialogue to spontaneous speech (Quaglio 2009 and Richardson 2010), showing that features of naturally occurring speech are observable to a similar extent in scripted dialogue. Other scholars take as given a great degree of similarity, working from the assumption that television dialogue is constructed with the explicit goal of being a very close approximation of naturally occurring speech (see for example Benz's 2007 analysis of the historical accuracy of the language of *Deadwood*). In other words, instead of being artificial because of the constraints of television production, scripted dialogue is assumed to be realistic or to aim for realism as a function of these same constraints (Bednarek 2010, 2012; Berliner 1999; Georgakopoulou 2000; Kozloff 2000; Piazza, Bednarek, and Rossi 2011). It is not the parameters of television production, but the underlying rules, linguistic principles, and conversational conventions of naturally occurring speech that determine the form of television dialogue (Dynel 2011a; Herman 1995; Richardson 2010). Marta Dynel (2011a) summarizes the relationship between scripted dialogue and naturally occurring speech as operating according to similar, underlying processes: "Whether intuitively employed by regular language users or carefully constructed by a script writer . . . an interaction always operates on the same linguistic resources, in accordance with deeply ingrained, and frequently only intuitively felt, communication rules" (Dynel 2011a, 44).

It is not the agenda of *Watching TV with a Linguist* to develop the authenticity debate further, but the discussion certainly underlines the relevance of this volume. It acknowledges the fact that the constraints imposed by the television context affect such aspects as the timing, delivery, clarity, and economy of interaction and dialogue, and it openly appreciates the intrinsic value of television language as concentrated, illustrative evidence of specific linguistic processes in action. This volume reminds the reader that television language is encountered on a regular basis, and thus it is a very real feature of our everyday linguistic lives. Regardless of how authentic or artificial, casual or careful, spontaneous or specifically scripted television dialogue may be, it encourages us to think about and become more aware of language: Which aspects of talk make us believe that depicted conversation is realistic or artificial? What role does language play in constructing characters, giving them identities, and distinguishing them from each other? How many of our own linguistic practices are recreated and recognizable? What kind of language use do we experience as appealing, entertaining, or innovative? In an effort to answer these questions, the need to determine conclusively the extent of realism or authenticity of television language is perhaps diminished, and instead we discover an even more significant aspect of scripted dialogue, which remains valid regardless of its form or content, namely, its dual function as both reflecting and influencing our own language use. Television language is a representation of what scriptwriters, and by extension we the viewers, understand about language, how we think it works, how we think it is used, how we think it sounds. But television dialogue can also be a model for language use: how it should work, how it should be used, how it should sound. Furthermore, the language to which we are exposed on television often works its way into our everyday interactions and discourses (Ayass and Gerhardt 2012; Dynel 2011b; Kozloff 2000; Richardson 2010), such that scripted dialogue may be based on naturally occurring speech, and naturally occurring speech may incorporate elements of scripted dialogue. Television both represents and influences our ideas about and usage of language and linguistic resources, and thus in this volume, the authors approach the language of television as one of many sources of linguistic input and exposure, all the while emphasizing its significance as a mirror of and possibly an influence on the viewer's own usage (Beers Fägersten 2012; Stuart-Smith 2011).

This volume is not the first of its kind to focus on television language, and thus its predecessors should be duly acknowledged. A few examples include book-length treatises of the characteristic language of specific series, such as the slang of *Buffy the Vampire Slayer* (Adams 2003), the Old West language of *Deadwood* (Lavery 2011), or the informal conversations of *Friends* (Quaglio 2009). Additionally, Monika Bednarek (2010); Roberta Piazza, Monika Bednarek, and Fabio Rossi (2011); and Kay Richardson (2010) all deal with television language in general, basing their analyses on various series. The scope of these previous books is deliberately narrow, in terms of either their focus on one series or their invocation of one linguistic field (such as corpus linguistics, discourse analysis, or sociolinguistics). In contrast to these and other large- and small-scale academic analyses of television language, the scope of *Watching TV with a Linguist* is broad, with regard to both the television series included and the disciplines of linguistics applied to television data. This volume also targets a broad reading audience: anyone who is interested in television *or* language. If the reader identifies as the former, then this volume will enrich the television viewing experience, making salient aspects of television dialogue that may have gone unnoticed or making clear the relationship between language and humor or drama, or identifying the role of language in character development. If the reader identifies as the latter, then this volume will serve as a wealth of examples of language in action, providing terminology and tools for description and analysis, and suggesting television resources for additional investigation. The authors hope that, by the end of the book, the television fans and the language enthusiasts will be indistinguishable.

Each chapter includes a number of different examples, in the form of transcribed extracts of dialogue. Unless otherwise indicated, all transcriptions were conducted by the chapter author(s), who accessed the featured extracts via means generally available to the reading audience, such as YouTube, network websites, paid streaming services, or on DVD. It should be noted that the transcriptions are a record of what was heard and noticed in the viewing process; scriptwriters are credited throughout the volume, but the transcriptions are not citations of a written script, from which the final, spoken dialogue in the broadcast episode can deviate. To increase accuracy, the transcribed extracts were often compared against other transcriptions available online. While there are many sites devoted to collecting episode transcripts, mostly in the form of user-generated content, the authors' transcripts in this volume were cross-referenced with those available on the websites Forever Dreaming[1] and Springfield! Springfield![2] Readers are welcome to consult both of these sites to access full episode transcripts, which often include stage directions or other paralinguistic information. However, readers are also strongly encouraged to conduct transcriptions on their own, which results in a more active and engaged viewing experience.

It is important to note that a familiarity with the featured series and episodes is not actually necessary to use and appreciate this book. The dialogue extracts featured in the examples and analyses are always introduced, explained, and contextualized, and the focus is on understanding the use and effects of language within the context of specific episodes, as opposed to developing a discussion about the series per se. Nevertheless, watching or revisiting the featured episodes subsequent to reading the chapters is recommended, because the television viewing experience promises to be even more fulfilling with the raised linguistic awareness this volume promotes.

1. http://transcripts.foreverdreaming.org/.
2. http://www.springfieldspringfield.co.uk/tv_show_episode_scripts.php.

With a Linguist, as a Linguist

Watching TV *as* a linguist means being acutely aware of just how much language permeates the television landscape. Although we watch television, thereby overtly focusing on the visual elements of the medium, we also simultaneously listen, constantly evaluating and reconciling what we see with what we hear. As a linguist-viewer, one cannot help but identify the myriad of examples of linguistic principles and phenomena that are constantly incorporated in television dialogue, sometimes simply because all language operates according to linguistic principles, but often owing to explicit construction and targeted manipulation of dialogue for dramatic and comedic effect. Watching TV *as* a linguist is thus an intensely active practice, in which the authors of this volume enthusiastically take part and which, with a bit of guidance, any viewer can learn as well.

Watching TV with a Linguist is an introduction to the study of English linguistics based on English-language television shows. Each of the chapters approaches linguistics as science in action, with comprehensive presentations of linguistic subfields, including clear explanations of relevant linguistic terminology, concepts, theory, and method, each of which is illustrated with examples from contextualized dialogues from one or more episodes of a specific drama or comedy series.

In chapter 1, "Watching the Detective: *Sherlock* and Spoken Television Discourse," Kay Richardson explains how the character of Sherlock Holmes is linguistically constructed, invoking fundamentals of spoken discourse, the ethnography of speaking, and conversation analysis. Richardson shows that, on the one hand, scripted dialogue is similar to naturally occurring speech with regard to the appearance of conversational norms. Once the norms are established, they can be exploited for dramatic purpose, such that deviations from the conventions of ordinary talk can in turn establish Sherlock as extraordinary.

In chapter 2, "Dealers and Discourse: Sociolinguistic Variation in *The Wire*," Joe Trotta introduces sociolinguistics as the study of the relationship between language and society. This chapter unpacks and explains the systematic use of nonstandard features in a social dialect, which many viewers of *The Wire* have found as compelling as it is challenging (Toolan 2011), namely African American Vernacular English.

Chapter 3, "'Back in St. Olaf . . .': Regional Variation in *The Golden Girls*," continues with sociolinguistics, but shifts the focus from social variation to regional variation. In this chapter, Jean Ann attends to the linguistic differences embodied by the series' four leading females, relating the variation in their language use to differences in their regional backgrounds.

Kristy Beers Fägersten and Hanna Sveen also consider the language use of four female friends, but from a gender perspective. In chapter 4, "SaMANtha: Language and Gender in *Sex and the City*," the authors provide a review of seminal work on gender and language, presenting qualities of male and female speech according to empirical evidence. With the help of copious examples, they explore the possibility that one of the series' four female characters is, linguistically, actually a man, and thus poses a challenge to some linguistic theories of gender.

In chapter 5, "The Pragmatics Explication: Making Sense of Nerds in *The Big Bang Theory*," authors Matthias Eitelmann and Ulrike Stange consider this popular sitcom from the perspective of pragmatic theory, illustrating how a preference for linguistic accuracy over social conventions of language use can make it difficult to be understood, and can challenge one's own ability to make sense of the other.

Michael Percillier's chapter, "Cunning Linguistics: The Semantics of Word Play in *South Park*," explores the role of lexical relationships in creating humor. The examples presented in chapter 6 illustrate how wordplay can function as a humorous aspect of an episode, or constitute its entire plot.

In chapter 7, "Word Formation in *HIMYM*," author Jessie Sams also considers how humor is achieved through linguistic means. This chapter focuses specifically on how to form new words in English, as observable in "HIMYM"—an example of a word formation process based on the featured sitcom series' title *How I Met Your Mother*.

In chapter 8, "What's the Deal with Morphemes? Doing Morphology with *Seinfeld*," Kristy Beers Fägersten picks up where chapter 7 leaves off, namely by showing how to deconstruct newly formed words. This chapter illustrates how the arc of an episode can revolve around the smallest meaningful unit of a language: the morpheme.

In chapter 9, "Channel Surfing: Tuning into the Sounds of English," Kristy Beers Fägersten presents the basics of phonetics and phonology, using the titles of a wide variety of television programs to illustrate the sounds of American English. Beers Fägersten also lingers on specific episodes that feature nonstandard pronunciations, showing how phonetic features contribute to establishing a television character's linguistic identity.

In chapter 10, "Syntax in Seattle," Gülşat Aygen demonstrates the simplicity of syntax using examples from two of television's most linguistically sophisticated characters, the Crane brothers from *Frasier*.

Once the basics of language are presented, chapters 11 and 12 introduce how language is learned. In chapter 11, "I'm Learneding! First Language Acquisition in *The Simpsons*," Kristy Beers Fägersten explores how children acquire their first language and how child(ish) language is represented on television, looking to the junior cast members of one of the longest-running American series, *The Simpsons*, for examples.

In chapter 12, "*Lost* and Language Found," Kristy Beers Fägersten and Ilaria Fiorentini then consider how people learn a second language, and how second language acquisition is represented on television, drawing from Korean speakers learning English in *Lost*.

Finally, the volume concludes with chapter 13, "The One Based on 738,032 Words: Language Use in the *Friends*-corpus." In this chapter, Paulo Quaglio explores corpus linguistics as both theory and methodology. Using a corpus composed of more than 700,000 words from the ten seasons of *Friends*, Quaglio shows how large quantities of language data can uncover significant patterns of talk in interaction. This chapter prepares readers for their own continued investigations of any of the series included in the volume, or any that are not.

Through its focus on television as the most accessible form of popular culture, this book aims to raise linguistic awareness among readers by identifying linguistics in action, thereby enabling the readers autonomously to recognize additional examples of linguistic concepts. Particular series or particular episodes illustrate linguistic phenomena, but once awareness is raised, the same phenomena can be observed in other television series and/or episodes. For this reason, each chapter concludes with suggestions for further viewing and analysis, but the reader is also welcome and encouraged to apply any of the linguistic principles or theories beyond the context of television dialogue.

Each of the chapters in *Watching TV with a Linguist* champions the use of the language of television series to learn about linguistics, and in so doing, the volume is a testament to the relevance and applicability of all linguistic fields to the analysis of television dialogue. In acknowledging its readers as active television viewers, this text has the ultimate goal of initiating them into the world of linguistics and demonstrating its relevance not only to television language, but also to any form of language use or interaction. The result each of the contributing authors aspires to is an educated reader-viewer who would not hesitate to proclaim, "I *do* watch TV!"

References

Adams, Michael. 2003. *Slayer Slang: A* Buffy the Vampire Slayer *Lexicon*. Oxford, UK: Oxford Univ. Press.

Attallah, Paul. 1984. "The Unworthy Discourse: Situation Comedy in Television." In *Interpreting Television: Current Research Perspectives*, edited by Willard D. Rowland and Bruce Watkins, 222–49. Beverly Hills, CA: Sage, 1984.

Ayass, Ruth, and Cornelia Gerhardt, eds. 2012. *The Appropriation of Media in Everyday Life*. Amsterdam: John Benjamins.

Bednarek, Monika. 2010. *The Language of Fictional Television: Drama and Identity*. London: Continuum.

———. 2012. "'Get us the hell out of here': Key Words and Trigrams in Fictional Television Series." *International Journal of Corpus Linguistics* 17(1): 35–63.

Beers Fägersten, Kristy. 2012. "Intertextual Quotation: References to Media in Family Interaction." In *The Appropriation of Media in Everyday Life*, edited by Ruth Ayass and Cornelia Gerhardt, 79–104. Amsterdam: John Benjamins.

Benz, Brad. 2007. "*Deadwood* and the English Language." *Great Plains Quarterly* 27(4): 239–51.

Berliner, Todd. 1999. "Hollywood Movie Dialogue and the 'Real Realism' of John Cassavetes." *Film Quarterly* 52(3): 2–16.

Bubel, Claudia. 2005. *The Linguistic Construction of Character Relations in TV Drama: Doing Friendship in* Sex and the City. PhD diss., Universität des Saarlandes.

Chovanec, J. 2011. "Humour in Quasi-Conversations: Constructing Fun in Online Sports Journalism." In *The Pragmatics of Humour across Discourse Domains*, edited by Marta Dynel, 243–64. Amsterdam: John Benjamins.

Claessens, Nathalie, and Alexander Dhoest. 2010. "Comedy Taste: Highbrow/Lowbrow Comedy and Cultural Capital." *Participations: Journal of Audience and Reception Studies* 7(1): 49–72.

Dose, Stefanie. 2013. "Flipping the Script: A Corpus of American Television Series (CATS) for Corpus-Based Language Learning and Teaching." In *Corpus Linguistics and Variation in English: Focus on Non-Native Englishes*, edited by Magnus Huber and Joybrato Mukherjee. Helsinki: Research Unit for Variation, Contacts, and Change in English. http://www.helsinki.fi/varieng/journal/volumes/13/dose/.

Dynel, Marta. 2011a. "Stranger than Fiction. A Few Methodological Notes on Linguistic Research in Film Discourse." *Brno Studies in English* 37(1): 41–61.

———, ed. 2011b. *The Pragmatics of Humour across Discourse Domains*. Amsterdam: John Benjamins.

Emmison, Michael. 1993. "On the Analyzability of Conversational Fabrication: A Conceptual Inquiry and Single Case Example." *Australian Review of Applied Linguistics* 16:83–108.

Georgakopoulou, Alexandra. 2000. "On the Sociolinguistics of Popular Films: Funny Characters, Funny Voices." *Journal of Modern Greek Studies* 18(1): 119–33.

Herman, Vimala. 1995. *Dramatic Discourse: Dialogue as Interaction in Plays*. London: Routledge.

Kozloff, Sarah. 2000. *Overhearing Film Dialogue*. Los Angeles: Univ. of California Press.

Lavery, David, ed. 2011. *Reading* Deadwood*: A Western to Swear By*. London: I. B. Tauris.

Marshall, Jill, and Angela Werndly. 2002. *The Language of Television*. London: Routledge.

Piazza, Roberta, Monika Bednarek, and Fabio Rossi, eds. 2011. *Telecinematic Discourse: Approaches to the Language of Films and Television Series*. Vol. 211. Amsterdam: John Benjamins.

Quaglio, Paulo. 2009. *Television Dialogue: The Sitcom* Friends *vs. Natural Conversation*. Vol. 36. Amsterdam: John Benjamins.

Richardson, Kay. 2010. *Television Dramatic Dialogue: A Sociolinguistic Study*. Oxford, UK: Oxford Univ. Press.

Schegloff, Emanuel. 1988. "Goffman and the Analysis of Conversation." In *Erving Goffman: Exploring the Interaction Order*, edited by Paul Drew and Anthony Wotton, 89–135. Oxford, UK: Polity Press.

Short, Mick. 1989. "Discourse Analysis and the Analysis of Drama." In *Language, Discourse and Literature*, edited by Ronald Carter and Paul Simpson, 139–68. London: Unwin Hyman.

Stuart-Smith, Jane. 2011. "The View from the Couch: Changing Perspectives on the Role of the Television in Changing Language Ideologies and Use." In *Standard Languages and Language Standards in a Changing Europe*, edited by Tore Kristiansen and Nicholas Coupland, 223–39. Oslo: Novus.

Thompson, Robert J. 1997. *Television's Second Golden Age: From* Hill Street Blues *to* ER*:* Hill Street Blues, Thirtysomething, St. Elsewhere, China Beach, Cagney & Lacey, Twin Peaks, Moonlighting, Northern Exposure, LA Law, Picket Fences, *with Brief Reflections on* Homicide, NYPD Blue *&* Chicago Hope, *and Other Quality Dramas*. Syracuse, NY: Syracuse Univ. Press.

Toolan, Michael. 2011. "I Don't Know What They're Saying Half the Time, but I'm Hooked on the Series: Incomprehensible Dialogue and Integrated Multimodal Characterisation in *The Wire*." In *Telecinematic Discourse: Approaches to the Language of Films and Television Series*, edited by Roberta Piazza, Monika Bednarek, and Fabio Rossi, 161–83. Amsterdam: John Benjamins.

Tulloch, John. 2002. *Television Drama: Agency, Audience and Myth*. London: Routledge.

1

Watching the Detective

Sherlock *and Spoken Television Discourse*

KAY RICHARDSON

The successful TV drama series *Sherlock* (BBC 2011–present) is the latest in a long sequence of dramatizations of Conan Doyle's short stories and novels, chronicling the adventures of the eponymous detective and his assistant, John Watson. This newest version is a British-made production, created by Steven Moffatt and Mark Gatiss, starring Benedict Cumberbatch as Sherlock Holmes and Martin Freeman as Dr. John Watson. This chapter will show how spoken discourse helps in the creation and maintenance of 'Sherlock Holmes' as a plausible character in this specific textual context, and does so drawing on three main approaches to the analysis of spoken discourse:[1] the ethnography of communication, in which I consider what kind of talk TV drama dialogue might be in relation to its context(s); Erving Goffman's dramaturgical model of social interaction, in which I focus on impression management, stance, and identity/persona; and conversation analysis, focusing on turn-taking and turn-sequencing, including the communicative effects to be derived from different ways of orienting to principles of talk-construction.

The 'spoken discourse' referred to in the title of the chapter is of interest not only to linguists and sociolinguists. Anthropologists, sociologists,

1. Despite its obvious relevance, I have left out the approach known as pragmatics, with Herbert Paul Grice's (1975) theory of conversational implicature as a key reference, because chapter 5 of this volume is specifically concerned with the discussion of television dialogue from the perspective of linguistic pragmatics.

philosophers, literary critics, and others have also contributed to this research field, and so this chapter is intentionally interdisciplinary. It helps to think of this topic as the study of talk—and to remember that there is more to talk than just its words. It is multimodal, because speakers use their faces and their bodies as well as their voices. Some 'conversations', in real life or in drama, can take place without any words at all. When Sherlock and John are separately transported to Buckingham Palace by the British security services ("A Scandal in Belgravia"[2]), their first encounter in this new location involves nonverbal expressions from John that ask, 'Why are we here?' and responding expressions from Sherlock that answer, 'No idea'. Despite the lack of words, it is hard to misunderstand the meaning of the interchange.

Spoken discourse is a more theoretical expression for 'talk', and like all theoretical terms, there is an academic rationale for it. Because this is a linguistics book, I will explain the rationale in linguistic terms. The high-level term 'discourse' is needed to cover *all* forms of extended linguistic expression, and to do so in a way that prioritizes the study of language *use* (see, for example, Johnstone 2008). But there are only a few generalizations that can be made about discourse at this overarching level. The really interesting studies of discourse find it essential to discriminate, and one important discrimination is between different *modes* of language use. Speech is a sound-based mode whereas writing is a sight-based mode. Spoken discourse can be *monologic*, like lectures and political speeches. Or it can be *interactive*, co-constructed by two or more people whose contributions are created in response to one another and to their communicative situation. Or it can be a mixture of both—a short address, followed by questions and answers, for example. In literate cultures like ours, a lot of monologic 'talk' is actually composed in advance, in writing.

I want to start from the question of what kind of talk we can expect to find in TV drama. It should already be obvious from my account of spoken discourse in the preceding paragraph that TV drama talk complicates the simple picture in which it is the monologic talk, which is likely

2. Written by Steven Moffat.

to be pre-scripted, and the dialogic, interactive talk, which is composed in real time. TV drama dialogue is pre-scripted interactive talk. The first approach to spoken discourse I will discuss is the one known as the ethnography of communication or ethnography of speaking, because this is the approach best suited to the discussion of talk in context.

Spoken Discourse in Context

Although there is now an expanding literature on the language of drama (see references in this volume's introductory chapter, and also Mandala 2007), many analysts do not provide any specific discussion of drama dialogue within their general accounts. The artificiality of drama dialogue seems to disqualify it for particular attention. It is pretend talk, not the real thing: if we discuss it at all it might be in terms of how 'realistic' it is, how faithful to the real-world genres on which it is based. But this is only part of the story. Drama talk is only artificial at one level. Audiences may watch and listen to a police interview in an episode of *Law and Order*; it's undoubtedly artificial in its relation to real police interviews, but it is real enough in relation to other programs and other dramas. In media-saturated societies, we are exposed to enormous amounts of discourse of this sort, which has contextual parameters of its own. So the obvious place to begin is not directly by discussing the language, but by discussing *contexts* of spoken language use. The ethnographic approach to spoken discourse is specifically designed for this purpose.

Sociolinguistic research in the ethnographic tradition focuses on particular social communities, studying how they use language and paying as much attention to the context as to the words. To facilitate comparisons (both of different communities and of different uses), it is valuable to have a standard set of categories for identifying and discussing the parameters of the social context. The most well-known category schema is the one originally developed by Dell Hymes in the 1970s. Hymes's schema uses the word *SPEAKING* as a mnemonic device for differentiating the important contextual variables: the 'S' refers to the physical setting of the speech event; the 'P' refers to its participants; the 'E' to its ends (purposes); the 'A' to the Act Sequence or order in which things are done/said; the 'K' to the Key, for example, serious or joking; the 'I' to the Instrumentalities or choices of modes, channels, language varieties, and so forth; the 'N' to the Norms of interaction (what's allowed and disallowed, what interpretations are permissible); and the 'G' to Genres (Hymes 1974). Obviously there is an element of contrivance in this schema, artfully manipulated to fit the mnemonic device: nevertheless it has proved its heuristic usefulness over the years and is still widely cited.

How might the SPEAKING schema apply to talk in TV drama? It has a double application, first to the context of the drama and second to the varying contexts of the fictional events depicted in that drama as a communicative event. I will refer to these as the outer and the inner contexts respectively. Because TV drama is mediated communication, not face-to-face, any idea of a *single context* is very problematic. For media artifacts, there are contexts of production, and there are quite separate contexts of reception. Both have been studied ethnographically (though by media scholars, not sociolinguists); ethnographies of production trace the processes by which creative decisions are made and put into practice, while ethnographies of reception sample individuals or households and inquire into their viewing practices, experiences, and readings. Features of the audiovisual text might be 'communicative' as between drama and audience but not as between characters. When Sherlock is in the act of deducing, his mental processes are sometimes rendered as untethered written words moving around the screen, like animated versions of the thought bubbles in cartoon strips. This is a use of mode that would come under Hymes's category of instrumentalities.

Within the dramatization, the inner contexts are creations of the fiction. There are scenes set in hospitals, in morgues, out on the streets, in Sherlock's apartment, in hotels, in police stations, and so on. Participants include journalists, police officers, taxi drivers, pathologists, newspaper proprietors, members of the security services, politicians, and others. Purposes, keys, and genres vary too; the latter include press conferences, speeches, interviews, and conversations of different kinds.

Elizabeth Stokoe's 2008 research interestingly shows how an outer context, in the form of studio audience laughter, is responsive to features of turn management by the characters (inner context), thus operating across the boundary separating the inner and the outer. For example, 'odd' patterns of interaction, especially when juxtaposed with more appropriate ones, cue laughter in recordings of *Friends* episodes. Stokoe's research paradigm works for certain kinds of sitcoms, which typically (though not universally) are filmed before a live studio audience whose audible responses are accessible on the broadcast soundtrack, even though these responses are also susceptible to 'enhancement' in the interests of entertainment values. Data of this type are not available for other kinds of TV production, and of course the reactions of the studio audience and those of the domestic audience are not necessarily the same.

Dramatists have to consider not only where to set the action but also how audiences will recognize the settings and bring to bear the appropriate interpretative *schemata*. A schema is a cluster of properties that readers, listeners, and audiences already know about generic situations, entities, and events. Because they already have this 'default' information, they can supply it even when the text does not. They know what to expect, though their expectations can be disrupted. This approach to textual interpretation has roots in the cognitive theory of Roger Schank and Robert Abelson (1977), though it has been developed and used in a variety of ways including in relation to drama (Culpeper 2001). Using schematic knowledge in this way represents a kind of collaboration between dramatist and viewer. The knowledge comes from the viewer but the dramatists must work to trigger it, in the ways that they configure the scene, the participants in it, and the language they use.

Drama dialogue has to make sense to an audience (outer context) while displaying characters who make sense to one another (inner contexts). Characters know who they are and what their business is. If audiences can apply a schema to what they are hearing, they too should be able to understand events that would otherwise be cryptic to outsiders (though schematic association is only one way to make cryptic exchanges comprehensible). Audiovisual drama has resources of set design and costume, as well as language, to ensure that audiences apply the appropriate schema, and sometimes there are very few gaps to be filled in.

Toward the start of episode 1 of *Sherlock* ("A Study in Pink"[3]) there is a police press conference. The configuration of the scene—with privileged speakers behind a desk, a seated audience facing them, cameras clicking, mobile phones chirruping, statements from the key speakers followed by question-and-answer sequences—makes it easy to identify the scene for what it is and therefore to understand its purposes.

If dramatists rely on audiences' schematic knowledge, do characters within the drama similarly rely on one another? In fact, it is better to ask whether dramatists have any interest in showing them doing so, given that characters only exist to serve the purposes of their creators. The answer is that there can be dramatic value in showing characters come up with *mistaken* schemata, as when Sherlock and John visit a restaurant so that they can spy on a neighboring establishment. The host at the restaurant reads the scene schematically as a romantic date, and attempts to enhance the occasion with flowers and candles. John in particular is very keen to correct this misinterpretation.

Spoken Discourse as Social Interaction

Another approach to spoken discourse is rooted in the work of Erving Goffman, and sociolinguists are indebted to his dramaturgical model for the understanding of impression management in everyday social interaction (Goffman 1955), to his use of the frame concept (Goffman 1974) and to his ideas on footing (Goffman 1981). The account offered in this section is indebted to ideas about participation in dramatized media discourse developed by, among others, Claudia Bubel (2005), Marta Dynel (2011a), and Monika Bednarek (2011a).

There is some irony in starting from Goffman in the context of a book about talk in drama productions, because one of the things that Goffman fostered was the idea of everyday behavior, including talk, as itself a matter of performance. Drama, for Goffman, was a source metaphor that helped us to better understand real life, particularly the efforts that speakers make in impression management. We as humans listen to what each other is

3. Written by Steven Moffat.

saying, but we don't take it all at face value, and so we are also attentive to unconscious meanings given off through choice of words, through pronunciation (accent), through paralinguistic cues (broadly speaking 'tone of voice', in everyday parlance), through facial expression, and through body language, that tell us more about who the other person 'really' is, what s/he 'really' thinks, and what s/he 'really' feels—which might be very different from what is actually said in so many words. Impression management is the idea that, actually, those other signs can also be controlled, can be made to say—that is, convey—what their producer means them to say. The producer may prefer that the recipient does not realize the extent of the control. If people form impressions of one another through tuning in to aspects of their interactional behavior, then so too do audiences, in the outer context, as they 'eavesdrop' on character speech. As Bubel (2005) has shown, audiences can also form impressions of relationships *between* characters, as they witness both sides of interactional exchanges.

There may be limits to impression management. Sherlock Holmes apparently thinks there are, but with Irene Adler (the initial villain in "A Scandal in Belgravia") he has to access the physiological level to find the truthful signs, those that have escaped their producer's conscious control. Irene has previously given the impression that she is romantically/sexually interested in Sherlock Holmes. However, as example 1 shows, it is important for her to project in the denouement that she countermands that impression.

Example 1:

IRENE: Oh dear God. Look at the poor man. You don't actually think I was interested in you? Why? Because you're the great Sherlock Holmes, the clever detective in the funny hat?

(He steps even closer to her, their bodies almost touching.)

SHERLOCK: *(softly)* No.

(He reaches out and slowly wraps the fingers of his right hand around her left wrist, then leans forward and brings his mouth close to her right ear.)

SHERLOCK: *(in a whisper)* Because I took your pulse.

(Flashback to Irene kneeling in front of him at the flat and putting her hand on top of his, then him turning his hand over and resting his fingertips on the

underside of her wrist. In the present, Irene frowns in confusion, while Sherlock tightens his grip a little around her wrist.)

SHERLOCK: *(softly into her ear)* Elevated; your pupils dilated.

(Dialogue transcript provided by Ariane DeVere, http://arianedevere .livejournal.com/; used by permission.)

Within the drama, the racing pulse and the dilated pupils tell the truth; the words may not. Impression management cannot command biology—though in the flashback scene there would have been no need for Irene to try. The physiological evidence then corroborated the overt discourse, so it is the current denial that is incredible. It takes the presence of mind of a character like Sherlock—rationally in control, 'detecting' when others are succumbing to emotional reactions—to focus on biological evidence at what was ostensibly a tender moment.

The question of Sherlock's own impression management is interesting too. His job of course requires him to lie and to adopt disguises as the occasion demands (for instance, posing as a mugged clergyman in "A Scandal in Belgravia," a persona designed to gain admittance to Irene Adler's house). In counterpoint to these strategic self-creations is the 'real' Sherlock, and he is meant to come off as a person who is indifferent to one particular subtype of impression management, because he is indifferent to other people's feelings. He seemingly lacks the sensibility that makes most people try to respect others' faces, dignity, and moral standing, as they expect their own to be respected, and to manage their interpersonal relations accordingly. This kind of impression management is known as 'facework,' and its use in spoken discourse analysis also goes back to Erving Goffman (Goffman 1955; see also Brown and Levinson 1987). From this interpretative perspective, Sherlock's rudeness to other people is unintentional; it is just a consequence of his lack of effort with respect to ritual aspects of spoken interaction. This is evidence, perhaps, of a slightly autistic disposition; in "The Hounds of Baskerville,"[4] sidekick John Watson refers to Sherlock's Asperger's condition, albeit behind his back and

4. Written by Mark Gatiss.

not entirely seriously. But it is more complicated than that, given that there is no doubt that Sherlock is aware of this character 'defect', suggesting that he could control it if he wanted to.

In "His Last Vow,"[5] John has to take Sherlock to get tested for drug consumption, and there are a number of people involved in the visit, for different reasons. After the drug test, the group breaks up; John and Sherlock take a taxi together back to his apartment.

Example 2:

(Sherlock frowns and looks around the cab and then out of the back window.)

SHERLOCK: Hang on—weren't there other people?

JOHN: Mary's taking the boys home; I'm taking you. We did discuss it.

(Sherlock raises his eyes upwards as if trying to remember.)

SHERLOCK: People were talking, none of them me. I must have filtered.

JOHN: I noticed.

SHERLOCK: I have to filter out a lot of witless babble. I've got Mrs. Hudson on semi-permanent mute.

(Dialogue transcript provided by Ariane DeVere, http://arianedevere.livejournal.com/; used by permission.)

Our hero understands his own behavior; indeed he talks as if it is justified. Much of other people's talk is just "witless babble" that has to be filtered out. Facework and politeness are evidently for Sherlock not relevant considerations against the strength of this conviction.

Another of Goffman's contributions to the study of social interaction is the concept of footing to describe the different alignments that participants can have to the talk they are producing and receiving. It turns out that the everyday term *speaker* is too simplistic, and Goffman invites us to think in more accurate ways about what he terms the "production format" of talk. For any speaker, alignment is partly a question of one's social role—teacher, customer, friend, significant other, and so forth. But it is also a question of discursive responsibility. Whenever the character Sherlock delivers a line in the drama, he, Sherlock, as well as Benedict Cumberbatch

5. Written by Steven Moffat.

and the writers (credited writers include Steven Moffatt, Mark Gatiss, and Stephen Thompson) all have some responsibility. Cumberbatch's voice and body are used to deliver the lines. He is thus the animator in Goffman's terms. Moffatt, Gatiss, or Thompson compose the language: that makes them the authors. 'Sherlock' is the 'person' who has decided what to say and is responsible for the thought that it conveys. In that respect he is the principal. These three communicative roles are all part of speakerhood: frequently, perhaps normatively, they combine in the same person for any given utterance, but they can be analytically separated and they can also be separated in practice. Anyone can be an 'animator' and repeat words composed by others, though there is a difference between reciting words with commitment to the meaning (a poem at a funeral, perhaps) and reciting them in a wholly detached way, as when reading newspaper articles out loud to a visually impaired companion. Following Goffman's logic, the poem-reader would be not only an animator, but also a principal, though not an author—the sentiments of the poem would represent the sentiments of the speaker, as a mourner. The news-article reader would be just an animator—neither author nor principal. Other permutations are also possible. In the context of a literate culture, authorship can exist without animation/performance; that is, 'utterances' can be written rather than spoken, and they can combine with principality (my story, my words) or be separated from principality/principalhood (in professional contexts this is called ghostwriting).

Of course, because 'Sherlock' does not exist (hence the scare quotes) and his lines of dialogue are just part of a larger whole, his principality is of a devolved kind. The true principal, of the text as a whole at the outer level, is the author: Moffat, Gatiss, Thompson, or a combination thereof, depending on the episode. This underscores the important theoretical point that although the default production format for talk in general may be the one in which author, animator, and principal coincide in the same individual, this is not a necessary state of affairs. The communicative roles can be distinct, as they are for *Sherlock* in the ways I have described.

Within the inner world of the drama, Sherlock and others do exist, and for these characters-as-people, the default production format applies most of the time. Sherlock and the others are usually author, animator, and principal of their own words. Occasionally one of them might read out a newspaper headline or a text message (John Watson does some of this at the start of "The Hounds of Baskerville"). They then become animators of texts in which principality and authorship belong with someone else. But these cases are the exception, not the rule, and the footing shifts are always very clearly signaled. This kind of disjuncture is put to extraordinary use in "The Great Game" episode.[6] The villain, Moriarty, abducts innocent people and booby-traps them with explosives. He keeps them hostage until Sherlock solves a crime-puzzle. Each hostage in turn then telephones Sherlock to set the puzzle and taunt him. The words and thoughts are those of Moriarty, but the speech is that of the hostage, reading aloud a word at a time, with a distinctive reading-style intonation that would be puzzling without this contextualization.

There are comparable complexities to take into account in thinking about what it means to be a hearer of spoken discourse. Goffman deals with these under the heading of participation framework. He is particularly interested in differentiating between various kinds of listening work, given that not everyone who hears speech is intended to do so, or expected to respond. In multiparty settings, the idea would be that any utterance takes account of a virtual 'line' between those who are understood to be giving some attention to a speaker—the ratified hearers, and those who are present but excluded from the speech event—the bystanders whose access to the occasion is recognized by the participants, and the overhearers, whose access is not acknowledged. Among the ratified hearers, one or more of them would be an addressee, specifically targeted as the person(s) for whom the utterance is intended. Among the overhearers, a subgroup might be wholly invisible to the participants—these would be the eavesdroppers. Not everyone is satisfied with the classification as originally proposed by Goffman (see, for example, Dynel 2011a), but everyone recognizes that 'listening to' and 'hearing' talk have an organizational complexity that is important to acknowledge. For an example of how production format can be exploited dramatically, consider the following:

6. Written by Mark Gatiss.

Sherlock has been pretending he is not interested in a case that Mycroft wants him to investigate. Instead, John takes on the inquiry. A body was found on a railway line, but with very little blood, considering the nature of the injuries. John muses out loud about the possible reasons for this. There is no addressee, no ratified participant, no apparent bystander, either to him or to the TV audience. Then Sherlock comes into the shot. He has been listening, and now joins in.

Example 3:

SHERLOCK: Points.

JOHN: Yes.

SHERLOCK: Knew you'd get there eventually. West wasn't killed here, that's why there was so little blood.

(Dialogue transcript provided by Ariane DeVere, http://arianedevere.livejournal.com/; used by permission.)

As with production format, there are considerations here that relate to the outer level of the drama and its audience, questions, perhaps as to whether and when audiences should be regarded as overhearers rather than ratified listeners in Goffman's terms, especially now that TV productions can be consumed in such a variety of ways: via broadcast experience (first run or repeat), via hard disk distribution, or via digital download. Are all of these consumers ratified listeners, for all time, or only some of them? Where should the line be drawn?

Within the fiction, considerations of listenership become potentially relevant in scenes involving more than two of the characters. In some of these scenes, all the bodies who populate the scene are participants to the talk in some sense, even if they have no lines. When the talk takes place in locations displayed as 'public' (on the streets and in bars, cafés, and restaurants), the bodies and voices of characters are distinct from the bodies and voices in the surrounding space—these 'others' are actors hired as extras to create the necessary visual and aural realism.

Dell Hymes's contextual SPEAKING mnemonic, discussed earlier, invites us to think, in the first instance, about how parameters of the context influence the forms of language that are used in the talk. Discourse analysts are aware, though, that the influence can run in the other direction. The forms of the talk may contain within them clues about how the context should be understood. If participants and witnesses can be brought to agree, or deemed to agree, then the talk can be heard as *constituting* the context. The material environment can be bracketed out, or else (re)interpreted in terms of what fits the talk. Contexts, given or constructed, provide interpretative frameworks for episodes of interaction, within which utterances can be inserted that break frame or otherwise disrupt that context. Such utterances will be marked in some way through their form, their content, or some combination of the two. This is part of what Hymes understands as keying. The matrix will be in one key, the embedded sequence in a different one, and there will be clues to signal transitions. As language users we learn to recognize, for example, the clues that separate serious statements from comic or ironic ones, even if we are unable to say exactly what those clues are.

The concept of stance (Englebretson 2009; Jaffe 2009) is closely related to that of key. Stance-taking is defined by Jaffe as "taking up a position with respect to the form or content of one's utterance" (Jaffe 2009, 3): like key, stance needs not remain constant throughout a whole text. Jaffe also sees a relationship between stance and identity, which is very pertinent here: that social identity may be seen as the accumulation of stances taken over time (Jaffe 2009, 11). For example, cumulative expression of a cynical stance on the part of a speaker creates, for people who know him/her, the identity of a cynic as a personality trait. While 'identity' is the preferred term when talking about real people, in order to maintain the distinction I will use the term 'persona' in relation to fictional ones for the rest of this section. For other published research on characterization in TV drama, see Bednarek 2010, 2011b; Pearson 2007; Richardson 2010.

Deriving identity/persona from stance should be easier for drama than it is for real life, for two reasons. First, audiences know that a dramatic mastermind is controlling his or her characters' behavior: audiences are intended to draw particular conclusions about persona, as part of understanding the drama as a whole. Second, it is presumed that the encounters between audience and characters are complete: the audience has all the relevant evidence to form an appropriate character assessment (this presumption is not beyond question, however, especially in relation to soap opera and other long-form serial drama in which viewers may dip in and out rather than watch every episode).

The art of the dramatist is in judging just how much stance repetition is sufficient to underwrite a character-construct, and to do so while balancing the need for characterization against some of the other demands on dialogue such as: advancing the plot, explicating the narrative, identifying the characters, creating humor and other special effects, allowing performers to give virtuoso performances, anchoring the production in time and place, and sustaining realism (see Kozloff 2000 for a full list of functions for dramatic dialogue in movies). If there has been sufficient investment by dramatists in that repetition, their payoff will be that they will then be able to surprise us by meaningfully showing a participant acting 'out of character', speaking and acting in ways that violate the construct, inviting our speculation on what lies behind the deviation.

Earlier in this chapter I raised the possibility that the 'autistic' persona presented by Sherlock was for him a choice, not a pathological condition beyond conscious control, a by-product of privileging truth and knowledge over relationships. The stance he adopts routinely gives off signs of indifference toward the feelings of other people. Because the dramatists have invested so much effort into making sure viewers understand that Sherlock is reliably like this, they can from time to time surprise audiences by showing that he can be more like other people.

The following example, from "A Scandal in Belgravia," displays both 'autistic' Sherlock and 'sensitive' Sherlock. The scene takes place at a Christmas cocktail party held in Sherlock and John's Baker Street apartment. One of the guests is Molly Hooper, a pathologist who works professionally with Sherlock from time to time and who has a crush on him. She has brought Christmas gifts to the party and Sherlock notices one of them:

Example 3:

SHERLOCK: I see you've got a new boyfriend, Molly, and you're serious about him.

MOLLY: Sorry, what?

SHERLOCK: In fact, you're seeing him this very night and giving him a gift.

JOHN: *(quietly, exasperated)* Take a day off.

LESTRADE: Shut up and have a drink.

SHERLOCK: Oh, come on. Surely you've all seen the present at the top of the bag—perfectly wrapped with a bow. All the others are slapdash at best. It's for someone special, then. The shade of red echoes her lipstick—either an unconscious association or one that she's deliberately trying to encourage. Either way, Miss Hooper has lurrrve *[sic]* on her mind. The fact that she's serious about him is clear from the fact she's giving him a gift at all. That would suggest long-term hopes, however forlorn; and that she's seeing him tonight is evident from her make-up and what she's wearing.

(Smiling smugly across to John and Jeanette, he starts to turn over the gift tag attached to the present.)

Obviously trying to compensate for the size of her mouth and breasts . . .

(He trails off as he looks down at the writing on the tag. Written in red ink, the greeting reads:

Dearest Sherlock

Love Molly xxx)

MOLLY: You always say such horrible things. Every time. Always. Always.

(As she fights back tears, Sherlock turns to walk away . . . but then stops and turns back to her.)

SHERLOCK: I am sorry. Forgive me. *(softly)* Merry Christmas, Molly Hooper.

(He leans forward and gently kisses her on the cheek. It's a sweet and beautiful moment, which is instantly ruined by the sound of an orgasmic sigh. Molly gasps in shock.)

(Dialogue transcript provided by Ariane DeVere, http://arianedevere.livejournal.com/; used by permission.)

The audiences can be expected to experience a powerful appreciation of Sherlock's gesture because of the contrast with his normal behavior, including the behavior immediately preceding it. It had not occurred to him that he was the intended recipient of the carefully prepared gift. And now the dramatists lay on the character surprise: Sherlock apologizes.

There is sincerity in the performance. He then gives Molly a ritual peck on the cheek, as any friend might do on being given a Christmas gift. But what is ritual for normal people can be understood as much more meaningful when performed by 'autistic' Sherlock. Genuine contrition for interpersonal offense is an extraordinary stance for the Sherlock that we have come to know, and even ritual politeness, from him, is rather shocking.

Spoken Discourse: Taking Turns

A change of perspective is required now in order to engage with the next set of concepts, all of which have to do with the sequencing of utterances in interactive talk. It is important to start from a recognition of how interactive talk in drama differs from its counterpart in real life. The difference originates from the fact that dialogue is pre-scripted, and the authorship separated from the animation in Goffman's terms (see above), whereas everyday talk is composed in real time, with authorship and animation conflated. As a result, while interactive everyday talk is genuinely co-constructed, its dramatic equivalent is not, though it must sustain an illusion of co-creation in the interest of realism and credibility.

Sociologists became interested in conversation when they realized that it was a form of human social behavior that was essentially orderly, even though there was no top-down, authorized set of rules that speakers had been taught to follow. Explaining the basis of this orderliness then became a major project, under the auspices of Conversation Analysis (CA). The basic principles that research uncovered include, for instance, the precept that conversationalists follow a one-person-at-a-time convention, with self-selection of the next speaker when a turn ends, unless the current speaker pre-selects the next one: "What do you say to that, Mr. Holmes?" would be a question that pre-selects Sherlock as the next speaker. If Sherlock does take the next turn, this satisfies the conversation's local organization, and if anyone else takes Sherlock's turn, something accountable has happened. Because speakers cannot always judge correctly when a turn has ended, and because in multiparty groups more than one speaker may self-select at the same time, the occurrence of overlapping talk is something that the model predicts, though it also recognizes orderly ways of restoring the floor to a single person. These ideas date back to a key 1974 article by Harvey Sacks and his colleagues (Sacks et al. 1974); it's important to add that the universality of this set of principles has been contested (for example, Coates 1996).

All of this is hard to demonstrate in drama dialogue in which the one-person-at-a-time rule is even more strictly observed than in its everyday counterpart. This is partly because dramatists work with a simpler mental model of what real conversation is like than the one proposed by Sacks and colleagues. It is also because anything more realistic would be at the expense of comprehensibility by the audience. When talk overlaps, it is not really possible to give equal attention, in real time, to what all participants are saying. In dramatic contexts, if it is important for the audience to hear everything, then it is also important to ensure that the macro conditions make that possible. And so the dramatist, not the characters, creates the order of speaking turns. There is no need for characters to compete for the floor, because the participants that the dramatist keeps silent have nothing to say that the audience needs to hear. To be convinced of the extent of the difference between drama talk and its counterpart, it's interesting to compare the dialogue in a *Sherlock* episode with a production commentary. These commentaries have become familiar bonus material in DVD box sets, where a finished production is overlaid with an additional sound recording of people (normally actors, directors, and other members of the production team) discussing the text scene by scene. The *Sherlock* DVD commentaries are very hard to follow at points, because of the extent of competition for the floor and the resulting overlap of turns.

The CA study of turn-taking principles has also paid attention to the relations between turns, noting, for example, that when a speaker designs an utterance as a question, this sets up an expectation that the next speaker will design their utterance as an answer to this question. Pairs of related utterances such as question-answer or greeting-greeting have been termed 'adjacency pairs'. The most orderly kinds of sequence that can be produced by this system are the ones that so obviously and naturally conform to this default option that it seems there is nothing to say about them:

Example 4:

JOHN: What are we doing here, Sherlock? Seriously, what?
SHERLOCK: I don't know.
("A Scandal in Belgravia")

But non-answers can be orderly too: when a question receives another question by way of response, the implication is that the second question is relevant to the first question's answer in some way. They can, for example, be requests for clarification of the first question. Instances of this pattern can be found in dramatic data, including *Sherlock*:

Example 5:

SHERLOCK: Where is she? -> FIRST PAIR PART OF ADJACENCY PAIR ONE.
JOHN: Where's who? -> START OF FIRST SIDE SEQUENCE. FIRST PAIR PART OF ADJACENCY PAIR TWO.
SHERLOCK: The woman. That woman. -> END OF FIRST SIDE SEQUENCE. SECOND PAIR PART OF ADJACENCY PAIR TWO.
JOHN: What woman? -> START OF SECOND SIDE SEQUENCE. FIRST PAIR PART OF ADJACENCY PAIR THREE.
SHERLOCK: The woman. The *woman* woman! -> END OF SECOND SIDE SEQUENCE. SECOND PAIR PART OF ADJACENCY PAIR THREE.
JOHN: What, Irene Adler? She got away. No one saw her. -> END OF SEQUENCE. SECOND PAIR PART OF ADJACENCY PAIR ONE.
("A Scandal in Belgravia")

When the second question has been answered, the ground has been cleared for an answer to the first. John can't answer the question "Where is she?" until he knows whom Sherlock is talking about. Sherlock eventually gives enough information for John to work that answer out for himself, and then John can answer the original question. This pattern involves an embedded adjacency pair, a side sequence, consisting of the second question and its follow-up turns, and is one of the recognizable more extended structures that we can expect to find in supposedly 'free-flowing' talk as well as in dramatic imitations of such talk. Stokoe (2008) has applied this kind of analysis to talk exchanges in the American sitcom *Friends;* as mentioned previously, Stokoe's interest is specifically in how particular exchange patterns cue laughter on the part of the TV audience.

The existence of rules for turn exchange and turn sequence provides a basis for understanding how speakers become accountable for the choices they make in their interactional exchanges. Other things being equal, when speaker A in a conversation asks a question, the next utterance by speaker B is the answer to that question, unless it can be heard as doing ground-clearing work in the manner of a side sequence. Speaker A's question sets up an interpretative frame from which there is no real escape for speaker B. Whatever she says will be interpreted in terms of that frame. Not speaking does not escape the frame. It becomes an accountable action in its own right. Speaker A (or someone else) can choose to request an account or assume it: "Did you hear me?" or "Why are you refusing to talk to me?" are both very plausible responses to a non-answer. Taking a turn, but talking about a different topic, will also be treated as accountable: "Don't change the subject!"

Although talk in TV drama does proceed according to the same basic principles, as comprehensibility requires, dramatists have additional options. They can, for example, cut away in the middle of an ongoing conversation to another scene in a different time/place. In those cases, audiences won't know if a question was answered or an account requested for a non-answer. Dramatic considerations may also favor giving audiences rather than characters the responsibility for deciding what kind of account makes sense of a non-response or an unsatisfactory one.

The following sequence is offered partly as an example of an unsatisfactory talk exchange, that is, one that requires some repair work as it progresses to bring the talkers back to order, and partly as an example in which the interpretative work is slightly different for the participants and for the audience. The context for this sequence is from the episode "His Last Vow," when Sherlock enlists John's help on a case. John meets Sherlock at the apartment that the two of them shared before John got married. Despite the early morning hour, John finds a woman in the apartment: his wife's friend Janine. Janine is obviously very comfortable in the apartment, even helping John navigate what was once his own kitchen. Janine and Sherlock are behaving like lovers, and when John asks, incredulously, "You have a girlfriend?" Sherlock promptly and frankly replies, "Yes, I have." While John tries to process this informat ion, Sherlock debriefs him dramatically on the case. Before Janine heads off to work, she suggests that John and his wife join Sherlock and her for dinner some evening. She and Sherlock then share an intimate good-bye, after which the following dialogue between Sherlock and John ensues (lines numbered for ease of reference):

Example 6:

1 SHERLOCK: You know Magnussen as a newspaper owner, but he's so much more than that. He uses his power and wealth to gain information. The more he acquires, the greater his wealth and power. I'm not exaggerating when I say that he knows the critical pressure point on every person of note or influence in the whole of the Western world and probably beyond. He is the Napoleon of blackmail and he has created an unassailable architecture of forbidden knowledge. Its name is Appledore.

(During this monologue, Sherlock moves across the room, to his computer, where he pulls up a picture of Appledore and shows it to John)

2 JOHN: Dinner.

3 SHERLOCK: Sorry, what, dinner?

4 JOHN: Me and Mary, coming for dinner . . . with . . . wine and . . . sitting.

5 SHERLOCK: Seriously? I've just told you that the Western world is run from this house, and you want to talk about dinner?

6 JOHN: Fine, talk about the house.

Conversation analysts have a procedure that involves looking at the next utterance to see how a preceding one was interpreted: speakers have to display, in their utterances, what they took previous utterances to be doing, and those displays constitute the orderliness of the talk, including any necessary repairs when someone indicates that something disorderly has happened. In this case, analysts might say something along these lines:

- Sherlock's "Sorry, what, dinner?" (line 3) displays that he has heard John's "Dinner" as an unsatisfactory/incomprehensible response to his own prior monologue about Magnussen and Appledore.

- John's utterance in line 4 displays that, for him, line 3 was Sherlock's request for elaboration of a cryptic line 2.
- Sherlock's line 5 displays first that he now understands John's point, but second that he rejects it as a satisfactory contribution to the conversation (indeed, as an attempt to change the subject).
- John's line 6 displays his abandonment of the 'dinner' topic and acceptance of the 'Appledore' topic.

However, this account of the moves in the dialogue is incomplete without a (speculative) assessment of the interpretative work that the TV audience is asked by the dramatists to do as they engage with this sequence. The audience needs to hear "Dinner," line 2, as a perfectly understandable response by John not to the monologue—which, the exchange suggests, has barely penetrated his consciousness—but by what John has seen and heard just before that interruption. Sitting on Sherlock's lap, Janine had suggested that the two couples get together for a meal one evening, at her place. So, for the audience, if not for Sherlock, "Dinner," line 2, displays John's astonishment at what Janine's invitation suggests about Sherlock. This is an incomprehensible change not only in Sherlock's persona, from celibate to the male half of a heterosexual couple, but also in John's own social relationship with Sherlock's, which might now include suburban socializing. The request for clarification at line 3 does not disrupt this focus of attention: line 4 is just a more elaborate display of John's incomprehension. Only after Sherlock's repair work in line 5 does John put his incomprehension aside to collaborate in a more orderly way with his colleague.

The foregoing discussion suggests that CA procedures on their own may not be very well suited to the recognition of such double-layered interpretative work, when the set of hearings that are present in the manifest data themselves needs to be understood in a larger context of hearings that analysts and audiences make. (See also Mick Short's [1981] influential study of dramatic dialogue with reference to its layered character). Conversation analysts are interested in hearings that, in being displayed by participants, affect the *construction* of the talk, move by move. The hearings of audience members, whether these are discourse analysts or regular consumers of the TV show, appear to have no such constitutive effects: the published text was completed long before they became involved.

The relevance of the CA approach here is that it gives us a way to discuss the kind of repair work that goes on in talk. Speakers' displays of incomprehension and dissatisfaction are signs of their reactions to conversational disorderliness, and evidence that disorder can and should be repaired. They collaboratively remedy disorder in the ways that they hold one another accountable for deficiencies, as Sherlock holds John accountable for the incomprehensible "Dinner." In the wider, dramatic context it then becomes appropriate to relate particular realizations of disorder and repair to the narrative context that has produced it. In this case, Sherlock's established celibacy and bohemian lifestyle form a context against which John's sudden discovery that he may be repudiating both allows audiences to enjoy not only the sidekick's astonishment, but also the discursive form in which this astonishment is realized and negotiated in the scene. (It turns out that Sherlock has strategically cultivated a relationship with Janine, actually a chaste one, despite her willingness to take it further, because her status as personal assistant to Magnussen will help Sherlock's investigation. But that's another story.)

Discussion

It does not matter how many characters describe Sherlock as a genius or as a sociopath (as he describes himself). For such descriptions to be credible, he has to be shown *being* those things, partly in what he does, in solving crimes, and partly in how he uses talk. His intellect is performed through rapid-fire monologues of deductive inference from physical clues, cross-referenced with his own general knowledge and some occasional help from the Internet. A good example of how Sherlock does this can be witnessed in the first phase of the scene in which he offends Molly, cited previously. To display his (debatably) pathological traits, it is not just his own language that we need to examine, but his patterns of interaction with other characters. When Sherlock apologizes to Molly for the face-threatening implications of his deductions about her love life, audiences appreciate the significance of such out-of-character sensitivity. When John produces disorderly talk by saying "Dinner" at that particular point in the exchange, viewers use his breach of the conventions to appreciate just how stunned the doctor is at the very idea of Sherlock and Janine as a couple behaving in conventional, sociable ways. Spoken discourse in drama has been contrived so as to produce these effects, and the extent of the contrivance should not be forgotten. But the contrivances are based on principles and constraints that are the same for this form of talk as for its real life correlates. All talk is created in negotiation with a context, which requires some kind of ethnographic grounding. All talk accommodates considerations of face and impression management, which Goffman's dramaturgical principles can help us to understand. And all talk is constructed in reference to the goal of orderliness, though arguably it is the disorderly talk that is the most interesting, because of the reflections it can provoke on the reasons for the disorder. That these principles can be exploited to create characters like Sherlock is an indication of their value as shared communicative resources.

Suggestions for Further Viewing and Analysis

1. Benedict Cumberbatch's Sherlock has some character traits in common with Jim Parson's Sheldon from *The Big Bang Theory* (see chapter 5). Both have a level of intelligence at or approaching genius, and both are either uninterested in and/or unaware of social customs that ideally are accompanied by ritualistic talk. In both *Sherlock* and *The Big Bang Theory,* Sherlock and Sheldon are often responsible for communicative breakdowns, such that others do not understand their contributions or Sherlock and Sheldon do not understand others' contributions. Consider how such breakdowns are constructed in talk, as well as how their repairs are initiated and executed.

2. In the *Seinfeld* episode "The Merv Griffin Show,"[7] Kramer discovers (in a dumpster) studio furniture and set décor that he recognizes from *The Merv Griffin Show,* a daytime talk show, which ran during the late 1960s until the mid-1980s. Kramer installs the studio set in his own apartment, and thereafter proceeds to socialize according to the conventions of

7. Written by Bruce Eric Kaplan.

a daily talk show, in other words, the cluster of properties that one associates with this talk show context. What are these properties or features of the talk show schema that Kramer invokes in "The Merv Griffin Show"? What kind of indications are there that Kramer's interlocutors are not aware or accepting of the talk show schema, and how are these repaired?

3. The title characters of the series *The Gilmore Girls* (2000–2007) are thirtysomething Lorelai Gilmore and her teenaged daughter, Rory. Lorelai is particularly verbose and prone to bouts of frantic speech, while Rory is an adept and accustomed conversational partner, who easily engages with Lorelai in rapid-fire interaction. Speedy spoken discourse is a hallmark of *The Gilmore Girls,* as evidenced by the series' tagline, "Life's short. Talk fast." This tagline also presupposes talk, and the plethora of conversations between Lorelai and Rory cover the range of banal to intimate. It is obvious that Lorelai and Rory share a close personal relationship, to which their perfectly aligned verbal behavior attests. In the excerpt below from "Kiss and Tell,"[8] Rory does not want to be alone in the living room with her date, Dean, so she comes to the kitchen to fetch Lorelai. Consider how form and content contribute to establishing and identifying the intimacy of Lorelai and Rory: What do they talk about? What kind of self-disclosure does Rory engage in? What kind of sentence structure characterizes Rory's contributions, and how are they conducive to fast-paced speech? How do Lorelai's side-sequences in lines 4 and 6 suggest new information?

1 RORY: He's sitting there and he's watching the movie and he's perfect and he smells really good.

2 LORELAI: What?

3 RORY: He smells really good and he looks amazing and I am stupid. I said thank you.

4 LORELAI: Whoa, whoa, whoa. You—you said thank you?

5 RORY: When he kissed me.

6 LORELAI: Wai— he kissed you again? What is he just out of prison or something?

8. Written by Jenji Kohan.

7 RORY: No, not now. Yesterday? At the store?

8 LORELAI: Oh alright, strike the prison comment. So wait he kissed you and you said thank you?

9 RORY: Yes.

10 LORELAI: Well that was very polite.

11 RORY: No it was stupid. And I don't know what I'm doing here. You're sitting in the kitchen. What kind of chaperone are you?

12 LORELAI: Me? I'm not trying to be a chaperone. I'm trying to be a girlfriend.

13 RORY: Well switch gears 'cause I'm freaking out here!

(Transcribed by Kristy Beers Fägersten)

References

Becnarek, Monika. 2010. Telecinematic Discourse: Approaches to the Language of Films and Television Series. Amsterdam: John Benjamins.

———. 2011a. "Expressivity and Televisual Characterisation." *Language and Literature* 20(1): 3–21.

———. 2011b. "The Stability of the Televisual Character. A Corpus Stylistic Case Study." In *Telecinematic Discourse: Approaches to the Language of Films and TV Series,* edited by Roberta Piazza, Monika Bednarek, and Fabio Rossi, 185–204. Amsterdam: John Benjamins.

Brown, Penelope, and Steven Levinson. 1987. *Politeness. Some Universals in Language Usage.* Cambridge, UK: Cambridge Univ. Press.

Bubel, Claudia. 2005. *The Linguistic Construction of Character Relations in TV Drama: Doing Friendship in* Sex and the City. PhD diss., Universität des Saarlandes.

Coates, Jennifer. 1996. *Women, Men and Language: A Sociolinguistic Account of Gender Difference in Language.* London: Pearson Education.

Culpeper, Jonathan. 2001. *Language and Characterization: People in Plays and Other Texts.* London: Routledge.

Dynel, Marta. 2011a. "Revisiting Goffman's Postulates on Participant Statuses in Verbal Interaction." *Language and Linguistics Compass* 5(7): 454–65.

———. 2011b. "'I'll Be There for You!' On Participation-Based Sitcom Humour." In *The Pragmatics of Humour Across Discourse Domains,* edited by Marta Dynel, 311–33. Amsterdam: John Benjamins.

Englebretson, Robert. 2009. *Stancetaking in Discourse.* Amsterdam: John Benjamins.

Goffman, Erving. 1955. "On Face-Work: An Analysis of the Ritual Elements in Social Interaction." *Psychiatry: Journal for the Study of Interpersonal Processes* 18:213–31.

———. 1974. *Frame Analysis: An Essay on the Organization of Experience*. London: Harper and Row.

———. 1981. *Forms of Talk*. Philadelphia: Univ. of Pennsylvania Press.

Grice, Herbert Paul. 1975. "Logic and Conversation." In *Syntax and Semantics 3: Speech Acts*, edited by Peter Cole and Jerry Morgan, 41–58. New York: Academic Press.

Hymes, Dell. 1974. *Foundations of Sociolinguistics: An Ethnographic Approach*. Philadelphia: Univ. of Pennsylvania Press.

Jaffe, Alexandra. 2009. *Stance: Sociolinguistic Perspectives*. Oxford, UK: Oxford Univ. Press.

Johnstone, Barbara. 2008. *Discourse Analysis*. 2nd ed. Malden, MA: Blackwell.

Kozloff, Sarah. 2000. *Overhearing Film Dialogue*. Oakland: Univ. of California Press.

Mandala, Susan. 2007. *Twentieth-Century Dialogue as Ordinary Talk*. Farnham, UK: Ashgate.

Pearson, Rebecca. 2007. "Anatomising Gilbert Grissom: The Structure and Function of the Televisual Character." In *Reading* CSI: *Crime TV Under the Microscope*, edited by Mary Allen, 39–56. London: I. B. Tauris.

Richardson, Kay. 2010. *Television Dramatic Dialogue: A Sociolinguistic Study*. New York: Oxford Univ. Press.

Sacks, Harvey, Emmanuel Schegloff, and Gail Jefferson. 1974. "A Simplest Systematics for the Organization of Turn-Taking for Conversation." *Language* 50(4): 696–735.

Schank, Roger, and Robert Abelson. 1977. *Scripts, Plans, Goals, and Understanding: An Inquiry into Human Knowledge Structures*. Oxford, UK: Lawrence Erlbaum.

Short, Mick. 1981. "Discourse Analysis and the Analysis of Drama." *Applied Linguistics* 2(2): 180–202.

Stokoe, Elizabeth. 2008. "Dispreferred Actions and Other Interactional Breaches as Devices for Occasioning Audience Laughter in Television 'Sitcoms'." *Social Semiotics* 18(3): 289–307.

2

Dealers and Discourse

Sociolinguistic Variation in The Wire

JOE TROTTA

As a way of introducing this chapter, consider the following excerpt from the television series *The Wire*, in which a young, African American resident of Baltimore, Maryland (portrayed in the show as a low-level drug dealer on a street corner) recalls an encounter he had with a white family who were sightseeing in the city:

Example 1:

> YOUNG MAN: Yeah, so we out on Carrollton, this ol' white motherfucker and his wife roll up, he's like, "young man, you know where the Poe House is?" I'm like, "Unc, you kiddin'? Look around, take yo' pick." So, the old man, he's like, "the Poe House. The Edward *[sic]* Allen Poe House." . . . I'm like, "I don't know no Edward Allen Poe." The man look at me all sad and shit like I let him down . . .

("All Due Respect"[1])

How do we interpret this reported discourse and how do we make sense of the response to the question about the location of the Poe house? Those who are familiar with the dialect of American English known as African American Vernacular English (or simply AAVE) will surely appreciate the skill of the scriptwriters in producing the dialogue in this

1. Written by Richard Price and David Simon.

example. In AAVE, the word *poor* would be pronounced in a way almost identical to *Poe*,[2] giving a satirical twist to the exchange; that is, the young man's answer to the question posed by the tourist can be seen as meaning something like 'You must be kidding me. Just take a look around, everybody in this neighborhood is poor, just choose any house'.

This example also shows that when the creative staff involved in producing a TV series works on scripted speech, the ways in which languages and dialects are used are often not only very striking and innovative, but also illustrative. In example 1 above, the variation in pronunciation that would lead an AAVE speaker to saying *Poe* rather than *poor* does not derive directly from a simple correlation with a regional variant of the language, as we discover in chapter 3; the dialect in question is related to at least one social variable. In this case it is most likely linked to ethnicity. This assumption is supported by the presence of other linguistic features of AAVE in example 1, namely so-called copular deletion (the dropping of a copular verb BE) that results in *we out on Carrollton* rather than *we were out on Carrollton*, the double negative *I don't know no Edward Allen Poe*, and the irregular subject-verb agreement in *the man look at me* rather than *the man looks at me*.

In this chapter, we examine the linguistic subdiscipline of sociolinguistics with the aid of the television program *The Wire*. The series, written and produced for the premium cable network HBO, which intentionally defines itself in opposition to ordinary network TV as summed up in its famous *it's-not-TV-it's-HBO* catchphrase, and broadcast between 2002 and 2008, pivots around typically interrelated criminal cases worked by the Major Crimes Unit in the predominately African American city of Baltimore.[3] *The Wire* is known for its narrative complexity, its broad and varied characters from all layers of society, its shifting thematic arcs, and, not least, its gritty realism and attention to detail. Be it the minutiae of criminal investigations, the spirit-crushing dysfunction of various

2. Compare these pronunciations with that of *auditor* in chapter 3.

3. According to the 2009 US Census Bureau statistics, the black population of Baltimore, Maryland, is 63.2 percent (quickfacts.census.gov/qfd/states/24/24510.html).

institutional machines, the rules of 'the game' (incarnated as street life, political maneuvering, the legal system, police loyalty, the school-system, the media, and so forth) or the subtleties of various linguistic milieux, *The Wire* uncompromisingly immerses the viewer in the world of its protagonists.

The main author and creative force behind the series is David Simon, who is not only a Baltimorean himself, he also worked for twelve years as a reporter for the *Baltimore Sun* newspaper, primarily on the police beat, giving him an insider perspective to almost all the institutions explored in the show. Simon's goal was to create an engaging, true-to-life portrayal of the city and the streets of Baltimore; it was filmed in Baltimore, many of its characters are based upon real personages from the city, and numerous actors are, in fact, from Baltimore.[4] The language is replete with colloquial speech, slang, nonstandard grammar, colorful metaphors, and local humor. Blake Ethridge (2008) comments on Simon's choice of Baltimore for the show in the following manner:

> Locating *The Wire* in Baltimore gives the show particularity and character, or as locals might say, charm. Baltimore is a poor, second-tier city that has seen rough times since World War II. De-industrialization, suburbanization, segregation and globalization have not been kind to the city. At least 40,000 buildings are now vacant, many abandoned as the population shrank to less than two-thirds of its peak. Also, crime and drugs have besieged the city, and the homicide rate is a constant problem. It is also a city with a long, fascinating history and a quirky, vital culture. Yet, stepping back a bit, Simon is as much interested

4. Interestingly enough, despite the number of genuine Baltimore residents, several of the actors who play main characters are from elsewhere, most notably Dominic West who plays James "Jimmy" McNulty, and Idris Elba, who plays Russell "Stringer" Bell, both of whom are from England. In personal appearances and interviews, both West and Elba have clearly British accents, which are very different from those of their characters on *The Wire*. West's character is central to the show, but not to this study, so his language is not examined here. Speech delivered by Elba has been avoided if possible, or alternatively, included if the usage is not controversial.

> in accurately and caringly depicting the character and difficulties of his city as he is in projecting a criticism of the ideas and myths of America. (152–53)

Lisa Kelly (2009, 4), on a similar note, mentions the relation between the use of local actors and the dialect used in *The Wire*: "the use of locals within the supporting cast of *The Wire* lends an authenticity to the programme that marks it out as distinctive. The often impenetrable accents and highly specific colloquial vernacular make no concessions to the average viewer but instead demand their attention and commitment."

Given this background and the integral role of language and dialects in the series, *The Wire* provides an excellent platform to discuss selected regional and social dialect features and how these examples can be used to illuminate some important concepts in sociolinguistics.

Sociolinguistics

Phrased as simply as possible, sociolinguistics is the study of the interrelationship between language and society. It studies how language varieties differ between groups of people in relation to specific social variables, such as ethnicity, socioeconomic status, religion, profession, gender, level of education, age, and so forth. One of the fundamental tenets of sociolinguistic research is that language is variable and changing, which logically entails that in this discipline, language is not viewed as homogeneous—not for the individual user and not within or among groups of speakers who use the same language. Thus a sociolinguistic perspective on language use and variation will examine how regional, social, and situational variables relate to how we choose to package a message (sometimes intentionally, sometimes not) in terms of dialect, style, and register, and, conversely how such packagings affect the ways in which we assess, interpret, and often judge communication and the speaker(s) behind it.

Consider now the following exchange in which a character in *The Wire* called Snoop Pearson (an African American female and hardened, ruthless hit-woman for the Stanfield drug organization) discusses the different qualities of nail-guns with a store employee, presumably a clerk, who is an unnamed, middle-aged white male with no gang connections (in this example, turns are numbered for easier reference):

Example 2:

1 CLERK: Ah, I see you got the DeWalt cordless. Your nail gun . . . Clerk gestures to Snoop's nail gun . . . DeWalt 410.

2 SNOOP: Yeah. The trouble is, you leave it in a truck for a while, need to step up and use the bitch, the battery don't hold up, you know?

3 CLERK: Yeah, cordless'll do that. You might want to consider the powder-actuated tool. The Hilti DX 460 MX or the Simpson PTP . . . these two are my Cadillacs. Everything else on this board is second-best, sorry to say. Are you contracting, or just doing some work around the house?

4 SNOOP: No, we work all over.

5 CLERK: Full time?

6 SNOOP: No, we had about five jobs last month.

7 CLERK: Ah. With that rate, the cost of the powder-actuated guns justifies itself.

8 SNOOP: You say "power"?

9 CLERK: Powder.

10 SNOOP: Like gunpowder?

11 CLERK: Yeah. The DX 460 is fully automatic, with a .27-caliber charge. Wood, concrete, steel to steel . . . she'll throw a fastener into anything. And for my money, she handles recoil better than the Simpson or the P3500. Now, you understand what I mean by recoil?

12 SNOOP: Yeah, the kickback. I'm wit you.

13 CLERK: That's right.

14 SNOOP: .27 caliber, huh?

15 CLERK: Yeah, not large ballistically, but for driving nails, it's enough. Any more than that, you'd add to the recoil.

16 SNOOP: Man, shit. I seen a tiny-ass .22 round-nose drop a nigga plenty of days, man. Motherfuckers get up in you like a pinball, rip your ass up. Big joints, though . . . big joints, man, just break your bones, you say, "Fuck it." I'm gonna go with this right here, man. How much I owe you?

17 CLERK: $669 plus tax. *(Snoop hands clerk money)* No no, you just pay at the register.

18 SNOOP: Nah, man, you go ahead and handle that for me, man. 'N keep the rest for your time.

19 CLERK: This is $800.

20 SNOOP: So what, man? You earned that buck like a motherfucker. Keep that shit.

("Boys of Summer"[5])

Both speakers are from the same city, so the linguistic differences here are not regional, and of the social variables that could be of interest, many, like gender and age, are not of any observable relevance. For most people, it is immediately obvious that the different language variants used by the clerk and by Snoop are primarily related to social class and ethnicity. Judging from this snippet, the store clerk seems to master a higher linguistic style and his language in this example conforms more closely to mainstream English, more precisely to a variant that is typically referred to as 'Standard English' (a concept that is discussed in more detail in the sections below). The clerk also appears to show a better awareness of the appropriate register for this situation, namely the type of language use one might expect from a specific professional community, such as doctors, lawyers, bankers, and sales clerks, or among any discourse community (professional or otherwise) that has shared interests or hobbies, for example chess enthusiasts, video gamers, skateboarders (see below for further clarification). Most notably, the clerk displays a greater repertoire of topic-related jargon, which, in contrast to register, refers more specifically to terminology/vocabulary associated with a profession, a hobby, or simply a topic. Examples of jargon in example 2 would be terms like *powder actuated, recoil, ballistically,* among others.

In contrast, Snoop's language is peppered with slang and vulgarisms (like *bitch, ass, fuck, nigga,* and *motherfucker*), and it is packaged in nonstandard grammatical forms (*the battery don't hold up* [line 2], *I seen a tiny-ass*

5. Written by David Simon and Ed Burns.

.22 round-nose [line 16], *How much I owe you?* [line 16], and so forth). She also relates some of the technical jargon (for example, *recoil, clerk* [line 11]) to her own informal or slang understanding of the relevant term (*kick-back* [line 12]). Without any prior knowledge of the interlocutors involved and based only on this example, most people would, rightly or wrongly, assume that the clerk is the speaker with the better education (and possibly better occupational status given that he could be the store manager), whereas the opposite assumption would be made about Snoop. The store clerk himself may be uncertain about Snoop's educational background given that he feels it is necessary to explicitly ask if she understands the word *recoil* (line 11).

Accent and Dialect

Because this chapter is about variation, specifically social variation, it includes an analysis of social dialects. 'Dialects' are language varieties that can be identified by distinguishing features on all levels of language, that is, pronunciation, grammar, and vocabulary. This means that 'accents', or variations in pronunciation, count as aspects of dialects, but they are not the same thing as dialects. In other words, someone may speak with an accent, while not speaking a dialect, but if someone is speaking a dialect, then that person is, by definition, exhibiting an accent. If, for example, I say *to-MAY-toe*, and you say *to-MAH-toe*, we probably have different accents. However, a person who says *to-MAH-toe*, lives in a flat, and goes *on holiday* probably speaks a dialect of British English, whereas someone who says *to-MAY-toes*, lives in an *apartment*, and goes *on vacation* is probably a speaker of an American dialect of English. Unfortunately, the distinction between accent and dialect is often muddled by the fact that many people, including some professionals, use the two terms interchangeably. Furthermore, given that accent and dialect are often used incorrectly or carelessly to refer to how 'others' talk (often in a disparaging way, as highlighted in the first of the Suggestions for Further Viewing and Analysis in chapter 3), it is worth noting that all speakers of a language speak with a particular dialect—which entails a particular accent. In other words, all language users speak in a dialect and they all have an accent that is a part of that dialect.

Style and Register

In contrast, 'style' and 'register' are labels used to describe variations in language use that a given speaker may choose to employ depending on context, situation, and the speaker's personal preferences. Style refers to the ways in which a speaker can vary an utterance in terms of formality—it is a scalar notion with 'informal' and 'formal' at either ends of the scale. For example, the following expressions vary in their formality going from most informal to most formal: *the old man is knackered -> Dad is shattered -> Dad is tired -> father is exhausted*. Register is the variant of language used in association with the discourse practices of a particular speech community, that is, a group of people who share certain norms and expectations about language use (see also below for more discussion). Register is often associated with shared interests or a specific topic (say, for instance, stamp collecting, football, politics, ballet, music, finances, and so on), communicative situation (one register might be appropriate for a public speech or a courtroom appearance, yet another when chatting with friends online), or professional activity (the specific language choices made within the spheres of different professions such as banking, computer programming, academics in a specific discipline, and so forth). In principle, a register can be a reflection of the linguistic conventions of any speech community that is united by some mutual activity and whose speakers share certain core assumptions/values associated with that activity.[6] The term *jargon* may also be used this way and it is a widely recognized synonym to register,

6. It is worth noting that in much of the literature, *register* and *style* are used interchangeably. In the present context, however, the terms overlap but are not identical. A given register, as the term is used above, includes all aspects of language such as grammar, pronunciation, vocabulary, and so forth, and thus can correspond with a formal or informal style, but the two terms are best used to cover different perspectives on language use. For example, the register of doctors, lawyers, and bankers would typically be characterized as a formal style, whereas the register of, say, skaters and hip-hoppers might be labeled as informal. However logical it might seem to equate style with register, it would be more accurate to say that a formal style is a part of the professional register of bankers, lawyers, and doctors, and an informal style is a part of the register of skaters and hip-hoppers.

though here it is reserved for specific vocabulary choices/terminology rather than for other aspects of language.

Standard English

One of the central concepts of English sociolinguistics is so-called Standard English (or SE), not because SE is a pure, ideal form of the language against which other variants should be measured, but rather because it is a nebulous notion that causes confusion about what the appropriate model is (or should be) for 'correct' English usage. The problems of defining terms like 'standard' and 'nonstandard' dialect are well noted in the literature and there is no simple, straightforward way to differentiate between them. More often than not, when one labels a dialect as standard or nonstandard, that distinction is based on a social judgment of the dialect in question rather than on its linguistic merits.

Questions of style, register, and even medium (namely, the channel of communication, such as spoken vs. written) can also confuse the issue, that is to say one can speak of 'informal' Standard English or standard 'spoken' English that many speakers may mistakenly view as nonstandard. Considering the limited scope of this chapter, it is not necessary, desirable, or practical for the present purposes to present a categorical and complete definition of Standard English or Nonstandard English (NSE), but rather we can take as our starting point a commonsense definition of SE as the (officially or unofficially) recognized 'prestige' dialect used primarily in written language and formal speech situations. It is typically the variant that has been codified in school grammars, usage books, dictionaries, and other reference works and perpetuated in schools and other formal institutions as the norm to which language learners should aspire. A working definition of NSE can then be established in opposition to this basic notion of SE; broadly speaking, nonstandard English is any dialect (for example, regional or social) that differs from Standard English.

It is worth noting in connection with the purpose of this chapter that the use of nonstandard English dialects in scripted speech and other fictional texts is by no means a new phenomenon. Classic authors such as Shakespeare, Dickens, and Twain often put a great deal of effort into creating credible dialogue for characters with various regional and social backgrounds. Unfortunately, however, the nonstandard language used in these and similar works is often not only intended to make the speech more realistic, it may also be intended to reveal something about the characters' other traits and moral qualities. As such, fictional representations of nonstandard dialects are well worth studying, especially when they occur in so-called popular culture contexts because these representations play an important part in the social construction of certain group identities (like, for example, ethnicity), and they can serve a crucial role in shaping, communicating, and understanding social categories such as race, gender, and social class, among others (see also Bucholtz [2001] and Bucholtz and Lopez [2011] for further discussion on the portrayal of race in Hollywood films).

Speech Community and Social Networks

A speech community (sometimes also referred to in the literature as a discourse community) is, as mentioned above, a group of people who typically interact with each other through some shared activity (for instance, a sports activity, a profession, a political belief, fandom, pet ownership, music, role-playing, and so forth), and they often share specific forums for communicating with each other (such as regular meetings, e-mail lists, and message boards). Members of any given speech community will typically have ways of communicating with each other that are characterized by explicit and implicit conventions, and because of this the linguistic packaging of a message by the group's members will, intentionally or not, mark them as belonging to that particular community (most notably via vocabulary choices, but also through other language choices). A speech community will typically have shared values, assumptions, and beliefs, at least in terms of the group members' relationship to the activity that defines and unifies the group. An activity that seems to create a speech community in *The Wire* is street crime, which is a part of the everyday lives of many of the characters in the show (consider, for instance, the numerous terms used in connection with drugs and drug dealing,[7] for

7. *Re-up* means a delivery of drugs to a dealer (dealers keep a limited amount of drugs at any given time; when that supply runs out, they then need a *re-up*), a *package* is a large shipment of drugs (usually to gang middlemen who store it and distribute it to dealers), and

example *re-up, package, product, slinging, grinding, bangin'*). It is important to keep in mind in this context that a person is almost always a member of more than one speech community.

In contrast to a speech community, a social network is a less tangible system of connections between people whose links to each other are not necessarily based on a shared activity. In other words, some individuals within the same social network may also share the same speech community; for instance they may be linked together through the same workplace or university course in which they participate, but because the structure of the social network is based on social interactions between individuals, the network will typically bridge several different speech communities. Clusters in the network (which can be considered micro-networks in themselves) can be organized based on specific, key individuals or groups, but a large-scale envisioning of a social network would include many connections that go beyond any individual speech community. An example of a social network in *The Wire* would be the group of dockworkers featured in season 2 of the series, some of whom are involved in smuggling activities (like Frank Sobotka or Thomas "Horseface" Pakusa), others of whom are involved in drug dealing (like Ziggy and Nicky Sobotka), and others who are simply relatives (like Joan Sobatka) or just ordinary dockworkers (for example, Nat Coxson or Vernon "Ott" Motley) and are not active in the smuggling or drug businesses.

In sociolinguistics, a social network can be characterized as 'tight' or 'loose' depending on how members interact with each other. For example, a small business whose employees are also friends who interact with each other outside of work would be a tight social network, whereas a loose network could be group who are unified for some limited purpose, say a charity-based online community, but in which most people only interact with one or two other members. In a tight network, links between members are typically strong and deliberate and usually maintained and

---

product is the particular variant of a drug that is available at a given time. *Slinging, grinding,* and *bangin'* can all be used to refer to selling drugs on the street, though *bangin'* is often used as a larger concept referring to criminal activities in general (cf. *gang bangin'*).

renewed through social contact, but in a loose network the links are normally not as clear or deliberate and may arise by chance, for example via an online dating service or based on an invitation to an event from an online social network (like Facebook or Instagram). A social network as a theoretical construct can be viewed from several angles, and the exact scope of a given network, in terms of relationships between its members, will depend on the perspective of the analyst and one's purpose in devising a model of the network: a micro-perspective of a social network might focus on the tight-knit connections of a particular cluster of individuals in the network. For the sake of simplicity, let's say that for a specific family (for example, the Barksdale family), a meso-perspective would widen that scope, taking into account, for example, a whole neighborhood or extended group (for example, the Barksdale drug organization), and a macro-perspective would increase the scope even further, for example viewing the network relationships in even larger groups (such as the criminal underground of Baltimore or the population of an entire city).

Consider now figure 2.1, which provides a visualization of the hierarchical organization of the Barksdale social network.

As one might expect, the relative looseness or tightness of a given network or speech community may affect the way individuals communicate within that network/community. In a tight network with a clear network identity, individuals who are central to (or who want to be perceived as central to) that network may speak a certain way, and those ways of speaking will influence others. In other words, certain language choices will relate to an individual's desire to be identified with that network. Members who have a looser connection to the network will typically not adopt such conventions or may only use them in specific situations (see also style-shifting, below). In this way, the use of an extreme variety of AAVE, along with other aspects of a register related to crime and drug dealing, is positively reinforced and becomes self-perpetuating. Because central, key members of the gang use such language, it becomes prestigious and thus serves as a model for imitation by other gang members.

Another relevant concept is that of so-called in-groups and outgroups. A member of an in-group is someone who belongs to the group under examination. In our case it would be an AAVE from Baltimore with

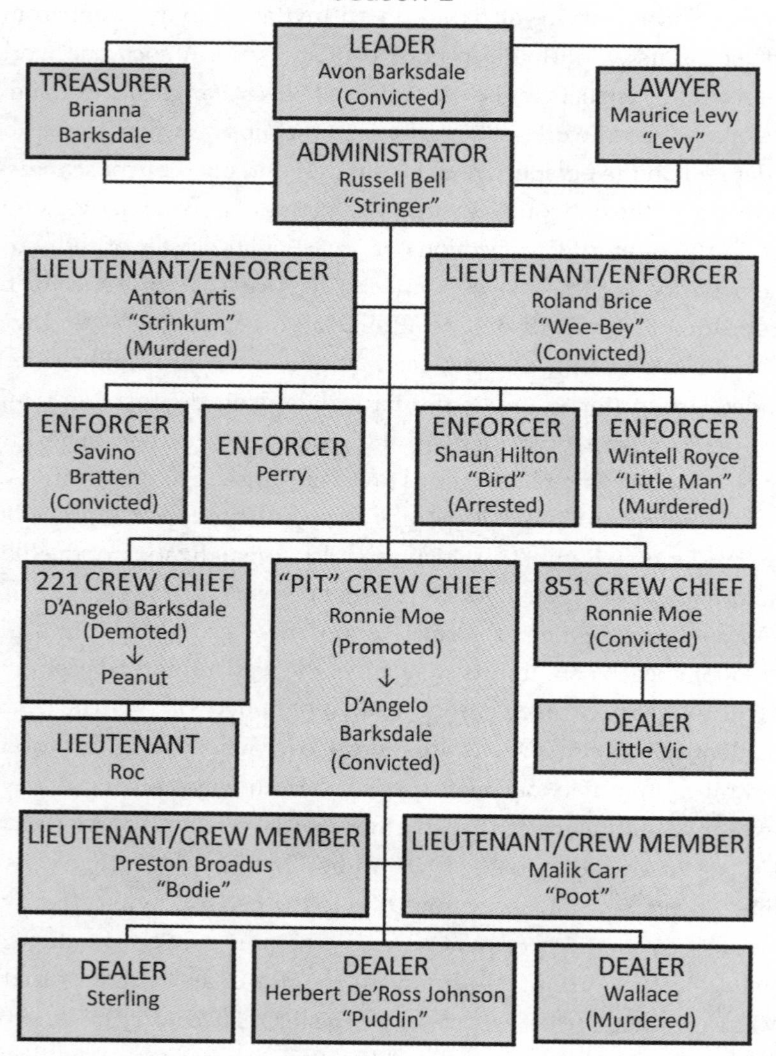

Figure 2.1. Visualization of the Barksdale social network. Image by Andyshades82 via Wikimedia Commons on https://commons.wikimedia.org/wiki/File%3ABarksdale1.jpg.

knowledge of the typical gang activities; a member of an out-group is someone who does not belong to that group (which may or may not include audience members). In-group members often have an advantage because they have an insight into the group's behavior and shared assumptions, whereas this is typically not the case for an out-group member. Sociolinguists who are studying a particular dialect, but do not belong to the in-group, frequently rely on previous research and in-group testing to verify, support, or refute their findings.

Style-Shifting and Accommodation

The speakers of any given language typically have a linguistic repertoire that allows them to alternate (to varying degrees) between dialects, styles, and registers. When a speaker chooses to blend or switch between features of formal and informal styles, that type of switching is referred to as 'style-shifting' (unfortunately, as previously mentioned, the terms 'style' and 'register' are often used interchangeably, but for our purposes a shift in register will generally involve a shift in style, so the point is moot in this context).

Switching of this type will depend on contextual and situational factors as well as on the motivation of the speaker and his/her ability to switch. Traditional views of style-shifting have seen it as a way for the speaker to react to normative pressures on the stylistic expectations of a given situation. However, other research has shown that such switching may also be an attempt to construct social meaning and that speakers may proactively switch styles in order to maintain or present to others a public self-image.

As a way of exemplifying style-shifting, consider example 3 in which Stringer Bell (the de facto leader of the Barksdale gang while Avon Barksdale is in prison) attempts to change the routines for ways the gang members meet and discuss their criminal activities:

Example 3:

(*The Barksdale gang has gathered for a meeting—the scene opens with a close-up of one of the higher-ranking members of the gang skimming through a copy of* Robert's Rules of Order)

1 BODIE: With these towers down, we need to take the rest of them low-rises an' all them Fayette Street corners.

2 STRINGER: Take 'em? Take 'em how, Mr. Bodie?

3 POOT: Ya say fuck it and take 'em.

4 SHAMROCK: Nigga, you ain't got the floor. The chair don't recognize your ass.

5 STRINGER: Take 'em how?

6 BODIE: I dunno, just . . . let them Fayette niggers know, you know, we serious, right? You know, get or get got.

7 STRINGER: Yeah, yeah, like you did on McCulloh Street last year? Snatch the real estate, and just wait for some shit to happen, right? Naw, man, we done worryin' about territory, man. What corner we got, what project. Game ain't about that no more. It's about product.

8 SHAMROCK: Yeah.

9 STRINGER: And we got the best goddamn product so we gonna sell no matter where we are, right? Product, motherfuckers. Product.

10 SHAMROCK: Chair recognize Slim Charles.

11 SLIM CHARLES: Chair, our people got to stand somewhere, don't it? I mean, all the product in the world don't mean nothin' if you constantly getting your ass whooped for standin' on another fool's corner.

12 . . .

13 STRINGER: We had six of the towers of the Terrace right, all running 24/7, but three of those we had to give to Prop Joe's people to upgrade the package that we was puttin' out there, right? Now how much you think we lost in the deal? *(pause)* Alright, the answer is we made more. Half the real estate, twice the product. And our profit went up like eight, nine percent. Yo, get it straight. Your territory ain't gonna mean shit if your product's weak. Go ahead and ask them motherfuckers tryin' to sell them Ford Tempos an' you got niggas ridin' around in Japanese and German cars in America all day. Territory ain't shit. Especially when you consider it's the fight for the territory that be bringin' the bodies. And the bodies that bring the police.

14 BODIE: Yeah, but how we gonna stand . . .

15 SHAMROCK: Yo, chair ain't recognize your ass, man.

16 BODIE: How we gonna stand on some . . .

17 SHAMROCK: Come on, man.

18 BODIE: How we gonna stand on some corner that's not ours?

19 STRINGER: Well, we got the best product, right? So the chances are, we gonna be able to bring in the competition by offering the re-up with us from our package. Feel me? Everybody makin' money, sharing the real estate.

20 SHAMROCK: Slim Charles?

21 SLIM CHARLES: What if they don't cop our re-up though?

22 STRINGER: Well, I'ma worry about that when it happen. Until then, Mr. Charles, we gonna handle this shit like businessmen. Sell the shit, make the profit and later for that gangster bullshit.

23 POOT: Yeah? Do the chair know we gonna look like some punk-ass bitches out there?

24 STRINGER: Motherfucker, I will punk your ass for sayin' such shit!

25 SHAMROCK: Yo, String.

26 STRINGER: What?!

27 SHAMROCK: Poot did have the floor, man.

28 STRINGER: Shut the fuck up, man! This nigga too ignorant to have the fuckin' floor. Y'all niggas need to start lookin' at the world in a new fucking light. Start thinkin' about this shit like some grown fucking men, not some niggas off the fuckin' corner. You heard me? Adjourn your asses.

("Time After Time"[8])

Stringer Bell has aspirations to leave the criminal world and make a move into the real estate trade; he takes business classes at night and is studying hard in order to shift his criminal activities into legitimate businesses. In the above exchange, he is obviously still managing and discussing drug-dealing and other criminal activities, but his new interests in the ways of the business world have rubbed off on his other activities and he is trying to run his gang through meetings like those from a professional organization. The dialogue in line 3, though it is deadly serious and

8. Written by David Simon and Ed Burns.

delivered in a serious manner, has a comical quality about it because of the way informal styles and slang are mixed with formal words/phrases such as *the chair* (the person presiding over a meeting); *the chair recognizes X* (the leader of the meeting is acknowledging that it is X who has formally shown his/her intention to speak and thus it is X's turn); *X has the floor* (it is X's turn to speak and he cannot be interrupted); and *adjourn* (used as an official way of marking the suspension or end of the meeting). When the language of a professional meeting is mixed with nonstandard English, the resultant clash can be quite striking and humorous, for example, *yo—chair ain't recognize your ass, man* (line 14), *this nigga too ignorant to have the fuckin' floor*, and *adjourn your asses* (both in line 27).

Speakers may shift or adjust their style of speaking also to accentuate social similarities or differences with regard to other interactional participants. Such accommodation can thus take the form of convergence, where similarities are emphasized, or divergence, where differences in communication strategies are maintained (Coupland, Coupland, and Giles 1991).

Overt Prestige and Covert Prestige

Different language variants will have more or less status in a given speech community or in a particular context, for example stigmatized, nonstandard language is socially dispreferred by mainstream society whereas variants of the standard typically garner respect and approval. The way in which an individual's language choices are valued in terms of the symbolic status they convey is expressed in sociolinguistics by the concept of prestige.

There are two variants of prestige: 'overt prestige' and 'covert prestige'. Overt prestige is the positive prestige associated with the dialects that are most established as being representative of the most correct usage in the language, namely those dialects spoken by the affluent, well-educated, and socially influential upper class. In this way, overt prestige is typically associated with the understood standard dialect of a country or region because the standard often becomes so by the very fact that it is associated with the most prestigious and influential speakers of the language/dialect in question, such as doctors, lawyers, educators, politicians, engineers, and so on.

In contrast, covert prestige is the prestige associated with nonstandard dialects. In other words, it is the prestige that can accrue to a speaker who uses explicitly nonstandard or stigmatized forms, typically for the very reason that they do not conform to the ideals of the standard. These situations occur when the speaker wants to gain recognition or acceptance, or show solidarity with one or more groups that identify themselves in opposition to the perceived prestige groups in society. Covert prestige is ordinarily evidenced among working-class men, but many social groups and/or subcultures attach a covert prestige or 'symbolic capital' to rough/nonstandard language because it is emblematic of rebelliousness and dissent. Such groups/subcultures, for example, may include criminal gangs but often covert prestige is also valued among groups whose identity is not necessarily related to criminal activities such as hip-hoppers, punk rockers, bikers, skaters, metal-heads, among many others. By association, because nonstandard dialects are often viewed as corrupted or debased variants of the standard, the desire to show covert prestige may incorrectly be seen as a sign of poor education, low intelligence, or bad morals, when actually in many cases it is simply a way of showing distance from the standard dialects and the social groups typically associated with it. As noted previously, popular culture representations of nonstandard dialects can promote/reinforce certain ways (typically negative ones) of thinking about speakers of nonstandard dialects.

Vernacular Language and AAVE

Among laypeople and sociolinguistic experts alike, the word *vernacular* is often used inconsistently; for some, it simply means an informal register or, as the founding father of sociolinguistics, William Labov (1972, 112), put it himself, "the least self-conscious style of people in a relaxed conversation," or "the most basic style" of a given speaker. In other words, for some people, the term is used synonymously with a casual style that is used spontaneously and without reflection rather than more formal styles that involve conscious reflection on the linguistic variants involved in packaging a particular utterance.

In contrast to the above definition, other people view the word *vernacular* as referring to the use of nonstandard dialects; that is, vernacular is used as an antonym to 'standard language'. As noted above, the concepts of 'standard' and 'nonstandard' are difficult to pin down, but for the sake of simplicity, we can say that here we are speaking of socially disfavored dialects (in terms of grammar, vocabulary, pronunciation, and so forth). In this view of the meaning of the term, vernaculars are primarily spoken and not written. For the present purposes, vernacular is used in this chapter to mean the casual, spontaneous speech of a speech community. It may or may not be socially dispreferred; this aspect of vernacular is not a crucial defining point for its use here.

African American Vernacular English

Because the term African American Vernacular English is used extensively in this chapter, it makes sense to take a closer look at the term itself. As noted above, much of the dialogue in *The Wire* is delivered in AAVE, which in the most concise terms possible is 'a form of American English spoken primarily by African Americans'. Though this expedient definition can provide a practical starting point for this study, it is well worth noting that not all African Americans speak AAVE, and for many who do, it is a scalar phenomenon, to be understood in degrees of (non-)standardness, rather than a rigid all-or-nothing usage. *The Wire* reflects this well; for example, some black characters (on both sides of the law), such as police lieutenant Cedric Daniels, Mayor Clarence Royce, or Brother Mouzone, use no socially marked features of AAVE whatsoever, while on the other end of the scale, characters such as Snoop, Avon Barksdale, or Wee-Bey speak almost exclusively in an extreme variety of AAVE. Yet other characters shift dialects seamlessly depending on the situation, the most notable figure being the corrupt Senator Clay Davis, who typically makes good use of his extraordinary rhetorical skills and supreme AAVE proficiency to garner himself a type of downhome street credibility with voters.

Moreover, AAVE is not an exclusively black phenomenon; some white Baltimoreans, especially the younger members of the working class, pick up the sociolect of their fellow blacks. Thus it is no surprise that some white drug-dealers in *The Wire* use AAVE grammar along with typical drug-related slang and criminal jargon, as they are living and 'working' in an environment that is dominated by African Americans. In this way, the scripted AAVE in the show not only creates an image of 'blackness' but also contributes to a linguistic representation of socioeconomic status and social class.

Examining Selected Features of AAVE via The Wire

In the narrow scope of this chapter, it is not possible to provide a comprehensive presentation of all the features of AAVE, but for the purposes of illustration, consider the exchange in example 4 below, in which some of the most salient features occur. The excerpt involves three characters, Proposition Joe (an AAVE speaker and high-level drug distributer); Sergey (a Russian gangster whose organization provides Proposition Joe with drugs); and Nicky (a working-class white male whose cousin, Ziggy, is an inept, low-level drug dealer). They are discussing a situation that nearly cost Ziggy his life at the hands of Proposition Joe's nephew, nicknamed 'Cheese'. In the following, Sergey is trying to help Nicky negotiate a settlement with Proposition Joe.

Example 4:

1 PROPJOE: Sergey, my nigger.

2 SERGEY: You're losing weight. Shit. You are down to nothing. In this country, supermarkets are cathedrals. I worry for you, buddy.

3 PROPJOE: How your peoples, dog?

4 SERGEY: Same, good.

5 PROPJOE: You talk to the man about that other thing, right? Because I can get behind that business in a big way.

6 SERGEY: We will talk later. Now, another business.

7 PROPJOE: Right. This the man with the raggedy-ass Camaro?

8 NICKY: Wasn't mine, it was my cousin's. It wasn't all that raggedy.

9 SERGEY: Sorry. Nicky is with us. His cousin . . . But family cannot be helped.

10 PROPJOE: Who you telling? I got motherfucking nephews and in-laws fucking all my shit up all the time. And it ain't like I can pop a cap in their ass and not hear about it Thanksgiving time. For real, I'm living life with some burdensome niggers.

11 NICKY: So what the fuck?

12 PROPJOE: You ain't pay my boy Cheese, and Cheese ain't paying me, right? I ain't talking about all the money in the world. But it ain't like Cheese be in a position out on that corner . . . to let your cuz exemplify shit, you feel? The man cut you some slack, and soon every fucking-up white boy be on his titty.

13 NICKY: We wanna pay what we owe. The $2,700 anyway. We're gonna have it soon enough. Your man doubled it, though. He also burned the car. Now the blue book on that Camaro was $5,100.

14 PROPJOE: Now, let me understand. You gonna come up in here, having fucked up a package . . . asking me to tell Cheese, who you fucked it up on . . . to pay you out $2,400.

15 NICKY: He gets to keep the Camaro.

16 PROPJOE: *(to Sergey)* Just how good a friend is this motherfucker to y'all? The Cheese ain't gonna be happy having to pay me back . . . so I would advise y'all to give him some distance.

17 NICKY: Just so he don't come back on my cousin. Anyway, thanks for being straight on this.

18 PROPJOE: Fool, if it wasn't for Serge here, you and your cuz both would be cadaverous motherfuckers.

("All Prologue"[9])

The passage contains plenty of grammar structures that are typical of (but not necessarily exclusive to) AAVE: The negation word *ain't*, common in most nonstandard varieties of English, is used six times in the passage (lines 10, 12, and 16). Twice in line 12 we can see examples of so-called aspectual *BE* (*it ain't like Cheese be in a position and soon every fucking-up white boy be on his titty*). In these cases an invariant form of auxiliary verb BE is used to indicate an action as occurring habitually, ordinarily, or customarily, a use of BE that is regularly noted as being a fairly specific characteristic of AAVE. Another typical AAVE feature mentioned in the literature is the omission or deletion of the copular (or 'linking') verb

9. Written by David Simon and Ed Burns.

BE (see *How your peoples, dog?* [line 3] rather than 'how *are* your people'). This phenomenon is evidenced four times in example 4, mostly in question forms, in lines 3, 7, 10, 14. The pronoun form *y'all,* a feature that is also common among white speakers in the American South (see chapter 3), is used twice in line 16. In line 3 Joe uses plural *people* with an additional, redundant *-s*. The so-called '*-ass* morpheme' (that is, the use of the word *ass* as a morphological affix typically with a reflexive meaning, for example, *your ass* = *yourself,* or as an intensifier in an adjective phrase, for example, *broke-ass city*) is used twice, once in line 10 meaning 'them' (*their ass* = 'them'), once in line 7 as a part of an adjective (*raggedy-ass Camaro*). Another general feature of nonstandard or informal English, the future indicator *gonna,* is used twice, once with a deleted *BE* (*You gonna come up in here,* line 14) and once with *ain't* in line 16 (*The Cheese ain't gonna be happy*). Finally, irregular subject-verb agreement (that is, the grammatical agreement between the subject of a sentence and its verb in terms of person and number) also occurs here, in line 12 in *the man cut you some slack,* in which *cut* could be understood as being in the past tense (and thus acceptable in terms of SE), but is better understood as reading something like '(if) the man cuts you some slack' in SE.

In terms of vocabulary, Joe uses the word *dog* (pronounced as *dawg*) as a synonym of 'friend' (line 3); the idiom *pop a cap,* another way of saying 'shoot a bullet' (line 10); *for real* as a disjunct meaning 'seriously' (line 10); and the confirmation tag question *you feel?* (line 12), meaning 'do you understand?' The word *nigger* is used twice, once in a positive sense toward a white person (line 1), and once in a negative sense (line 10). He also uses the word *motherfucker,* once as an adjective in line 10, once as a substitute for 'person' (line 16) and once in the creative phrase *cadaverous motherfuckers* (line 18), meaning 'you would be dead'; in all cases the word is intended in a negative sense. The word *boy,* meaning 'associate', can be found in line 12 as well as *fool* in line 18. Note that in the extract, Joe addresses two white characters, and while doing so, in a short space of time, he uses a fairly large number of the typical properties of AAVE along with other AAVE features that are not as obvious, such as, for example, *come* to express indignation in line 14.

Throughout the entire series, Proposition Joe is portrayed as a highly articulate character, capable of adjusting his speech to the situation at hand. His ease in using his AAVE linguistic identity with Nicholas and Sergey could be an indication that in Joe's eyes, there is a type of solidarity among them. Even though all of the characters present are criminals, they have more things in common than just that: Joe, as mentioned before, is an African American. Sergey is an immigrant. Nicholas is a second-generation stevedore working in a dying harbor. All of them are struggling, disenfranchised, lower-class outsiders. Finally, the exchange given above can be used to show that the level of depth and sophistication that can be expressed through AAVE is dependent on the speaker (which includes, among other things, a good awareness of many of the concepts discussed above, such as prestige, style-shifting, and accommodation).

Discussion

The language of *The Wire* presents us with a high-fidelity, albeit densely packaged, reflection of African American Vernacular English and thus provides us with some insight into the workings of sociolinguistics. Having said that, *The Wire* is a specific show based on a specific area with specific themes. Because AAVE is central to the series, it is easy to use this dialect as a way of discussing sociolinguistic concepts, but this use also means that many other sociolinguistic variables, such as language and gender, language and age, and so forth, cannot be covered within the scope of this chapter. The reader is encouraged to investigate such topics in relation to other TV programs.

It is also worth mentioning that no scripted representation of speech will ever reproduce all the characteristics of naturally occurring spoken language exactly or in exactly the same proportions; scripted language is created with the intention of entertaining an audience and thus some features will be exaggerated or heightened for effect, while others, such as repetitions, false starts, conversational overlaps, and so forth are played down or 'disaccentuated', partly because of the time constraints and practicalities of television and partly because they would make the viewing experience tedious. It is also crucial to keep in mind that ethnicity is not the only relevant variable for the way AAVE speech is represented in *The Wire*; the specific subject matter of the show, its Baltimore location, and the social class membership of many of its characters surely affect the language and vocabulary and thus also have a great significance for the types of features found and their relative frequencies (on a similar note, see also Toolan [2011], which also explores the scripted dialog of *The Wire*).

The Wire is an extremely powerful television series, which manages to present the bleak reality many citizens of Baltimore face daily. The poverty, violence, isolation, neglect, and despondence are apparent not only in the actions, but also through the speech and dialogues of many characters. Ethridge (2008) explains that, according to the show's creator David Simon, *The Wire* received its title not only because of the show's focus on high-end police investigations and wire taps, but also because it illustrates a metaphorical wire of separation:

> The title really refers to almost an imaginary but inviolate boundary between the two Americas, between the functional, post-industrial economy that is minting new millionaires every day and creating a viable environment for a portion of the country, and the other America that is being consigned to a permanent underclass, and this show is really about the vagaries and excesses of unencumbered capitalism and what that has wrought at the millennium and where the country is and where it is going and it is suggestive that we are going to a much more divided and brutish place, and I think we are, and that really reflects the politics of the people making the show. It really is a show about the other America in a lot of ways, and so *The Wire* really does refer to almost a boundary or a fence or the idea of people walking on a high wire and falling to either side. . . . (154)

In the five-year-long stretch of sixty episodes, we see how in a city abandoned by the general American public the dialect is becoming the norm, while the 'norm' is becoming the margin: we see it with politicians and community leaders, we see it with the young white working class and with the black police officers—there is no clear 'wire' that neatly divides them up into AAVE and non-AAVE speakers.

Suggestions for Further Viewing and Analysis

1. Consider examples of other television series that prominently feature African American characters:[10] *Good Times* (1974–79), *The Jeffersons* (1975–85), *What's Happening* (1976–79), *Diff'rent Strokes* (1978–85), *The Cosby Show* (1984–92), *Family Matters* (1989–98), *Living Single* (1993–98), *Chappelle's Show* (2003–6), *The Tracy Morgan Show* (2003–4), *Everybody Hates Chris* (2004–9), and *Black-ish* (2014–). Are there features of AAVE present in any of the characters? How does the language of African American television characters vary: between the characters themselves, between series, and over time?

2. Other social variables can be reflected in a character's language use or, conversely, can be constructed and foregrounded by language use. In the suggestion above, the variable of race can be explored in a number of television series, and in chapter 4, the relationship between language and gender is investigated. Consider the relationship between language and other sociolinguistic variables that are prominent in television series, including:

- Age, such as teenagers in *Beverly Hills 90210* (1990–2000), *Buffy the Vampire Slayer* (1997–2003), *One Tree Hill* (2003–12), *Freaks and Geeks* (1999–2000), *The Inbetweeners* (2008–10); and the elderly in *The Golden Girls* (1985–92), *Murder, She Wrote* (1984–96), *Matlock* (1986–95), and *One Foot in the Grave* (1990–2000).
- Sexuality, primarily the LGBT characters in *Three's Company* (1977–84), *Will and Grace* (1998–2006), *Queer as Folk* (2000–2005), *The L Word* (2004–9), *Modern Family* (2009–), *Orange Is the New Black* (2013–), and *Looking* (2014–).
- Ethnicity, such as Italian-American in *The Sopranos* (1999–2007), *Everybody Loves Raymond* (1996–2005), *Mama's Boys of the Bronx*, (2012–); Jewish-American in *Seinfeld* (1989–98), *Brooklyn Bridge* (1991–93), and *Curb Your Enthusiasm* (2000–2011); Hispanic-Americans in

10. Note that the suggestions listed here include not only fictional television series with purely scripted dialogue but also reality TV shows in which the language may be considered more genuine and spontaneous.

Resurrection Boulevard (2000–2002), *Greetings from Tucson* (2002–3), *The George Lopez Show* (2002–7), and *Ugly Betty* (2006–10).

3. Medical, legal, law enforcement, and investigative television series often include formal registers and profession-specific jargon in the episode scripts. Identify and consider the role of each in dramas versus comedies, such as *ER* (1994–2009), *House* (2004–12), and *Scrubs* (2001–10); *The Good Wife* (2009–), *Law and Order* (1990–2010), and *Night Court* (1984–92); *True Detective* (2014–), *Monk* (2002–9), and *Barney Miller* (1974–82); and finally *Hill Street Blues* (1981–87), *Life on Mars* (2006–7), and *Reno 911!* (2003–9).

References

Bucholtz, Mary. 2011. "Race and the Re-Embodied Voice in Hollywood Film." *Language and Communication* 31(3): 255–65.

Bucholtz, Mary, and Quiana Lopez. 2011. "Performing Blackness, Forming Whiteness: Linguistic Minstrelsy in Hollywood Film." *Journal of Sociolinguistics* 15(5): 680–706.

Ethridge, Blake. 2008. "Baltimore on *The Wire*: The Tragic Moralism of David Simon." In *It's Not TV: Watching HBO in the Post-Television Era*, edited by Marc Leverette, Brian L. Ott, and Cara-Louise Buckley, 152–64. New York: Routledge.

Coupland, Justine, Nikolas Coupland, and Howard Giles. 1991. "Accommodation Theory: Communication, Context, and Consequence." In *Contexts of Accommodation*, edited by Howard Giles, Justine Coupland, and Nikolas Coupland, 1–68. Cambridge, UK: Cambridge Univ. Press, and Paris: Éditions de la maison des sciences de l'homme.

Kelly, Lisa. 2009. "Casting *The Wire*: Complicating Notions of Performance, Authenticity, and 'Otherness'." *Darkmatter*. Accessed Sept. 19. http://www.darkmatter101.org.

Labov, William. 1972. "Some Principles of Linguistic Methodology." *Language in Society* 1:97–120.

Toolan, Michael. 2011. "I Don't Know What They're Saying Half the Time, but I'm Hooked on the Series: Incomprehensible Dialogue and Integrated Multimodal Characterisation in *The Wire*." In *Telecinematic Discourse: Approaches to the Language of Films and Television Series*, edited by Roberta Piazza, Monika Bednarek, and Fabio Rossi, 161–83. Amsterdam: John Benjamins.

3

"Back in St. Olaf . . ."

Regional Variation in The Golden Girls

JEAN ANN

The Golden Girls can be succinctly summarized as a situation comedy about a group of elderly women living out their retirement years together as housemates in Miami, Florida. Each half-hour episode concerns their everyday activities and the ways in which they support each other and keep active in their community through good times and bad. The four female leads include Blanche Devereaux, played by Rue McClanahan: a sexually adventuresome widow from Atlanta, Georgia; Dorothy Zbornak, played by Bea Arthur: a practical, sensible divorcée who works as a substitute teacher and cares for her mother; Estelle Getty's Sophia Petrillo: a Sicilian immigrant who doesn't suffer fools gladly—both Dorothy and her mother, Sophia, come from New York City; and finally Rose Nylund, played by Betty White: a tender-hearted and naïve widow from a rural Minnesota community called St. Olaf.

The Golden Girls ran from 1985 to 1992. The series enjoyed immediate popularity, was quick to garner critical acclaim, and remains a beloved television series over three decades since its premier.[1] It consistently received nominations and awards for areas such as writing, directing, and editing,

Thanks to John Lalande, Curt Rice, Espen Rice, Susan B. Brown, Chris Walsh, Bobbi Schnorr, Sharon Kane, Barb Beyerbach, Mary Harrell, Bonita Hampton, and Tania Ramalho for discussing the contents of this chapter with me. Thanks also to Kristy Beers Fägersten for a good deal of additional data.

1. See, for example, Farr (2015) and Yuko (2015).

as well as for individual performances and for the series itself. Weekly audiences looked forward to the show's treatment of lighter-hearted topics such as Blanche's experiences with her numerous sexual partners; the dating experiences of Dorothy, Rose, and Sophia; and attempts of all of the aging women to be present in and make sense of a changing world, while trying new experiences such as going back to school, getting part-time jobs, and doing stand-up comedy. But the show also took on racism, illness, death, homophobia, looks-ism, able-ism, ageism, and jealousy in ways that spoke deeply to American society.

Among the many aspects of *The Golden Girls* that make it appealing to television viewers is the very fact that the dialogue includes language use that is familiar to the viewer, but that illustrates particular linguistic phenomena that may be unfamiliar. This chapter aims to identify and explain these linguistic phenomena, and in so doing to raise the viewer's linguistic awareness.

Most interesting to the linguist is how *The Golden Girls* relates to sociolinguistics, that is to say the branch of linguistics that investigates the relation between language and society, as explored in part in chapter 2. Sociolinguistics, at its heart, is about variation, arising from the deceptively simple idea that all speakers of a given language do not speak with each other in the same way all the time. This means that language varies between individual speakers, and among groups of speakers of a given language, in this case, English. The conditions under which language varies are what sociolinguists study; in this chapter, we explore geographical conditions.

Regional Variation

As illustrated in chapter 2, social variation can manifest itself in accents and dialects, but these linguistic phenomena are perhaps more readily recognized as indicators of regional variation, or differences in language use as a function of geographical influences. The distinction between accents and dialects bears repeating now, before we consider their relationship to regional variation. While accents refer only to variations in pronunciation, dialects refer to language varieties that can be identified by distinguishing features of pronunciation *and* vocabulary *and* grammar. In this chapter, we want to make a further distinction: one between dialect and language. Let's consider the adage "A language is a dialect with an army and a navy."[2] This statement is a way of expressing that there may be no obviously linguistic aspects differentiating the two concepts of 'language' and 'dialect'. In fact, sociolinguistic research posits that there are only extra-linguistic differences between a language and a dialect, such as geographical, political, and perhaps religious or social considerations. For example, Swedish and Norwegian are considered two different languages, given that they each belong to a different country. And yet native speakers of Swedish and Norwegian can understand and communicate with each other reasonably well. At the same time, it is also true that the Chinese language has many dialects, such as Cantonese and Mandarin, but these dialects are mutually unintelligible. Although a folk-linguistic interpretation of the term 'dialect' may reflect an assessment of imperfectness or inadequacy, this is not the linguist's understanding. Rather, a linguist uses the term 'dialect' objectively, to refer quite straightforwardly to a variety of language associated with a particular region (regional dialect) or social standing (social dialect) and with identifiable features of pronunciation, grammar, and vocabulary. The focus of this chapter, then, will be the regional dialects that characterize the leading ladies of *The Golden Girls.*

Blanche, Dorothy, Rose, and, to a certain extent, Sophia share similar characteristics: they are all elderly, single, middle-class women who have come to retire in Miami. Their broad similarities allow for an easy identification of their differences. For example, this identification can be considered in terms of their overall characterizations, representing one of the four main stages of a woman's life: virgin, spouse, mother, and wise woman (Kaler 1990, 49). But these representations "fluctuate among the characters," a strategy that allows for easy relation to "the right mix of archetypal patterns which the viewers . . . recognize . . . subconsciously, but the producers have consciously planned" (Kaler 1990, 49).

2. This quote is commonly attributed to the sociolinguist Max Weinreich, but others have also been credited with this statement; see en.wikipedia.org/wiki/A_language_is_a_dialect_with_an_army_and_navy.

A more specific aspect of variability between the characters that was overtly exploited throughout the series is their different regional backgrounds. This particular variation constituted a major theme of the show, and it was reflected most obviously through the language that each of the characters used. While the dialogue throughout the series often included explicit reminders of this variation—for example, in Rose's recurring prelude to her anecdotes, "Back in St. Olaf . . ."—the linguistically minded viewer notices how the characters' regional variation is otherwise established and maintained in their speech. Blanche, Rose, Dorothy, and Sophia represent the linguistic (and social and cultural) norms of different geographical areas, and as such their speech patterns illustrate different regional dialects.

Regional Dialects

Three of the major American dialects (Labov, Ash, and Boberg 2006) are represented by the speech of the characters in *The Golden Girls*. Each of their recognizable speech patterns is associated in people's minds with those geographic areas. Rose speaks in a way that is characteristic of the North Central part of the United States, Blanche's speech is associated with the South, and Sophia and Dorothy speak in ways that are typical of New York City. That the women speak differently is clear enough, but what is the scope of these differences, and is it enough to identify distinct regional dialects?

It is important to remember that the term 'dialect' refers to a variety of language that exhibits unique features in three dimensions, specifically grammar, pronunciation, and vocabulary. If differences between any two groups of people are solely limited to pronunciation, for example, then it is simply a question of accent. However, once differences in vocabulary and grammar are also noticeable, then linguists can identify a dialect. When linguists explore regional dialects, they actually map out areas of variation, identifying, as accurately as possible, the geographical area where one feature ends and another begins. These particular meeting points are traced on a dialect map and referred to as 'isoglosses', or geographic boundaries of dialectal features. Isoglosses can be identified for aspects of pronunciation, grammar, or vocabulary, and when all three features can be identified within a particular region, a regional dialect is said to exist. In the next sections, we'll consider the grammar, pronunciation, and vocabulary features of various regional dialects that are observable in *The Golden Girls.*

Grammar

Most television series feature speakers of a standard English dialect so as to appeal to and be understood by as broad an audience as possible. Diversity in terms of regional or social variation will most likely be in the form of accent or vocabulary features, but even these will be subtle so as not to veer into incomprehensibility. (A noteworthy counter-example to this, however, is examined in the previous chapter, in which the grammar, pronunciation, and vocabulary of the social dialects featured in the HBO series *The Wire* severely challenge the uninitiated; see also Toolan [2011]). Generally, the female leads of *The Golden Girls* produce little to no non-standard English grammatical forms, with the exception of some common spoken English forms such as *gonna* or *wanna*. These, however, are not necessarily associated with any one particular regional dialect. Instead, we'll focus on a widely recognized feature of several dialects: the plural form of the second-person pronoun *you*.

As early as season 1, Blanche reveals the form *y'all* as a part of her linguistic repertoire. In the episode "Adult Education,"[3] Blanche has decided to take a course, the teacher of which has propositioned her: Blanche can receive a passing grade if she sleeps with him.

Example 1:

BLANCHE: I asked my teacher for help like y'all told me to. He said the only way I would get an A on his final is if I sleep with him.

ROSE: No!

BLANCHE: Oh yes! I just don't know what to do!

SOPHIA: Get it in writing.

(Transcribed by Kristy Beers Fägersten)

3. Written by James Berg and Stan Zimmerman.

In a subsequent episode, "Bedtime Story,"[4] the women meet a stationmaster from (fictional) Appalappichobee, who informs them of the town's train schedule:

Example 2:

STATIONMASTER: Oh, all the trains out of Appalappichobee leave early. That's what our town's famous for! Now, y'all may think this sounds kinda silly, but we actually printed "Our Trains Leave Early" right on the town seal!

(Transcribed by Kristy Beers Fägersten)

Here we see that the form *y'all* is used to identify the stationmaster as having a regional background that may be similar to Blanche's. This is because the isogloss *y'all* helps to define the American dialect of the South, which extends as far west as Texas,[5] and to as far north as Virginia. Speakers for whom the plural of *you* is *you all* or *y'all* tend to reside in or come from this area, which includes Blanche's hometown of Atlanta and even the Appalachian area, which, presumably, includes the fictional home of the stationmaster, Appalappichobee. There are other plural *you*-variants, including dominant *you guys*, which occurs from the Northeast to the West, including the Midwest, where Rose is from. Variants such as *yous(e)* or *yous(e) guys* constitute isoglosses in more concentrated areas of the United States. While Sophia and Dorothy themselves do not produce either of these forms throughout the series, they both represent New York City dialects, where both the *yous(e)* or *yous(e) guys* forms are common. Additional variants of *you* include *you'uns* from the Ohio River Valley, and *yinz*, a plural-*you* form unique to Pittsburgh.[6]

4. Written by Kathy Speer and Terry Grossman.

5. The use of *y'all* is a defining feature of Tami Taylor's speech in *Friday Night Lights*, which is based in Texas.

6. In the opening sequence of *Parks and Recreation* episode "Fluoride" (written by Matt Hubbard), Pawnee, Indiana, resident Tom tells two Indiana Colts running backs that he doesn't 'run', saying, "That's your guys's [gaIzəs] job," clearly indicating not only another alternative plural form, *your guys*, but also illustrating a common reanalysis of a possessive marker ('s) on a plural form (*guys*), realized as a second syllable.

Pronunciation

Many people commonly locate the differences between one dialect and another in the area of pronunciation. Differing pronunciations of the same words are commonly known as accents, and most of us have heard the speech of people who have a different accent from ours either in person or on television. And while accents, that is, pronunciation differences, are part of what constitutes a dialect, it is important to remember that a dialect can be said to exist only when pronunciation differences are accompanied by both grammatical and lexical differences.

To see how the same word is pronounced in a different way by different characters, we can consider an example from *The Golden Girls* in which both Blanche and Sophia pronounce the word *auditor* or *auditors*, allowing us to compare their pronunciations. In "Comedy of Errors,"[7] Sophia and Dorothy are seated on the couch following a somewhat unpleasant conversation about Dorothy's upcoming attempt to try her hand at stand-up comedy. In the scene, Blanche enters the living room having just returned from a visit to her accountant. Blanche's entrance is a good excuse to drop the topic and move on to other things.

Example 3:

BLANCHE: But Dorothy, you don't get it, my accountant reminded me I've been audited before and I've never had to pay a penny in back taxes. I have a way with auditors. The last time I was audited, I got money back from the government.

SOPHIA: Blanche, it's not a refund when the auditor leaves two twenties on your nightstand.

We'll focus on a well-known phenomenon in both Blanche's and Sophia's speech: a conspicuous lack of an r-sound after a vowel. Interested readers can listen to this part of the episode as many times as necessary to have Blanche and Sophia's pronunciations of *auditor/s* clearly in mind.

Because our task here is to compare the pronunciation of the same word of two speakers who speak two different dialects, we'll need a bit

7. Written by Don Reo.

more linguistic information. When linguists talk about the sounds of someone's English, they can't rely on using English spelling to point out the exact sound or sounds in question. This is because though both speakers would spell a word in the same way, they would pronounce it differently. If linguists wanted to discuss the pronunciation of what some might call the *r* in a word like *park*, we would quickly discover that some speakers in fact produce no corresponding r-sound in this word. And if we had to talk about what is pronounced instead of the *r*, we would quickly find ourselves in a quagmire of descriptions of sounds and no way to write down what we are discovering. So, if we can't use spelling to pinpoint and represent in writing exactly what we're talking about, what can we do? Linguists make use of the International Phonetic Alphabet (IPA) to represent graphically the sounds that people say. The IPA assigns one pronunciation to one phonetic symbol. These symbols are used to represent in writing the sounds of any language or dialect in the world. We'll make use of the IPA to represent what's going on in Blanche and Sophia's *auditor/s*; more about the IPA, phonetics, and phonology is included in chapter 9.

Let's compare the pronunciation of *auditors*, spoken by Blanche, and *auditor* spoken by Sophia, focusing just on the last syllable of each of the words. If we listen more closely, we notice that the last syllable (corresponding to *-tors* for Blanche and *-tor* for Sophia) sound different from each other—even if we don't consider the word-final plural marker *-s* on Blanche's variant. The discovery is that neither Blanche nor Sophia produces a sound corresponding to the letter *r* after the vowel *o* in the final syllable. In other words, there is no production of a post-vocalic [ɹ]. Furthermore, each of them pronounces this final vowel differently, which can be represented by a phonetic transcription. Here, IPA transcriptions are used to represent what each speaker produces; the rest of the word appears in regular English spelling: Blanche's *auditors* audi[tɨz] vs. Sophia's *auditor* audi[tə].

Two generalizations are captured about Blanche's and Sophia's pronunciations. First, because neither produces a post-vocalic [ɹ] sound, we do not see the symbol for the sound 'r' (which is [ɹ]) in the phonetically transcribed last syllable of the word. The fact that neither speaker produces a post-vocalic [ɹ] shows a similarity between these two dialects. In fact, the dialects of the South and of New York City, of the American dialects, are both characterized by a lack of post-vocalic [ɹ].

A second generalization is that Blanche and Sophia produce a different vowel in the last syllable. Blanche produces what linguists call a 'barred i', represented in IPA as [ɨ]. Sophia produces a schwa, represented in IPA as [ə]. The difference between [ɨ] and [ə] has to do largely with the height of the tongue: the tongue is higher in [ɨ] than it is in [ə]. The fact that these vowels are different for each speaker suggests that if we investigate further and check on more speakers, we would find that these two dialects, not just these two speakers, differ in this way. And if we examined the pronunciations of people who speak other American English dialects, such as Rose, we would find that when they produce the word *auditor*, they are likely to produce a post-vocalic [ɹ], and a different vowel from those that Sophia and Blanche produce.

Summarizing our inquiry so far, it is clear that some American speakers do not produce a post-vocalic [ɹ] (such as Blanche and Sophia) and that this pronunciation feature also affects vowel quality, exemplified by [ɨ] for Blanche and [ə] for Sophia. At the same time, it can be assumed that speakers of the North Central dialect, such as Rose, and many other speakers of American English do produce post-vocalic [ɹ]. This linguistic variation actually occurs in predictable patterns, according to geography. Because pronunciation differences are part of what makes up a dialect, we would expect that any given dialect represents a myriad of pronunciations that are distinct from those of other dialects.

Lexis

Considering that *The Golden Girls* features characters from different areas of the United States, it is reasonable that dialectal differences even on the level of lexis would be represented—and indeed they are. However, instead of each of the main characters representing a distinct regional dialect characterized by wildly different vocabulary items, it is only Rose whose 'idiolect' (that is, whose particular speech habits) is most notably constructed by lexical features of a regional dialect. While the viewer encounters some evidence of lexical variation among all the characters—for example, Blanche refers to her parents as *mama* and *daddy* (or, as an alternative to this latter term, *big daddy*) and Dorothy uses the terms *ma* and *pop*—it is, significantly, Rose who characteristically employs words that are strikingly unfamiliar to Blanche, Dorothy, and Sophia as well as to the viewing audience. This is mainly owing to the fact that Rose Nylund, who is of Norwegian descent, comes from the fictional Minnesota town of St. Olaf. This town, like much of the northern Midwest, has a Scandinavian history, which is particularly evident in the lexical aspects of the corresponding regional dialect.

It is important for character development to foreground Rose Nylund's regional background, and throughout the seven seasons of *The Golden Girls*, the tagline "Back in St. Olaf . . ." is often invoked by Rose to introduce a story of hometown illogic or silliness that is commonly punctuated with unfamiliar, Scandinavian-sounding words. It is thus both the cultural and the linguistic strangeness that is capitalized on for humor, each firmly anchored in regional background. So consistently does Rose tell tales of St. Olaf that both befuddle and exasperate her friends with Scandinavian vocabulary that she is effectively represented as embodying a particular northern Midwest dialect.

To illustrate Rose's regional dialect in terms of lexical features, we'll consider the continuation of example 3, in which Rose enters after Sophia's remark about "two twenties" on the nightstand.

Example 4:

BLANCHE: But Dorothy, you don't get it, my accountant reminded me I've been audited before and I've never had to pay a penny in back taxes. I have a way with auditors. The last time I was audited, I got money back from the government.

SOPHIA: Blanche, it's not a refund when the auditor leaves two twenties on your nightstand.

ROSE: *(enters from the kitchen holding a cake)* You wanna see my vanskap kaka?

SOPHIA: As long as I don't have to show you mine.

ROSE: It's a St. Olaf friendship cake.

Most notable in example 4 (as a continuation of example 3) is the unfamiliar, or at least unfamiliar-sounding, term *vanskap kaka*. The novelty of this word is suggested by Sophia's reaction to it, which indicates that she has misunderstood, and this misunderstanding is addressed in Rose's final turn, which includes a clarification of the term. In this turn, Rose not only explains what a *vanskap kaka* is ("friendship cake"; see the section "Borrowing" below), but, crucially, she makes explicit reference to St. Olaf, thereby establishing the term as a feature of a regional dialect. Example 5 is similar, in which two new terms are introduced and general misunderstandings establish Rose's background and her associated dialect as unfamiliar. In this scene of "Long Day's Journey into Marinara,"[8] the women have just eaten a delicious meal prepared by Sophia and her sister, Dorothy's Aunt Angela. They are getting ready to have dessert, which Blanche expects was also prepared by Sophia and Angela, before discovering it was in fact made by Rose.

Example 5:

ROSE: I made dessert.

BLANCHE: Damn.

ROSE: What'd you say, Blanche?

BLANCHE: Yum, I said yum.[9]

DOROTHY: Rose, is this another one of those Scandinavian Viking concoctions?

ROSE: Yes, it's called genueckenfluegen cake. It's an ancient recipe, but I Americanized it.

DOROTHY: Yeah, so one might say you brought geflueckennuegen into the '80s?

ROSE: Yes, but I'm not one to blow my own vetuevenfluegen.

SOPHIA: I can't even reach mine.

In example 5, Dorothy's labeling of Rose's dessert as "another one of those Scandinavian Viking concoctions" foregrounds Rose's regional

8. Written by Barry Fanaro and Mort Nathan.

9. Note that much of the reason that Blanche is able to rather seamlessly replace *damn* with *yum* is owing to another characteristic feature of her Southern regional dialect, namely the diphthongization (see chapter 9) of the [æ] vowel sound of *damn* such that it is pronounced as two syllables, ['dejʌm], with the final syllable, [jʌm], pronounced in almost the same way as *yum*.

background and highlights its foreignness and strangeness. This evaluation is immediately rewarded as accurate when Rose introduces the decidedly concocted words *genueckenfluegen* and *vetuevenfluegen*. If we take the context and co-text into consideration, that is, the situation in which the interaction occurs and the surrounding textual cues (see chapter 5 for more information), we can infer that *genueckenfluegen* is a type of cake, while *vetuevenfluegen* is analogous to *horn* in the idiom *to blow one's own horn*. However, in order to further establish the strangeness of Rose's lexis, Dorothy mispronounces *genueckenfluegen* as *gefluecken-nuegen*, while Sophia implies that *vetuevenfluegen* is a body part (a guess similar to the one she makes in example 4), which she can neither blow nor reach.

It should be noted here that, in the absence of any official episode transcripts and the fact that *geneuckenfluegen* and *vetuevenfluegen* do not actually exist, the transcript above represents merely an orthographical approximation. On the site http://goldengirls.wikia.com, the words are instead spelled *genügenflürgen* and *vertugenflürgen*, suggesting a slightly different aural reception of Rose's pronunciation. It is worthwhile to point out that the differently transcribed realizations of Rose's words further establish the unfamiliarity that confronts Blanche, Dorothy, and Sophia—as well as the viewing audience. Additionally, while there may be some difficulty in recognizing, capturing, and phonetically representing exactly what Rose said, the focus is nevertheless on the words as distinct lexical items and their status as lexical features of a regional dialect. Neither *geneuckenfluegen* nor *vetuevenfluegen* are recognizably English, and being uttered by Rose, they are assumed to be Scandinavian terms, quite possibly unique to the St. Olaf dialect. While evidence of Blanche's, Dorothy's, and Sophia's regional dialects is mainly in the form of accent and even features of grammar, Rose's regional dialect is most obviously characterized by a Scandinavian lexis. In the next section, we will examine the idea of language contact and its outcomes.

Language Contact

Though Rose is a native speaker of English, she is also a member of an immigrant community in the United States. In an American context, immigration is often responsible for a phenomenon known as 'language contact'. Language contact refers to a situation in which speakers of one language come into sustained contact and a need to communicate with speakers of another language. Language contact produces linguistic outcomes for both individuals and communities. Among them are borrowing, bilingualism, and bidialectalism.

Borrowing

'Borrowing' is a linguistic phenomenon that originates from language contact situations in which linguistic entities from one language are used by people who speak the other language. Borrowing is the most common result of language contact (Thomason 2001, 10). That a native speaker of English such as Rose might pepper her speech with words from another language may be somewhat surprising to some, but Rose is in good company; people from all linguistic backgrounds do this. And her particular tendency to use Scandinavian or Scandinavian-sounding words is not farfetched, given that in reality, for the hundred years between 1830 and 1930, large numbers of Scandinavians immigrated to the United States and settled in various places throughout the northern Midwest. Minnesota had the second largest percentage of Norwegian immigrants in 1940 (Haugen 1969, 31), thus resulting in language contact between English and Norwegian. Einar Haugen identified the dialect of American Norwegian, a variety of Norwegian spoken in the settlements of the Midwest (Haugen 1969) that resulted from intense contact between English and Norwegian. A speaker of Rose Nylund's presumed age might very well have been part of St. Olaf's linguistic life in which English and American Norwegian coexisted. The idea that Rose and other members of her community would use words and phrases that originated from Norwegian thus makes sense, as does the unlikelihood that speakers from outside this community or region would have these words in their own linguistic repertoires. The words of Scandinavian origin that Rose uses were presumably borrowed into English as a result of language contact, and eventually came to lexically characterize the St. Olaf dialect, as constructed for and represented in *The Golden Girls*.

Bilingualism

Another linguistic consequence of language contact, or in the case of Sophia coming into contact with another language, could be 'bilingualism', the state of having competence in two (or more) languages. Interpretation of 'competence' in a language is a controversial issue. While for some bilingualism refers to very high proficiency in all skills (reading, writing, speaking, listening), for others it may be enough to just know a few phrases in two or more languages. This is a debate that is beyond the scope of this chapter, but it is worth considering the bilingual status of the character of Sophia, who came to the United States from Palermo, Sicily, at the age of fourteen. Sophia has no discernible Italian accent; instead, her style of speech conjures up the character of a tough-talking New Yorker. Throughout the seven seasons of *The Golden Girls*, however, there are indications that Sophia is bilingual. For example, in the example below, Sophia translates for an elderly Italian contractor. In the episode "Rose's Big Adventure,"[10] both Dorothy and Sophia herself claim that Sophia's Italian is "rusty," but nevertheless Sophia accomplishes the following translation:

Example 6:

DOROTHY: Wait a minute, what does he want to charge us?

SOPHIA: I'll ask him.

(Sophia asks a simple question in Italian, and the contractor gives her a lengthy answer.)

SOPHIA: He says he'll do it for nothing, he likes getting away from the center, he also likes working, and most of all he likes being in the company of pretty young girls.

(Dorothy, Blanche, and Rose are flattered)

DOROTHY: Oh, well, since he puts it that way how can we refuse? It's a deal.

SOPHIA: Good. Here's a list of the pretty young girls he wants you to get for him.

(Transcribed by Kristy Beers Fägersten)

10. Written by Jeff Abugov.

In the episode "Foreign Exchange,"[11] two of Sophia's friends visiting from Sicily, Philomena and Dominic, arrive at the house, where introductions to Dorothy, Rose, and Blanche are made in English. When Blanche offers an effusive welcome, Philomena switches to Italian to speak to Dominic. In example 7, it is clear that Sophia teases about just how competent in Italian she is.

Example 7:

> BLANCHE: Oh what a charming old-world couple. Welcome to Miami!
>
> *(Philomena speaks in Italian to Dominic.)*
>
> BLANCHE: What did she say?
>
> DOMINIC: Eh, she says she wants to thank you for your gracious welcome.
>
> SOPHIA: Oh my Italian must really be rusty, I could swear she asked if you were a streetwalker.
>
> (Transcribed by Kristy Beers Fägersten)

Unlike Sophia, there are no indications that Rose is bilingual. Although she partakes in only a few Italian-language exchanges throughout the series, her translations and her own as well as Dorothy's observations that her Italian is "rusty" establish an underlying competence. Rose, on the other hand, does not engage with speakers of any Scandinavian languages nor does she allude to any linguistic abilities. Furthermore, the borrowings that characterize her St. Olaf dialect tend to reflect Americanized pronunciations, suggesting a distance to or a lack of competence in the language(s) of origin. However, both Sophia and Rose hail from regions known for their immigrant communities (Scandinavians in the northern Midwest, and Italians [among other nationalities] in the greater New York City area), where varying degrees of bilingualism can be assumed.

Bidialectalism

'Bidialectalism' refers to the ability to speak two or more dialects of the same language and also arises out of language (or language variety)

11. Written by Harriet B. Helberg and Sandy Helberg.

contact. For example, a person who could speak both British and Australian English would be considered bidialectal. Otherwise, bidialectalism is more critically discussed in terms of regional or social dialects in opposition to standard dialects. Bidialectalism is actually quite difficult to attain (Siegel 2010), particularly in terms of production abilities (Weener 1969), and researchers suspect that it may be more challenging to learn two dialects of the same language than two different languages.[12]

Bidialectalism often arises out of a need for speakers of a low-prestige social or regional dialect to be able to use a high-prestige, standard dialect (see chapter 2). While each of the characters of *The Golden Girls* exhibits characteristics of having regional dialects, they all speak a more or less standard, and thus overtly prestigious, social dialect. In the series finale, the two-part episode "One Flew out of the Cuckoo's Nest,"[13] Sophia adopts a Southern dialect when she learns that Dorothy will be marrying Lucas, a true Southern gentleman who also happens to be Blanche's uncle. Sophia dons a Southern servant's outfit and performs an exaggerated version of a Southern dialect, which is markedly in contrast to Blanche's higher-class, genteel dialect. The transcript in example 8 reflects an orthographical approximation of Sophia's turns.

Example 8:

(Sophia enters the living room from the kitchen; Lucas, Dorothy, and Blanche are seated.)

SOPHIA: Well, if it ain't the kinfolk.

DOROTHY: Ma, where did you get that outfit?

SOPHIA: I bought it. Figured, five Halloweens, it'll pay for itself. *(To Lucas)* Hope you brought your appetite, young fella. I know you gonna be pleased with the dinner [ˈdɪnə]: corn pone, succotash, collard greens—and them's just the appetizers.

(Rose enters)

12. In the episode "Rose's Big Adventure," Sophia blames the complicated regional dialects of Sicily for her communication problems with the contractor.

13. Written by Mitchell Hurwitz, Don Siegel, and Jerry Perzigian.

ROSE: Sorry to interrupt everybody, but I have an announcement *(notices Sophia)* . . . to make.

SOPHIA: A mess a somethin. I'll scare [ski:r] us up a mess a somethin.

(Transcribed by Kristy Beers Fägersten)

Sophia is of course merely appropriating a Southern servant persona and performing an associated Southern dialect to complete the pretense. Her performed regional (and social) Southern dialect can easily be deactivated (as it is, briefly, in response to Dorothy's question), and it is in contrast to Lucas's and Blanche's own Southern dialects by being overtly inferior in its stereotypical features, including nonstandard pronunciation (such as [skir] as a variant of *scare* [sker]), grammar (*them's* as a variant of *those are*), and lexis (*kinfolk, mess a somethin*). Although many people can similarly reproduce or perform approximations of regional or social dialects, the term 'bidialectal' is usually reserved for those who have natively or naturally acquired and/or use two or more dialects.

Discussion

The Golden Girls stands out in the television landscape as a long-running, successful series that featured four main characters who were similar in many ways but significantly different with regard to regional background. In fact, the characters' regional variation was highlighted in the series and foregrounded in their identities: Blanche was a Southern belle from Atlanta, Dorothy was a tough Brooklynite, Sophia was a Sicilian immigrant, and Rose was a proud former resident of St. Olaf, Minnesota. These regional backgrounds shaped the characters' linguistic identities.

The regional variation of *The Golden Girls* was not conveyed one-dimensionally, that is, by just one linguistic aspect. Instead, regional variation was indeed manifested as regional dialects, with examples of grammatical, phonological, and lexical features. In the context of a prime-time television series with a broad audience, it is important that dialectal features not jeopardize intelligibility. Not surprisingly, neither regional accent nor grammar deviated to any extreme extent, and regional vocabulary, which characterized Rose's speech, was instead capitalized on for humor. Words specific to the St. Olaf speech community had a distinct

Scandinavian sound and structure, which is evidence of a linguistic history characterized by language contact, which in turn can result in borrowing, bidialectalism, and bilingualism. Examples of each of these can be observed on *The Golden Girls*, distinguishing it as a series that drew from rich linguistic resources, oftentimes from all the way back in St. Olaf.

Suggestions for Further Viewing and Analysis

1. The four lead characters in *Designing Women* (1986–93), Julia Sugarbaker, Suzanne Sugarbaker, Mary Jo Shively, and Charlene Frazier, run an interior decorating firm in Atlanta, Georgia. Like Blanche Devereaux from *The Golden Girls*, Julia and her sister Suzanne both grew up in Atlanta. How do their regional dialects compare to Blanche's? How do they compare to the dialects of Mary Jo and Charlene, who come from Franklin, Kentucky, and Poplar Bluff, Missouri, respectively? Both Mary Jo and Charlene were to varying extents characterized as having less social finesse than the Sugarbakers: how much of this characterization was a function of their regional dialects? Are different Southern dialects associated with different values or prestige?

2. *King of the Hill* (1997–2010) centered around Hank Hill, a propane salesman living in Arlen, Texas. Each of Hank's family members and two of his three main friends speak a similar type of familiar Southern dialect, with the exception of the character Boomhauer, whose speech is nearly unintelligible. However, in the episode "A Firefighting We Will Go,"[14] the four friends recount their own versions of how the firehouse burned down. In Boomhauer's version, he is the only one who speaks intelligibly, while the other three sound like Boomhauer normally does. Consider how this may be evidence of bidialectalism.

3. Series taking place in the US South have long been a popular staple of American television production, with many titles explicitly referring to their Southern settings: *The Dukes of Hazzard* (1979–85) were not only recklessly dangerous as the series title teases, but also lived in Hazzard County, Georgia; *Evening Shade* (1990–94) took place in Evening Shade,

14. Written by Alan R. Cohen and Alan Freedland.

Arkansas; the series *Dallas* (1978–91) foregrounded its Dallas, Texas, setting; *One Tree Hill* (2003–12) took place in Tree Hill, North Carolina; while the series name *The Beverly Hillbillies* (1962–71) hints at the incongruence of Ozarks hillbillies in Beverly Hills, California. Compare the speech of characters in these series with characters from similarly named series taking place in other regions of the United States: *WKRP in Cincinnati* (1978–82), *LA Law* (1986–94), *NYPD Blue* (1993–2005), *Chicago Hope* (1994–2000), *South Park* (1997–), *Boston Legal* (2004–8), *Hot in Cleveland* (2010–), or *Fargo* (2014–). Are there any regional dialects that are as easily identifiable as the Southern dialect?

References

Farr, David T. 2015. "The Farr Side: Celebrating the 30th Anniversary of 'The Golden Girls'." *Pocono Record*, Sept. 17. Accessed Sept. 19, 2015. http://www.poconorecord.com/article/20150917/NEWS/150919546.

Haugen, Einar. 1969. *The Norwegian Language in America: A Study in Bilingual Behavior*. Bloomington: Indiana Univ. Press.

Kaler, Anne K. 1990. "*Golden Girls*: Feminine Archetypal Patterns of the Complete Woman." *Journal of Popular Culture* 24:49–60.

Labov, William, Sherry Ash, and Charles Boberg. 2006. *Atlas of North American English: Phonetics, Phonology and Sound Change*. New York: Mouton de Gruyter.

Siegel, Jeff. 2010. *Second Dialect Acquisition*. New York: Cambridge Univ. Press.

Thomason, Sarah G. 2001. *Language Contact*. Edinburgh: Edinburgh Univ. Press.

Toolan, Michael. 2011. "'I Don't Know What They're Saying Half the Time, but I'm Hooked on the Series': Incomprehensible Dialogue and Integrated Multimodal Characterisation in *The Wire*." In *Telecinematic Discourse: Approaches to the Language of Films and Television Series*, edited by Roberta Piazza, Monika Bednarek, and Fabio Rossi, 161–83. Amsterdam: John Benjamins.

Weener, Paul D. 1969. "Social Dialect Differences and the Recall of Verbal Messages." *Journal of Educational Psychology* 60:194–99.

Yuko, Elizabeth. 2015. "Op-ed: Why The Golden Girls Never Lost Its Luster." *Advocate*. Accessed Sept. 8, 2015. http://www.advocate.com/commentary/2015/09/08/op-ed-why-golden-girls-never-lost-its-luster.

4

SaMANtha

Language and Gender in Sex and the City

KRISTY BEERS FÄGERSTEN AND HANNA SVEEN

Sex and the City premiered on cable network HBO in 1998, which broadcast the last of the series' ninety-four episodes in 2004. Throughout its six-season run, *Sex and the City* enjoyed consecutive Golden Globe Award nominations for Best Television Comedy/Musical Series and Emmy Award nominations for Outstanding Comedy Series, eventually winning the former in 2000, 2001, and 2002, and the latter in 2001. Additionally, the series and its cast members were nominated for more than seventy other broadcast awards, including seven Emmy Award nominations for Outstanding Writing for a Comedy Series.

Although the title accurately summarizes the series' basic goal of depicting sexual relationships in New York City, *Sex and the City* can more correctly be said to be about friendship, specifically female friendships. At the start of the series, characters Carrie Bradshaw, Miranda Hobbes, Charlotte York, and Samantha Jones were all single, in their thirties, and fully employed: Carrie as a writer of "Sex and the City," a newspaper column about sex and relationships; Miranda as a lawyer; Charlotte as an art gallery curator; and Samantha as a public relations executive. In each episode, Carrie mused about a specific aspect of relationships for the purpose of her column, most often guided by her own and her friends' experiences. Hookups and breakups, promiscuity, abstinence, infidelity, and sexual positions, practices, trends, and deviations, among other things, were often depicted in provocative detail. As Janna L. Kim and colleagues note, the four female leads "defy the Heterosexual Script by exhibiting sexually agency, prioritizing their sexual pleasure, and valuing their independence from men" (2007, 155). This defiance is enabled by their privileged status as white, educated, upper-class, heterosexual females, which also allows them to believably deviate from stereotypical language use. Thus, while the female leads would separately navigate their own sexual relationships, in each episode they would interact with each other in various constellations (but most commonly all four together) and discuss their experiences in, for television at that time, an unusually open manner. While the sex scenes helped to distinguish *Sex and the City* as groundbreaking television, the intimacy and explicitness with which the female lead characters interacted with each other garnered the series a wide and loyal audience. If language use were totally and absolutely determined by gender, we could expect that each of the four female characters of *Sex and the City* (and, by extension, all females) would communicate in the same or very similar ways. This, however, is simply not the case, as illustrated best by the character of Samantha, who represents the most obvious deviation from conventional notions of how women speak. Indeed, so stereotypically masculine is Samantha's communicative behavior that one wonders if the name *Samantha*, with its second-syllable emphasis, isn't essentially a tongue-in-cheek indication of her true linguistic identity. By comparing Samantha's typical speech practices to examples from Carrie, Charlotte, and Miranda, we illustrate that gender is not an absolute variable but rather exists on a continuum, and that language use is neither determined by gender nor a function of gender alone, but rather can be considered the representation or construction of one's position within a social group and one's role in a social context.

Throughout this chapter, we consider examples of talk and interaction in *Sex and the City* (also referred to as *SATC*) from a gender perspective, proposing that the series both supports and challenges theories about the relationship between gender and language, specifically with regard to women's language. The chapter thus provides tools for recognizing and understanding gender roles in television series by highlighting linguistic strategies of gender construction.

Folk-linguistic Beliefs about Gender and Language

In a fictional television series, all characters' talk is constructed, mainly by writers, actors, or directors, so as to create, develop, and reflect a recognizable identity. Biological sex is one of the most salient features of an identity, but the state of being male or female is not achieved simply through talk. Gender, on the other hand, referring to how 'masculine' or 'feminine' a person behaves, or to what degree a person orients to masculinity or femininity, can be conveyed via linguistic means. Gender is thus a performance: it can be said that one behaves like a woman or like a man.

When it comes to gender as constructed and performed by the speech of fictional characters, it is the real people around the character, including the viewers, actors, or writers, who have conscious or subconscious ideas of what is traditionally considered typical masculine or feminine traits in talk. These ideas can be based on research and/or experience, and can be considered to represent a hegemonic discourse about gender differences, that is, the dominant, and often blindly accepted, way of thinking and talking about gender. If we assume that there are perceived gender differences in talk, and that some features are considered more feminine and others more masculine, these features can be arranged along a continuum or scale ranging from very masculine to very feminine and everything in between. In that way we stress that gender does not consist of two binary features, female or male. Nevertheless, by performing gender along this continuum every time we speak, we construct or perform a gender identity that is often perceived, by ourselves and/or by others, as being predominantly feminine or masculine.

As an obvious forum for performance, television constitutes a relevant vista for investigations of identity construction, not in the least those that pertain to gender and language. Investigations of fictional characters allow us to observe the application of folk linguistics, or how nonlinguists perceive, relate to, and evaluate language use. Folk-linguistic beliefs about language guide writers in constructing characters who are easily identifiable by viewers, and thus the construction of masculinity and femininity both draws from and perpetuates stereotypes about language and gender. According to Jennifer M. Rey (2001, 138), "while language used on television is obviously not the same as unscripted language, it does represent the language scriptwriters imagine that real women and men produce," and as such can reveal perceived differences in women's and men's speech. By way of example, let us consider the following bits of dialogue, which were extracted from six different episodes of *Sex and the City*.

a. Oh god. There goes my hard-on.
("The Perfect Present"[1])

b. 97 percent of them can't fuck you worth a damn!
("The Man, the Myth, the Viagra"[2])

c. I totally should've seen this coming, but of course I didn't, because they wait for you to get relaxed and comfortable, before they bring the ice pick down right between your eyes.
("The Fuck Buddy"[3])

d. Don't bust my balls. If you're a head-hunter, get me a good assistant.
("Boy, Girl, Boy, Girl . . ."[4])

e. No, *we're* friends, but I don't put my dick in you.
("Where There's Smoke . . ."[5])

f. I totally believe that love conquers all. Sometimes you just have to give it a little space, and that's exactly what is missing in Manhattan—the space for romance.
("Sex and the City–Pilot"[6])

If we consider this list of conversation excerpts, albeit taken out of situational context, which ones would we attribute to male speakers and which ones to female speakers? Presented in this way in a chapter on language and gender, it is not too difficult to suspect that this is a trick question. In an idealized exercise, however, extracts a, b, d, and e would be identified as statements from men, and extracts c and f as statements from

1. Written by Jenny Bicks.
2. Written by Michael Patrick King.
3. Written by Merrill Markoe and Darren Star.
4. Written by Darren Star and Jenny Bicks.
5. Written by Darren Star.
6. Written by Darren Star.

women. These conclusions would then shockingly be revealed as incorrect, and any preconceived notions of the relationship between gender and language would be dramatically challenged.

Extracts a, b, d, and e were, in fact, uttered by Kim Catrall, portraying the *Sex and the City* character Samantha: promiscuous, free-spoken, opinionated, and socially fearless. Examples c and f were lines delivered by Ben Weber, portraying the male character Skipper, a sensitive and romantic web designer who had an on-again, off-again relationship with Miranda. In the first quote, Samantha expresses her disappointment and reduced sexual attraction to a waiter she has been flirting with, when he insists that he is actually an aspiring actor. In the second quote, Samantha is complaining about the men of New York City. In quote c, Skipper is lamenting his experience with women and yet another bad break-up. In quotes d and e, respectively, Samantha is on the phone berating a recruiter for not finding her a worthy assistant, and taking issue with the use of the word "friend" to describe a sexual partner. In the sixth quote (f), Skipper is waxing romantic in a discussion about love and relationships.

Despite the answer key having been revealed at this point, why is it that we can still assume that the examples from Samantha would more stereotypically be identified as typical of a male speaker, while the examples from Skipper would be considered more typically female? While there are implications of gender via anatomical references ("hard-on," "balls," "dick"), it is also likely that many people would base their conclusions on folk-linguistic beliefs about gender and language, for example that men are more direct and more likely to swear, while women are indirect and insecure in their speech and often complain, such as illustrated by Skipper's quotes.

In the following sections, we present an overview of past and current research on gender and language, and highlight and illustrate the main theories, conclusions, and controversies with further examples of language use in a range of episodes from *Sex and the City*.

An Overview of Language and Gender Research

Language and gender as an academic field can be divided into two areas of interest: on the one hand, investigations of potential differences in language use *about* males and females, which include studies of sexism in language, and on the other hand, investigations of potential differences in language use *by* males and females. While this chapter focuses on the latter area, it is worth briefly considering *SATC* even as an illustration of the former, before moving on to examples of talk.

Talk about Men and Women

While much of what Carrie, Miranda, Charlotte, and Samantha, as well as other characters, talk about in *SATC* revolves around notions of men and women, the dialogue does not immediately lend itself to investigations of how men and women are talked *about* in the sense of language and gender. Instead, it is perhaps more effective to illustrate language about gender by looking at how the female characters themselves are discursively treated in the media. For example, in a recent critique of *SATC*, the lead characters were dismissed as revisited "types" already embodied by *The Golden Girls*, and easily identified as "the Slut, the Prude, the Career Woman, the Heroine" (that is, Samantha, Charlotte, Miranda, and Carrie [Martin 2013]). Emily Nussbaum (2013) problematizes these and similar labels for the characters of *SATC*, such as "man-haters or gold-diggers," and also discusses the problem with simply labeling *SATC* and its ilk as "chick-centric series." Terms such as *slut*, *prude*, *man-hater*, *gold-digger*, and *chick* are commonly, if not exclusively, used to refer to females, and as such constitute sexist language. *Slut* and *prude* furthermore suggest a damned-if-you-do, damned-if-you-don't conundrum with regard to female sexuality. Men are rarely referred to as sluts or prudes, but rather their sexual activity is normally positively evaluated in terms such as *bachelor*, *ladies' man*, *stud*, and so forth. A comparison of these and similar terms for men and women reveals a problematic relationship, in which "a woman is a sexual being dependent on man, whereas man is simply defined as a human being whose existence does not need reference to woman" (Pauwels 2003, 553). In other words, language perpetuates the idea of that which M. R. Schulz (1975) refers to as the "generic man" and the "sexual woman."

Reinforcing the notion of the male as the norm is asymmetry, or an inequality in gender-marked terms. A particularly clear example of asymmetry can be found in the form of gender-marked pairs, such as *Mr.* vs. *Ms./Mrs./Miss*. While the singular term for males allows no room for speculation of age or marital status, the existence of three terms for females imposes such categorization on women and even invites a disparaging use of these terms. For example, while Samantha is respectfully referred to several times throughout the series as *Ms. Jones* ("Belles of the Balls,"[7] "The Ick Factor,"[8] "Pick-a-Little, Talk-a-Little"[9]), in "Four Women and a Funeral"[10] she is addressed as *Miss Jones* by a disdainful hostess at a high-class restaurant, who informs Samantha she is no longer welcome there. The use of *Miss* conveys a pretense of respect, while at the same time denying Samantha any real significance or power. This singular deviation in address terms thus surely reflects a deliberate writing decision, which in turn can be considered a reflection of the realistic consequences of asymmetry.

Asymmetry is also evident in a lack of female-marked equivalents for terms such as *man*, *he*, or *fellow*, used in their generic senses. And, at the same time, there are also a number of disparaging words for females that do not seem to have male-marked equivalents. Two noteworthy examples from other television series reflect an attempt to rectify the asymmetry in part: *mimbo*, a male bimbo (*Seinfeld*, "The Stall"[11]) and *mastress*, a male mistress (*How I Met Your Mother*, "Slap Bet"[12]). Such instances raise our awareness of the asymmetry and ultimately the inequality of language, which is the essential focus of language and gender studies, even when the focus is on language use *by* men and women, as we see in the next section.

Talk by Men and Women

Linguistics has long been characterized by an approach to language use that positions male speech as the norm. In fact, as early as 1922, linguist

7. Written by Michael Patrick King.

8. Written by Julie Rottenberg and Elisa Zuritsky.

9. Written by Julie Rottenberg and Elisa Zuritsky.

10. Written by Jenny Bicks.

11. Written by Larry Charles.

12. Written by Kourtney Kang.

Otto Jespersen infamously pronounced women's language as not only significantly different from men's language, but also inferior to it, thereby reflecting women's inferior social status and lesser abilities (Jespersen 1922). Jespersen's many generalizations about gender and language and his dismissive attitude toward women and women's linguistic behavior more or less permeated the collective linguistic subconscious until the 1970s. Since then, the study of language and gender has developed from both introspection and empirical evidence, resulting in a number of notable interactionist theories, or theories based on language use in conversation or other interactional forms of communication. These include the theories of deficit, dominance, and difference. While these theories have contributed significantly to a better understanding of the relationship between language and gender, their shared focus on a gender dichotomy (Baxter 2011), which contrasts and polarizes men and women and their linguistic behaviors, presupposes similarities within the genders and differences between them. Variation in language use, referring to the facts that not all women speak the same, that not all men speak differently from women, and that not just gender influences language use, is more fully acknowledged by the social constructionist approach.

The Deficit Theory

The deficit theory is attributed to Robin Lakoff, who suggested in the 1975 text *Language and Woman's Place* that the place a woman then occupied in American society was subordinate to that of a man's, and so her language use was similarly viewed as unequal, or deficient. Lakoff theorized that this subordinate status was reflected in and a function of language, with females being socialized from a young age to use language in a ladylike way, which in turn served to maintain subordination. A woman's style of language was characterized as "more tentative, hesitant, indirect, and therefore a more powerless version of men's [language]" (Baxter 2011), and can be recognized by features such as hedges and questions. As we shall see, this theory is very similar to the dominance theory, because it too focuses on power relationships between speakers. However, historically in language and gender research, the dominance theory was primarily applied to mixed-sex conversations, to explain the immediate indirect power relationship between the interlocutors in the conversations (interpreted as a reflection of inequality in society). For the sake of simplicity, we make the same distinction in the present chapter.

It Might Possibly be Hedging, Maybe

'Hedges' are words or phrases that mitigate or lessen the impact of what is being said by invoking possibility or uncertainty. Hedges such as *maybe*, *I think*, or *could* are thus often associated with a lack of knowledge, conviction, or power. In example 1, Miranda employs multiple hedges as a way of not showing complete commitment or to indicate uncertainty. She had previously run into Skipper, a former boyfriend with whom she broke up because of his youth, immaturity, and gentle nature. At their chance meeting, however, Skipper was with a new woman, thereby triggering feelings of jealousy in Miranda. Later in the evening, Miranda called Skipper to explore the possibility of dating again. Unbeknownst to Miranda, Skipper and his date were having sex at the time of her call, and thus, in example 1, Miranda first speaks to the answering machine.

Example 1:

MIRANDA: Hi Skipper it's Miranda. Umm, I just wanted to say it was great running into you today. And, uh . . . you looked great! Did you do something different to your hair?

SKIPPER: *(interrupting the sexual activity)* Um, hello? Miranda. Hey. Uh, yeah, I can't talk right now.

MIRANDA: That's ok. I just wanted to say maybe, you know, I thought we could have dinner some night.

SKIPPER: Seriously?

("The Monogamists"[13])

In Miranda's second turn, she mitigates her proposition, essentially one of asking Skipper out on a date, via a total of six hedges, marked in

13. Written by Darren Star.

italics: I *just* wanted to say *maybe, you know,* I *thought* we *could* have dinner *some night*. Examples of similar hedges expressing uncertainty and/or minimizing the speaker's commitment to a statement include *just/only/simply, maybe/perhaps, you know/I mean, could/would/should, thought/was thinking, some night/some day/some time.*

In example 1, Miranda's use of hedges identifies her as the subordinate of the two interlocutors, and signals her proposition as subject to rejection from Skipper. Her use of hedges could thus also signal nervousness, an emotion triggered by the situation rather than by the gender of the speaker. The observed or even believed high frequency of hedges in women's speech is associated with their subordinate roles in mixed-sex conversations, constructed by and reflected in speech that is tentative and nonassertive.

Examples of hedging can also be found in many of *SATC*'s same-sex interactions. In example 2, all four friends are discussing soul mates. Charlotte believes there is one soul mate for everyone, an opinion in direct opposition to that of her three friends. Initially, Charlotte acknowledges the disagreement and states her opinion assertively: "I disagree. I believe that there is that one perfect person out there to complete you." As the discussion continues, however, her opinion is called into question, and Charlotte resorts to hedging by qualifying her statement with the nonaffirmative expressions *got to be* and *maybe* in the final turn.

Example 2:

CHARLOTTE: No that is not how it works.

CARRIE: *(turning to face Charlotte and holding her gaze in mock challenge)* Oh. Okay.

MIRANDA: But you're still looking outside yourself. It's saying that you're not enough.

. . .

CHARLOTTE: But there's got to be that someone out there who's just perfect for me. Maybe I should keep looking.

("The Agony and the Ex-tacy"[14])

14. Written by Michael Patrick King.

What's with All the Questions?

Questions are also a hallmark of women's speech, according to the deficit theory. Conventionally, questions are asked by people who seek knowledge and are thus unsure of an answer. Conventional questions are salient in the language of *Sex and the City*. In fact, Claudia Bubel (2005) found that the female characters engaged in 'doing' friendship primarily via two different alignment practices: asking questions and using terms of address (see the next section, "The Dominance Theory"). Lakoff (1975) claimed that women's speech contained more questions, question intonation, and tag questions than men's speech, and subsequent research in support of her deficit theory (such as Brouwer, Gerritsen, and de Haan 1979; Fishman 1978; Fishman 1980b) also revealed a greater frequency of questions among women than men. Question-laden speech was duly attributed to the status of women as insecure and powerless, occupying subordinate positions, which these linguistic features constructed, reflected, and maintained.

At the heart of each episode is one of Carrie's constant musings about sex and relationships, often in the form of questions and often introduced by the phrase "I couldn't help but wonder . . ."; according to one tally, Carrie 'wondered' aloud forty-two times over six seasons (Sharma 2013). Carrie's inquisitive nature as a writer prompts her to question her friends and herself, and she likewise fields questions from her friends. Example 3 illustrates a typical question-prompted conversation between the female friends. In this example, Carrie is concerned about where she stands with Mr. Big after seeing him out with another woman. The example begins with Carrie's voice-over narration.

Example 3:

CARRIE: *(voice-over narration)* There were so many questions I wanted him to answer, but would not ask. Not tonight at least. No, tonight I would ask Miranda.

CARRIE: He said, "I miss you baby." Do you think that was meant to be some kind of coded mea culpa?

MIRANDA: You mean like what he really meant was, "I've been a complete idiot, please forgive me for having dinner with that other woman"?

CARRIE: Exactly.

MIRANDA: Could be.

CARRIE: Well, no, because that would mean that everything he ever said that I interpreted as sincere is subject to interpretation, and in that case, what I perceive as his feelings for me may only really be reflected projections of my feelings for him.

MIRANDA: What?

CARRIE: Oh God, I'm freaking. I gotta stop. I'll stop.

This example illustrates the conversational style of Carrie and Miranda in their same-sex interactions. They are eager to engage each other in discussion and explore each other's thoughts and opinions via questions (such as "Do you think . . ." in Carrie's first turn), or through the use of questioning intonation (for example, Miranda's first turn). It is interesting to note that one question can trigger another, as Carrie's question does, and that the question format may serve not just to elicit answers and opinions from others, but rather to allow the questioner to supply her own answers, such as in Carrie's third turn. Questions can also signal confusion, misunderstanding, or even rejection of a proposition, such as in Miranda's final turn.

Unlike conventional questions, 'tag questions' come at the ends of declarative statements, essentially turning the declarations into questions, which invite a response. Tag questions such as *isn't it?* or *don't you?* are asked in order to receive confirmation of a statement and can indicate a lack of certainty as well as a desire to be supported or an attempt to engage others in conversation (see next section). In comparison to conventional questions, tag questions are used less frequently by the female leads of *SATC*, especially by Samantha. Example 4, however, showcases one of these rare occasions, and features Samantha as linguistically out of character. Her current lover, James, suspects something is troubling Samantha because of her lack of interest in sex, and he has suggested that they attend couples counseling. James does not know that, although Samantha is emotionally attached to him, she is neither sexually attracted to nor satisfied by him, owing to his small penis. In the counseling session, Samantha tries to avoid revealing this as the reason for her loss of interest in sex.

Example 4:

JAMES: I've noticed that our sex-life has diminished.

SAMANTHA: That's normal, isn't it? I mean, after a while—

COUNSELOR: How long has it been?

JAMES: A month.

. . .

SAMANTHA: I'm just not feeling very sexual these days.

("The Awful Truth"[15])

Contrary to her last statement, Samantha is always feeling very sexual, and neither a diminished sex life nor attending counseling is normal for her. Nonetheless, she must pretend not to know what is at the root of her and James's problems. Her tag question, *isn't it?*, is an overt attempt to enlist the support of the counselor with regard to the claim of normalcy. It can also be considered an indication of her subordinate, defensive position vis-à-vis the counselor and James, which is further suggested by the hedges *I mean* and *just* in her subsequent utterances. In the end, Samantha is unwilling to maintain the charade and reverts back to her normal style of talk, bluntly telling James that his penis is too small. In the next section, we will consider further examples of the more typical aspects of Samantha's interaction style.

The Dominance Theory

The deficit approach to language that began with Jespersen and was further explored and socially contextualized by Lakoff asserts a dichotomy between women and men with respect to language use that ultimately serves to promote men's speech as the norm and women's speech as deficient. However, while Lakoff and others explored the supposed subordinate status of women, others have focused on patriarchy and the assertion of male power and superiority as contributing factors to differences in language use. The dominance theory of language and linguistic inequality reflects this perspective, and proposes that, in mixed-sex conversations,

15. Written by Darren Star.

all participants co-construct a pattern of male dominance and female submission, represented and enacted in terms of quantity of talk vs. silence, interruptions, use of questions to engage other speakers, or frequency of conversational back-channeling (that is, using minimal responses such as *mm-hmm* or *yeah* to signal attention to the speaker).

By way of example, we can consider how *SATC* reflects the folk-linguistic belief that women talk more than men, and that men are more reticent. This is, in fact, not the case (Cameron 2007; Fishman 1978; James and Drakich 1993), but the stereotype persists, and it is capitalized on in the series' fourth season, when Samantha dates a lesbian, Maria. In example 5, extracted from the season's fourth episode, Samantha is talking on the phone with Carrie. Previously that same evening, Samantha had introduced Maria to Carrie, Miranda, and Charlotte, and the telephone call to Carrie was to inquire about their reactions to Samantha's dating a lesbian.

Example 5:

CARRIE: Hello?

SAMANTHA: So, did you and the girls run down the street talking about me?

CARRIE: Maybe.

SAMANTHA: How many blocks?

CARRIE: Ohhh . . . 2. Okay, 9.

SAMANTHA: Honestly, I'm a little hurt. I mean, all the hours I listen to you people talking about your relationships.

CARRIE: You do that?

SAMANTHA: I make the courtesy call, "Do you think you love him, blah, blah, blah."

("What's Sex Got to Do with It?"[16])

Here, Samantha's turn-final "blah blah blah" hints at an extension to the folk-linguistic belief that women talk a lot, namely, that their abundant talk tends to focus on interpersonal relationships. In example 5, Samantha represents the male norm by expressing contempt for too much talk

16. Written by Nicole Avril.

and for relationships as a valid topic of conversation. This stereotypical representation and the identification of Samantha as ever more obviously embodying a (linguistically) male persona are further developed as Samantha and Maria continue their courtship. By the end of the fourth episode (from which example 5 is extracted), Samantha was exhilarated by her new lesbian relationship; her enthusiasm seems to have diminished, however, by the beginning of the fifth episode, as illustrated in example 6. Here Samantha has agreed to accompany Miranda to the opening of a bar, and Miranda assumes Samantha will bring Maria.

Example 6:

MIRANDA: I'm going out with Samantha and her lesbian lover and I am proud.

SAMANTHA: Let's not invite Maria. I could use a night away from the ole ball-and-chain.

CARRIE: Oh, don't tell me you're in a sapphic slump.

SAMANTHA: All we ever do is lie around, take baths together, and talk about feelings.

CHARLOTTE: I think they call that a relationship.

SAMANTHA: I don't know how you people do it. All that emotional chow-chow, it's exhausting.

MIRANDA: I know, don't you just hate that?

CARRIE: Mm, women.

("Ghost Town"[17])

Samantha does not seem to focus on dating *as* a woman, but rather dating *a* woman, whom she refers to with the classically sexist expression "ball and chain," thereby identifying as a male and imposing a heteronormative construct on her lesbian relationship. Moreover, with the phrase "you people" Samantha overtly distances herself from (and belittles) women/the female gender, serving to establish or even confirm men as the norm. She further aligns with this norm by complaining about and ridiculing stereotypical female behavior, such as 'bathing' and 'discussing

17. Written by Allan Heinberg.

feelings'. In their final turns, Miranda and Carrie acknowledge Samantha's self-identification as a man, ironically co-constructing women as the other.

Samantha's irritated tone that accompanies the phrases "all we ever do" and "talk about feelings," and her dismissal of such talk as "emotional chow-chow," succeed in constructing her as a stereotypical male, while, at the same time, capitalizing on and perpetuating such folk-linguistic beliefs that women talk more than men. However, empirical studies suggest that the opposite is the case, and that it is men who, in fact, talk more in terms of total time of talk or words uttered (Cameron 2007; Fishman 1978; James and Drakich 1993), often interrupting women (West and Zimmerman 1983) or neither responding to women's efforts to develop a topic (DeFrancisco 1991) nor making equal efforts to engage women in conversation via, for example, questions (Fishman 1980a). According to the dominance theory of gender and language, men achieve and maintain conversational control and power in this way.

Further dominance is enacted by a speech style that can be characterized as direct, assertive, and competitive. Men's talk demonstrates expertise and orients toward problem-solving more so than discussion (Butler 1999; Eckert and McConnell-Ginet 1992), and men hold "center stage" and position themselves in a hierarchy through shows of knowledge and skill (Tannen 1990, 77). Conversational dominance can also be exerted via rejection of a topic of conversation, or overt introductions of new topics. In the next example, all four women are seated around a table at a café, and Charlotte is lamenting her difficulties in choosing a wedding dress. Samantha's participation in the interaction illustrates a direct, assertive style of speech, a demonstration of expertise, an orientation toward problem solving, and a rejection of Charlotte's topic of conversation via an introduction of Samantha's own. It is interesting to note that, prior to the featured exchange, the scene began with Charlotte presenting a stack of bridal magazines and distributing them to her friends with instructions. Charlotte had managed to engage Carrie and Miranda in the physical task and an accompanying discussion, while Samantha was unresponsive to Charlotte's efforts. Instead, Samantha changes the topic by asking if the others have ever had an AIDS test. Carrie notes the abrupt conversational shift, but she and Miranda dutifully reply and orient themselves to Samantha and away from Charlotte. Charlotte politely asks Samantha not to talk about AIDS testing while they are looking at wedding gowns, but she is ignored as Carrie and Miranda continue the topic introduced by Samantha. Charlotte makes a second attempt to redirect the conversation, and, in example 7, a third.

Example 7:

CHARLOTTE: There are 1,400 gowns in this magazine and I have only seen 600 of them. I need help.

SAMANTHA: Okay, listen, you need to chill the fuck out and hire yourself a stylist.

CHARLOTTE: A stylist?

SAMANTHA: Yeah, some little minion to run around town and do your dress bidding.

CHARLOTTE: I can hire someone to do that for me?

SAMANTHA: Oh, honey, this is New York City, you can hire someone to do anything. I'll fax you some names.

CHARLOTTE: Oh thank you thank you thank you!

("Running with Scissors"[18])

Samantha's first turn is direct and assertive, and it includes swearing, a practice stereotypically associated with dominance and masculinity (de Klerk 1991, 1992; Stapleton 2010). This turn is also goal-oriented, as Samantha focuses on solving Charlotte's problem. In her second and third turns, Samantha displays her knowledge and expertise by addressing Charlotte's questions regarding what she means by "stylist" and what is a feasible action to take. Samantha further secures her expertise by referring to "some names," indicating that she not only knows what can be done, but she knows who can do it.

Example 7 also includes a characteristic feature of Samantha's speech, namely, her practice of addressing her friends and others as *honey*. This

18. Written by Michael Patrick King.

term of endearment, along with *sweetie* and *sweetheart*, occurs frequently in *SATC*. For example, in her analysis of the series' first two seasons (thirty episodes), Bubel (2005, 161) notes that Samantha used *honey* twenty-two times, and *sweetie* and *sweetheart* three times each. By comparison, Carrie used *sweetie* twenty-one times, *sweetheart* once, and *honey* eight times, while Miranda and Charlotte used none of these terms during the first two seasons. Bubel's analyses indicate that Carrie uses terms of endearment to initiate intimacy, apologize, mitigate directives, and offer comfort or support (in line with Bednarek's [2011] analysis of *honey* as an affiliative device in *The Gilmore Girls*). Samantha's use of *honey*, on the other hand, is associated with knowledge displays. This observation applies throughout all six seasons of the series, with Samantha addressing Carrie, Miranda, Charlotte, and others as *honey* in nearly every episode, as a prelude to knowledge display, an expert evaluation, or a speech act, that is, an utterance designed to cause another to perform an action.

Research on gender and language has shown that women tend to avoid expressing expertise or engaging in other overt displays of knowledge or power (Bubel 2005; see also Coates 1996; Lakoff 1975; Tannen 1990), and thus by repeatedly advising, evaluating, opinionating, and commanding, Samantha again linguistically aligns with a dominant male speaker. This alignment via knowledge display is emphasized by her use of *honey*, consistently uttered with noticeable emphasis on the first syllable and a falling or steady word-final intonation. *Honey*, in turn, simultaneously serves to frame the addressee as a non-expert, novice, subordinate, or otherwise unequal and thus an appropriate target for Samantha's exhibitions of knowledge and power. Other forms of address delivered in this way, including terms of endearment such as *sweetie* and *sweetheart*, can also serve to patronize, condescend, or disrespect (Lerner 2003; Goodwin 1990; Sidnell 2011) their targets. However, throughout the six seasons of *SATC*, there is a distinct difference in communicative function between Carrie's frequent use of *sweetie* to signal intimacy, and Samantha's frequent use of *honey* to signal superiority. This is just one of many ways that the series indexes the different communicative styles between Carrie, Miranda, and Charlotte, on the one hand, and Samantha on the other.

The Difference Theory

The deficit and dominance theories can broadly be considered two sides of the same coins, in which the former focuses more on women's language and the latter more on men's. Both theories, however, highlight differences in language use, serving to confirm or recognize male language as the norm, thereby establishing it as the default basis for comparison. The difference theory, articulated and popularized by Deborah Tannen (1990), reflects an approach to language and gender that highlights a different-but-equal perspective. In other words, the difference theory proposes that, based on presumed differences in their use of language, men and women constitute two different cultures, each with their own communicative styles, one neither inferior nor subordinate to the other.

According to Tannen's difference theory, men's language reflects an orientation toward status, problem-solving, communicating information, giving orders, engaging in confrontation, and maintaining independence. Women's language, on the other hand, reflects orientation toward showing support, seeking understanding, building relationships, being polite, avoiding or resolving disagreement, and achieving intimacy. The different cultures are learned at a young age, with boys competing to grab and hold the floor, and speaking for a distinct purpose, while girls learn to cooperate and express their feelings (Maltz and Borker 1982). The cultural differences are manifested in communicative styles that Tannen (1990) neatly summarized as report-talk vs. rapport-talk—which, in scripted television language, can be recognized as informational vs. involved production (Rey 2001).

In the previous section, example 7 illustrated typical men's speech according to the difference theory, whereby Samantha makes a status display (rejecting/introducing a topic), problem-solves, communicates information, gives orders, engages in confrontation, and remains independent (for example, makes a decision without consulting Charlotte). Samantha's different communicative style is made more evident when compared to how the speech of Carrie, Miranda, and Charlotte can be considered to represent women's language according to the difference theory, as the next two examples illustrate. First, in example 8, the four women are gathered in Carrie's apartment, paging through fashion magazines and commenting on the female models featured within. Charlotte and Miranda express self-dissatisfaction in comparison with the models, which prompts Carrie to allay their insecurities.

Example 8:

> CARRIE: What are you talking about? Look at you two, you're beautiful.
>
> CHARLOTTE: Awnh, I hate my thighs.
>
> MIRANDA: Oh come on!
>
> CHARLOTTE: I can't even open a magazine without thinking, thighs thighs thighs.
>
> MIRANDA: Well, I'll take your thighs and raise you a chin.
>
> CARRIE: I'll take your chin and raise you a hmm *(points at nose).*
>
> *(Carrie, Miranda, and Charlotte look at Samantha)*
>
> SAMANTHA: What?
>
> CARRIE: Oh, come on!
>
> SAMANTHA: Hey, I happen to love the way I look.
>
> ("Models and Mortals"[19])

In this example, Carrie, Miranda, and Charlotte co-construct a complaining event and engage in a form of self-disclosure, which can be likened to what Tannen (1990) calls "troubles talk," that is, the sharing of problems, worries, or concerns. While men may react to troubles talk by offering advice or a solution, women are more likely to share or disclose their own troubles, thereby supporting their conversational partner through alignment, and achieving intimacy through mutual disclosure. In example 8, Samantha overtly refrains from taking part in troubles talk, which signals her as a nonpractitioner of this 'genderlect', or the style of speech associated with women. Example 8 also illustrates the supportive nature of women's talk: Carrie, Miranda, and Charlotte support each other by establishing that they are not alone in their dissatisfaction with their appearances. The fact that Samantha does not volunteer any criticism of

19. Written by Darren Star.

her own appearance can thus be interpreted not only as nonsupportive but as an affirmation of the other women's self-criticisms.

Example 9 illustrates, however, that Samantha does participate in support exchanges, but in a way different from her friends. In this example, Carrie has decided she has come to terms with the fact that her ex-boyfriend, Mr. Big, will be marrying another woman, Natasha. Until this scene, Carrie's negative feelings toward Natasha had made her reluctant to even say Natasha's name aloud, and thus her eventual acceptance of the relationship is symbolized by her uttering of the name in conversation with her friends. Although Carrie claims to be handling the situation well, her sadness is obvious, prompting Samantha to initiate a supportive interaction.

Example 9:

SAMANTHA: Natasha. What a bullshit name.
MIRANDA: Totally.
CHARLOTTE: Stupid.
CARRIE: Complete bullshit.
("Ex and the City"[20])

Samantha supports Carrie by orienting toward Natasha (represented by her name) as a common target of ill will. While the force of her turn is therefore one of support, it is delivered in a manner characteristic of men's language: that is, assertive, aggressive, and framed as an expert evaluation. The subsequent turns by Miranda, Charlotte, and Carrie, however, illustrate women's linguistic behavior as supportive and understanding. Not only do their turns offer Carrie support and understanding with regard to her situation, but they also support Samantha's evaluation, aligning with it via synonym (*stupid*), emphasizer (*totally*), and emphasized repetition (*complete bullshit*), thereby co-constructing rapport and intimacy.

Social Constructionist Theory

The deficit, dominance, and difference theories successfully ushered in a long-overdue investigation of the relationship between gender and

20. Written by Michael Patrick King.

language. However, while they represent critical explorations of apparent gender differences in language use, they have not been without controversy (Coates 1998). The theories have been criticized or even rejected for focusing on differences between women's talk and men's talk, promoting an essentialized perspective on gender, that is, that women and men represent two distinct binary categories with inherent, essential properties. Further, several initial academic claims of gender differences in talk were based only on folk-linguistic beliefs and lacked empirical evidence. Once researchers set out to provide empirical evidence, the primary object of study, namely the participants in the investigations, often turned out to be a limited number of white, middle-class, heterosexual Anglo-Americans (not seldom college students, who were easily accessible to the researcher). Thus the essentializing theories of deficit, dominance, and difference fail to take into account what has more recently come to be known as intersectionality, namely that additional factors such as interlocutors' class, age, ethnicity, or even social positions and relationships interact with their gender. It is therefore naïve to assume that language use is the function of only one of these variables, and it is difficult to reliably isolate one variable from another.

The lively debate and criticism within the field of language and gender has led to a new wave of research and investigation (Cameron 2005; Holmes 2007). The social constructionist approach to gender and language makes the observation that previous theories contribute to and perpetuate a polarization of the genders, such that differences are highlighted to a greater extent than similarities, and that an extreme adherence to these theories would promote a view of language use as being determined by one's gender. Proposing that language usage is not so much an inherent function of gender as it is a social construction reflecting outside influences, social constructionist theory repositions the role of gender in language use, reevaluates any potential or evident linguistic differences, and challenges the traditional views of gender and language. Gender identity is viewed as the result of performance: one behaves as a male or a female, and this behavior has both physical and linguistic manifestations. A gender identity is not automatically assigned; instead, one learns how to socially construct and enact it through repeated interactions. Certain linguistic practices become associated with one gender or the other, such that ideas of masculine and feminine language use become culturally engrained. All linguistic practices, however, are potentially available to all language users, and thus we can all align differently with masculinity or femininity through our own language use. Gender, then, is not viewed as an either/or category of identity, but a scalar construction, such that one person's language use may vary according to their varying social roles, at times aligning with stereotypically masculine or feminine identities, or no readily identifiable gender identity at all.

Discussion

By highlighting the interactional practices of four women, *Sex and the City* illustrates how talk is not determined by gender, but that certain linguistic practices contribute to constructing gender. Carrie, Miranda, Charlotte, and Samantha each linguistically performs and occupies varying positions on the gender-identity scale, while together performing and negotiating their in-group roles. Among the four women, Samantha aligns most consistently with a stereotypically masculine identity, accomplished in part through her sexually aggressive behavior, but even more significantly through her language use. Nonetheless, her identity as a woman is neither ambiguous nor compromised, ultimately providing more support for the social constructionist view of gender roles as both shifting and contradictory (Baxter 2011). Ultimately, the linguistic variation exhibited by the female characters of *Sex and the City*, most salient between Samantha and the others, illustrates the fact that not all women speak in the same way, and not all women speak differently from all men.

The role of television and other forms of popular culture should not be underestimated when it comes to their reflection of and ultimate influence on our own conceptions of gender. On the one hand, we have seen in this chapter that *Sex and the City* capitalized on, and thereby potentially perpetuated, stereotypical linguistic manifestations of gender. On the other hand, as the writers of the series play around with gender identities via the language they put in the mouths of their characters, such as having a female character appropriate stereotypically male language, the series also forced its viewers to confront their own folk-linguistic beliefs about the relationship between gender and language. *Sex and the City* thereby contributes significantly to the general conversation of gender identity (Baxter 2009), ultimately rendering it vulnerable to further re-conceptualizations. Feminist and queer linguistics, both aiming at avoiding the use of binary categories as a starting point altogether, are leading the way. The episode "Boy, Girl, Boy, Girl . . ."[21] seems to foreshadow this development, as Carrie questions the concept of gender:

> If women can transform into men, and men into women and we can sleep with everyone, then maybe gender doesn't exist anymore. If we can take the best of the other sex and make it our own, has the opposite sex become obsolete?

Suggestions for Further Viewing and Analysis

1. In this chapter the categories of Slut, Prude, Career Woman, and Heroine as applied to *The Golden Girls* and *Sex and the City* were presented. Do these categories apply to other television series featuring four female leads, such as *The Facts of Life* (1979–88), *Designing Women* (1986–93), *Sisters* (1991–96), *Desperate Housewives* (2004–12), *Cashmere Mafia* (2008), or *Girls* (2012–)? Consider other terms specific to females that may be applied to characters not immediately conforming to one of these four categories.

2. In the *30 Rock* episode "Standards and Practices,"[22] Liz Lemon decides to use the men's bathroom when the women's bathroom is closed for cleaning. She hears crying from the neighboring stall (occupied by Kenneth) and initiates a conversation, pretending to be a man. In addition to adopting a very low voice, consider how else Liz enacts a male persona via language use, and what theory or theories of language the interaction best illustrates:

> LIZ: Dude. What's up?
>
> KENNETH: I'm just having a bad day sir.

21. Written by Jenny Bicks.

22. Written by Vali Chandrasekaran.

LIZ: Alright, bro-bro. Let's just . . . be cool and sit down and pee in silence, like dudes do.

(Kenneth simultaneously sobs and vents his work troubles, caused by Liz)

. . .

LIZ: Bro, you should just smack that Liz in the mouth.

3. In the *Modern Family* episode "Two Monkeys and a Panda,"[23] Phil Dunphy is clandestinely visiting a spa when he receives a phone call from his wife, Claire. The purpose of the phone call is for Claire to ask Phil to take care of dinner, because she is handling a problem between two of the children. Phil offers Claire advice and claims to be able to solve the problem, which upsets Claire, who only wanted to inform Phil that he would be responsible for dinner. Several women at the spa hear the entire exchange between Phil and Claire, and proceed to school Phil on how to communicate with women.

PHIL: Okay I'm confused. You're saying to me that if she tells me she has a problem I'm not supposed to help her?

WOMAN 1: Not unless she asks for your help.

PHIL: But if she lets me help her I can make her problem go away.

(The women laugh)

WOMAN 2: That is such a male thing to say.

PHIL: Well forgive me for being a man.

SPA WORKER: *(holding up skin creams)* Mango or kiwi?

PHIL: Oooh, kiwi!

WOMAN 2: When you say, "do this" or "do that," all she's hearing is, "I'm smarter than you."

PHIL: Believe me, she doesn't think that.

WOMAN 2: She doesn't want you to solve her problems. She just wants you to give her support, so that she can solve her problems herself.

WOMAN 1: Yes, and sometimes, sometimes she just wants a sympathetic ear.

23. Written by Carol Leifer.

PHIL: Woah, woah. Maybe it's all the creams, but that just made sense, girlfriends.

The scene continues with Phil summarizing for the women what he's learned, and later in the episode he successfully practices his new knowledge on Claire. In the extract above and throughout the remainder of the scene, identify examples of language use that support different theories of gender and language.

4. Series that feature an equal number of male and female characters of comparably equal status who frequently engage in mixed-sex interactions can allow for testing of the different theories of language and gender. Consider shows such as *Friends* (1994–2004), *That 70s Show* (1998–2006), *How I Met Your Mother* (2005–14), *Brothers & Sisters* (2006–11), *Happy Endings* (2011–13), *Cougar Town* (2009–14), or *Glee* (2009–15), among many others. Are there recognizable patterns of language use that can be attributed more to gender roles than to social roles?

5. Consider how gender identity is linguistically performed or constructed in series that feature gay, lesbian, or transgender characters, such as *Buffy the Vampire Slayer* (1997–2003),[24] *Will and Grace* (1998–2006), *Queer as Folk* (2000–2005), *The L Word* (2004–9), *Glee* (2009–15), or *Looking* (2014–), or in series that feature characters pretending to be another gender, such as *Bosom Buddies* (1980–82), *Game of Thrones* (2011–), the *Dr. Quinn, Medicine Woman* (1993–98) episode "Life in the Balance,"[25] or *The Simpsons* (1990–) episode "Girls Just Want to Have Sums."[26] How much gender identity work is accomplished through linguistic means, as opposed to physical or otherwise behavioral means?

References

Baxter, Judith. 2009. "Constructions of Active Womanhood and New Femininities: From a Feminist Linguistic Perspective, Is *Sex and the City* a Modernist or a Post-Modernist TV Text?" *Women and Language* 30(2): 91–97.

24. Gender roles in Buffy have been written about in *Sex and the Slayer* (Jowett 2005).

25. Written by Chris Abbott.

26. Written by Matt Selman.

———. 2011. "Gender." In *The Routledge Handbook of Applied Linguistics*, edited by James Simpson, 331–43. London: Routledge.

Bednarek, Monika. 2011. "The Stability of the Televisual Character: A Corpus Stylistic Case Study." In *Telecinematic Discourse: Approaches to the Language of Films and Television Series*, edited by Roberta Piazza, Monika Bednarek, and Fabio Rossi, 185–204. Amsterdam: John Benjamins.

Brouwer, Dédé, Marinel Gerritsen, and Dorian De Haan. 1979. "Speech Differences Between Women and Men: On the Wrong Track?" *Language in Society* 8(01): 33–50.

Bubel, Claudia. 2005. *The Linguistic Construction of Character Relations in TV Drama: Doing Friendship in* Sex and the City. PhD diss., Universität des Saarlandes.

Butler, Judith. 1999. *Gender Trouble*. New York: Routledge.

Cameron, Deborah. 2005. "Language, Gender, and Sexuality: Current Issues and New Directions." *Applied Linguistics* 26(4): 482–502.

———. 2007. *The Myth of Mars and Venus*. Oxford, UK: Oxford Univ. Press.

Coates, Jennifer. 1996. *Women Talk: Conversation Between Women Friends*. Oxford, UK: Blackwell.

———. 1998. *Language and Gender. A Reader*. Malden: MA: Blackwell.

DeFrancisco, Victoria Leto. 1991. The Sounds of Silence: How Men Silence Women in Marital Relations. *Discourse and Society* 2(4): 413–24.

Eckert, Penelope, and Sally McConnell-Ginet. 1992. "Think Practically and Look Locally: Language and Gender as Community-Based Practice." *Annual Review of Anthropology* 21:461–90.

Fishman, Pamela M. 1978. "Interaction: The Work Women Do." In *Language, Gender and Society*, edited by Barrie Thorne, Cheris Kramarae, and Nancy Henley, 89–101. Rowley, MA: Newbury House.

———. 1980a. "Conversational Insecurity." In *Language: Social Psychological Perspectives*, edited by Howard Giles, William Peter Robinson, and Philip Smith, 127–32. Oxford, UK: Pergamon.

———. 1980b. "Interactional Shitwork." *Heresies* 1(2): 99–101.

Goodwin, Marjorie H. 1990. *He-Said-She-Said: Talk as Social Organization Among Black Children*. Bloomington: Indiana Univ. Press.

Holmes, Janet. 2007. *What Is Gender? Sociological Approaches*. London: Sage.

James, Deborah, and Janice Drakich. 1993. "Understanding Gender Differences in Amount of Talk: A Critical Review of Research." In *Gender and Conversational Interaction*, edited by Deborah Tannen, 281–312. Oxford, UK: Oxford Univ. Press.

Jespersen, Otto. 1922. *Language: Its Nature, Development and Origin*. London: George Allen and Unwin.

Kim, Janna L., C. Lynn Sorsoli, Katherine Collins, Bonnie A. Zylbergold, Deborah Schooler, and Deborah L. Tolman. 2007. "From Sex to Sexuality: Exposing the Heterosexual Script on Primetime Network Television." *Journal of Sex Research* 44(2): 145–57.

Jowett, Lorna. 2005. *Sex and the Slayer: A Gender Studies Primer for the Buffy Fan*. Middletown, CT: Wesleyan Univ. Press.

de Klerk, Vivian. 1991. "Expletives: Men Only?" *Communications Monographs* 58(2): 156–69.

———. 1992. "How Taboo Are Taboo Words for Girls?" *Language in Society* 21(2): 277–89.

Lakoff, Robin. 1975. *Language and Woman's Place*. New York: Harper and Row.

Lerner, Gene. 2003. "Selecting Next Speaker: The Context Sensitive Operation of a Context-Free Organization." *Language in Society* 32:177–201.

Maltz, Daniel N., and Ruth A. Borker. 1983. "A Cultural Approach to Male-Female Miscommunication." In *Language and Social Identity*, edited by John A. Gumperz, 195–216. Cambridge, UK: Cambridge Univ. Press.

Martin, Brett. 2013. *Difficult Men: Behind the Scenes of a Creative Revolution: From* The Sopranos *and* The Wire *to* Mad Men *and* Breaking Bad. New York: Penguin.

Nussbaum, Emily. 2013. "Difficult Women." *New Yorker*, July 29. Accessed Aug. 22, 2015. http://www.newyorker.com/magazine/2013/07/29/difficult-women.

Pauwels, Anne. 2003. "Linguistic Sexism and Feminist Linguistic Activism." In *The Handbook of Language and Gender*, edited by Janet Holmes and Miriam Meyerhoff, 550–70. Malden, MA: Blackwell.

Rey, Jennifer M. 2001. "Changing Gender Roles in Popular Culture: Dialogue in *Star Trek* episodes from 1966 to 1993." In *Variation in English: Multi-dimensional Studies*, edited by Douglas Biber and Susan Conrad, 138–56. London: Longman.

Schulz, M. R. 1975. "How Serious Is Sex Bias in Language?" *College Composition and Communication* 26(2): 163–67.

Sharma, Neha. 2013. "Everything Carrie Ever Wondered About on *Sex and the City*." *Vulture*, Mar. 13. Accessed Aug. 22, 2015. http://www.vulture.com/2013/03/carrie-sex-city-couldnt-help-but-wonder.html.

Sidnell, Jack. 2011. "'D'you understand that honey?': Gender and Participation in Conversation." In *Conversation and Gender*, edited by Susan A. Speer and Elizabeth Stokoe, 183–209. Cambridge, UK: Cambridge Univ. Press.

Stapleton, Karyn. 2010. "Swearing." In *Interpersonal Pragmatics*, edited by Miriam A. Locher and Sage L. Graham, 289–306. Berlin, Germany: De Gruyter Mouton.

Tannen, Deborah. 1990. *You Just Don't Understand: Women and Men in Conversation*. London: Virago.

West, Candace, and Don H. Zimmerman. 1983. "Small Insults: A Study of Interruptions in Cross-Sex Conversations Between Unacquainted Persons." In *Language, Gender and Society*, edited by Barrie Thorne, Cheris Kramarae, and Nancy Henley, 102–17. Cambridge, MA: Newbury House.

5

The Pragmatics Explication

Making Sense of Nerds in The Big Bang Theory

MATTHIAS EITELMANN AND ULRIKE STANGE

The US sitcom *The Big Bang Theory* (CBS, 2007–) centers around four highly intellectual yet extremely nerdy scientists. Even if each of them has at least one master's degree in natural sciences, they fail to master the everyday traps and pitfalls of human communication. This lack of mastery becomes evident as early as the beginning of the pilot episode,[1] when physicists Leonard, a brainy experimental physicist who has more or less successfully adapted to society, and Sheldon, a brilliant mind tinged by obsessive-compulsive disorder, meet their new neighbor Penny, an aspiring actress. The following exchange introduces viewers to the male protagonists' nerdiness.

Example 1:

PENNY: Oh, hi!

LEONARD: Hi.

SHELDON: Hi.

LEONARD: Hi.

SHELDON: Hi.

PENNY: Hi?

LEONARD: We don't mean to interrupt, we live across the hall.

PENNY: Oh, that's nice.

1. Written by Chuck Lorre and Bill Prady.

LEONARD: Oh . . . uh . . . no . . . we don't live together . . . um . . . we live together but in separate, heterosexual bedrooms.

PENNY: Oh, okay, well, guess I'm your new neighbor, Penny.

LEONARD: Leonard, Sheldon.

PENNY: Hi.

LEONARD: Hi.

SHELDON: Hi.

PENNY: Hi.

LEONARD: Hi. Well, uh, oh, welcome to the building.

PENNY: Thank you, maybe we can have coffee sometime.

LEONARD: Oh, great.

PENNY: Great.

SHELDON: Great.

LEONARD: Great. Well, bye.

PENNY: Bye.

SHELDON: Bye.

LEONARD: Bye.

Leonard and Sheldon are unable to manage the conventions for meeting new people, and instead create a potentially infinite greeting loop—twice. The more socially adept Penny ends the first loop with a rising intoned *Hi*, which serves to question the interaction, and then ends the second loop with a decidedly falling intoned *Hi*, signaling it as the final contribution. Nevertheless, Leonard and Sheldon are unable to avoid similar loops as the conversation continues and eventually ends. Furthermore, they create a highly awkward situation as they feel the need to disambiguate the implied meanings of their living together—and bluntly state their sexual orientation. Of course, Penny does not know how to react to the blatant violation of the social conventions for this setting. In this short but meaningful first scene of the series, the premise of *The Big Bang Theory* as a show about socially challenged geeky geniuses is effectively established.

Communicative mishaps such as in example 1 raise the viewers' awareness of principles at work in conversations. Indeed, watching TV as a linguist is extremely worthwhile in the case of a sitcom like *The Big Bang Theory*: the episodes abound with social and communicative disasters that are continuously exploited for humoristic effects.[2] These are caused by sheer incompetence in the sphere of social interaction and/or utter ignorance of conversational principles, with Sheldon as a "cornucopia of social awkwardness" being particularly prone to putting his foot in it.[3] The linguistic subfield of interest here is pragmatics, which can be defined as follows:

> Pragmatics is concerned with the study of meaning as communicated by a speaker (or writer) and interpreted by a listener (or reader). . . . This type of study necessarily involves the interpretation of what people mean in a particular context and how the context influences what is said. It requires a consideration of how speakers organize what they want to say in accordance with who they're talking to, where, when, and under what circumstances. (Yule 1996, 3)

In contrast to (lexical) semantics, which is primarily concerned with the meaning of linguistic items in isolation (see chapter 6), pragmatics considers language use in actual context (on the distinction between semantics and pragmatics, see Cruse 2011). In this chapter, we will discuss key notions of pragmatics, whereby we will not only broaden our understanding of this branch of linguistics, but also gain an insight into how humor works in *The Big Bang Theory*. Furthermore, owing to a heightened awareness of communication mechanisms, we will also benefit on a metalinguistic level, namely in that we confront what we seem to know about our own everyday conversations, and thus call into question our own communicative skills.

Inferencing: The Art of Determining Meaning

The starting point for our discussion of various pragmatic principles will be "The Loobenfeld Decay,"[4] an episode that focuses on the topic of

2. For an introduction to the television genre of sitcoms, see Mills (2005).

3. Ironically, it is Sheldon himself who uses the expression "cornucopia of social awkwardness" in "The Desperation Emanation" (written by Bill Prady, Lee Aronsohn, and Dave Goetsch) to refer to Leonard, although his housemate is definitely less socially awkward than he is.

4. Written by Bill Prady and Lee Aronsohn.

lying. Penny invites Leonard and Sheldon to come and see her perform in a one-night showcase of the musical *Rent*, but they do not want to go and pretend they have to attend a symposium on that night. Sheldon then becomes paranoid about Penny finding out that they lied to her, so he weaves a web of an "un-unravelable lie." This masterpiece of a lie includes (a) him admitting they lied, but (b) lying about why they lied in the first place, and (c) providing more substance to the second lie by introducing a fake drug-addicted cousin.

One important pragmatic issue concerns the fact that there is often a significant difference between what speakers say ('sentence meaning') and what they mean ('utterance meaning'); most often, "what is meant in a speaker's utterance" is not an explicit "part of what is said" (Horn 2004, 3). For example, if a speaker asks, "Do you know how to get to the Empire State Building?" it would not suffice to answer "yes" or "no," but rather the question has to be interpreted as a request for directions. In order to bridge the gap between sentence meaning and utterance meaning, we as hearers have to draw correct inferences; these inferences are interpretations that we arrive at by going beyond the literal meaning of an utterance. What guides us in our inferencing activities is consideration of what surrounds the respective utterance—more specifically, the co-text and the context of an utterance—and to rely on our background knowledge. The term 'co-text' covers all those utterances or words by which the utterance in question is accompanied. 'Context' refers to the specific communicative setting in which an utterance is embedded, including the time and place of the utterance, the level of intimacy between the interlocutors, the topic and purpose of the conversation, and so forth. Importantly, the setting plays a decisive role in the form of a conversational contribution and causes a great deal of variation. Lastly, the term 'background knowledge' refers to automatic interpretations based on knowledge gained from previous experiences.

The Big Bang Theory illustrates again and again how communication can go wrong when interlocutors do not draw the correct inferences. Sheldon in particular is notorious for his inability to infer the intended meaning, as the following exchange between him and Penny demonstrates.

Example 2:

PENNY: Do you have any idea what time it is?

SHELDON: Of course I do. My watch is linked to the atomic clock in Boulder, Colorado.

("The Loobenfeld Decay"[5])

Troubled by Leonard's lie and unable to sleep, Sheldon decides to talk to Penny to ease his conscience. After knocking on her door in his characteristic manner (that is, exactly three times, accompanied by the threefold repetition of her name), he is greeted by Penny's half-sleepy, half-annoyed question—not meant, of course, as an enquiry as to what time it actually is, but rather as an expression of her disapproval of Sheldon's waking her up in the middle of the night. Consequently, the sentence meaning (the question taken literally, that is, "I want to know whether you know what time it is") fails to concord with the utterance meaning ("It is inappropriate to wake me up in the middle of the night").

When it comes to the interpretation of an utterance, there is more to its correct understanding than simply dealing with its precise wording. The different strands coming into play have been disentangled by means of the concepts 'locution', 'illocution', and 'perlocution' (Levinson 1983, 236, based on Austin 1962). Locution and illocution correspond to form and intention of the utterance respectively, while the term 'perlocution' refers to the effect of the utterance on the hearer. Thus the question "Do you have any idea what time it is?" constitutes the locution, and its communicative intent would normally be interpreted as an expression of annoyance (illocution). Again, in a normal speech situation, the perlocutionary effect on the hearer would be, for instance, an apologetic reaction. In Sheldon's case, however, the rather unusual reaction is one of indignation.

In Sheldon's reply, a number of pragmatic issues become apparent that result from his misunderstanding Penny's question. First, as regards co-text, Sheldon's answer is a direct reply to Penny's question, correlating with co-text and context. After all, strictly speaking, this is in accordance with question-answer structures. However, if we take into consideration the situational setting, his contribution turns out to be inappropriate

5. Written by Bill Prady and Lee Aronsohn.

because, second, he ignores the context. "Do you know what time it is?" is a perfectly normal question at a perfectly normal time of day (or early night), but not at a time when people usually sleep. Sheldon does not take heed of this and thus lacks an essential clue for inferring the correct utterance meaning. Third, he fails to activate his background knowledge. This is in fact linked to the previous aspect: you need to be aware of the fact that it is inconsiderate to wake people up in the middle of the night. Fourth, he solely relies on a literal interpretation of Penny's question, so there is no inferential activity on his part. The sum of these factors (not minding the context or background knowledge, taking the question word for word) explains why Sheldon fails to draw the correct inference from Penny's utterance.

Interestingly, even if Penny had asked him what time it was, Sheldon would still have failed to interpret her question correctly by faithfully answering, "Yes, I do." Admittedly, on the surface, the sentence is indeed a question that can be answered with yes or no, but the utterance meaning of this question is usually a request in the sense of "I want you to tell me what time it is." In everyday conversations, however, indirect requests (in this in case in the form of a question) are preferred as they sound more polite. As we shall see later on, Sheldon has considerable problems with politeness conventions, which require an increased inferencing activity.

Speech Acts: Words as Actions

The discussion so far has shown that Sheldon is generally unaware of the power of speech. After all, "*by* saying or *in* saying something," language users are actually "doing something" (Austin 1962/1955, 12; emphasis J. A.), an idea rendered explicit in the term 'speech act'. Originally introduced by John Austin (1955), this concept has been considerably elaborated by John Searle (1969), who regards speech acts as "the basic or minimal units of linguistic communication" (1969, 16).

Speech acts may differ in their degree of directness, an issue that is closely linked to the relation between sentence meaning and utterance meaning. In 'direct speech acts', the sentence meaning equals the utterance meaning (SM = UM). Whenever the utterance meaning and the sentence meaning clash, as in the example above, we speak of 'indirect speech acts' (SM ≠ UM).

Searle (1977, 34) distinguishes between five kinds of speech acts:

1. representatives (or assertives)
2. expressives
3. commissives
4. declaratives
5. directives

In 'representatives' or 'assertives', "[t]he point or purpose . . . is to commit the speaker (in varying degrees) to something's being the case" (Searle 1977, 34) in that the speaker may simply produce statements that are true in an objective sense: "water boils at 100° Celsius," "a fry-up is the traditional breakfast in Britain," and so forth. Assertives are always direct speech acts, that is, the sentence meaning and the utterance meaning match.

'Expressives' convey the speakers' feelings. This type of speech act may be direct or indirect: in "I love you" the sentence meaning and the utterance meaning are the same, but in "I could eat a horse" the utterance meaning is "I feel very hungry." Other types of expressives are, for instance, apologies ("I am sorry I smashed your favorite vase," SM = UM); congratulations ("Congrats on getting your driving license"—"I feel happy for you because you have passed your driving test," SM ≠ UM); condolences ("I am so sorry for your loss," SM = UM); and compliments ("Well done!"—"I am happy that you are doing a good job," SM ≠ UM). In a nutshell, any utterance that provides an insight into the speaker's emotional state of mind is an emotive speech act.

'Directives' typically aim at making the interlocutor(s) do something (Searle 1977, 35). Like expressives, directives can be direct or indirect: "Close the window, please" (SM = UM) is considered less polite than "There's a draft in here" (SM ≠ UM). In general, speakers prefer indirect directives because they are more polite. In the example above, Penny meant "Don't wake me up in the middle of the night," but expressed it indirectly by asking Sheldon whether he knew what time it was.

'Commissives' can be performed in utterances in which the speakers commit themselves to "some future course of action" (Searle 1977, 35).

Again, we distinguish between direct and indirect speech acts: for example, "I promise to take the rubbish out before I leave for work" (SM = UM), or "You can count on me" meaning "I guarantee that I will help you" (SM ≠ UM). Threats are also classified as commissives, as in "I swear I will fire you if you don't do your job properly" (SM = UM).

'Declaratives' are a special kind of speech act in that they "bring about some alternation in the status or condition of the referred-to object or objects solely by virtue of the fact that the declaration has been successfully performed" (Searle 1977, 37). This regards, among others, baptisms, marriages, prison sentences, declarations of war, and so forth. It is essential that speakers producing declaratives usually need to have certain powers bestowed upon them in order to be able to actually bring about this change of affairs in the external world: you need to have a special license or hold a particular office to baptize children, to send a criminal to jail, to declare war on another nation, and so on. Furthermore, to undo the new situation, corresponding declaratives can again only be issued by a person having the right to perform these speech acts: by producing an utterance such as "I hereby pronounce you husband and wife," two people are suddenly legally bound to one another and can only alter this state of affairs by addressing a lawyer and filing for divorce. Similarly, if a president of a given nation declared war, only they or their successors can declare peace again. A judge may send murderers to death row, but only the governor of a state can pardon them. Declaratives are always direct speech acts, as the sentence meaning always equals the utterance meaning.

To briefly sum up, assertives and declaratives are always direct speech acts, in that the intended meaning is expressed literally (for instance, "I christen thee Mary Ann"). Expressives, commissives, and directives, on the other hand, may be expressed directly or indirectly. Indirectness may be seen as being more polite in the case of directives, but it can also be interpreted as evasiveness in the case of expressives and commissives.

Turning again to "The Loobenfeld Decay," we will see that it is especially indirect speech acts that cause problems for Sheldon. In the following scene, Penny is excited about what happened (namely getting the chance to perform in a musical) and wants to share this with Sheldon:

Example 3:

PENNY: You'll never guess what just happened.
SHELDON: I don't guess. As a scientist, I reach conclusions based on observation and experimentation.

On the surface Penny's utterance looks like an assertive—that she thinks that Sheldon will not guess what just happened. As is to be expected, Sheldon again only relies on the literal meaning of what Penny says and tells her that he does not hazard guesses. On the level of utterance meaning, however, a number of interpretations are available: 'I'm so excited about this, I can't wait to tell you' (indirect expressive), 'I want you to listen to this' (indirect directive), 'I want you to ask me what just happened' (indirect directive), 'I promise to tell you every little detail' (indirect commissive). As is the case with most everyday conversations, speakers constantly need to determine whether there is a mismatch between sentence meaning and utterance meaning or not, and to interpret the respective utterances by making the correct inference. Evidently this is a challenging task, which can cause communication to go wrong. It is essential to always take into account the co-text, context, and background knowledge when drawing inferences, and even then all pitfalls cannot be avoided.

More instances of communication going wrong can be found throughout the episode.[6] After his confession in the early morning, Sheldon again misinterprets the illocutionary force of a speech act:

Example 4:

SHELDON: He lied, and I'm feeling very uncomfortable about it.
PENNY: Well, imagine how I'm feeling.
SHELDON: Hungry? Tired? I'm sorry, this really isn't my strong suit.

6. Of course, communicative mishaps can be found throughout the whole series. For example, in "The Spaghetti Catalyst" (written by Chuck Lorre, Bill Prady, Lee Aronsohn, and Steven Molaro, even a highly formulaic expression such as "How have you been?" is taken literally, prompting Sheldon to reply, "Well, my existence is a continuum, so I've been what I am at each point in the implied time period." For an interpretation of this exchange, see Pötzsch (2012, 163).

Sheldon takes Penny's utterance literally, namely as a prompt to put himself in her shoes: he interprets "imagine how I'm feeling" as a direct directive. What Penny actually means, however, is 'I'm feeling sad because Leonard lied to me'. Thus she produces an indirect expressive in the form of an imperative. Again Sheldon fails to draw the correct inference, which results in his guessing wildly what her feelings in this particular situation might be.[7]

Felicity Conditions: The Secret of Success

As sentence meaning often differs from utterance meaning, the question arises as to which factors still guarantee the ultimate success of a speech act, or, as Austin (1955, 16) puts it, which factors prevent a speech act from "misfiring." These factors have been formulated by Searle (1969), who calls them "felicity conditions": criteria that need to be met for a speech act to be successful. All in all, there are five conditions to be satisfied:

1. the general condition
2. the propositional content condition
3. the preparatory content condition
4. the sincerity condition
5. the essential condition

Importantly, if one or more of the felicity conditions are not met, the result is often a misunderstanding between the speaker and the listener.

The 'general condition' takes into account external factors of a speech event and states that the listener must be able to hear and understand the locution. This condition implies that the utterance is produced in a communicative-friendly environment: any surrounding noise like loud music, traffic, and the like must not exceed a certain level for the utterance to be clearly audible. Furthermore, the speaker and the listener need to share a common language. If the speaker produces an utterance in English and the interlocutor only speaks French, the speech act cannot be successful per se.

7. Sheldon's inability to read Penny's emotions and his taking her words literally once more is also reminiscent of Asperger's syndrome (Bednarek 2012, 210).

The 'propositional content condition' refers to the fact that the speaker must render the content of the utterance in a clear and comprehensible manner. The production of lengthy, incoherent sentences full of fancy words will result in an unsuccessful speech act.

The 'preparatory content condition' prepares the ground for a successful speech act in that the speaker and the listener need to be in a certain state of mind for the speech act to be realized. Thus it focuses on the internal factors concerning the speaker and the interlocutor themselves. In the case of apologies, for instance, the speaker needs to regret what they have done and the listener needs to be willing to forgive. If the speaker or the listener is not in the right state of mind that is required for this speech act, it cannot be felicitous.

The 'sincerity condition' states that the speaker must mean what they say, namely, that apologies, promises, declarations of love, and so forth need to be sincere. If the speaker lies, the speech act is not successful.

The 'essential condition' finally states that the speaker and interlocutor must consider the speech act itself as the realization of the intended speech act. For instance, if the speaker makes a promise, the speech act itself—the promise—is considered as a binding contract, and not as empty words.

Let us consider these conditions in turn in another scene from "The Loobenfeld Decay." After Sheldon and Leonard have lied to Penny about not being able to come to the showcase, Sheldon knocks on Leonard's door in the middle of the night (again in his notorious way) because he wants to discuss their lie. Leonard, who does not want to get up to talk, tells Sheldon to go away. As Sheldon can hear Leonard's command very clearly and as they speak the same language, the general condition is satisfied. Leonard's choice of words, namely "Go away!" is brief and comprehensible, so the propositional content condition is met as well. The sincerity condition is also complied with in that Leonard means what he says: he does want Sheldon to go away. The comic effect of the whole exchange results from the fact that Sheldon's nature is detrimental to the successful realization of this speech act. After all, the preparatory content condition is not fulfilled: while Leonard wants Sheldon to leave him alone until morning, Sheldon is in no state of mind to be sent away, even though he is disturbing his roommate's sleep. Thus it is Sheldon's lack of willingness to oblige that proves disadvantageous for the realization of the speech act. Second, the essential condition is also problematic because Leonard's command is not reacted upon appropriately. Therefore, the speech act itself does not count as the realization of the speech act for Sheldon.

In sum, while Leonard can be observed to comply with all felicity conditions, preparing the ground for a successful speech act, it is Sheldon who fails to satisfy the preparatory content and the essential condition, which results in the speech act misfiring: Leonard's saying "Go away!" does not have the desired effect on his roommate. Leonard suspects that his directive speech act is infelicitous, as his follow-up question "Are you still there?" demonstrates—and indeed, Sheldon has not moved an inch.

The Cooperative Principle: It Takes Two to Communicate

Sheldon's communicative impediments can also be seen to result from his constantly not observing one of the most crucial pragmatic principles governing natural conversations: the so-called Cooperative Principle. Originally postulated by H. Paul Grice (1975), the principle asserts that interlocutors should make all efforts to cooperate with each other when communicating, namely by making "your conversational contribution such as is required, at the stage at which it occurs, by the accepted purpose or direction of the talk exchange in which you are engaged" (Grice 1975, 45).

More precisely, speakers follow four highly interrelated maxims, which are associated with the Cooperative Principle (Grice 1975, 45–47):

1. Maxim of Quantity: A conversational contribution should provide as much information as is needed, no more nor less. For the sake of this maxim, a speaker will not, for instance, explicitly mention facts that they assume the hearer already knows.
2. Maxim of Quality: A speaker's contribution should be based on solid facts, thus qualifying it as truthful. Following this maxim, a speaker will not only refrain from lying blatantly but will also avoid producing utterances made up out of thin air or for which they lack ample evidence.
3. Maxim of Relation: What a speaker says should be relevant in that it relates to the previous discourse. In other words, a speaker is

expected to make a contribution to the speech situation that befits the context and displays a clear reference to the current topic and the communicative goal.

While the first three maxims refer more or less to the contents of a speaker's contribution, the fourth maxim—in Grice's view a "supermaxim"—focuses on *how* these contents are presented, instructing speakers to "[b]e perspicuous" (Grice 1975, 46):

4. Maxim of Manner: Ideally, a speaker will make their contribution clear and orderly, thereby maximizing transparency and cohesion—or, to put it in other words, a speaker will avoid wordings that are vague, ambiguous, or exuberantly verbose.

In an ideal world, then, speakers will opt for efficiency by complying with all the aforementioned maxims. However, this challenging task is potentially constrained by the aforementioned more general principle to "[m]ake [one's] contribution such as is required" (Grice 1975, 45); in other words, speakers are expected to encode their communicative intents in a way that befits the speech situation, which may mean that a maxim is violated for the benefit of being polite or provoking a specific response from the hearer.[8] What speakers thus do when violating a maxim on purpose is called, in pragmatic terms, flouting the maxims: they may produce utterances that are not as informative as necessary, not true, seemingly irrelevant, and rather obscure. It is exactly in such situations of discrepancy where the role of the hearer becomes important within the context of the Cooperative Principle: In order to maintain effective communication, it is the hearers' task to make sense of any violations of the maxims, for example, by interpreting sentences in a non-literal way or by inferring utterance meaning from sentence meaning.

In this respect, then, the apparent non-observance of a maxim typically triggers a conversational implicature, that is, an implication deduced from the conversational context. Assuming that the speaker's contribution

8. As Jacob L. Mey (2001, 70) succinctly puts it, "Given that I *want* to communicate, what I *do* communicate depends on what I *can* communicate, given my circumstances, and on what I *must* communicate, given my partner's expectations."

is essentially guided by the wish to cooperate rather than to impede or counteract communicative efficiency, a hearer will still interpret the speaker's contribution as meaningful and fill in the blanks where necessary. This hearer-related capacity is exactly the reason why most of us will not answer a question such as Penny's "Do you know what time it is?" truthfully with "yes" or "no." Rather, by relating the utterance to the speech situation, we would interpret the question (in the middle of the day) as a speaker's enquiry for the time or (having woken somebody up in the small hours) as an expression of annoyance that could have been worded much more aggressively.

It does not come as a complete surprise that Sheldon, who fails to infer utterance meaning from sentence meaning (as shown above), generally misses the point of the Cooperative Principle. Even though Grice originally formulated his conversational maxims as imperatives, they are not to be mistaken as strict rules or norms underlying communication. Rather, they are to be seen as the pragmatic key to the question of why communication is in most cases so efficient, even though communicative intentions are made explicit only rarely. Sheldon, then, proves to be uncooperative in two respects. As a hearer, he is oblivious to any pragmatic implications and therefore incapable of drawing necessary inferences. Correspondingly, as a speaker, he adheres to the conversational maxims in an almost slavish manner, but is obviously unaware that effective communication requires more than simply obeying elementary rules and principles.

This lack of awareness becomes evident in "The Loobenfeld Decay" as Leonard and Sheldon discuss the benefits of a white lie. After overhearing Penny practicing her song for her stand-in performance in the musical *Rent*, Leonard dodges Penny's invitation to attend the Friday show by violating the Maxim of Quality, namely by claiming that he and Sheldon would have to attend a "symposium on molecular positronium." Sheldon, on the other hand, strictly follows the Maxim of Quality, as he corrects Leonard on the spot, truthfully remarking that the congress actually takes place "a week from Tuesday, at 6:00." Only with Leonard reinforcing the lie by insisting that the symposium is indeed scheduled for this very Friday can Leonard and Sheldon circumvent Penny's invitation and spare all of them the embarrassment of telling Penny that she can't sing at all.

Sheldon, however, would not hesitate to tell Penny the bitter truth as he makes clear back in their flat; strictly applying the Gricean maxims, he suggests the following answer:

Example 5:

> SHELDON: Singing is neither an appropriate vocation nor avocation for you, and if you disagree, I'd recommend you have a CAT scan to look for a tumor pressing on the cognitive processing centers of your brain.

Of course, by this time, we as TV viewers have also already overheard Penny's feeble attempts at mastering the solo number "Over the Moon" and can therefore agree that the above remark is fitting albeit very impolite.

Once more Sheldon displays a preference for linguistic accuracy over social conventions of language use by strictly following the four maxims of the Cooperative Principle. First, his comment definitely constitutes a truthful statement, fully adhering to the Maxim of Quality. Second, as an answer to the question of how Leonard and Sheldon like Penny's musical skills, it would also perfectly comply with the Maxim of Relation (and quite ironically, Sheldon alludes to this maxim on a metalinguistic level by doubting that the intention to not hurt Penny's feelings is a "relevant factor"). Third, the way Sheldon phrases his statement certainly leaves no doubt that Penny is a terrible singer, so that the Maxim of Manner is definitely obeyed—for sure, his statement put in such unequivocal words could not be any clearer. As concerns the fourth maxim, the Maxim of Quantity, we might object that Sheldon's recommendation for a brain scan provides too much information. However, the way Sheldon delivers the message, namely in a rather neutral tone without any emotions, points to the fact that at least in his opinion he has absolutely followed the Maxim of Quantity and provided exactly as much information as needed, no more nor less.

Ultimately, Sheldon's supposedly "un-unravelable" lie that replaces Leonard's comparatively harmless white lie also completely adheres to the maxims of the Cooperative Principle. In Sheldon's view, a concocted story can only pass off as believable if it is not possible in any way to disprove even one minor detail that forms part of the lie. In this respect, Leonard's lie could be easily exposed if Penny googled the date of said symposium (that is, if Penny could memorize the topic of the symposium, which she seems unlikely to do based on her facial expression when confronted with the term "molecular positronium"). In stark contrast, Sheldon's much more complicated lie involves not only a fictive drug-addicted cousin but also requires his laboratory assistant Loobenfeld to actually impersonate the cousin after an equally fictive family intervention in Long Beach went terribly wrong. The background story that Sheldon devises with meticulous detail meets the requirements of the conversational maxims in an absurd manner—which is typical of his obsessive-compulsive disorder: It is cohesive (Maxim of Manner), consisting of as many details as needed (Maxim of Quantity) in order to give not merely an excuse but a plausible explanation for Sheldon's and Leonard's missing out on Penny's performance. Sheldon and Leonard even act out some of the details—such as actually driving to Long Beach—to turn some of the fictitious elements of Sheldon's story into true facts (Maxim of Quality). Needless to say, Sheldon's lie is completely blown out of proportion and, despite being un-unravelable, inevitably unravels itself into what the episode under investigation is aptly called: "The Loobenfeld Decay."

Politeness: The Face of Pragmatics

Sheldon's communicative behavior clearly demonstrates that it is not always appropriate, let alone effective, to stick to the maxims of the Cooperative Principle. On the contrary, there are circumstances in which it is preferable to produce a white lie even though in this way the maxims are blatantly violated. Obviously, in order to maintain good social relations, and thus to be cooperative in another sense, it takes more than merely the four maxims postulated by Grice as they blank out interpersonal relations for the most part. This issue has been addressed by Geoffrey Leech (1983; 2014), who emphasizes the need to expand the Cooperative Principle by a Politeness Principle, which comprises, among others, maxims of tact, generosity, and modesty (Leech 1983, 104ff., 131ff.). Against this background, it is rewarding to take a closer look at what we do exactly when we are polite.

Politeness from a linguistic perspective involves face-work, as Penelope Brown and Stephen C. Levinson (1987) have argued in their fundamental study on politeness universals. Drawing on Erving Goffman's (1967) notion of face, they use this crucial term to refer to "the public self-image that every member [of society] wants to claim for himself [or herself]" (Brown and Levinson 1987, 61). This self-image is essentially characterized by two intrinsically human motivations, which Brown and Levinson differentiate as positive face and negative face. Positive face implies that we have a positive self-image of ourselves that we want others to acknowledge; after all, all of us want to be perceived by others in a favorable way. At the same time, as 'competent adults', we want to be as free and unlimited in our actions and choices as possible, and this "basic claim to . . . freedom of action and freedom from imposition" (Brown and Levinson 1987, 61) constitutes our negative face.

In this respect, impolite behavior boils down to what pragmatics call face-threatening acts: speech acts that may pose a threat to an interlocutor's positive or negative face. It is important to note that such face-threatening acts do not reduce to rude language or plain insults that certainly do not correspond with one's positive self-image; potential face-threatening acts may also be at hand in the case of simple requests. Let's take the following situation for illustration: Imagine you want someone to share his/her sandwich with you. Of course, you could say quite bluntly, "Share your sandwich with me," which, in the form of a straightforward imperative, would surely be conceived of as highly inappropriate. Probably even the addition of "please" would only slightly change the degree of impoliteness associated with the request as the linguistic form of the utterance is still an imperative (in speech act terms: a direct directive) that does not give the addressee any explicit choice.[9] In this sense, the utterance "Share your sandwich with me (please)" constitutes a (negative) face-threatening

9. Etymologically, the politeness marker *please* goes back to a more lengthy phrase used in sixteenth-century English, *(and) if you please*, as for example in Shakespeare's *Love's Labour's Lost*: "Let me say no my liedge, and yf you please" (OED). In contrast to the reduced form *please*, the conditional clause gives the addressee a clear choice as to whether to fulfill the request or not, so that the direct directive is less face-threatening.

act in that the request frankly disturbs the addressee's aforementioned 'freedom of action and freedom from imposition'.

The question now is which linguistic strategies can be applied in order to mitigate the imminent face-threatening act. One strategy might be to appeal to the addressee's positive face: "I know you are such a generous person—so share your sandwich with me." However, such a compliment could potentially challenge the addressee's positive face in that a decline of the request would compromise or threaten the requestee's positive self-image insinuated by the requester's flattering remark. Another strategy involves making use of indirect speech acts in the form of an interrogative statement such as "Could you share your sandwich with me?" Strictly speaking, this question literally asks about the addressee's physical disposition as to whether or not they are able to share a sandwich with me, and what is more, the modal auxiliary *could*—morphologically speaking, the past-tense form of *can*—focuses a situation not in the here and now, but rather in a hypothetical realm. In sum, then, the speech act verbalized by "Could you share your sandwich with me?" is less face-threatening owing to its shift of focus (straightforward request to share > enquiry about the addressee's capability of sharing) and its linguistic form (interrogative, use of *could*). However, this utterance of a request in the disguise of an interrogative violates the Maxim of Manner for the sake of being more polite, constituting yet another case of flouting as described above.

Not surprisingly, with Sheldon's understanding of social interactions being clouded by his widespread ignorance of pragmatic principles, he struggles with conversational practices that require a constant renegotiation of the Cooperative Principle and politeness strategies. When asked for an honest opinion, for instance, speakers have to consider whether adhering to certain conversational maxims (being relevant, telling the truth, and so on) will result in a face-threatening act—and if it does, they might prefer to flout the maxims by telling a white lie in order to save the interlocutor's face. In the episode discussed here, Penny's positive face would be at stake if Leonard and Sheldon had to give their honest opinion on her singing skills. Sheldon's spontaneous response cited above would not only be face-threatening but utterly face-destroying. Therefore, Leonard has to go to great lengths to explain to Sheldon that under certain circumstances, the Cooperative Principle may be overruled by the Politeness Principle. As Leonard points out, according to "social protocol," an appropriate response to Penny's singing and subsequent invitation to see her stage performance would be to tell her that she was "terrific" and that they couldn't "wait to hear [her] sing again." Or, put differently:

Example 6:

> LEONARD: It's what you do when you have a friend who's proud of something they really suck at.

Once made aware of this politeness strategy, Sheldon proves to be a quick learner and compliments Leonard on his qualities as a chess player, repeating Leonard's fake approval by rote: "When we played chess earlier, you were terrific, and I can't wait to play you again." Of course, Sheldon's compliment could be interpreted as a sarcastic remark, uttered with the intention to serve Leonard his own medicine. However, given Sheldon's general misconception of pragmatic principles, we can rather conclude that he once more misses the crucial point, namely that politeness strategies are not polite per se. On the contrary, being polite evidently depends on the interlocutor's sensitivity to the appropriate conversational practice required by the respective social context.

Watching "The Desperation Emanation" as a Pragmatist

After having introduced the most important aspects of pragmatics in the previous sections, we will now apply this knowledge to another episode, "The Desperation Emanation."[10] Season 4 introduces new series regular Amy Farrah-Fowler, Sheldon's girlfriend, who is Sheldon's (almost) perfect match, at least communicatively speaking. In Amy's speech, the utterance meaning equals the sentence meaning more often than not. As a consequence, most of the speech acts she performs are direct ones, so they do not require any inferencing on the part of the hearer. Considering that Sheldon lacks inferential abilities, this facilitates any communication the two of them have.

10. Written by Chuck Lorre, Steven Molaro, and Steve Holland.

However, since the beginnings of *The Big Bang Theory*, Sheldon has improved his communicative skills in that he now knows that what people say and what they mean is not necessarily the same thing and that social protocols may put restrictions on what language may be used in a certain communicative event. While this increase in communicative competence proves advantageous in interaction with 'normal' people, it is Sheldon's feeble attempt at reading between the lines that puts their relationship at stake in the episode "The Desperation Emanation." He suspects that Amy's straightforward request "I'd like you to meet my mother" means more than that, especially as Leonard, drawing on background knowledge, has constantly bantered about their relationship turning into something more serious.

Paranoid that Amy wants to take their relationship to the next level, Sheldon goes to great lengths to break off contact with her. Fortunately, Amy realizes that a misunderstanding must have occurred between them and addresses the issue. Thus she deduces from his reaction that he must have drawn the wrong inference from her utterance "I'd like you to meet my mother," namely, something along the lines of 'I want you to be my proper boyfriend and I want to make our relationship official'. Her true intention, however, is concordant with the literal meaning of the utterance: she simply wants Sheldon to meet her mother, positive that she will then stop nagging at her about not having a boyfriend. That Amy and Sheldon are usually on the same communicative wavelength is nicely illustrated by the following brief exchange in which Amy has no problems at all decoding Sheldon's figure of speech:

Example 8:

SHELDON: I don't want to be joined to another object by an inclined plane wrapped helically around an axis.

AMY: In what way are you screwed?

What is more, they turn out to be equally inapt in regard to social conventions, which becomes obvious in their video chat with Amy's mother. They share information with her that no ordinary couple would share with their parent:

Example 9:

SHELDON: I'm having regular intercourse with your daughter. . . . We're like wild animals in heat. It's a wonder neither of us has been hurt.

MRS. FOWLER: *(aghast)* Amy . . . what is he saying?

AMY: You wanted me to have a boyfriend, Mother. Well, here he is. Have to sign off now. My hunger for Sheldon is stirring in my loins.

SHELDON: Oh, yes, it's time for me to make love to your daughter's vagina.

They simultaneously violate all of the four maxims of the Cooperative Principle. First, they lie as concerns their relationship status, thus not complying with the Maxim of Quality. Second, they provide more information than necessary, which runs counter to the Maxim of Quantity. Third, the content of the conversation is entirely irrelevant because unasked for (Maxim of Relation). After all, a mother's interest in the man her daughter spends time with does not entail interest in the details of their sex life—which they readily concoct.[11] The Maxim of Manner is not violated at first sight. Yet, their choice of words ("intercourse," "stirring in my loins") is inappropriate as is the mismatch between the content of utterance and the way in which it is rendered (impassive faces and monotonous intonation). It is the sum of these factors that renders their whole exchange highly awkward for Amy's mother but humorous for the viewers.

Discussion

The discussion of the pragmatic principles in the two episodes has shown that the intended meaning of an utterance is rendered only implicitly more often than not, which raises the question of how we still manage to communicate successfully most of the time. By saying that "[c]ommunicators and audience need no more know the principle of relevance to communicate than they need to know the principles of genetics to reproduce," Dan Sperber and Deirdre Wilson (1986, 162) attribute the mystery surrounding

11. This invasion of the (m)other's space can also be interpreted as a specific impoliteness realization in the sense of Bousfield (2008, 99–143). The question is, however, whether Sheldon and Amy are really making a conscious effort to be impolite, or whether they wrongly assume that this is indeed what the social protocol requires from them in such a situation.

successful communication to innate and intuitive knowledge. Watching *The Big Bang Theory* as a linguist and especially as a pragmatist has shed some light on this mystery by revealing the various principles at work and by drawing attention to the potential traps and pitfalls in everyday communication. With Sheldon as a prime example of a person who displays communicative and social incompetence, we have seen the intricate complexity that characterizes speech events. Any discourse is characterized by an exquisite web of utterance meanings in need of correct inferences, a web that for Sheldon, as a "cornucopia of social awkwardness," proves un-unravelable time and time again. At the same time, it is exactly this linguistic (mis)behavior that links Sheldon intertextually to other TV characters that are impolite to a certain extent or particularly inept at inferring utterance meaning from sentence meaning, such as the android Data, the Vulcan Spock, or the Cyborg Seven of Nine (Bednarek 2008, 214).[12] As demonstrated above, the various instances of (mis)communication in *The Big Bang Theory* provide plenty of room for both entertaining and instructive discussions of pragmatic principles from a linguistic perspective.

Suggestions for Further Viewing and Analysis

1. The pilot episode of *Modern Family* (2009–) introduces homosexual couple Mitchell Pritchett and Cameron Tucker, who have secretly adopted a baby girl and want to share the news with Mitchell's extended family, including Mitchell's father, Jay.[13] In order to increase the surprise effect, Cameron hides with baby Lily, while Mitchell gathers his family in the living room. As Mitchell announces, "I have something that I need to tell you," Jay's rather conservative views on his son's gay relationship and his opinion of Cameron come to the fore: "You're a little better off because he was kind of a drama queen." Cameron now enters the room and, in drama queen fashion, presents their newly adopted daughter in a pose reminiscent of *The Lion King* and contextualized as such with the score playing in

12. Interestingly, all these fictional characters are from the *Star Trek* universe, a TV show that Sheldon as a sci-fi geek highly cherishes. Particularly on Seven of Nine's linguistic behaviour, see Mandala (2011).

13. Written by Steven Levitan and Christopher Lloyd.

the background. Embarrassed, Mitchell tells him to "turn it off," which Cameron answers with "I can't turn it off. It's who I am." Consider how these interaction couplets (and others you can identify throughout the series) illustrate how false inferences and interpretations of utterances are exploited for humoristic purposes.

2. Awkward first encounters are not exclusive to *The Big Bang Theory*. In the first episode of *Buffy the Vampire Slayer* (1997–2003),[14] Xander Harris introduces himself to Buffy Summers, who has just joined Sunnydale High School, in the following way:

> XANDER: I don't know you, do I?
> BUFFY: I'm Buffy. I'm new.
> XANDER: Xander . . . is . . . me. Hi. Well, um . . . Maybe, I'll see you around. Maybe at school, since we both go there.

How is this first-time meeting different from and similar to the one between Penny, Leonard, and Sheldon? Which Gricean maxims does Xander flout, and to what effect?

Note that *Buffy the Vampire Slayer* also abounds with relations to speech act theory, as Buffy's actual power lies within her witty speech. Interested readers (and viewers) are referred to Karen Eileen Overbey and Lahney Preston-Matto (2002, 83), who argue that Buffy is *the* ultimate speech act in which word equals deed, namely, her words are actions in best Austin/Searle tradition.

3. The pilot episode of *30 Rock* opens with utter chaos behind the scenes of the Saturday night live comedy show *The Girlie Show*,[15] which is represented by the following exchange between Liz Lemon, head writer of the show, and her assistant Cerie:

> LIZ: Cerie, do you want to go get some coffee?
> CERIE: *(lying on the sofa in the writers' room, reading a magazine)* No, thank you.

14. Written by Joss Whedon.

15. Written by Tina Fey.

This interaction serves to establish and characterize the working relationship between Liz as a boss and her team. Consider this and similar examples in terms of speech acts (how does Liz give orders?) and felicity conditions (is the authority of Liz recognized?).

References

Austin, John L. 1962. *How to Do Things with Words*. In *The William James Lectures delivered at Harvard University in 1955*, edited by J. O. Urmson. Oxford, UK: Oxford Univ. Press.

Bednarek, Monika. 2012. "Constructing 'Nerdiness': Characterisation in *The Big Bang Theory*." *Multilingua* 31:199–229.

Bousfield, Derek. 2008. *Impoliteness in Interaction*. Amsterdam: John Benjamins.

Brown, Penelope, and Stephen C. Levinson. 1987. *Politeness: Some Universals in Language Usage*. Cambridge, UK: Cambridge Univ. Press.

Cruse, Alan. 2011. *Meaning in Language. An Introduction to Semantics and Pragmatics*. Oxford, UK: Oxford Univ. Press.

Goffman, Erving. 1967. *Interaction Ritual: Essays in Face-to-Face Behavior*. New York: Doubleday.

Grice, H. Paul. 1975. "Logic and Conversation." In *Syntax and Semantics*. Vol. 3: *Speech Acts*, edited by Peter Cole and Jerry L. Morgan, 41–58. New York: Academic Press.

Horn, Laurence R. 2004. "Implicature." In *The Handbook of Pragmatics*, edited by Laurence R. Horn and Gregory Ward, 3–28. Oxford, UK: Blackwell.

Leech, Geoffrey. 1983. *Principles of Pragmatics*. London: Longman.

———. 2014. *The Pragmatics of Politeness*. Oxford, UK: Oxford Univ. Press.

Levinson, Stephen C. 1983. *Pragmatics*. Cambridge, UK: Cambridge Univ. Press.

Mandala, Susan. 2011. "*Star Trek: Voyager*'s Seven of Nine: A Case Study of Language and Character in a Televisual Text." In *Telecinematic Discourse: Approaches to the Language of Films and Television Series*, edited by Roberta Piazza, Monika Bednarek, and Fabio Rossi, 205–23. Amsterdam: John Benjamins.

Mey, Jacob L. 2001. *Pragmatics: An Introduction*. Oxford, UK: Blackwell.

Mills, Brett. 2005. *Television Sitcom*. London: British Film Institute.

Overbey, Karen Eileen, and Lahney Preston-Matto. 2002. "Staking in Tongues. Speech Act as Weapon in *Buffy*." In *Fighting the Forces: What's at Stake in* Buffy the Vampire Slayer, edited by Rhonda V. Wilcox and David Lavery, 73–84. Oxford, UK: Rowman and Littlefield.

Pötzsch, Janelle. 2012. "Wittgenstein and Language Games in *The Big Bang Theory*." In *The Big Bang Theory and Philosophy. Rock, Paper, Scissors, Aristotle, Locke*, edited by Dean A. Kowalski, 161–74. Hoboken, NJ: John Wiley and Sons.

Searle, John R. 1969. *Speech Acts: An Essay in the Philosophy of Language*. Cambridge, UK: Cambridge Univ. Press.

———. 1977. "A Classification of Illocutionary Acts." In *Proceedings of the Texas Conference on Performatives, Presuppositions and Implicatures*, edited by Andy Rogers, Bob Wall, and John P. Murphy, 27–45. Arlington, VA: Center for Applied Linguistics.

Sperber, Dan, and Deirdre Wilson. 1986. *Relevance*. Oxford, UK: Blackwell.

Yule, George. 1996. *Pragmatics*. Oxford, UK: Oxford Univ. Press.

6

Cunning Linguistics

The Semantics of Word Play in South Park

MICHAEL PERCILLIER

"Oh my God, they killed Kenny! You bastards!" This dialogue is without a doubt the most iconic catchphrase of the American animated sitcom South Park, which has aired on the Comedy Central television network since 1997.[1] Created by Matt Stone and Trey Parker, the show follows the adventures of four foul-mouthed schoolboys living in the quiet mountain town of South Park, Colorado.

The core group of characters consists of Stan Marsh, who represents the average American kid; Kyle Broflovski, the only Jewish kid in town; Kenny McCormick, who is from a poor family and dies on a regular basis; and Eric Cartman, who is obese, racist, anti-Semitic, and greedy but uncannily resourceful. Further characters deserve to be introduced because they appear in the passages discussed below. Leopold "Butters" Stotch, a classmate of the central characters, is a cheerful but naïve boy, characteristics that are often exploited by Eric Cartman. Tweek is a paranoid, anxious, and hyperactive classmate of the main characters. He is the son of the town's coffee shop owners, who attribute his mental state to ADHD and give him coffee to "calm him down." Herbert Garrison is the boys' schoolteacher. In the course of the show, he undergoes a range of identity crises, starting out

1. *South Park* episodes can be viewed legally and free of charge at the creators' website *South Park Studios*, http://www.southparkstudios.com/. Users from outside the United States may be redirected to a local version of the website.

as a gay-bashing homosexual in denial who then embraces his sexuality, subsequently becomes a woman (Janet Garrison) by means of gender reassignment surgery, then becomes a lesbian, and finally completes the "full cycle" by having renewed surgery in order to become a man again.

The show is notorious for its crude and irreverent humor, as well as for its tendency to generate controversy by frequently addressing thorny or even taboo issues and ridiculing both sides of the debate. In addition to the surreal, shocking, and satirical brand of humor characteristic of the show, South Park also features more sophisticated comical elements, some of which are based on language play. While an analysis of linguistic humor in South Park would require touching on a variety of linguistic disciplines, such as word formation or sociolinguistics, this chapter focuses on the field of semantics and discusses central notions of the discipline by analyzing dialogues and plot elements from the show, ranging from short puns to linguistic phenomena pivotal to the plot of an episode.

Lexical Ambiguity

Lexical ambiguity refers to lexemes (or lexical words) sharing a common linguistic form but having distinct semantic content (or meaning). Mainly owing to its potential for puns, lexical ambiguity features in various episodes and is a staple of South Park comedy. Four passages from the series in which lexical ambiguity plays a central role are presented below. Different types of lexical ambiguity will be introduced to make a semantic analysis of the passages possible.

Homonymy

In "Fun with Veal,"[2] the boys save weakened baby cows, that is, calves, from a local cattle farm. Because the animals were kept in chains, their muscles are not developed enough to allow them to run away. The boys therefore hide the calves in Stan's house. They hope to enable the animals to walk free by using a device that Butters claims "makes baby cows strong again."

2. All episodes featured in this chapter were written by Trey Parker.

Example 1:

STAN: Butters! Did you bring it?

BUTTERS: I sure did. We'll have those poor baby cows in shape in no time!

KYLE: All right!

BUTTERS: *(reads the box)* Suzanne Somers' Calf Exerciser.

STAN: What?

BUTTERS: *(reads the box)* Makes your calves stronger in just two days.

KYLE: Oh, Goddamn it! That's your plan?

In example 1, the boys are with the rescued and weakened calves and waiting for Butters, who has said he has something at his house that "makes baby cows strong again." Kyle is understandably puzzled that Butters should have such a device at home. When Butters finally arrives and presents them with "Suzanne Somers' Calf Exerciser" that "[m]akes your calves stronger in just two days," the other boys are duly disappointed.

Butters's confusion is owing to a phenomenon called homonymy, which refers to multiple words with different meanings that happen to have the same linguistic form. In this case, the homonyms are calf, a young bovine animal, and calf, the back part of the lower leg. The words share a linguistic form in pronunciation and spelling (homo meaning same and nym meaning name), which applies to both the singular form calf and the plural form calves. Homonyms are distinct words of separate origin that happen to have merged their pronunciation and spelling in the course of their history. The two words are not related, as calf (animal) goes back to Old English cealf (OED Online 2013, "calf, n.1") while calf (body part) appears to stem from the Old Norse borrowing kálfi (OED Online 2013, "calf, n.2"). As such, homonyms are normally given separate main entries in dictionaries (see Cruse 2011, 115). Butters misunderstands the compound calf exerciser as a device to exercise young cows rather than a part of the human body. The other boys do not make the same mistake, as the ambiguity caused by the homonyms calf/calf can easily be resolved in this context. Given that a device designed to exercise young cows would be a peculiar contraption, the word calf denoting a body part remains the only plausible option.

Homophony

In "Jared Has Aides," the boys meet Jared Fogle, famous for his significant weight loss attributed to eating Subway sandwiches.[3] After the boys question the veracity of this claim, Jared admits having had additional help.

Example 2:

> JARED: Well, eating sub sandwiches was a big part of it. But the way that I lost so much weight was that I got aides.
>
> ERIC: A— AIDS?
>
> JARED: That's right. I got aides about two years ago and I've been losing weight ever since. It's amazing how slim you can get with aides.
>
> STAN: I'll bet you can.
>
> JARED: Would you like to meet them?
>
> KYLE: *(puzzled)* Them?
>
> JARED: My aides. Scott, Tyler! *(Scott and Tyler enter)* Scott is my personal trainer and Tyler is my dietician.
>
> SCOTT & TYLER: Hello.
>
> KYLE: Oh, a-i-d-E-s aides.

In the course of the episode, Jared wants to come clean about the fact that it was not just the sandwiches that helped him lose weight. He announces publicly that he lost weight thanks to aides and decides to launch the "Aides for everyone" foundation that will make sure everyone, including children, has aides in order to lose weight. The shocked audience turns into an angry mob and is about to execute him by hanging. The boys rush onto the gallows platform and rescue Jared by clearing up the misunderstanding.

In example 2, Jared tells the boys that he achieved his spectacular weight loss not only thanks to a diet of sandwiches, but also thanks to aides, using the plural form of aide, a synonym for assistant. The boys, however, think he refers to the disease AIDS, an acronym of Acquired Immuno-Deficiency Syndrome. Aides and AIDS share a common pronunciation

3. Since August 2015, Fogle is perhaps more notorious for having committed sex crimes against minors.

but are spelled differently, and as such are homophones (homo meaning same and phone meaning sound). Homophony is a case of partial homonymy, as the words share only a common pronunciation but differ in spelling. Homophony is unproblematic in written communication, but is as ambiguous as homonymy in spoken language. As the conversation is entirely oral, the difference in spelling cannot serve to disambiguate the two words. Given that the disease AIDS is known to cause significant weight loss, the boys assume that Jared refers to the disease rather than to his assistants. In addition, the word aide is less frequent than both its synonym assistant and the term AIDS. A quick consultation of the Corpus of Contemporary American English (Davies 2008–), a collection of 450 million words of authentic American English texts, reveals that the word assistant (in both its singular and plural form) occurs 26,958 times and the term AIDS 21,368 times, while aide (both singular and plural) occurs only 11,454 times. As such, the word aides is not recognized for two reasons: first, it has the homophone AIDS that is more frequent and also fits in the current context, and second, it has the preferred synonym assistant. Given the relative rarity of the word aide(s), the intended meanings of the successive ambiguous sentences are too remote to even cross the listeners' minds (see Zimmermann and Sternefeld 2013, 15).

The ambiguity arising from the homophony of aides and AIDS starts being resolved when Jared asks the boys if they want to "see them." While this is a perfectly normal question from Jared's point of view, the use of them seems incongruous to the boys: first from a grammatical perspective, as the singular noun AIDS should not concord with the plural personal pronoun them; second from a semantic point of view, as a syndrome is not something one can actually see. Only when Scott and Tyler enter the room do the boys realize that Jared had been referring to his aides all along, and the ambiguity is finally overcome. The boys spell the word to confirm that they have now resolved the ambiguity, thereby highlighting that homophones can easily be distinguished in writing, but are just as ambiguous as homonyms in spoken communication.

While the boys (and the audience) are now in the know, the rest of the town's population still assumes that Jared refers to AIDS rather than aides, a source of confusion that lays the ground for the episode's plot.

With Jared apparently oblivious to the homophony between AIDS and aides, his attempts to help others shed pounds the way he did by providing them with aides are misunderstood as an intention to infect everyone with the deadly disease: he tells his fiancée that he has had aides since before they met, and that after their wedding his aides will be her aides as well as their future children's aides; he also announces the launch of his "Aides for everyone" foundation, whose mission includes giving aides to underprivileged children around the world. Given that these conversations are oral, the word aides is consistently mistaken for AIDS. As a consequence, his fiancée leaves him and the townspeople plan to hang him. Only the intervention of the boys, who disambiguate the homophony to everyone, can save Jared's life. Jared finally realizes how others understood his previous statements, and the townspeople realize what Jared actually meant. Everyone breaks into hysterical laughter about what is called "the biggest misunderstanding EVER!"

Lexical Ambiguity and Its Effects on Syntax

In the episode "D-Yikes," the boys hired Mexicans to do their homework for them. The assignment was to read Ernest Hemingway's The Old Man and the Sea and write an essay about it. In the extract below, the boys are meeting the Mexicans again in order to collect their homework.

Example 3:

ERIC: All right, did you write the four essays?
MEXICAN #1: Sí, we all wrote éses for you.
BOYS: All right!
ERIC: OK, let's have 'em.
MEXICAN #2: Have what?
KYLE: You said you all wrote essays. Where are they?
MEXICAN #1: Well, my ése lives in Miami. I wrote to him like you said, but I don't think he got the letter yet.

In a similar vein to the passage discussed above, the ambiguity in example 3 is based on homophony, this time between the words essay, a written piece of moderate length, and ése, a Mexican Spanish and Chicano English word, meaning friend. Besides being an example of homophony, the misunderstanding of ése for essay showcases the interface between semantics and syntax: both to write an essay and to write an ése share the same formal make-up, which is the syntactic structure " [VP write] + [NP an essay/ése]" (see chapter 10 for more information on phrase structures). However, the noun phrases an essay and an ése serve different syntactic functions as well as semantic roles. These differences are owing to the semantic properties of the noun phrase heads and their relation to the transitivity of the verb to write.

The verb to write can be used ditransitively; that is, it can have two objects. These objects cannot be randomly assigned, but have to hold specific semantic properties. The direct object refers to what is written, which coincides with the semantic role of the 'patient', namely that on which the action of the verb is performed. As such, only nouns whose semantic properties refer to written messages or written works qualify, for example, sentence, letter, e-mail, book, novel. The indirect object coincides with the semantic role of the 'recipient', that is, the entity to whom the direct object is intended. As essay refers to an inanimate written piece, the structure to write an essay uses the noun phrase an essay in the syntactic function of a direct object and in the semantic role of a patient. In contrast, ése refers to an animate human being, so that the structure to write an ése uses the noun phrase an ése in the syntactic function of an indirect object and in the semantic role of a recipient. In this case, the direct object does not need to be mentioned as it can be inferred as any written message, such as a letter or a postcard. As a result, the misunderstanding based on homophony between the boys and the Mexican laborers results in more than just lexical ambiguity, but also structural ambiguity (see Zimmermann and Sternefeld 2013, 29), all based on the different semantic properties of two homophones, specifically regarding their animacy.

Polysemy

In "Free Hat," the boys found the "Save films from their own directors" club to prevent directors such as Steven Spielberg and George Lucas from releasing altered versions of their classic films. To advertise their first meeting, they put up a cardboard sign that reads "We must save our nations [sic] films! Rally tomorrow in the school gymnasium 12:00 pm!"

Eric insists on writing "Free Hat" on the sign, thinking that offering prizes should attract a larger crowd. Tweek is tasked with making paper hats for the meeting but has only managed to make fifteen pieces. To his dismay, the gymnasium is packed with a thousand people shouting "Free Hat" repeatedly. In spite of this, the boys decide to begin with the meeting.

Example 4:

STAN: Uh, one thing before I continue. Unfortunately we don't have enough of the free hats for everyone.

. . .

WOMAN: We don't care about that.

TWEEK: You don't?

STAN: You mean, you just came because you believe in our cause?

SKEETER: Yeah. Free Hat.

TWEEK: What?

MAN: Hat McCollough. He was sent to prison in '82, and we believe he should be released!

Unlike the two previous passages, the ambiguity in example 4 occurs in written language. However, this case is also different from the calf exerciser in the first passage, where spelling was equally ambiguous. Like calf, free can hold different meanings while maintaining the same pronunciation and spelling. The written message as intended by its author Eric Cartman used the word free as an adjective, meaning that hats would be handed out for free at the advertised meeting. The message as understood by the crowd used the word free as a verb in its imperative form, thereby forming a call to release Hat McCullough from prison.

The major difference between the cases of calf and free is that while the common linguistic form of the two words calf/calf is an accident of successive sound changes in the history of English, the adjective free and the verb to free have etymological and semantic links. This phenomenon is called polysemy and refers to a single word having multiple meanings. Unlike homonyms, polysemous words have their meanings listed under a common main entry in dictionaries. From a synchronic perspective, the verb to free appears to be a conversion (or zero-derivation) from the adjective free. However, the relation between the two words is more complex:

both words go back to the same Indo-European root and have developed separate meanings, so that the Old English adjective frēo had the same meaning as the present adjective, while the Old English verb freogan/freon had the primary meaning to love. This meaning was lost in Middle English with the current meaning developing because of the influence of the adjective free (OED Online 2013, "free, v."). The polysemy of free may be considered a bit tenuous, but the etymological links as well as the close semantic relationship (see Zimmermann and Sternefeld 2013, 17) between the adjectival and verbal forms of the word clearly set it apart from cases of homonymy such as calf/calf.

Semantic Feature Analysis

Now that we have seen how words with similar linguistic forms but varying semantic contents are used for language play and plot development in the show, it is time to turn our attention to semantic content itself. Two passages that illustrate semantic feature analysis will be given below, accompanied by a brief introduction to different approaches to semantic feature analysis, and a discussion of the passages in light of these approaches.

Defining Meanings

We return to the episode "Fun with Veal," in which the boys visit a local cattle farm during a school trip. After having been shown the cattle ranch and the slaughterhouse, they are taken to the veal ranch, where they make a startling realization.

Example 5:

STAN: Wait a minute. Veal is little baby cows?

RANCHER: Yeppir.

KYLE: Then why the hell do they call it "veal"?

RANCHER: Well, if we called it "little baby cow" people might not eat it.

STAN: Yeah, I wouldn't have.

The boys later capture the calves in order to save them, which leads to a week-long hostage crisis. One of the conditions for releasing the calves is the official change of the word veal to "tortured baby cow," a demand that is accepted and carried out by the police negotiator. Eventually the boys are arrested and the calves returned to their owner, who cannot sell them as veal anymore because people abstain from ordering "tortured baby cow" when they see it on the menu.

In example 5, the boys are shocked to learn, during their visit to the local farm, that veal is in fact the meat of young cows. The reason why the actual definition of the word veal was unknown to them goes back to an unusual lexical distinction between words denoting animals and their meat. In most European languages, the same word can denote the live animal as well as its meat, for example Kalb in German or veau in French. In English, the existence of both the Germanic word calf and the Romance word veal led to a lexical distinction between the animal and the meat, so that the relation between animal and meat is obscured and one does not automatically know the origin of the meat from its name alone.

The boys view this as a euphemism intended to conceal the fact that veal is in fact "little baby cow." Their attempts to kidnap the calves and bring them to safety are thwarted, and what saves the animals in the end is the official renaming of veal to "little tortured baby cow." Basically, what the boys did was to perform a semantic feature analysis of the semantic concept 'veal'. This analysis, which David Alan Cruse (2011, 54) calls the classical approach to semantic concepts, defines a set of necessary and sufficient conditions to determine membership to the category at hand. For veal, the necessary conditions are that it must be meat, it must be from a cow or bull, and that cow or bull must be young. If any of these conditions are not met, we are not dealing with veal. If for example the cow or bull is not young, the concept of 'beef' will be better suited. The boys explicitly use the necessary conditions of 'veal' as a basis for the new denomination of the meat. The printing of this semantic feature analysis on restaurant menus was enough to put consumers off veal altogether, which points toward the obscured relationship between animal and meat in English.

Your Wife's a Dude: Limits of the Classical Model

In the episode "Eek, a Penis!" the boys' teacher, Mrs. Garrison (formerly Mr. Garrison), regrets her previous gender reassignment surgery and wishes to become a man again. When she learns about the Vacanti mouse, a laboratory mouse used to grow a human ear using cartilage scaffolding, Mrs. Garrison spends all her money to use the same procedure to have her original male genitals grown in the lab in order to make a renewed gender reassignment surgery possible. Later on, the mouse with the genitals growing on its back escapes from the lab, and Mrs. Garrison's attempts to find it form one of the two major plot lines of the episode. Finally the mouse is found and the organ transplantation is performed, reverting Janet Garrison to Herbert Garrison, who is then welcomed back to his school.

Example 6:

PRINCIPAL: Students and faculty, please put your hands together and help me in welcoming back, Mister Garrison.

(everyone claps)

MR. GARRISON: Thanks everyone. It's great to be back. I'm a man again. Thanks to my very special new friend. *(The lab mouse climbs onto his right shoulder.)* But you know, I've learned that I've really been a dude all along. Because the key difference between men and women is that women can have babies. If you can't have babies, then you're a man.

A TEACHER: Whoa, uh wait, uh, hang on a second. My wife had ovarian cancer, so she can't have babies.

MR. GARRISON: Well then get an AIDS test, Thompson, 'cause your wife's a dude, faggot! *(Thompson is dumbfounded.)* Yeah! I'm back!

After reverting to a man, Mr. Garrison rationalizes his tumultuous gender history in example 6 by denying ever having been a woman, claiming he was always a man. He argues that the defining feature of womanhood is the ability to give birth, and because his first surgery did not provide him with this ability, he was never a woman and therefore remained a man all along. One of his colleagues points out an error in Mr. Garrison's line of thought by giving a clear counterexample: his own wife has lost the ability to bear children because of ovarian cancer. Mr. Garrison does not concede the point, but instead maintains his definition of woman and applies it to the counterexample, thereby rudely claiming that his colleague's wife must be a man.

This passage is noteworthy because it clearly highlights the limits of the classical approach to semantic feature analysis. The feature 'ability to give birth' is not a necessary condition for the concept 'woman', as not all women possess this trait. As such, it cannot be used to describe the concept 'woman', although it is a feature that many speakers would readily associate with the lexeme woman to set it apart from the lexeme man. This showcases that a checklist of necessary features is not how speakers usually represent the meaning of lexical items in their minds. The cognitive approach to semantic features analysis is an attempt to remedy this problem by treating semantic concepts not as a set of necessary and sufficient conditions, but as 'prototypes' (Geeraerts 2010, 183–203). The term refers to categories containing typical as well as peripheral members. Typical members are characterized as possessing all of the semantic features associated with the concept, and most speakers would cite typical members when asked for examples of the concept ('apple' as a typical example of the concept 'fruit' as opposed to 'olive'). Peripheral members lack certain features of the category 'core', but this does not exclude them from the category. Mr. Garrison somewhat mixes up the two approaches by using semantic features relevant to a cognitive analysis, but treating them as necessary conditions. The ability to give birth is without a doubt one of the most striking semantic features of the lexeme woman that distinguishes it from the lexeme man. However, this does not mean that the ability to give birth is a necessary condition for being a woman, which would also imply that a man is nothing other than a woman without the ability to bear children. The semantic feature 'ability to give birth' is therefore a central feature of the prototypical concept 'woman', meaning that it is commonly associated with the lexeme, but lacking this feature will not in itself lead to an exclusion from the category. By using a prototypical feature as a necessary condition, Mr. Garrison wrongly categorizes a woman as a man. An appropriate classical semantic feature analysis would require specific features that apply to all women, regardless of whether they are central or peripheral members of the category 'woman', for example the absence of a Y chromosome in the karyotype, which is how a specialist, but not a layperson, might conceptualize the category.

Shift Happens: How Meanings Develop

As we have seen how semantic meaning can be disambiguated and described, we can now look at the various ways in which the meaning of words can form, change, and develop. Four passages dealing with various aspects of semantic change will be introduced below, accompanied by a brief theoretical introduction to these aspects and an analysis of the passages.

Pirate Ghosts Packing Fudge: How New Word Formations Gain Their Meaning

In the episode "Korn's Groovy Pirate Ghost Mystery," the members of the rock band KoЯn arrive in a haunted South Park in what is an obvious parody of the series Scooby-Doo. The presence of pirate ghosts as well the disappearance of the body of Kyle's grandmother lead the KoЯn members to the conclusion that something is amiss.

Example 7:

JONATHAN: Well, that does it. Something funny is going on here. Your missing grandma must be connected somehow to those creepy pirate ghosts.

DAVID: They're not pirate ghosts, Jonathan, they're ghost pirates.

JONATHAN: Huh?

DAVID: "Pirate ghost" would suggest that a pirate died, and became a ghost, but a ghost pirate is a ghost that later made a conscious decision to be a pirate.

MUNKY: No, David. Then they are pirate ghosts, because they're the ghosts of pirates.

FIELDY: You're wrong, because there were no pirates in Colorado. So these must be ghosts that have decided to become pirates after the fact.

In example 7, the members of the band KoЯn debate whether the apparitions haunting the town are pirate ghosts or ghost pirates. While this distinction is trivial in comparison to the characters' ongoing concerns, the order of the individual elements does indeed make a difference. As we learn in chapter 7, a compound is a new lexeme formed by the combination of two free lexical morphemes. In our example, the lexemes pirate and ghost can be combined to form the compounds pirate ghost and ghost pirate. English uses the 'modifier-head structure', so that a compound of word A and word B yields an A type of B. In other words, the last element determines the semantic outcome of the compound. As such, a pirate ghost is a type of ghost, namely the ghost of a pirate, while a ghost pirate is a type of pirate, in this case a ghost that decided to become a pirate. The debate is not brought to a conclusion, as it cannot be determined which of these positions is accurate. As is appropriate for a Scooby-Doo tribute, the pirate ghosts (or ghost pirates) turn out to be neither pirates nor ghosts at the end of the episode.

In the episode "200," the boys are on a field trip to a fudge factory. When they visit the room in which the fudge is put into boxes to be shipped, they notice, to their surprise, that the actor Tom Cruise is working there.

Example 8:

BUTTERS: Hey Stan, isn't that Tom Cruise?

STAN: Huh? Oh wow it is! Hey guys check it out, Tom Cruise is a fudge-packer!

TOM CRUISE: What did you call me?

ERIC: Hey, that is Tom Cruise! *(takes a picture)*

BUTTERS: How come you're packin' fudge, Mr. Cruise?

TOM CRUISE: I'm not a fudge-packer!

KYLE: Dude, you don't have to be ashamed or anything.

TOM CRUISE: But I'm not a fudge-packer! *(packs a block of fudge into a box)*

When the boys see Tom Cruise working in the fudge factory in example 8, they call him a fudge-packer because he is packing fudge into boxes for shipping. Tom Cruise is offended and asks them to stop, then proceeds to sue the entire town for defamation. The cause of this misunderstanding is the fact that not all compounds follow the A type of B pattern. Depending on their semantic properties, compounds can be grouped into two main categories: endocentric and exocentric compounds. With endocentric compounds, the meaning of the resulting lexeme remains within the domain of one of the original words, as in the pirate ghost/ ghost pirate example above. In contrast, an exocentric compound creates meaning that lies outside its components, so that a combination of A and B results in a new lexeme that is neither A nor B. The cause of the misunderstanding between the boys and Tom Cruise lies in the ambiguity of the compound fudge-packer. While the boys use the term as an endocentric compound, that is, a person who packs fudge into boxes as a profession, Tom Cruise understands the term as an exocentric compound, which does not refer to a specific type of packer, but by metaphorical extension is a derogatory term for a male homosexual. The root of the problem is therefore a case of polysemy originating in the application of the two main compounding strategies on the same set of lexemes.

A Lot of Fags Aren't Gay: When Meanings Change

The plot of "The F Word" revolves entirely around the concept of semantic change, as the boys seek to have the meaning of the word fag officially changed to reflect their use of the word, as denoting "annoying Harley riders" rather than being a pejorative term for homosexuals. When the town is beleaguered by excessively loud Harley riders, the boys call them "fags" and spray-paint the message "Fags get out" all over town. The town's adults are outraged by what they misunderstand to be the children's sudden and proud display of homophobia. The boys now have to explain their case in front of a panel of judges.

Example 9:

JUDGE #1: We are really trying to understand this. How is it that you boys think referring to gay people as fags in today's world is acceptable?

KYLE: Because we're not referring to gay people! You can be gay and not be a fag.

STAN: Yeah, a lot of fags aren't gay.

. . .

STAN: All right, look, you're driving in your car, okay? And you're waiting to make a left at a traffic signal. The light turns yellow, should be your turn to go, but the traffic coming at you just keeps coming. And even when the light turns red, a guy in a BMW runs the red light so you can't make your left turn. What goes through your mind?

JUDGE #2: Fag.

STAN: Right. But you're not thinking "Oh, he's a homosexual," you're thinking "Oh, he's an inconsiderate douche-bag like a Harley rider."

At the beginning of "The F-Word," there is a generational gap as the word fag means something else to children and adults. For children, the word refers to an "annoying, inconsiderate douche," while for adults it is a pejorative term for homosexuals. For this reason, the adults become worried that the children have become homophobes, a concern the children do not understand, because for them the term has nothing to do with homosexuality. The boys' appearance before the panel of judges in example 9 is the turning point of the episode in which adults begin to understand the word's new meaning and later adopt it too.

Statements such as "a lot of fags aren't gay" seem contradictory to the adults but are perfectly coherent from the boys' perspective. The ongoing semantic shift becomes clear to the adults after one of the boys performs an elicitation test on one of the judges, prompting him to use the word fag to insult a hypothetical driver who cut him off, not in the sense of homosexual but in the sense used by the children. As such, adults had applied this semantic shift as well but were not aware of it. In the course of the episode, the Harley riders themselves embrace the word fag to describe themselves, followed by the dictionary editor, who is the very last person to acknowledge the new definition. The fact that the dictionary is the very last instance to register the semantic shift is an allusion to the lag between language change and its codification in written grammars and dictionaries.

While the semantic shift presented in the episode is fictional, it bears parallels to the semantic change that the word gay is going through. Younger generations have recently begun using the adjective to refer to things they deem "uncool," without any implication of homosexuality. This usage has often been misunderstood as homophobic by older generations, although the emergence of a word used to express negative assessments based on a reference to homosexuality can be seen as indicative of homophobia on a cultural level, at least in the period in which the new meaning developed. The word fag too has undergone some major semantic shifts, which is alluded to in a scene in which the Harley riders look up the word's etymology at the library. It is a clipped form of the word faggot and not to be confused with its homonym fag, which refers to the loose end of objects such as a cigarette or a rope. The word faggot is originally a French loanword denoting "a bundle of sticks," a meaning it still holds in present-day French. Through a series of semantic shifts triggered by metaphorical extensions, the word came to refer to cumbersome bundles in general, old unpleasant women, and finally male homosexuals (OED Online 2013, "faggot | fagot, n."). The show's creators evidently made the effort to look up the word's etymology but mixed the chronological order of the various meanings by listing "old unpleasant woman" as the oldest meaning.

In the episode "It Hits the Fan," the word shit is used uncensored for the first time on television, which leads to an inflationary usage of the words shit and shitty. A counter in the lower left corner of the frame keeps track of how often the words are uttered in the episode (162 times). Because of this surge in usage, the elementary school and kindergarten teachers have to brief their pupils on the new guidelines for using these words.

Example 10:

(At the elementary school)

MS. CHOKSONDIK: You can only use it in the non-literal sense. For instance, *(writes on the board)* "That's a shitty picture of me" is now fine. However, the literal noun form of *(writes)* "This is a picture of shit" is still naughty. *(crosses out the sentence)*

. . .

ERIC: Wow, this is gonna be great! A whole new word!

KYLE: It's not new! I'm gonna look "shit" up in the encyclopedia and prove it!

ERIC: Don't mind Kyle, everyone, he's just got a little sand in his vagina.

KYLE: There's no sand in my vagina!

MS. CHOKSONDIK: Boys, watch your language! Shit!

(Scene changes to the kindergarten classroom)

MR. GARRISON: And so, children, instead of saying "Hand in your papers," I may now say, "Hand in your shit." Any questions?

FILMORE: What about, "I have to take a shit"?

MR. GARRISON: No! No, Filmore! You can say "I have to poop and shit" or "Oh, shit, I have to poop," but not "I have to shit." Are we all clear?

KINDERGARTENERS: No.

In the episode "It Hits the Fan," the word shit becomes acceptable, but not in its core meaning. The word is polysemous, with a core meaning denoting feces and two further meanings, one that is an expletive, the other that refers to objects not specifically defined, akin to stuff. These two additional meanings have developed via 'extension', which is the rise of new meanings when a word is used in new contexts (Heine and Kuteva 2007, 34). The semantic extension of a word to hold new meanings is followed by a process called 'semantic bleaching', or 'desemanticization', which is a shift to a meaning increasingly void of its original semantic content (Heine and Kuteva 2007, 39–40). Extension and semantic bleaching are part of a larger process called 'grammaticalization' (see Heine and Kuteva 2007, 32–53), in which the semantically blank word can eventually fulfill a grammatical or discourse function, and no longer holds the semantic properties of the core definition. While the core definition remains taboo, the bleached meanings have become acceptable in the show. The teachers attempt to explain the difference between core and additional meanings by giving example sentences such as "I have to poop and shit" and "Oh shit! I have to poop." One teacher uses the word as an expletive outside an example sentence by ironically saying "Boys! Watch your language! Shit!"

Discussion

As we have seen, South Park contains many examples of language-based humor and word play that cover a wide range of semantic topics. The various phenomena described are concerned with the relation between a single word form and its multiple meanings. Whether this relation consists of lexical ambiguity, literal/figurative usage, or shifting meanings, language users are typically able to resolve any communicative impasse by consciously or unconsciously engaging in semantic analysis. The creators of South Park purposely explore the limits of our ability to resolve these semantic deadlocks by confronting characters and viewers alike with such ambiguous setups. The realizations we as viewers (are forced to) make about these incongruities, as well as their resolution, are something we perceive as humor. The characters' repeated inability to resolve ambiguities that should not pose any problems in real-life communication constitutes pragmatic failures through which humor is created. This is valid not only for South Park, but for other television shows such as Friends, as noted by Paulo Quaglio (2009, 147; see also chapter 13).

Most interestingly, semantic phenomena are not limited to isolated puns, but are often plot catalysts or even at the very heart of an episode's plot. In other words, language is not simply a vehicle for the plot, but is the plot. A case in point is "The F-word." The excerpt given in example 9 and its analysis do not do justice to the overarching treatment of semantic change throughout the episode, which would best be served by viewing and analyzing the episode in its entirety, a task I gladly recommend to the reader.

While the linguistic humor of the show can certainly be enjoyed by laypeople, even a basic understanding of semantics can greatly improve the appreciation of humorous elements, as viewers will be able to understand the exact reasons for which they are laughing. It can further be argued that understanding the mechanics of linguistic humor not only improves the viewing experience, but also enhances our own humorous creativity.

Beyond enriching the viewing experience, an understanding of linguistic topics, semantics being only one of them, can also be helpful in the writing process of television episodes. As commercially available manuals on how to write television dialogue contain "virtually no linguistic information" (Quaglio 2009, 10), television writers can benefit from acquiring relevant linguistic knowledge and thereby becoming fully aware of the possibilities at their disposal for creating language-based humor.

Linguistic understanding also applies to the academic study of television. Given the multimodal nature of the medium, language is but one of the many sources of humor (see Lieberman et al. 2009, 501), and as such, it is understandable that the study of television cannot delve too deeply into linguistic matters. Still, describing linguistic humor in television with blanket terms such as word play restricts any analysis. As the discussion of the passages from South Park has shown, word play can in fact refer to many diverse processes, and television scholars do not have to be content with superficial analyses, especially when the observed linguistic phenomena are not simply punctual jokes, but central to an episode.

Suggestions for Further Viewing and Analysis

While the field of semantics is not the only linguistic topic treated in South Park, the reverse holds true as well, as many other TV series make use of semantic phenomena in comical and/or fascinating ways. I encourage readers to watch (or re-watch) their favorite TV series and look out for such elements. The three excerpts below are suggestions for getting started.

1. In the Two and a Half Men (2003–15) episode "The Price of Healthy Gums Is Eternal Vigilance,"[4] Charlie and Alan are at a restaurant with their mother, Evelyn, and Alan's son Jake. Evelyn asks her grandson what he would like to order.

> JAKE: I don't know. What's venison?
> EVELYN: Deer.
> JAKE: What?
> EVELYN: Deer.
> JAKE: What?
> EVELYN: Deer! D-E-E-R.
> JAKE: What? W-H-A-T.

Notice that even when Evelyn spells out the word she is saying, Jake still does not understand, so convinced he is that he has heard another word. Consider the cause of Jake's misunderstanding, and which lexical relation is illustrated in this example.

4. Written by Chuck Lorre, Lee Aronsohn, Mark Roberts, and Eddie Gorodetsky.

2. In the Friends (1994–2004) episode "The One Where Joey Speaks French,"[5] Rachel and Ross (who is a paleontologist with a PhD degree) visit Rachel's father at the hospital.

> RACHEL: (stops a nurse) Oh, uhm, excuse me, I'm here to see my father. My name is Rachel Green.
>
> ROSS: And I'm Doctor Ross Geller.
>
> RACHEL: Ross, please, this is a hospital, okay? That actually means something here.

Ross's usage of the title "doctor" refers to a university degree regardless of the field of study. Which semantic aspect of "doctor" allows Rachel to reprimand him? Considering the hospital setting of this interchange, which meaning of "doctor" is most likely to be inferred? The situational context influences the choice of one meaning over the other, and thus for readers interested in delving further into such phenomena, I recommend reading up on the concept of frame semantics (for example, Geeraerts 2010, 225–29).

3. We return to Two and a Half Men. In the episode "Big Flappy Bastards,"[6] Charlie is sitting at the piano while his nephew Jake is drinking from a juice box.

> CHARLIE: Okay, we're done here. *(They get up.)* Hey, hey, don't leave your juice box on the piano, it leaves a ring.
>
> JAKE: *(picks up the box)* How could a box leave a ring?

Jake poses an interesting question: How indeed could a rectangular box leave a ring? Consider the polysemy of the word ring and the fact that most drink containers such as glasses, bottles, and cans have a round bottom. Can the meaning of "ring" be extended beyond formal properties of shape, as Charlie's use of the word suggests?

References

Cruse, David Alan. 2011. Meaning in Language: An Introduction to Semantics and Pragmatics. Oxford, UK: Oxford Univ. Press.

5. Written by Sherry Bilsing-Graham and Ellen Plummer.

6. Written by Chuck Lorre, Lee Aronsohn, Eddie Gorodetsky, and Jeff Abugov.

Davies, Mark. 2008–. The Corpus of Contemporary American English: 450 Million Words, 1990–present. Accessed June 20, 2013. http://corpus.byu.edu/coca/.

Geeraerts, Dirk. 2010. Theories of Lexical Semantics. Oxford, UK: Oxford Univ. Press.

Heine, Bernd, and Tania Kuteva. 2007. The Genesis of Grammar: A Reconstruction. Oxford, UK: Oxford Univ. Press.

Lieberman, Evan A., Kimberly A. Neuendorf, James Denny, Paul D. Skalski, and Jia Wang. 2009. "The Language of Laughter: A Quantitative/Qualitative Fusion Examining Television Narrative and Humor." Journal of Broadcasting and Electronic Media 53(4): 497–514.

OED Online. 2013. Oxford, UK: Oxford Univ. Press. Accessed June 24, 2013. http://www.oed.com.

Quaglio, Paulo. 2009. Television Dialogue: The Sitcom Friends vs. Natural Conversation. Amsterdam: John Benjamins.

Zimmermann, Thomas Ede, and Wolfgang Sternefeld. 2013. Introduction to Semantics: An Essential Guide to the Composition of Meaning. Berlin: Mouton de Gruyter.

7

Word Formation in *HIMYM*

JESSIE SAMS

How I Met Your Mother is a half-hour sitcom series created by Carter Bays and Craig Thomas, which began in 2005 and ran until its ninth and final season in 2013. While the series was not particularly ground-breaking in its premise of chronicling the romantic adventures of five white, educated, heterosexual males and females in their twenties and thirties living in New York City, the execution of its narrative can certainly be considered innovative. The series actually unfolded in the future, the year 2030, when Ted Mosby, the titular "I," tells his two teenaged children the story of how he met their mother. Ted's narrated memories are presented as flashbacks to what is actually present time for the viewer, namely, when the series started in 2005, future Ted told his children stories, which took place in 2005. These stories featured the series' four other main characters: Ted's friends from college Marshall and Lily, whose long-term relationship and mutual devotion motivate Ted in his own romantic quests; Ted's on-again, off-again girlfriend Robin, a television journalist from Canada; and Barney, a committed bachelor and womanizer. Neither linear nor condensed, the story of how Ted met his children's mother unfolds over nine seasons, with viewers having to wait until the final seconds of the season 8 finale to actually see the mother's face.

Ted is a hopeless romantic and initially thinks of each woman he dates as the potential future Mrs. Mosby. While his friends Marshall and Lily are in a committed relationship with each other, Barney is infamous for his one-night stands and plots to pick up women. Ted meets Robin in the first season, and throughout the show, their relationship oscillates between romantic and platonic. At first, this causes viewers to wonder if Robin will ultimately turn out to be the mother, but it is soon made clear that this is not the case.

How I Met Your Mother has enjoyed popularity and success as a television sitcom by distinguishing itself in both form and content. The signature flashback sequences of the series provide the viewers with background knowledge, allowing them to cultivate a relationship with the characters, follow their development, and, crucially, recognize recurring themes and references to past events. The success of the series is, to a large extent, also owing to the fact that it created a recognizable linguistic identity for the characters. In other words, the language used in certain episodes managed to transcend the plots, such that what the characters said often made a greater impression than what they did. This chapter considers the characters' linguistic ingenuity; specifically, it presents examples of new words and analyzes the word formation processes behind them. Dialogue extracts from several different episodes are included,[1] but the chapter draws mainly from the episodes "Slap Bet"[2] and "Game Night."[3] For this reason, the next section is devoted to episode summaries, before we move on to introducing and illustrating word-formation processes.

"Slap Bet"

In this episode, Lily, Marshall, Ted, and Robin are together at their local bar when Barney enters and excitedly reports that the Sharper Image has opened its 500th store. In celebration, Barney explains, he wants to invite his friends to accompany him there, where he will treat them to a product of their choice. As everyone rushes to follow him out the door, he announces that they're off to the mall, which stops Robin in her tracks. She blankly refuses to go, and the remainder of the episode centers on

1. Unless otherwise indicated, episodes referred to in this chapter were written by Carter Bays and Craig Thomas.

2. Written by Kourtney Kang.

3. Written by Chris Harris.

Robin's secret and the mystery of her aversion to shopping malls. Marshall convinces Ted that Robin's secret is that she is married, having had her wedding ceremony in a shopping mall. Barney, on the other hand, is sure that Robin is a former pornographic film star. Marshall and Barney agree to a slap bet: whoever is right about Robin gets to slap the face of the other as hard as he can. The slap bet between Marshall and Barney is revisited throughout the series.

"Game Night"

In this episode, it is revealed that whenever the friends partake in their regular game night, Marshall always wins. The group thus decides to have Marshall run game night instead of participate in it, but Marshall instead understands this as an invitation to invent his own game, called Marshgammon. This game is actually a ploy to pose personal questions to Ted's new girlfriend, Victoria, whom Ted had explicitly asked Marshall not to interrogate.

While playing Marshgammon, Lily tells Barney that she has met an old acquaintance of his, a woman named Shannon, who gave Lily a videotape to return to Barney. Barney violently destroys the videotape and storms out of game night, leaving the others puzzled over his reaction. Some days later he shows up at the bar willing to tell the story of the video, but only on the condition that the others also share embarrassing stories from their pasts.

Barney himself reveals that when he was younger, he led a bohemian lifestyle, working in a coffee shop with his girlfriend, Shannon. They had planned to spend their life together, starting by joining the Peace Corps, which, Shannon claimed, would be "legendary." Loyal viewers of *How I Met Your Mother* recognize *legendary* as Barney's signature adjective. Instead, Shannon left Barney for a rich businessman, ultimately breaking Barney's heart and triggering an abandonment of the hippie lifestyle for one of well-dressed womanizing. Just prior to this abandonment, however, Barney records on videotape a weepy love song dedicated to Shannon, who, years later, would meet Lily and give her this same videotape to return to Barney.

Word Formation Processes

In this chapter, we will explore some of the most common English word formation processes. We focus on so-called derivational neologisms; that is, "new complex words, coined according to some well-established and productive patterns" (Szymanek 2003, 430). Our goal is to explore common and widely acknowledged (see for example Adams 1973; Bauer 1983; Plag 2003) English word formation processes without entering into a discussion of their theoretical robustness. Nevertheless, the analytical exercises presented here (and in the following chapter) assume the theoretical concept of a morpheme, and as such are most easily identified within morpheme-based morphology and the work of Morris Halle (1973); John J. McCarthy (1981); Rochelle Lieber (1992); and Halle and Alec Marantz (1995).[4] Chapter 8 provides more information on morpheme-based morphology.

The episodes "Slap Bet" and "Game Night" provide many examples of common English word formation strategies, which are assorted into four categories below: (1) additive processes, in which (parts of) words or morphemes are attached; (2) subtractive processes, where (parts of) words or morphemes are removed; (3) combinatory processes, including both additive and subtractive strategies; and (4) shifting processes, where existing words assume new functions.

Additive Processes

Forming new words can be like building; words or morphemes can be concatenated, that is, added or glued together to create something larger (compare with morpheme-based morphology, chapter 8). In this section, we will consider the additive processes of derivation, infixing, and compounding.

4. The reader is also invited to consider the examples presented here in terms of word- and lexeme-based word formation, as well as according to an onomasiological theory of word formation, which rejects "traditional notions" of word formation, and instead proposes that new words are formed according to a series of categorizing and naming processes that, in turn, are determined by societal needs and linguistic demands (Štekauer 2001, 81–84).

One example of derivation is *affixation*, which is treated in more detail in chapter 8. English uses the affixes known as *prefixes* and *suffixes*, which can be added to a stem or root morpheme to form a new word. Derivational affixes are not fully productive; that is, they cannot freely attach to just any morpheme when being used to form new words. On the other hand, indiscriminate affixation may be possible, if not always acceptable to native speakers. At one point in the episode "Slap Bet," Ted has just been told that his girlfriend, Robin, is married. In response, he tries to figure out how Robin's marital status would affect his own status as her current boyfriend.

Example 1:

> TED: I'm the mistress. No, not the mistress. The mastress. Master. What do you call it?

Understanding Ted's statement relies on two premises: (1) there is a gap in the English lexicon for the male counterpart of the female *mistress*; and (2) he tries to fill the gap by using a derivational affix on an existing word. The *-ess* suffix is used (now mostly archaically) to create a female version of what was historically considered a male word: *author* becomes *authoress*; *actor* becomes *actress*; *waiter* becomes *waitress*; and so on. Ted's usage of the *-ess* suffix is quite different, though, as he uses a female-gendered suffix to derive a new male-referential word. The resulting incongruity between the female marker and the male referent is what prompts us to experience Ted's use of this new word as humorous.

In "Game Night," Ted tells his own embarrassing story of how, after bidding good-bye to Robin at the end of a date, he fails to kiss her. He gets drunk and decides to return to Robin's apartment not once but twice, in pursuit of the goodnight kiss. Ultimately, however, Ted only manages to vomit outside her door.

Example 2:

> ROBIN: You re-returned for me. That's really sweet. Though you kind of ruined my customized Scherbotsky doormat.

Here we have another example of deriving a new word via affixation. In recognition of Ted's two-time attempt to find and kiss Robin, the verb *re-returned* is used: the prefix *re-* indicating an action is done again, and the inflectional suffix *-ed*, indicating past tense. It is important to note that both the derivational prefix and the inflectional suffix combine with and maintain verb forms only. We will return to *re-return* later in the chapter, to witness yet another word formation process.

While English derivation does rely on prefixes and suffixes, infixing is also possible in English, in terms of how whole words can be inserted into other words (such as *fucking* in *absofuckinglutely*; see Suggestions for Further Viewing and Analysis, chapter 8).[5] *How I Met Your Mother* is responsible for popularizing the infix "wait for it." This is, in fact, one of the most salient linguistic features of Barney's speech. He is best known for infixing "wait for it" in the equally frequently used "legendary," resulting in *legen—wait for it—dary.*

Aside from as an infix to "legendary," Barney also uses "wait for it" in other situations. In "Slap Bet," Barney announces what he believes Robin's secret to be:

Example 3:

BARNEY: Our friend Robin used to do porn—wait for it—ography!

Like an infix, the "wait for it" phrase is inserted into the middle of words, and it usually occurs at syllable boundaries and between a nonstressed and stressed syllable. In the episode "The Rough Patch,"[6] however, those placement 'rules' are broken, resulting in an instance of infixing that is incongruous with Barney's standard practice. In this example, Barney is describing a movie he had seen the night before:

Example 4:

BARNEY: It was Legen—wait for it—ds of the Fall.

The word *legends* has a stressed syllable followed by a nonstressed syllable (*le*-gends), which is not the typical environment for an infix.

5. For a discussion of (non-)expletive infixing, see Adams (2001; 2004) and McMillan (1980).

6. Written by Chris Harris.

Furthermore, Barney actually inserts "wait for it" inside the second syllable (rather than *le-wait for it-gends*).

Another additive method of forming new words is to combine two or more free morphemes (that is, words) resulting in what is known as a *compound*. In "Slap Bet," when Ted is frustrated over not knowing Robin's secret, Barney assures him it is actually a good thing: if Ted knows too much about Robin, he might hit "the fatal oh-moment." Marshall questions Barney on what the "oh-moment" is, which Barney defines.

Example 5:

BARNEY: That moment when you find that one detail about a person that is going to be a dealbreaker.

Thus we have two compounds: *oh-moment*, with the two free morphemes *oh* and *moment* joined together to represent a specific concept; and *dealbreaker*, comprised of *deal* and *breaker*, with the latter in turn being derived from *break* and *-er*.

As example 5 demonstrates, compounds in English can be written in different ways: with a hyphen between the individual free morphemes (*oh-moment*), as one word with no spaces (*dealbreaker* or even *deal-breaker*), or, as in the episode title, with a space between the individual free morphemes (*slap bet*). Because compounds are not written uniformly, they can be difficult to identify. One typical characteristic of English compounds is initial stress; for instance, when saying *slap bet*, *oh-moment*, or *dealbreaker*, the primary stress is on the first word in the compound.

The term 'slap bet' is defined in the episode by Marshall as a bet in which the winner "gets to slap the other person in the face as hard as they possibly can." When Lily at first scoffs at the slap bet Marshall and Barney make about guessing Robin's secret (Marshall bets she is married while Barney bets she was in pornography), Marshall tells Lily she can be "slap bet commissioner"—yet another compound. This example suggests that compounds can get rather long. Particularly in casual speech, speakers are wont to create compounds out of long strings of words, as in the following example from "Game Night." Robin speaks up to share a humiliating story of her own, about a time when she was live-interviewing a hansom cab driver, and Barney's response demonstrates his familiarity with the story.

Example 6:

BARNEY: Not the slipping-in-horse-poop story!

In example 6, Barney uses "slipping-in-horse-poop" as a compound adjective to describe the story Robin is about to tell.

Other examples can be found in the episode "Ring Up,"[7] such as the *I-got-caught-cheating diamond* and *Who's your "couldn't find mild salsa but said screw it and went with medium salsa" bad boy*? In writing, hyphens can be used to indicate that the words are working together as a unit (as in the first example) or quotation marks can be used in the same way (as in the second example).

Subtractive Processes

Not only can new words be formed by the addition of morphemes, but also by subtractive processes, that is, the removal of parts of words, which in turn creates new forms. In this section, we consider clipping and back-formation.

In example 3 above, Barney's infixed "wait for it" in "porn-wait for it-ography" is easily recognized as anticlimactic, owing to the fact that *porn* is a conventional and more common alternative term for *pornography*. The word *porn* is, in fact, the result of the word formation process known as 'clipping'. A 'clip' is a shortened version of a longer word. Clips retain the same meaning and part of speech category as their original form, but either the beginning or the ending (or, in some cases, both beginning and ending) of the word is removed.

In the next extract from "Game Night," we see examples of clipping from both the front and the back of a word. It is in a flashback to Barney's younger years as a long-haired hippie working at a coffee shop and in love with his co-worker, Shannon, that we see Barney kiss Shannon before turning to serve the next customer in line: a rich, arrogant, well-dressed businessman. He and Barney engage in the following conversation:

Example 7:

7. Written by Jennifer Hendriks.

BUSINESSMAN: Dude, that your g-friend? All right, high five!

BARNEY: *(giving a peace-sign)* Sorry, I only give high twos.

BUSINESSMAN: Whatevs. As long as you're nailing that.

BARNEY: Listen to you. That? You know, women aren't objects. They're human beings. And FYI, Shannon and I have decided to wait till we're married. You can read about it in my zine.

The businessman's use of *whatevs* and Barney's use of *zine* illustrate word-final (*whatever*) and word-initial (*magazine*) clipping. Note, however, the plural inflectional affix (*-s*) in *whatevs*. While *whatever* retains its adverb part of speech status even when clipped to *whatev*, the plural inflection suggests that *whatevs* is being grammatically treated as a noun—similar examples from youth and Internet slang suggest this to be the case, such as *forevs* (from *forever*) and *totes* (from *totally*).

Words can also be clipped both from the front and the back, leaving only a middle section. Such middle-clippings are less common, but two well-known examples are *fridge* from *refrigerator* (see, for example, "Pilot" and "Miracles"[8]) and *flu* from *influenza* ("Brunch"[9] and "Do I Know You?").

Finally, it should be mentioned that clippings are not the same as abbreviations. While clippings result in proper new words, abbreviations are simply shortened forms of words, and not immediately recognized as separate words. For example, *lab* is a clipping of *laboratory* and thus a word in its own right; *dept.* is merely an abbreviation for *department* and not recognized as an independent word. Like dept., most abbreviations are marked with a period: *corp., ltd.*, or *abbrev.* In the episode "Definitions," Ted takes a position as an adjunct professor. On his first day of class, he decides to write his name on the chalkboard, presenting himself as Professor Mosby, but is unable to spell *professor.* Ted could have saved himself the struggle by using the clipping *prof*, the abbreviated title *Prof.* or, had he actually had a doctoral degree, the abbreviation *Dr. Mosby.*

Like clips, 'back-formations' are shortened versions of words; however, unlike clips, the shortened form takes on a new meaning and a new

8. Written by Craig Thomas and Carter Bays.

9. Written by Stephen Lloyd.

part of speech. For example, in "Slap Bet," Lily begs Ted to tell her Robin's secret; *beg* is an example of a back-formation. *Beggar* was a noun in English that had no verbal form directly related to it. The phonological properties of the word were similar to those of other examples of English nouns such as *writer* and *painter,* where the derivational *-er* suffix changes a verb (like *write* and *paint*) into a noun, meaning 'one who does VERB'. The word *beggar* was assumed to be analogous such that a beggar must be 'one who begs'. This back-formation resulted in the verb *to beg.*

An example of back-formation that might not be so obvious comes from an episode that continues the slap bet theme, "Slapsgiving 3: Slap-pointment in Slapmarra"; as the title indicates, this episode also provides many examples of blending words with *slap,* which will be discussed in the next section. In derision of Marshall's suit, Barney tells him, "A suit like that only needs one button, self-destruct." Later in the episode, as Marshall is learning to master the art of slapping, he exclaims, "I've just got a slappetite for destruction." While we may normally see *destruction* as a derived form of *destruct,* it is in fact *destruct* that is a back-formation of *destruction.* Back-formations can often be difficult to spot without knowing the history of a word.

Combinatory Processes

Some word formation processes are actually a combination of both putting parts of words together and taking parts of words away. In this section we will consider examples of this combining in the processes blending, clip-compounding, hypocorisms, acronyms, and initialisms.

A 'blend' results from taking parts of two words and making them into one word, the result of which is also known as a 'portmanteau'. In "Slap Bet," Barney shows a video that he erroneously assumes to be Robin's pornography video. He therefore believes he has won the slap bet about Robin's secret, and as the video starts playing, he slaps Marshall. However, the video turns out to be a music video: in her youth, Robin was a pop star who performed in shopping malls all over Canada. When the true secret is unveiled, Marshall confronts Barney about the undeserved slap.

Example 8:

MARSHALL: Looks like somebody suffered from premature slapulation.

Here the word *slap* is blended with the word *ejaculation*, and the resulting *slapulation* is used in a way analogous to the collocation *premature ejaculation*. As in this example, an entire word (*slap*) is blended with part of another word (*-ulation*); in the section above, we saw how slap was blended with other words, yielding *Slapsgiving*, *Slapmarra*, *slappointment*, and *slappetite*, the latter two being particularly good examples of a blend in which it is unclear where one word ends and another begins.

In "Game Night," Marshall presents his newly invented game as "Marshgammon," combining the first part of his name (which itself is a word formation process that we explore further on) and the last part of *backgammon*. Blending even constitutes the theme of the episode "The Broath," in which Barney creates several new words by blending *bro*, the first part of *brother*. He asks Ted to don a *brobe* and to take a *broath*, just like *Brotus* did in the *Broman* times.

'Clip-compounding' combines, as the term indicates, clipping (usually word-finally) and compounding. A good example of clip-compounding is the episode title "Dowisetrepla."[10] In this episode, Marshall and Lily are looking for an apartment in what is actually an undesirable area of New York City, "Downwind of a Sewer Treatment Plant," but which sounds attractive due to its clip-compound name, DoWiSeTrePla, in the tradition of TriBeCa and SoHo.

'Hypocorism' refers to the result of a clipping in combination with an affixation of the suffix [*-i*], a diminutive morpheme commonly spelled as *-y* or *-ie*. In "Game Night," Ted's new girlfriend, Victoria, is taking part in game night for the first time; Marshall thus invites her to start off the game by saying, "Newbie goes first. Roll." The etymology of *newbie* is unclear; it may come from *new boy*, in which case it is not a hypocorism at all but rather an alternative pronunciation. On the other hand, it may indeed be a hypocorism in the form of an *-ie* suffix attached to a compound and/or clip of *new beginner*, *new blood*, or *newborn*. Even if *newbie* is actually a

10. Written by Brenda Hsueh.

reverse-engineered hypocorism of *newboy*, it is interesting to note that it, in turn, has served as a base word for the form *noob*.

In "Slap Bet," as Barney and Marshall each become more assured that they know Robin's secret, they engage in psychological warfare:

Example 9:

MARSHALL: I can see my handprint on your face.
BARNEY: Don't get too cocky, Slappy.

Here, Barney uses *Slappy* as a nickname for Marshall, a diminutive form of "slap." This is not a hypocorism: there is no clipping involved to arrive at the word *slap*. Instead, it is simply a derivation via affixation of the *-y* suffix, similar to *cocky*.[11] However, in this example, "Slappy" is more likely to be mistaken for hypocorism than cocky, because it is used as a name or personal reference—just as "Newbie" was in example 8. Hypocorism is, in fact, frequently evident in people's pet names or nicknames. Barney's own name is a hypocorism of Barnabas or Barnaby; Ted is a clipping of Theodore, which commonly becomes the hypocorism Teddy; among Barney's many sexual encounters were Wendy, Abby, and Jenny, each a hypocorism of original names Gwendolyn, Abigail, and Jennifer.

An 'acronym' is formed by combining only the first letters of a string of words and pronouncing them as a new word. For example, in the episode "The Playbook," Barney explains the strategies, or plays, he uses to pick up women in bars. Each of his plays has a name, often derived from what props he needs to carry the play out or which persona Barney adopts, such as the "Scuba Diver." The word *scuba* is an acronym, formed by the first letters in *self-contained underwater breathing apparatus*. Another of Barney's plays involves him claiming to work for *SNASA*, that is, the

11. Hypocorism, which involves clipping and suffixing, is not to be confused with simple derivation via *-y* suffix. It is this latter kind of suffixing that is a salient feature of the language of *Buffy the Vampire Slayer* (1997–2003). While both the names *Buffy* and *Scoobies* (as her crew calls themselves) are examples of hypocorism, words such as *out-of-the-loopy*, *depressedy*, and *stammery* are derivations, which both Michael Adams (2003, 42) and Susan Mandala (2007, 56) consider a marked linguistic practice serving to establish in-group identity.

Secret National Aeronautics and Space Administration. In the same episode, Barney refers to a woman as a *MILSWANCA*, or a *Mother I'd Like to Sleep With and Never Call Again*.

'Initialisms' are similar to acronyms in that they, too, involve the combination of first, or initial, letters. However, because of phonotactically prohibitive letter combinations, initialisms are resistant to pronunciation as words. In other words, it is necessary to say the letters one by one. An example of an initialism can be found in example 7, when Barney says, "And FYI, Shannon and I have decided to wait till we're married." The initialism *FYI* stands for *your information*, and is not possible, or at least not easy, to pronounce as an English word.

Finally, let's consider the title of the television series *How I Met Your Mother*. As a rather long title, it is ripe for shortening, either by acronym or initialism, and in fact it is often referred to as *HIMYM*, which can be pronounced as a word [haimIm] or [hImIm], making it an acronym, or as a string of letters, in which case it would be an initialism.

Shift Happens

One of the easiest ways of forming new words is to use existing words in new ways. In the following sections, we will look at how this is achieved through conversion, eponymy, and borrowing.

It is not necessary to add to or take away from existing words to form a new word; in fact, English is especially fond of using existing words in new and novel ways without changing their forms at all, for example by using a noun as a verb or an adjective as a noun. We refer to this process of forming new words by assigning a new part of speech as 'conversion'. For example, when Barney announces in "Slap Bet" that he thinks Robin's secret is that she was involved in pornography, Lily admits it could be true:

Example 10:

LILY: She does have the fake orgasm noises down.

TED: Hey!

LILY: What? The walls are thin.

TED: That's not what I'm hey-ing you about.

In the last line of the excerpt above, Ted uses the interjection *hey* as a verb: *to hey someone* is realized as "I'm hey-ing you." This is perhaps not immediately recognized as a legitimate English word, but in this context, both its meaning and function are clear.

Another example of conversion can be seen in the same episode when Ted is complaining to Marshall that he wants Robin to admit her lie about being married, but Ted is reluctant to tell her how it is he knows she lied. Marshall advises Ted to "lawyer" her. *Lawyer* is a noun, yet Marshall has converted it to a verb without having to change its form. In this context, Marshall's use of *(to) lawyer* means the act of tricking someone into revealing the truth by clever questioning, much like the stereotypical film or television lawyer would do in a courtroom when a witness or defendant is suspected of lying.

Earlier, in example 2, we saw an example of derivation when Robin discovers in "Game Night" that Ted "re-returned" for her. At the end of the episode, Barney takes pleasure in the fact that he coerced all of his friends into sharing their embarrassing stories, especially Ted's story of re-returning:

Example 11:

BARNEY: Ladies, gentlemen . . . Ted. This has been a wonderful evening. I got great dirt on all you guys. I got Ted to tell the re-return.

In this example, Barney creates a new word by converting the verb *(to) re-return* (itself a new word by derivation) into a noun, identified as such by the definite article, *the*, resulting in *the re-return*. Returning to example 7 from "Game Night," we see one example of conversion in the businessman's use of *nailing* in "As long as you're nailing that." Here, the noun *nail* has been converted to a verb, *(to) nail*. This is normally understood as the process of fastening with a nail, but in example 7, the converted *nail* means to have sexual intercourse with someone.

If we continue the extract from example 7, we see yet another example of conversion.

Example 7 (from the section "Subtractive Processes"):

BUSINESSMAN: Dude, that your g-friend? All right, high five!

BARNEY: *(giving the peace-sign)* Sorry, I only give high twos.

BUSINESSMAN: Whatevs. As long as you're nailing that.

BARNEY: Listen to you. That? You know, women aren't objects. They're human beings. And FYI, Shannon and I have decided to wait till we're married. You can read about it in my zine.

Example 12 (continuing from example 7):

BUSINESSMAN: Hey, Haircut, right here. Open up your knowledge basket 'cause here it comes. Forget that touchy-feely crap. You get money, you get laid. End of discussion.

BARNEY: I feel sorry for you, man.

BUSINESSMAN: Peace out, hombre.

BARNEY: *(chuckling, shaking his head)* Suits.

The businessman's use of "Haircut" to refer to long-haired Barney reveals two processes of conversion. First, the verb *(to) cut* has been converted to a noun, *(a) cut*. This conversion can then be extended to *haircut*, a process of compounding that we explored in the section "Additive Processes." The common noun *haircut* is then converted to a proper noun, by virtue of the businessman's vocative use of the word, that is, to substitute as a name for Barney.

In the next section, we focus more on the role of names in word formation processes.

In the section "Combinatory Processes," we saw in the episode "The Playbook" that "The Scuba Diver" and "SNASA" were among Barney's plays for picking up women. Yet another of his plays is called "The Mosby," so named for Ted Mosby. In this play, Barney walks into a bar and pretends to have just been left at the altar, drawing from an event directly out of Ted's life, when he himself was stood up at the altar. The use of a proper noun, that is, a person's name, to signify not the actual person in a direct personal reference, but rather something associated with that person is called 'eponymy', a type of word formation process similar to conversion, in which a proper noun becomes a common noun or other part of speech.

In "Game Night," Marshall introduces his new game, Marshgammon. As the inventor of the game, Marshall has lent his own name to it, and thus *Marshgammon* is an example of eponymy. However, *Marshgammon* is clearly also an example of a blend, introduced in the section "Combinatory Processes," because only part of Marshall's name and part of another game name are used. However, an even clearer example of eponymy can be found as Marshall attempts to explain the rules of Marshgammon:

Example 13:

> MARSHALL: But if you roll an even number while adjacent to the Peppermint Forest, then you "Marshall out," and all your chips go into the pot,

In this case, Marshall has used his entire first name to refer no longer to himself, but to a specific circumstance and action. This is also a further example of conversion, as the proper noun *Marshall* becomes a verb, *(to) Marshall,* which in turn can accept verb particles such as *out*.[12]

Languages don't always rely on internal methods to form new words, but may instead borrow words from other languages. For instance, Ted mentions *crêpes* in the opening sequence of "Slap Bet," a word borrowed from the French. Later in the episode, when Barney is quizzing Lily, trying to prove that she doesn't know all of Marshall's secrets, he asks about the time Marshall went to the Pacific Northwest. Lily answers that Marshall has never been there because of his fear of Sasquatch, a word borrowed from Salish.

In example 12, the businessman concludes his interaction with Barney by saying, "Peace out, hombre." Borrowed from the Spanish, *hombre* used in this context can be compared to Barney's use of *man* in the previous turn. The "Game Night" episode concludes with Barney's own appropriation of this borrowed word, signaling the completion of his journey from a long-haired, love-sick hippie to a well-groomed chauvinist.

Example 14:

12. There are further examples in "Game Night" of noun-to-verb conversions that then take particles, such as when a distraught hippie-Barney runs from the coffee shop and receives a flyer for a suit sale, announced by the phrase "Suit up!" or when Barney urges Ted to tell his story, given that everyone else has "manned up."

BARNEY: Ladies, gentlemen . . . Ted. This has been a wonderful evening. I got great dirt on all you guys. I got Ted to tell the re-return. I finally nailed Shannon! Told her I'd call her tomorrow. Yeah, right. And I rediscovered just how awesomely awesome my life is. Peace out, hombres!

Discussion

Like other popular cultural artifacts, a unique linguistic identity is vital to the longevity and success of a television series. In *How I Met Your Mother,* language use clearly contributes to character development and differentiation, but also distinguishes the series as linguistically innovative. It can be safely assumed that explicit attention was paid throughout the series to crafting the speech of the *HIMYM* characters to support character development through creative language use, in particular by the use of new words. Such innovation, as this chapter shows, is the result of a variety of word formation processes.

The examples presented in this chapter have been extracted from only a fraction of the episodes included in the nine-season-long series. Nevertheless, together the examples capture some of the most salient and essential themes and plots of the series, as well as personality traits and background stories of the characters. By exploring word formation processes in action in *How I Met Your Mother,* this chapter has thus served as yet another example of the central role linguistic processes, principles, and theories play in television series and, by extension, in our daily lives.

Suggestions for Further Viewing and Analysis

1. In the episode "Murder? . . . Anyone? . . . Anyone? . . . Bueller?"[13] of *Psych* (2006–14) the two main characters, Shawn and Gus, have the following interaction:

GUS: Wasn't Howie the victim at one point?

SHAWN: Gus, that is so forty minutes ago. I bet you're still telling your friends to chillax.

13. Written by Steve Franks and Andy Berman.

Shawn's turn provides an example of a blend (*chill* and *relax* combine to form *chillax*) and also reminds us that many new words are not necessarily long-lasting. Consider examples of slang, both retro and modern words, and determine the word formation strategies (or combination of strategies) at work.

2. In the example below, extracted from the episode "The One with All the Resolutions"[14] from *Friends* (1994–2004), analyze the words in italics in terms of word formation processes.

> PHOEBE: Mine is to *pilot* a commercial jet.
> CHANDLER: That's a good one, too, *Pheebs.* Now all you have to do is find a *planeload* of people whose resolution is to plummet to their deaths.
> JOEY: Well, you know those special skills I have listed on my *résumé*? I would love it if one of those was true.
> PHOEBE: Do you want me to teach you? I'm a great *teacher.*

A viewing of the entire episode will yield more examples of word formation strategies, and the series itself, as evidenced in chapter 13, is ripe for extensive linguistic analysis.

3. In the episode "Moon Landing"[15] of *Modern Family* (2009–), real estate agent Phil Dunphy, upon discovering that his personalized bus-stop advertisements have been vandalized, says the following:

> PHIL: Some people call me a salesman. I call myself a "salesfriend," so obviously I need strangers to trust me. I don't take it kindly when someone Tom Sellecks my bus bench.

Aside from *salesfriend,* an obvious example of compounding, another new word is salient in this example, namely *Tom Sellecks.* Phil's personalized bus-stop advertisement features a photograph of his face on a bus-stop bench. What does Phil mean when he says someone "Tom Sellecks" his bus bench? Which word formation strategy (or strategies) has been

14. Written by Suzie V. Freeman.
15. Written by Bill Wrubel.

invoked? Consider also how this example illustrates the importance of background knowledge in word formation processes.

4. In the episode "The Publicity Agent"[16] of *I Love Lucy* (1951–60), Ricky is playing solitaire (with cards) when Lucy walks in and begins the following exchange.

> LUCY: What'll we do tonight, Ricky?
>
> RICKY: Nothing.
>
> LUCY: What do you mean nothing? Let's call the Mertzes and play some cards.
>
> RICKY: I don't feel like seeing the Mertzes, and I don't want to play cards.
>
> LUCY: What do you call what you're doing here?
>
> RICKY: Tiddly-winks.
>
> LUCY: Lay your black tiddly on your red wink.

Consider the word formation strategies at play in both Ricky's use of *tiddly-winks* and in Lucy's utterance, "Lay your black tiddly on your red wink." How do examples like these illustrate dependence on context and limits of productivity in some word formation strategies?

References

Adams, Michael. 2001. "Infixing and Interposing in English: A New Direction." *American Speech* 76(3): 327–31.

———. 2003. *Slayer Slang: A* Buffy the Vampire Slayer *Lexicon*. Oxford, UK: Oxford Univ. Press.

———. 2004. "Meaningful Infixing: A Nonexpletive Form." *American Speech* 79(1): 110–12.

Adams, Valerie. 1973. *An Introduction to Modern English Word-Formation*. London: Longman.

Bauer, Laurie. 1983. *English Word-Formation*. Cambridge, UK: Cambridge Univ. Press.

Halle, Morris. 1973. "Prolegomena to a Theory of Word Formation." *Linguistic Inquiry* 4:3–16.

16. Written by Jess Oppenheimer, Madelyn Pugh, and Bob Carroll Jr.

Halle, Morris, and Alec Marantz. 1994. "Some Key Features of Distributed Morphology." In *Papers on Phonology and Morphology*, edited by Andrew Carnie, Heidi Harley, and Tony Bures, 275–88. Cambridge, MA: MIT Working Papers in Linguistics.

Lieber, Rochelle. 1992. *Deconstructing Morphology: Word Formation in Syntactic Theory*. Chicago: Univ. of Chicago Press.

Mandala, Susan. 2007. "Solidarity and the Scoobies: An Analysis of the -y Suffix in the Television Series *Buffy the Vampire Slayer*." *Language and Literature* 16(1): 53–73.

McCarthy, John J. 1981. "A Prosodic Theory of Nonconcatenative Morphology." *Linguistic Inquiry* 12(3): 373–418.

McMillan, James B. 1980. "Infixing and Interposing in English." *American Speech* 55:163–83.

Plag, Ingo. 2003. *Word-Formation in English*. Cambridge, UK: Cambridge Univ. Press.

Štekauer, Pavol. 2001. "Fundamental Principles of an Onomasiological Theory of English Word-Formation." *Onomasiology Online* 2:1–42.

Szymanek, Bogdan. 2005. "The Latest Trends in English Word-formation." In *Handbook of Word-Formation*, edited by Pavol Štekauer and Rochelle Lieber, 429–48. Dordrecht, Netherlands: Springer.

8

What's the Deal with Morphemes?

Doing Morphology with Seinfeld

KRISTY BEERS FÄGERSTEN

Festivus. Sponge-worthy. Yada-yada-yada. No soup for you. Not that there's anything wrong with that. Master of my domain. One needs only to mention words and phrases such as these to find kindred spirits across the globe who can appreciate the reference to what has been heralded as the greatest television show ever.[1] *Seinfeld*, created by Larry David and comedian Jerry Seinfeld, starred Jason Alexander as Jerry's best friend, George; Julia Louis-Dreyfus as Jerry's ex-girlfriend Elaine; and Michael Richards as Jerry's eccentric neighbor, Kramer. During its nine-season run (1989–98), the series gained steadily in popularity, eventually garnering prime time's highest ratings. It has been famously branded as a "show about nothing," with plots centering on the mundane, everyday activities of a group of four single New Yorkers.

Seinfeld was appreciated as a series with identifiable but unusual story arcs, eccentric recurring characters, and neatly interwoven storylines. Throughout its production, however, it remained firmly a show about the minutiae of daily life as endured by the four main characters. Where *Seinfeld* distinguished itself from other series, however, was its characteristic focus on language and the intricacies and absurdities of communication.

1. #1 of TV Guide's 50 Greatest TV Shows of All Time, 2002.

Not only did dialogue serve as a vehicle to progress storylines, but language use itself was a significant plot feature, with characters expressing themselves in innovative ways or discussing language use in noteworthy detail. For example, in the excerpt below from the episode "The Label Maker,"[2] Jerry explains to Elaine how to interpret someone's reaction to a gift she has given.

Example 1:

JERRY: Well how did he react when you gave it to him?

ELAINE: Um, he said, "Oh. A label maker. How 'bout that?"

JERRY: He repeated the name of the gift?

ELAINE: Yeah, so?

JERRY: Oh, well, if you repeat the name of the gift, you can't possibly like it.

ELAINE: What do you mean?

JERRY: Oh, you know, like when someone opens something up and they go, "Oh. Tube socks."

Similar analyses of social interaction reflect an attention to linguistic conventions and absurdities that pervaded the series and endeared *Seinfeld* to the viewing audience. As Caryn James (1998) noted in the *New York Times*, dialogue in *Seinfeld* is foregrounded, such that "language becomes action." In many episodes, it was often language itself that comprised the plot. Metalinguistic awareness couched in creative language use, engaging dialogue, and innovative storylines established *Seinfeld* as a so-called water-cooler show, such was the extent to which it generated enthusiastic post-episode conversation. Not only did the audience talk *about* the (mis) adventures of the characters, they talked *like* the characters, freely appropriating their linguistic features and incorporating them into their own speech (see, for example, Beers Fägersten 2012, 93; Tompkins 2014). Examples of this appropriation abound in McFedries (2003), which includes a *Seinfeld* lexicon and documented usages of Seinfeldisms in the media. It can thus be claimed that the language of *Seinfeld* is arguably its greatest

2. Written by Alec Berg and Jeff Schaffer.

legacy. After nine seasons, the series has left an indelible mark on the language of popular culture.

The majority of *Seinfeld*'s linguistic contributions are in the form of now well-known words and phrases (McFedries 2003; Magnotta and Strohl 2011, 127). Among the most famous are *festivus*,[3] the name of an alternative winter holiday; *sponge-worthy*,[4] the state of being worth the use of a limited supply of birth control sponges; *yada-yada-yada*,[5] a phrase that allows one to avoid recounting details; *no soup for you*,[6] an admonishment from the owner of a soup stand toward any customer complicating a soup order; *not that there's anything wrong with that*,[7] a recurring commentary on homosexuality; and *master of my domain*,[8] one of several analogous phrases used to claim that one has refrained from masturbation. This list of memorable phrases provides just a glimpse of the significance and pervasiveness of linguistics in *Seinfeld*, in which the architecture of entire episodes was regularly centered around language: the creation of a particular word, the repetition of a phrase, the linguistic management of social conventions, or the manipulation of language to discuss taboo topics. The language of *Seinfeld* could readily illustrate many linguistic phenomena, from word formation processes to the conventions of discourse and pragmatics, and even metalinguistic commentary (as illustrated by the phrases *low talker*[9] or *close talker*.[10] This chapter, however, will focus on morphological analysis, considering two words from the episode "The Label Maker": *regifter* and *degifted*.

The Label Maker

In "The Label Maker," Jerry has two tickets to the Super Bowl, which he cannot use and would like to give away. While walking along the street,

3. "The Strike," written Alec Berg, Jeff Schaffer, and Dan O'Keefe.

4. "The Sponge," written by Peter Mehlman.

5. "The Yada Yada," written by Peter Mehlman and Jill Franklyn.

6. "The Soup Nazi," written by Spike Feresten.

7. "The Outing," written by Larry Charles.

8. "The Contest," written by Larry David.

9. "The Puffy Shirt," written by Larry David.

10. "The Raincoats," written by Tom Gammill, Max Pross, Larry David, and Jerry Seinfeld.

Jerry meets an acquaintance, dentist Tim Whatley. Jerry offers Tim the Super Bowl tickets, and as a token of appreciation, Tim later sends Jerry a label maker, a device for typing out words on tape. In Jerry's apartment, Elaine notices the new label maker. She tells Jerry how much she likes the product and claims they make great gifts, as she had just given one to Tim Whatley. Jerry informs Elaine that his label maker was sent by Tim Whatley, and they both wonder if Tim has given Jerry the same label maker that Elaine had given Tim. Elaine believes that Tim is a *regifter*:

Example 2:

ELAINE: Hey. Oh, is that a label maker?

JERRY: Yes it is. I got it as a gift. It's a Label Baby Junior.

ELAINE: Love the Label Baby baby. You know those things make great gifts. I just got one of those for Tim Whatley for Christmas.

JERRY: Tim Whatley?

ELAINE: Yeah. Who sent you that one?

JERRY: One Tim Whatley!

ELAINE: No! My Tim Whatley?

JERRY: The same. He sent it as a thank you for my Super Bowl tickets.

ELAINE: I think this is the same one I gave him. He recycled this gift. He's a regifter!

Jerry later finds out that he is, after all, able to attend the Super Bowl, and asks Tim Whatley for the tickets back, only to find out that Tim has already offered one of the tickets to Newman, a tenant in Jerry's building. However, while trying to discover if he has regifted the label maker, Elaine has managed to make a flirtatious impression on Tim Whatley, who invites her to the Super Bowl. To do so, however, Tim must thus take back the ticket he gave to Newman. When Jerry discovers this, he concludes that Tim cannot be trusted, claiming that he has both regifted and degifted:

Example 3:

ELAINE: Hey, guess what? I'm going to the Super Bowl with Tim Whatley.

JERRY: What?

ELAINE: We went out for coffee last night and he offered me a ticket.

JERRY: What about the label maker?

ELAINE: Ah, well.

JERRY: Wait a minute, that's my ticket! You didn't even want to go.

ELAINE: It was totally out of the blue. We went upstairs to his apartment, you know, to look for the label maker.

JERRY: So, how did you get up there? Did you say you had to use the bathroom?

ELAINE: No.

JERRY: Then how'd you get up there?

ELAINE: I said, "Do you wanna go upstairs?"

GEORGE: And there's your ticket.

ELAINE: What?

JERRY: That's why you're going to the Super Bowl.

ELAINE: Why?

JERRY: You go out with a guy one time, you ask him to go upstairs like you're Mae West? Of course he's gonna try and get you alone for the weekend.

ELAINE: You mean just because I asked him to go upstairs, he thinks he's going downtown?

JERRY: Obviously.

ELAINE: You're crazy.

GEORGE: Well, what happened when you got upstairs?

ELAINE: As soon as we walked in, he got a call from one of his patients with an impacted molar or something, so he had to leave. I didn't even get a chance to look for the label maker.

JERRY: Yeah, well, I don't trust this guy. I think he regifted, he degifted, and now he's using an upstairs invite as a springboard to a Super Bowl sex romp.

The plot of "The Label Maker" is built around the themes of receiving a gift and giving it away again, and giving a gift and asking for it back. These are recognizable concepts, and we have an established lexical field for expressing them, with words such as *gift, give (away), take (back),* or even *recycle.* What distinguishes the plot of this episode beyond the intriguing exploration of the social practice of gift-giving is the linguistic ingenuity of the terms *regifter* and *degifted*. Not only do these words succinctly capture the concepts of recycling gifts or taking back something that has been given away, but they also manage to illustrate exquisitely a full range of morphological processes. Before we subject each of the words to morphological analysis, however, we will need to learn the basics of morphology.

The Morphology

Generally, *morphology* can be understood as the study of words. However, that which distinguishes morphology from word formation, semantics, or even other disciplines of linguistics is the specific focus on the internal structure of words. Morphology and morphological analysis encourage a deconstructive approach to words in an effort to identify the smallest meaningful units that comprise any one word. It is helpful to consider morphology from another perspective than the one we adopted for word formation in the previous chapter. While word formation focuses on processes that create words, morphology is instead concerned with dissecting existing words to identify their meaningful parts. Morphology is thus "the study of the internal structure of words, and of the systematic form-meaning correspondences between words" (Booij 2012, 7). The most basic units of study in morphology are *morphemes*, "the morphological building blocks of words, [which] are defined as the minimal linguistic units with a lexical or grammatical meaning" (Booij 2012, 8–9).

Morphological analysis generally can be associated with one of three main approaches: morpheme-based morphology, word-based morphology, and lexeme-based morphology, each of which uses the concepts of stems and affixes. 'Stems' are the bases or roots of words, while 'affixes' are parts of words, known as 'prefixes' and 'suffixes', that are fixed, or attached, at the beginnings (prefix) or ends (suffix) of words.

In morpheme-based morphology, both stems and affixes are morphemes, which are concatenated, that is, linked together or otherwise arranged in a particular order to form a word (Bresnan 1982; DiSciullo and Williams 1987; Halle 1973; Kiparsky 1982; Lieber 1992; Selkirk 1982; Siegel 1974). For example, *regifter* would be imagined as *re* + *gift* + *er*, with each component having equal status as a morpheme.

While the morpheme is the basic analytical unit of morpheme-based morphology, in word-based morphology the unit is the word. Morphological processes and regular rules of word formation apply to already-existing words, generating new words (Aronoff 1976; Booij 1977; Scalise 1984). For example, *regifter* would be imagined as the word *gift* serving to generate a new word, *regifter*, via affixation processes.

In linguistics, a distinction can be made between words and lexemes. A word, or word form, is a single realization of the abstract lexeme. For example, if *give* is a lexeme, then *giver, givers, giving,* and *gave* are some of the words associated with this lexeme. In word-based morphology, each of these words is the result of processes, which generate words from words. In lexeme-based morphology, words are generated from lexemes via separate syntactic and phonological processes (Anderson 1992; Aronoff 1994; Beard 1995; Halle and Marantz 1993; Stump 1991; Zwicky 1989). For example, *degifted* would be imagined as the lexeme *gift* undergoing both lexical (*de-*) and inflectional (*-ed*) derivation, whereas affixation would refer only to the phonological realizations of these morphemes.

The step-by-step analyses of *regifter* and *degifted* presented below are not intended to either promote or challenge any of these singular approaches to the (dis)advantage of the others. Nevertheless, throughout the remainder of the chapter, it is the morpheme that is assumed to be the basic unit of lexical and grammatical meaning.

The Morpheme Types

Let's begin with some examples of fairly recognizable morphemes: *apple, teach, the, to, -ly, -ness, -s, -ing.* The first four morphemes are known as *free morphemes,* while the latter four are called *bound morphemes.* Free morphemes are actually proper words, which can stand alone freely and do not require attachment to any other morphemes, that is, words or parts of a word. Bound morphemes, on the other hand, are units of language that do in fact have meaning or grammatical function, but which cannot stand alone freely. Instead, bound morphemes are affixed, connected, joined, or—as the name suggests—bound to at least one free morpheme.

Both free and bound morphemes can be further divided into more specific morpheme types. Free morphemes can be either lexical or grammatical (sometimes called functional), while bound morphemes can be derivational or inflectional. Lexical morphemes are the free morphemes that are the content carriers. In other words, they both stand alone and convey meaning. Lexical morphemes can be nouns (such as *apple*), verbs (*teach*), adjectives (*round*), and even adverbs (*fast*). Because each of these word classes, also known as parts of speech, is open to receiving new members, they comprise what is called the 'open class' of words. Note that not all (new) words qualify as singular free morphemes, but may instead be words composed of two or more free and bound morphemes. For example, *teach* is both a word and a lexical morpheme; *unteachable*, however, is a word but not a singular lexical morpheme (that is, according to morpheme-based morphology). Instead, *teach* would now be identified as a root or the stem/base form of the word, onto which two bound morphemes (*un-* and *-able*) have been affixed.

'Grammatical morphemes', also known as 'functional morphemes', are words that do not convey meaning as lexical morphemes do, but rather provide grammatical support to or functional connections between lexical morphemes. Articles (such as *the*), prepositions (*to*), pronouns (*it*), and conjunctions (*and*) belong to the category of grammatical morphemes, and these parts of speech in turn belong to what is known as the 'closed class' of words, as these classes never or rarely accept new members. Parts of speech, lexical and functional words, and both open and closed word classes are presented in greater detail in chapter 10.

Moving on to bound morphemes, we focus on the two specific types of derivational and inflectional morphemes. Derivational morphemes consist of those classic Greek, Latin, and even Germanic prefixes and suffixes (Plag 2003) many of us learned about in school, for example, *pre-*, *re-*, *dis-*, *un-* or *-ness*, *-ful*, *-ly*, or *-ion*. Derivational morphemes allow us to derive new words; derivation is thus a word formation process, as presented in chapter 7. It is therefore important to consider that words created through derivation may belong to a different word class than the original root or base word. For example, the prefix *re-* is commonly affixed to verbs, and the affixation creates a new word that also is a verb:

re- + *do* = *redo*. In English, prefixation typically does not affect word class. Notable exceptions, however, are *a-*, *be-*, and *en-*. The prefix *a-* can create adjectives from base nouns or verbs, such as *a-* + *fire* (n) = *afire* (adj) or *a-* + *miss* (v) = *amiss* (adj); both *be-* and *en-* create verbs from noun bases, such as *beguile* and *bedevil* or *enrage* and *enslave*.

English derivational suffixes are more commonly recognized as class-changing, though there are exceptions here as well. Suffixes such as *-ness*, *-ful*, or *-ly* change the word class of the base word, such as *happy* (adj) + *-ness* = *happiness* (n), *wonder* (v/n) + *-ful* = *wonderful* (adj), or *quick* (adj) + *-ly* = *quickly* (adv). On the other hand, the derivational suffix *-ship* does not affect part-of-speech status: *friend* (n) + *-ship* = *friendship* (n).

Because derivational morphemes are affixed to root or stem words, they serve to derive new words, which in addition to possibly affecting the word class of the root word, also results in new meanings. For example, *happy* and *unhappy* have opposite meanings, and even *quick* and *quickly*, though similar in meaning, are lexically distinguishable thanks to the derivational morpheme, which also renders them significantly different in terms of word class membership and syntactic function.

There are other suffixes that only carry grammatical meaning and serve syntactic functions. These are the bound morphemes known as 'inflections'. In English, there are only eight inflectional morphemes, though these can have different realizations. Unlike derivational morphemes, the eight English inflectional morphemes do not create new words, but rather alter existing, fully created words for grammatical function. There are two inflectional morphemes for nouns, four for verbs, and two for adjectives, as shown in table 8.1:

Table 8.1 **English inflectional morphemes**

Nouns	*Verbs*	*Adjectives*
Plural marker *-s*	Third person singular *-s*	Comparative *-er*
Possessive marker *-s*	Past tense *-ed*	Superlative *-est*
	Progressive *-ing*	
	Past participle *-en*	

'Allomorphs' are variant forms of morphemes that have the same function, but apply in different environments. Allomorphs provide us with a catch-all category of morpheme. Because *allo-* means 'other', there is an implication that there is a set of morphemes that have 'other' realizations. We can think of the plural morpheme as /-s/, but it is not realized orthographically as 's' and phonetically as [-s] in conjunction with all words. Instead, there are other plural morphemes than /-s/, and we can express that by saying that plural /-s/ has a number of allomorphs. Two of the plural morpheme's allomorphs are a vowel change, known as an 'ablaut': *tooth-teeth*, and no change at all, known as a 'zero morpheme': *sheep-sheep*. These allomorphs apply as well to verbs, as seen in the forms of *drink-drank-drunk* or *cost-cost-cost*. As for the adjective forms, although the basic *-er* and *-est* forms can still be recognized in the irregular forms of *fun* and *bad* (that is, *more fun* and *worst*), the allomorphs of these inflections would include the free morphemes *worse, worst, more,* and *most*.

We are now equipped with a working knowledge of morphology and are thus ready to return to our regular programming, the *Seinfeld* episode "The Label Maker." The following sections illustrate the morphological analyses of the words *regifter* and *degifted*.

The Regifter

When Elaine suggested that Tim Whatley was a "regifter," she invoked a word that was created using a combination of word formation processes. While the meaning of *regifter* is made clear by the previous utterances—"I think this is the same one I gave him. He recycled this gift"—the word itself relies upon Jerry's, and by extension the audience's, tacit knowledge of word formation processes and recognition of common derivational morphemes. A step-by-step morphological analysis of *regifter* illustrates the processes involved in the successful interpretation of meaning.

Step 1: The Root Morpheme

In order to understand *regifter,* we need to focus on the root of the word: the free, lexical morpheme *gift*, belonging to the word class of nouns. Only once this root is identified can we continue by considering the remaining morphemes.

Step 2: The Additional Morphemes

The word *regifter* is composed of one root, which we have identified as the noun *gift*, and two affixes: the bound, derivational prefix *re-* and the bound, derivational suffix *-er.* Because there are two morphemes to be affixed to the root, it will be necessary to determine the order of their affixation. This, in turn, requires that we look more carefully at the affixes. When we consider the nature of the prefix and suffix in question, however, we make a startling discovery: *re-*, which basically means 'again', and *-er,* which means 'one who does', are verbal (or in the case of *-er,* deverbal) affixes. In other words, they are derivational morphemes that commonly or even exclusively affix to verbs, making new verbs (verbal affixation) or making nouns or adjectives out of verbs (deverbal affixation). Because neither *re-* nor *-er* can be affixed to a noun and because the root word *gift* is currently a noun, it is necessary that it be converted to a verb.

Step 3: The Conversion

Conversion is one of the most common word formation processes in English. As we saw in chapter 7, conversion does not alter the forms of words, but it does affect word class, allowing, for example, verbs to be created from nouns. For example, we may put butter (noun) on our bread, or we can butter (verb) our bread; the verb form is a result of converting the noun form. For the analysis at hand, the root morpheme *gift* must be converted from a noun to a verb in order for it to undergo the affixation of *re-* and *-er.*

Step 4: The Order of Affixation

After the conversion process, the word *gift* (verb) is ready to undergo affixation. We will need to resume our consideration of the nature of the prefix *re-* and the suffix *-er* to determine the correct order of affixation. Recall that the process of derivation may result in a change of word class, which, in turn, may affect the order of affixation. What happens to verbs that are prefixed with *re-*? What happens to verbs that are suffixed with *-er*? In the case of the prefix *re-*, verbs remain verbs: *do* (verb) + *re-* = *redo* (verb). In the case of suffix *-er,* verbs become nouns: *teach* (verb) + *-er* = *teacher* (noun). This means that the order of affixation is significant, because if we were to affix *-er* first, we would generate a noun, *gifter,* onto which *re-* could not be affixed. Thus *re-* must be affixed first, generating another verb that can then be affixed with *-er.*

Step 5: The Affix re-

After *gift* has been converted to a verb, it can be prefixed with *re-* resulting in *regift* (verb).

Step 6: The Affix -er

After the derivation of *regift*, it can be suffixed with *-er,* resulting in *regifter* (noun).

This morphological analysis of *regifter* illustrates the interplay between word formation processes, in this case conversion and derivation, and the importance of recognizing how the nature of derivational morphemes can affect the order in which each of the processes occurs. In the next morphological analysis, we will see another example of the interplay between word formation and morphology, and further explore the significance of the order of affixation.

The Degifted

In "The Label Maker," an utterance by George indicates that the morphological productivity of *regifter* has been recognized. When Jerry learns that he can in fact attend the Super Bowl and regrets having given away his tickets to Tim Whatley, George suggests that Jerry simply ask for the tickets back. When Jerry claims that this would not be in the spirit of giving, George suggests that it would nevertheless be justified:

Example 4:

JERRY: I can't call Tim Whatley and ask for the tickets back.

GEORGE: You just gave them to him two days ago, he's gotta give you a grace period.

JERRY: Are you even vaguely familiar with the concept of giving? There's no grace period.

GEORGE: Well, didn't he regift the label maker?

JERRY: Possibly.

GEORGE: Well, if he can regift, why can't you degift?

George's use of the word *regift* shows a tacit understanding of its verbal properties, including the conversion of *gift* from a noun to a verb and the affixation of a verbal prefix. His subsequent use (and the possibly spontaneous creation) of *degift* similarly shows a tacit understanding of derivation by analogy; from a morphological perspective, his final utterance suggests a conclusion along the lines of, "if you can say regift, why can't you say degift?" Jerry's announcement that he believes that Tim Whatley has both *regifted* and *degifted* further confirms the morphological productivity at work, which a step-by-step morphological analysis of *degifted* illustrates.

Step 1: The Root Morpheme

Similar to the analysis of *regifter*, we begin our analysis of *degifted* by identifying the root morpheme, which, as before, is the noun *gift*. We can now continue with step 2, identifying additional morphemes.

Step 2: The Additional Morphemes

Also similar to *regifter*, the word *degifted* is composed of one root, which we have identified as the noun *gift*, and two affixes: the bound, derivational prefix *de-* and the bound, inflectional suffix *-ed*. Because there are two morphemes to be affixed to the root, it will be necessary to determine the order of their affixation. This determination, in turn, requires that we look more carefully at the affixes. When we consider the nature of the prefix and suffix in question, however, we again realize that they are both verbal affixes. Because neither *de-* nor *-ed* can be affixed to a noun and because the root word *gift* is currently a noun, it is necessary that it be converted to a verb.

Step 3: The Conversion

In order for the root morpheme *gift* to undergo the affixation of *de-* and *-ed*, it must be converted from a noun to a verb.

Step 4: The Order of Affixation

After the conversion process, the word *gift* (verb) is ready to undergo affixation. We will need to resume our consideration of the nature of the derivational prefix *de-* and the inflectional suffix *-ed* to determine the correct order of affixation. Recall that inflection is a process applicable to complete word forms; it is thus subsequent to derivation and all other word formation processes. If we were first to inflect *gift* (verb) for past tense, generating *gifted* (verb), that would indicate that our word formation processes were complete, thereby excluding the possibility of forming the verb *degift*, to be used in the past tense as *degifted*. Thus *de-* must be affixed first, generating another (complete) verb that can then be inflected for past tense with *-ed*.

Step 5: The Affix de-

After *gift* has been converted to a verb, it can be prefixed with *de-*, resulting in *degift* (verb).

Step 6: The Affix -ed

After the derivation of *degift*, it can be inflected with the past tense suffix *-ed*, resulting in *degifted* (verb).

Discussion

Seinfeld distinguished itself as a language-based comedy (McFedries 2003, 1), evident in the number of novel words or phrases—that is, catchphrases, one-liners, euphemisms, and coinages—that continue to live on in our vernacular. The reason such "Seinfeldisms" (Magnotta and Strohl 2011; McFedries 2003) have thrived beyond the life of the series is owing not only to their ability to capture the spirit of situations ranging from the mundane and familiar to the absurd and unbelievable, but, significantly, also to the engaging, linguistic challenges they represent. That is to say, the most memorable or successful Seinfeldisms can be considered puzzles, requiring us to apply or invoke cultural and linguistic knowledge so as to solve or make sense of them. The writers of *Seinfeld* capitalized on the entertainment derived from this endeavor, and the audience was further rewarded with a sense of satisfaction upon comprehension of the Seinfeldism in question, reinforcing their overall appreciation.

The morphological analyses presented in this chapter aim to raise our awareness of how intricate these puzzles can be and help us recognize the unique combination of linguistic creativity and economy that characterizes the language of *Seinfeld*. It is not the intention of these analyses to suggest that language users are conscious of or even have explicit knowledge of specific word formation processes or the concepts of derivation and inflection. Without the information presented in this chapter, we could continue blissfully unaware of morphemes, but managing nevertheless to function, probably quite well, as language users. The analyses included here serve, rather, to prove our linguistic competence, by illustrating our remarkable ability to use language creatively and meaningfully despite *not* having metalinguistic awareness or a working knowledge of relevant linguistic terminology. It is furthermore argued that words such as *regifter* and *degifted* as used in "The Label Maker" assume our shared tacit ability to comprehend word meaning and, significantly, they capitalize on our ability to recognize and our propensity to appreciate linguistic innovation and play.

As the analyses indicate, both *regifter* and *degifted* have the same root morpheme, the noun *gift*. The analyses also stipulate that further derivational or inflectional processes require that the noun *gift* be converted to a verb. The obvious question arising from the morphological analyses is, "Why start with the noun *gift* and convert it to a verb, when there already is an available verb: the word *give*?" In other words, given that the analyses make clear to us that the words *regifter* and *degifted* are the results of what is ultimately an unnecessarily intricate combination of word formation and morphological processes, we have to wonder: what is the point? To answer this, we should acknowledge that *to give* and *to give a gift* mean different things, and it can be proposed that this distinction is made salient through the conversion of *gift* to a verb. There is also the possibility that in recognition of the irregularity of *give*, the use of this word was actively avoided, allowing for more transparent inflection in *degifted* as opposed to the alternative *degave*.

The most probable answer to the question of motivation, however, is simply because the process involving a conversion of *gift* is the most entertaining. It reflects a competent and playful linguistic creativity, the recognition and comprehension of which both stimulate and satisfy the audience. One of the reasons for the overall popularity and success of *Seinfeld* was its ingenuity, which extended to language use and linguistic innovation. The series played with language, resulting in memorable words, phrases, and conversations that have left an indelible mark on popular culture and on our collective linguistic repertoire. Whether Seinfeld was a show about nothing or actually a show about language, it was truly a gift.

Suggestions for Further Viewing and Analysis

1. A recurring linguistic practice among the characters of the series *Grey's Anatomy* is known as Mc-labeling. This is the prefixing of words with *Mc,* characteristically used in the nicknames *McDreamy* and *McSteamy,* referring to the characters Dr. Derek Shepherd and Dr. Mark Sloan, respectively. Mc-labeling serves to generate other words than nicknames, however. Consider the following examples:

Example 1:

(Meredith shows up at work)

IZZIE: Why are you back here tonight? You don't have a date with McDreamy?

GEORGE: More like McMarried.

IZZIE: McWhat?

("Raindrops Keep Falling on My Head"[11])

Example 2:

(A new doctor has joined the staff)

MEREDITH: McSexy wants an X-ray to check for fractures and I think it's a bad idea if I take him.

GEORGE: Why? Why?

ALEX: I'm on it.

11. Written by Stacy McKee.

GEORGE: Why is it uh—a bad idea—

CHRISTINA: —McSexy?

MEREDITH: No?

IZZIE: McYummy!

MEREDITH: [No.

CHRISTINA: [No.

MEREDITH: McSteamy.

CHRISTINA: Ah, there it is.

IZZIE: Yep.

GEORGE: Oh, there's a . . . I'm just choking back some McVomit.

("Yesterday"[12])

Example 3:

(Christina sees Meredith taking leave from Derek in the elevator)

CHRISTINA: Oh, great. I'm in the pit protecting smack-heads and gang-bangers from my idiot interns and you're getting McDreamied in the elevator?

("The Heart of the Matter"[13])

A simple Internet search will produce more examples, including the site http://greysanatomy.wikia.com/wiki/Mc_Labeling. In an analysis of Mc-labels, decide whether *Mc-* should be categorized as a lexical, functional, derivational, or inflectional morpheme. Determine also the class(es) of words that Mc-labeling applies to, and whether or not the process maintains or changes word class.

2. Toward the end of the episode "Stop or My Dog Will Shoot!"[14] of *The Simpsons,* Homer pretends to be a dog. Marge checks to make sure Homer does not actually believe he is a dog, to which Homer responds:

Example 1:

HOMER: Relax Marge, I'm just messing with you. I know I'm not a dog. I'm a people, like you.

12. Written by Mimi Schmir and Krista Vernoff.

13. Written by Allan Heinberg.

14. Written by John Frink.

The free, grammatical morpheme *a* is incorrectly used in conjunction with the word *people*, which is the noun *person* inflected for plural. Argue that Homer's pairing of *a* and *people* is encouraged because of the irregularity of the plural form: it neither looks nor sounds like a plural because it is not inflected with the regular plural *-s* suffix. The argument can be supported by a listing of the allomorphs of plural *-s*, where care should be taken to consider both other irregular forms and the different phonological realizations of /-s/.

3. The analysis in the exercise above instructs us to consider allomorphs of plural *-s*. Most often allomorphs are the result of phonological environment. For example, among the large number of English nouns that can be inflected for plural with *-s* or English verbs that can be inflected for third person singular with *-s*, there are some that result in the plural morpheme being pronounced as [s], while other plural *-s* morphemes are pronounced as [z] or [Iz]. Say the nouns *ghosts, goblins,* and *witches* or the verbs *lifts, listens,* and *watches* to hear the differences. Thus we can say that plural *-s*, realized as [s], has an additional two allomorphs, [z] or [Iz], as does third person singular /-s/. A similar situation can be observed with past tense inflectional suffix *-ed*, which is realized as [-d], but has the allomorphs [t] and [Id], as in *listened, watched,* and *lifted*.[15] In light of this information about allomorphs, consider the *How I Met Your Mother* episode "The Possimpible."[16] In this episode, Barney Stinson explains his life philosophy as daring to go past the impossible, to the place where the possible meets the impossible: the *possimpible*. The coinage of *possimpible* involves a transposition of the derivational morpheme *im-* and the root morpheme *poss*, originating from the Latin *posse*, meaning 'able'.[17] The prefix *im-* is actually an allomorph of the derivational *in-*, meaning 'not'. Additional allomorphs include *ir-* and *il-*. Make a list of words containing

15. Additional allomorphs include ablauts (*man-men; give-gave*) and zero-morphemes (*deer-deer; put-put*), as well as irregular forms (*person-people; think-thought*).

16. Written by Jonathan Groff.

17. Note the lingering *p*, which may be deliberate so as to make the word similar to *simple*.

these 'not' prefixes, *in-*, *im-*, *ir-*, and *il-*, and determine the different phonological environments that dictate the use of each of the allomorphs.

4. In this chapter, only prefixes and suffixes were presented as possible derivational or inflectional morphemes. In many languages, however, affixation also takes the form of infixing, that is, the insertion of a morpheme within a word, as opposed to the adding of a morpheme to the beginning or end of a word. Derivational or inflectional infixing is nonexistent or at least rare in English, with examples generally limited to the insertion of whole words within words, such as *absofuckinglutely*.[18] However, a rich and developed case of infixing can be found in *The Simpsons*, thanks to the character Ned Flanders, who typically riddles his utterances with *diddly* or other close variations. Consider the following examples (many more are available at http://www.simpsonsarchive.com/guides/flanders.file.html) to determine the basic form of Ned Flanders's infix and whether or not this form has any allomorphs. Analyze as well the placement of the infix, determining if there are any phonological or morphological conventions to the infixing and any irregularities or exceptions to these conventions. It may be useful to consult Adams (2001; 2004), McCawley (1978), McMillan (1980), and Zwicky and Pullum (1987): Skidaddily-doo, De-diddly-lighted, Scrumdiddily-umscious, Murdiddily-urder, Prediddily-ictable, Diddily-ifference, Pretty darn doodily-diddily good; Reverend . . . emergency! I—it's the Simpson kids, eedily! I, uh, baptism, oodily! Uh, doodily!, gotta be nice hostidididildilidilly, ah hell, diddily ding dong crap!

References

Adams, Michael. 2001. "Infixing and Interposing in English: A New Direction." *American Speech* 76(3): 327–31.

———. 2004. "Meaningful Infixing: A Nonexpletive Form." *American Speech* 79(1): 110–12.

18. One example of this infixed word in use on television is in the final scene of the pilot episode (written by Darren Star) of *Sex and the City*, when the character "Big" answers Carrie's question of whether he had ever been in love.

Anderson, Stephen R. 1992. *A-morphous Morphology*. Vol. 62. Cambridge, UK: Cambridge Univ. Press.

Aronoff, Mark. 1976. *Word Formation in Generative Grammar*. Cambridge, MA: MIT Press.

———. 1994. *Morphology by Itself: Stems and Inflectional Classes*. No. 22. Cambridge, MA: MIT Press.

Beard, Robert. 1995. *Lexeme-Morpheme Base Morphology: A General Theory of Inflection and Word Formation*. Albany: State Univ. of New York Press.

Beers Fägersten, Kristy. 2012. "Intertextual Quotation: References to Media in Family Interaction." In *The Appropriation of Media in Everyday Life*, edited by Ruth Ayass and Cornelia Gerhardt, 79–104. Amsterdam: John Benjamins.

Booij, Geert E. 2012. *The Grammar of Words: An Introduction to Linguistic Morphology*. Oxford, UK: Oxford Univ. Press.

Bresnan, Joan. 1982. *On the Mental Representation of Grammatical Relations*. Cambridge, MA: MIT Press.

DiSciullo, Anne-Marie, and Edwin Williams. 1987. *On the Definition of Word*. Cambridge, MA: MIT Press.

Halle, Morris. 1973. "Prolegomena to a Theory of Word-Formation." *Linguistic Inquiry* 4:451–64.

Halle, Morris, and Alec Marantz. 1993. "Distributed Morphology." In *The View from Building 20*, edited by Kenneth Hale and Samuel Jay Keyser, 111–76. Cambridge, MA: MIT Press.

James, Caryn. 1998. "All Right, Goodbye Already! Parting Is Such Sweet Sitcom." *New York Times*, May 12. Accessed Aug. 22, 2015. http://www.nytimes.com/1998/05/12/arts/critic-s-notebook-all-right-goodbye-already-parting-is-such-sweet-sitcom.html?pagewanted=all.

Kiparsky, Paul. 1982. "From Cyclic Phonology to Lexical Phonology." In *The Structure of Phonological Representations (I)*, edited by Harry van der Hulst and Norval Smith, 131–75. Dordrecht, Netherlands: Foris.

Lieber, Rochelle. 1992. *Deconstructing Morphology*. Chicago: Univ. of Chicago Press.

Magnotta, Elizabeth, and Alexandra Strohl. 2011. "A Linguistic Analysis of Humor: A Look at Seinfeld." *Working Papers of the Linguistics Circle* 21(1): 126–35.

McCawley, James. 1978. "Where You Can Shove Infixes." In *Syllables and Segments*, edited by Alan Bell and Joan Hooper, 213–21. Amsterdam: North-Holland.

McFedries, Paul. 2003. "Seinfeldisms." *Verbatim* 2:1–6.

McMillan, James B. 1980. "Infixing and Interposing in English." *American Speech* 55(3): 163–83.

Plag, Ingo. 2003. *Word-formation in English*. Cambridge, UK: Cambridge Univ. Press.

Scalise, Sergio. 1984. *Generative Morphology*. Dordrecht, Netherlands: Foris.

Selkirk, Elisabeth. 1982. *The Syntax of Words*. Cambridge, MA: MIT Press.

Siegel, Dorothy. 1974. *Topics in English Morphology*. PhD diss., Massachusetts Institute of Technology.

Stump, Gregory T. 1991. "A Paradigm-Based Theory of Morphosemantic Mismatches." *Language* 67(4): 675–725.

Tompkins, Stephen. 2014. "The 20 'Seinfeld'-isms You're Most Likely to Hear in Everyday Conversation." *Uproxx*, Aug. 11. Accessed Sept. 19, 2015. http://uproxx.com/tv/the-20-seinfeld-isms-youre-most-likely-to-hear-in-everyday-conversation/.

Zwicky, Arnold M. 1989. "Quicker, More Quickly,* Quicklier." *Yearbook of Morphology* 2:139–73.

Zwicky, Arnold M., and Geoffrey K. Pullum. 1987. "Plain Morphology and Expressive Morphology." In *Proceedings of the Thirteenth Annual Meeting of the Berkeley Linguistic Society*, edited by Jon Aske, Natasha Beery, Laura Michaelis, and Hana Filip, 330–40. Berkeley, CA: Berkeley Linguistic Society.

9

Channel Surfing

Tuning into the Sounds of English

KRISTY BEERS FÄGERSTEN

In this chapter, in which the subjects of phonetics and phonology are introduced and illustrated, no one single television series is featured. Rather, a number of different series and episodes are invoked, the reason being that phonetics and phonology are concerned with the sound system of a language, most readily observable in pronunciation. If, as in the other chapters of this volume, our choice of featured television series was based on which one distinguishes itself by illustrating phonetic and phonological features and the sound patterns of English, there would be many candidates: all of the television series included in this volume, for example, feature spoken dialogue, and thus their characters routinely produce and exemplify the sounds of English. However, phonetics and phonology are fundamentally about studying and describing the discrete features and properties of the sounds of a language, and to a large extent, this practice highlights the differences between sounds. As experienced speakers, we are accustomed to both producing and recognizing different sounds. We are furthermore able to process various combinations of different sounds, which we in turn recognize as different words. All of this we do constantly and probably without even noticing—until, that is,

I would like to thank Philip Carr, professor of linguistics at Université Paul-Valéry Montpellier 3, for his contribution to this chapter and guidance in identifying and explaining key terms and concepts of phonetics and phonology. Any errors or misrepresentations in this chapter are solely my own.

we encounter a deviation, for example a foreign accent or a mispronunciation. Our awareness of sounds and maybe even of their production process is suddenly raised when we encounter pronunciations very different from our own. Few television series, however, feature a cast of characters with wildly deviant pronunciation patterns—this would risk compromising intelligibility. But many series feature characters with noticeable accents, many series have included episodes in which an important mispronunciation occurs, and many series have developed story lines that highlight pronunciation or the production of sounds. Therefore, in this chapter, we will be engaging in the familiar pastime of channel surfing, encountering a number of different series whose titles will help illustrate the sounds of English, and some episodes of which will allow us to focus on differences between these sounds. This channel surfing will help us raise our awareness of the phonetic and phonological properties of English.

Before moving on, however, it is important to point out that this chapter differs from the other chapters of this volume in yet another way. The linguistic concepts presented here are, in comparison, not as obviously self-contained. That is to say, that despite the fact that background and contextual information are provided along with the dialogue extracts being analyzed, the actual sounds on which we wish to focus can only be represented graphically in this written medium. Ideally, the reader would have the possibility to actually listen to the featured episodes, but this chapter attempts to eliminate listening as a necessity by introducing and explaining both the sound system of English and the linguistic conventions used to capture and accurately represent pronunciation. This chapter thus involves the reader in a form of what is known as reduced listening (Chion 1994; Schaeffer 1968), which is a "listening mode that focuses on the traits of the sound itself, independent of its cause and of its meaning" (Chion 1994, 1). Proper reduced listening is thus actually a very abstract exercise in that it requires listeners to consider sounds extracted from their source and contextual meaning. As Michel Chion (1994, 2) observes, "it is no mean task to speak about sounds in and of themselves, if the listener is forced to describe them independently of any cause, meaning, or effect." This chapter does not require such extremely reduced listening, but its goals are nevertheless to encourage readers to focus on discrete sounds and to provide readers with linguistic tools that will allow them to talk accurately about what they hear on TV.

Phonetics vs. Phonology

It is common to distinguish between phonetics, the study of human speech sounds, and phonology, the study of human language sound systems. Phonetics is concerned with the descriptive representation of the articulatory aspects of sounds, focusing on consonants and vowels. Phonology, on the other hand, considers sounds as part of a greater system. The majority of English words, for example, represent a combination of sounds, and thus phonology is the exploration of how sounds combine, interact, influence each other, or retain their distinctive properties. In this chapter, we will start by addressing elementary phonetics, limiting our discussion to (mostly American) English, and using data from episodes of various fictional television series to illustrate essential sound properties and differences.

Before we may move on to phonetic representation and description, however, it is necessary to acquaint ourselves more thoroughly with the International Phonetic Alphabet, or IPA, mentioned in chapter 3. The IPA is a system of phonetic notation that represents the sounds of spoken language. The entire IPA includes more than one hundred symbols and dozens of additional notation devices for representing specific sound variations; for the purpose of this chapter, we will limit ourselves to the IPA symbols that represent the essential sounds of English.

According to phonetic convention, sounds, also known as 'phones', are represented by IPA symbols written within square brackets, such as [s], used to indicate the word-initial sound of *s*ound. Many of the symbols of the IPA, also such as [s], look like the letter commonly used when spelling out sounds. For this reason, it is all too easy to confuse phonetic transcription with ordinary spelling, called 'orthography'. As we see later in the chapter, so close is the relationship between letters and sounds that it often results in mispronunciations, which in turn call our attention to phonetic properties.

Phonetic Description: Consonants

Most human speech sounds involve some kind of modification of an airstream, normally air flowing up from the lungs and out through the mouth, but air can also be released through the nose. When air is obstructed in such a way before or while being released, consonants are produced. The production of consonants is thus primarily a function of how a sound is made with regard to different degrees of airstream modification along the vocal tract. Figure 9.1 depicts the vocal tract and the different parts that are engaged in sound production.

While all English consonants are the result of a modified airstream, they differ from one another based on their manner of articulation, place of articulation, and voicing. These terms refer to how consonants are produced with regard to (1) the degree of air constriction, (2) the placement of

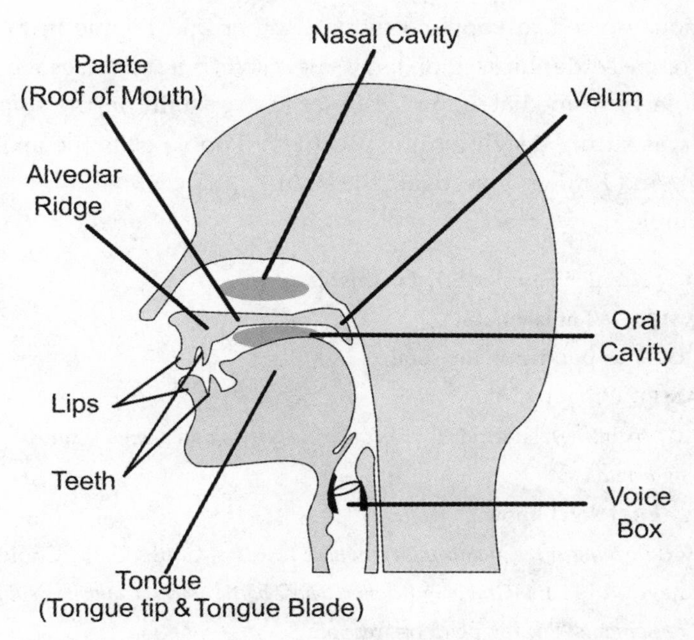

Figure 9.1. The vocal tract. Image by Tavin via Wikimedia Commons on https://commons.wikimedia.org/wiki/File%3ATract.svg.

the tongue in relation to the oral cavity, teeth, or lips, and (3) whether the vocal cords are engaged. Consonants tend to be grouped together based on their manners of articulation, as presented below.

Stops/Plosives

Consonant sounds with the most extreme modification of the airstream, which is complete closure, are called 'stops' because the airflow is completely stopped and then released. These sounds may also be referred to as 'plosives' because there is a slight expulsion of air from the mouth when the closure is released. Examples of stops/plosives in English are [p], [b], [t], [d], [k], and [g].

To get a feel for this plosive effect, our first example will draw on the *Seinfeld* episode "The Couch."[1] In this episode, Jerry welcomes into his apartment his neighbor, Kramer, and an elderly man called Poppie, who is Kramer's potential business partner. Jerry goes to his bedroom to fetch some money owed to Poppie, leaving Kramer and Poppie in his living room. Poppie settles himself on Jerry's new sofa, but then rises when Jerry returns. Jerry immediately notices a large, wet stain on the sofa where Poppie was sitting, leaving him speechless. Poppie exits the apartment, and Jerry and Kramer investigate the stain.

Example 1:

JERRY: Kramer, Kramer, what is this?!

KRAMER: What is what?

JERRY: This puddle on my sofa!

KRAMER: What puddle?

JERRY: *(pointing)* That puddle! *(Kramer sees the puddle, does a double-take, and shudders.)*

KRAMER: I don't know.

JERRY: *(looking at the puddle with Kramer)*: Is it . . . ? Could it . . . ? Could he have . . . ? IT IS! *(Grabbing Kramer, whose bottle of water splashes, spilling its contents)* Poppie peed on my sofa!

(Transcript from www.seinfeldscripts.com; used with permission.)

1. Written by Larry David.

In Jerry's final turn, the explosiveness of his [p]-sounds are visible in the spilled water from Kramer's bottle, such that it would appear that Jerry is actually spitting the words "Poppie peed on my sofa!"

Now that we have understood that the stops share a common explosive manner of articulation, we can move on to determining how they are different. We can begin by differentiating the sounds by pairs, focusing on [p]-[b], [t]-[d], and [k]-[g]. These three pairs differ from each other with regard to place of articulation, but the individual sounds in each of the pairs differ only with respect to voicing, as explained below.

In producing [p] and [b], both lips meet to close completely, so these two stops are called 'bilabials'. However, in the production of [p], the vocal cords are not vibrating; sounds with no vocal cord vibration are said to be voiceless, so [p] is a voiceless bilabial stop. The difference between [p] and [b] is that the vocal cords are vibrating in [b]: it is a voiced bilabial stop, illustrated three times in *Bob's Burgers* (2011–).

The sounds [t] and [d] are both produced by making a complete closure between the blade of the tongue (just behind the tip of the tongue) and the alveolar ridge, the bony ridge just behind the upper teeth and before the roof of the mouth begins arching upward. The sound [t] has no vocal cord vibration: it is a voiceless alveolar stop, as in the first and final sounds of *Tales from the Crypt* (1989–96). The [d] sound is a voiced alveolar stop, as in the word-initial, -central, and -final sounds of *Deadwood* (2004–6).

The sounds [k] and [g] are produced using the back of the tongue, which makes a complete closure with what is called the velum, or soft palate, which is the soft fleshy part at the back of the roof of the mouth. Sounds produced in this area are called 'velars'. The [k] sound is a voiceless velar stop, heard word-initially and word-centrally in *Californication* (2007–14), while the [g] sound is a 'voiced velar stop', occurring twice in word-initial position in *Gossip Girl* (2007–12).

The relationship between these last two stops is nicely illustrated by the *How I Met Your Mother* episode "Wait for It."[2] In this episode, the

2. Written by Craig Thomas and Carter Bays.

characters Ted, Barney, and Marshall are trying to comprehend the foreign name Gael, denoting a character played by Enrique Iglesias.

Example 2:

GAEL: Gael.

TED: I'm sorry, Gail?[3]

GAEL: Gael.

BARNEY: Kyle?

GAEL: Gael.

MARSHALL: Girl?

ROBIN: It's pronounced guy-el.

GAEL: It means joyful. That is why I live my life by bringing joy, good energy, and happiness to others. Especially those less fortunate than I.

TED: I'm sorry, so it's Gail?

The similar phonetic properties of [g] and [k] allow Barney to venture a guess that the name in question is "Kyle," the correct, voiceless pronunciation of which might be beyond Gael's phonetic abilities.

Fricatives

A less extreme degree of modification is close approximation, in which two parts of the vocal apparatus are brought very close together, but not close enough to create the complete closure that characterizes stops. The result is that turbulence is created, and this can be heard as audible friction. Sounds produced this way are thus called 'fricatives', and they include [f], [v], [θ], [ð], [ʃ], and [ʒ]. Much like the stops of English, fricatives can also be paired off, and compared in terms of places of articulation and voicing.

If the lower lip is brought into close approximation with the upper teeth, we produce labio-dental fricatives. The sound [f] is a voiceless labio-dental fricative, as in the word-initial and word-central sounds of *Firefly* (2003). The sound [v] is a voiced labio-dental fricative, as in the first word of *Veronica Mars* (2004–7).

3. Many online episode transcripts spell the name as "Gayle"; the spelling "Gail" is preferred here to more closely mimic that of the actual name.

If the tip of the tongue is brought into close approximation with the upper teeth, we produce what are known as 'dental fricatives', as in the voiceless dental fricative [θ], heard twice in *thirtysomething* (1987–91). The voiced dental fricative, [ð], can be heard in the first and third title words of *Father of the Pride* (2004–5).

If the blade of the tongue comes into close approximation with the alveolar ridge, we produce 'alveolar fricatives'. The voiceless alveolar fricative [s] can be heard in the first and last words of *Sex and the City* (1998–2004), and the voiced alveolar fricative [z] occurs word-finally in *Bones* (2005–), *Damages* (2007–12), and *Friends* (1994–2004).

Just behind the alveolar ridge is the palato-alveolar region, because it is in between the alveolar ridge and the hard bony roof of the mouth called the hard palate. Fricatives produced here are called 'palato-alveolar' (or 'post-alveolar') fricatives. The voiceless palato-alveolar fricative [ʃ] is the first sound in *Sherlock* (2010–). The voiced palato-alveolar fricative [ʒ] can be heard word-centrally in the second word of *Night Visions* (2001–).

Another fricative is known as a 'glottal' because it is articulated in the glottis, the space between the vocal cords. This is the glottal fricative [h], in which the vocal cords are in close approximation, creating friction in the glottis. This sound can be heard in the word-initial sounds of *Highway to Heaven* (1984–89).

Because of their similar manners of articulation, fricatives can often be confused or mistakenly be replaced with each other. And, because they share places of articulation, some fricatives and stops share a similar fate. As an example, we'll consider the title and an episode of *Da Ali G Show* (2000, 2003–6). This British-produced sketch series was written by Sacha Baron Cohen, who also played the titular character Ali G, an urban, hip-hop wannabe. Already in the title, *Da Ali G Show,* we see an example of a common feature of urban/AAVE dialects (see chapter 2), namely the pronunciation of 'th' as 'd', or more accurately, [ð] as [d]. These two sounds have similar places of articulation and are both voiced, facilitating this systematic replacement.

Another feature of this dialect is the alternation between [θ] and [f], two voiceless fricatives with close places of articulation. In the episode

"Rezurection," Ali G interviews the former US Surgeon General, C. Everett Koop, whom he engages in a discussion about death.

Example 3:

> ALI G: Let's talk about a big thing. Death, D-E-F. I is talking about the thing that happens to you, you know, a few weeks after you is alive. That's bad, innit?
>
> EVERETT KOOP: Yeah, you don't spell it that way, though, it's D-E-A-T-H.

Ali G pronounces *death* with a word-final [f][4] and then confirms this nonstandard pronunciation by spelling out the word with an *f*. This [f]-replacement is clearly not categorical, however, as Ali G does, in fact, pronounce the word *thing* with the voiceless dental fricative, [θ].

Affricates

There are sounds that are intermediate between stops and fricatives, in that they involve a complete closure followed by a fricative release. These are called 'affricates'. English has a voiceless palato-alveolar affricate, [tʃ], which occurs word-finally in the second word of *Third Watch* (1999–2005). English also has a voiced palato-alveolar affricate, transcribed [dʒ], which can be heard word-initially and word-centrally in the first word of *Judging Amy* (1999–2005). To understand the difference between fricatives and affricates, consider the name of one of the characters of *Arrested Development* (2003–6; 2013), Gene Parmesan, whose first name begins with the sound [dʒ], and whose last name includes a word-central [ʒ].

We have considered examples of how similarities in manner or place of articulation encourage alternations, which in turn can result in nonstandard pronunciations. Let's click back to *Seinfeld* again and consider another example, this time related to affricates. In the episode "The Wallet,"[5] Elaine talks to Jerry and George about her psychiatrist, whom she has been dating and is trying to break up with.

Example 4:

4. The clip may be viewed at www.youtube.com/watch?v=FUf06I_1Gpw.
5. Written by Larry David.

JERRY: So what happened, is it over?

ELAINE: Well not quite.

JERRY: Why not?

ELAINE: He was my psychiatrist, you know. He knows all my patterns. In my relationships I always try to find some reason to leave, so as my doctor, he can't allow me to do this, so he's not letting me leave.

GEORGE: What do you mean, "Not letting you?"

ELAINE: He has this power over me, okay. He has this way of manipulating every little word I say. He's like a svenjolly.

GEORGE: Svengali.

ELAINE: What did I say?

JERRY: Svenjolly.

ELAINE: Svenjolly? I did not say Svenjolly.

JERRY: George?

GEORGE: Svenjolly.

ELAINE: I don't see how I could have said Svenjolly.

JERRY: So maybe he's got like a cheerful mental hold on you.

(Transcript from www.seinfeldscripts.com; used by permission.)

This example can be considered to illustrate the effect that orthography can have on pronunciation. The letter *g* can be pronounced as [g], [dʒ], or [ʒ], depending on the context. The voiced, velar stop [g] can be produced when the letter *g* precedes the vowels *a, e, i, o,* or *u,* for example, *Game of Thrones* (2011–), *Get Smart* (1965–70), *Gossip Girl* (2007–12), and *Gunsmoke* (1955–75). A voiced palato-alveolar affricate [dʒ] can also occur when the letter *g* precedes an *e* or an *i,* as in *The George Lopez Show* (2002–7) or the reality show *Gigolos* (2011–). The voiced palato-alveolar fricative [ʒ] can occur if the letter *g* precedes the vowel *e,* but this occurs only in borrowed words such as *beige, rouge,* or *homage.* People sometimes impose this particular pronunciation pattern on other words ending in *-ge,* giving them a sophisticated, foreign flair. An example of this comes from *How I Met Your Mother* in the episode "Matchmaker."[6] The character Robin, a

6. Written by Sam Johnson and Chris Marcil.

television reporter, is doing a story on a matchmaking service, and she convinces her friends Barney and Ted to try it out. After they sign up, an employee of the service, Ellen, realizes that Barney's application is insincere, but she sees promise in Ted.

Example 5:

ELLEN: *(to Ted)* You're cute. You're an architect. Good career and you didn't use an obvious alias on your application like your friend, Jack Package.

BARNEY: *(through office door)* It's pronounced "pack-age."

Because the [ʒ]-sound has no orthographic counterpart, it is difficult to spell out Barney's exact pronunciation of *package*; many online transcripts use the spellings "pa-KAJ" or "pa-kojj" as approximations, which also highlight the second-syllable stress and nonstandard vowel sound in Barney's pronunciation. These features can be more accurately rendered with phonetic transcription, for example by representing the word final sound as [ʒ].

The fact that the phonetic realization of *g* before vowels is somewhat unpredictable increases the likelihood of error, as Elaine's mispronunciation suggests, or allows for deliberate manipulation, such as Barney practices.

Approximants

The least extreme degree of modification of the airflow is called open approximation, in which the articulators do not come close enough to produce any friction. These sounds of open approximation without friction are thus called 'frictionless continuants' or 'approximants', and include the sounds [r], [w], and [j]. The first of these, a voiced post-alveolar approximant, can be heard word-centrally and word-initially in *30 Rock* (2006–13); the second, a voiced bilabial approximant, can twice be heard word-initially in *The West Wing* (1999–2006), and the third, a voiced palatal approximant, can be heard in the first sound of *United States of Tara* (2009–11).

The similarity between [r] and [w] with regard to manner of articulation can cause mispronunciations. An example of this comes from *Parks and Recreation* (2009–15) in the episode "Park Safety."[7] Jerry, who is the object of ridicule for his frequent mishaps, is making a presentation before his colleagues, when he mispronounces the word *trout*.

Example 6:

> JERRY: Anyway, hunting and fishing season is winding down. And we all know that it's already closed season on twout. . . . So I said "twout," instead of "trout."
>
> DONNA: It happens to everyone.
>
> JERRY: My marbles are full of mouth today.

Jerry's final turn, which shows syntactic disorder, seems to confirm his nervous and befuddled state, causing him to confuse his approximants [w] and [r].

Lateral

One consonant sound is produced in a manner quite different from the other sounds, namely the 'alveolar lateral' [l]. The [l] sound is so named owing to closure between the blade of the tongue and the alveolar ridge, such that the air escapes over the sides of the tongue, thus lateral, meaning related to the sides. This sound can be heard in the first and final sounds of *Living Single* (1993–98).[8]

Difficulties in producing the post-alveolar approximant [r] and the alveolar lateral [l] are stereotypically associated with Asian accents, as the following example from *Modern Family* (2009–) suggests. In the pilot episode,[9] partners Cam and Mitchell are introducing their baby girl, whom they adopted from Vietnam, to Mitchell's extended family.

Example 7:

7. Written by Aisha Muharrar.

8. Readers might notice a different quality in the [l] of *living* compared to the [l] of *single*. The 'l'-sound is phonetically realized as a velarized lateral, [ɫ] (known informally as "dark l") when it appears at the ends of words or syllables.

9. Written by Steven Levitan and Christopher Lloyd.

CAMERON: Oh yes the music. Come say hello Lily.
HALEY: Oh, she's so cute!
PHIL: Let me see her. Hi Lily. Lily? Isn't that gonna be hard for her to say? No?

Phil's turn indicates that he assumes an Asian baby will have difficulty pronouncing the lateral sounds of the name Lily. Another example of this assumption can be found in the Seinfeld episode "The Chinese Woman,"[10] in which a Caucasian woman named Donna Chang causes ethnicity confusion by behaving stereotypically Asian, including pronouncing the [l] of "ridiculous" as [r].

Nasals

In all of the consonants we have described thus far, the soft palate (velum) is raised so as to prevent air from escaping through the nose. In nasal consonants, or 'nasals', the velum is lowered, and the air flows freely out through the nose. One example of a nasal is the bilabial nasal [m], in which the vocal cords are vibrating, the lips are closed, and the velum is lowered. This sound can be heard word-initially in *Mad Men* (2007–15).

Another common nasal is the alveolar nasal, transcribed as [n], in which the vocal cords are vibrating, the blade of the tongue is closed against the alveolar ridge, and the velum is lowered. This nasal can twice be heard word-initially and word-finally in *Brooklyn Nine-Nine* (2013–).

A third nasal that occurs in English is the velar nasal, transcribed [ŋ]. With this sound, there is closure between the back of the tongue and the velum, which is lowered so as to allow the air to escape through the nose. This sound can be heard word-finally and word-centrally in *Living Single* (1993–98).

Because the nasals are produced by releasing air through the nose, any blockage in the nasal cavity will impede their production. This is why, when one is suffering from a cold, it is difficult to pronounce words

10. Written by Peter Mehlman.

with the sounds [m], [n], and [ŋ]. Consider the following example from the *House* (2004–12) episode "Autopsy."[11]

Example 8:

HOUSE: Whoa . . . look at the time. I should have been outta here twenty minutes ago.

NURSE: You've only been here twenty minutes.

HOUSE: Can't slip anything by you, can I.

NURSE: There's a patient in one.

HOUSE: I'm taking a sick day.

In House's first turn, he pronounces two words that contain the letter *m*: time and minutes. Upon careful listening,[12] one will notice that House does not produce an [m], but rather a sound that more closely resembles a [b]. This is because both [m] and [b] are voiced bilabials, differing only in how air is released. If the nasal cavity is blocked, a speaker attempting an [m] sound is forced to open his/her mouth to release the air, in other words, release air that was previously blocked by the two lips, resulting in the production of the voiced bilabial stop [b]. A blocked nasal cavity similarly turns [n] sounds into [d] sounds.

All of these consonants, their places and manners of articulation, and their voicing features are presented in table 9.1. Voiceless variants appear to the left, while voiced sounds are on the right.

Phonetic Description: Vowels

In contrast to consonant sounds, there can be considerable variation in the vowel sounds uttered by speakers of different accents of English. The most standard accent in the United States is known as General American (GA).[13] GA tends to be defined in terms of the geographical location, rather than the social class, of its speakers. The term itself is an idealization

11. Written by Lawrence Kaplow.

12. A clip of this scene is available at www.youtube.com/watch?v=0-GuhHL4VRA.

13. This chapter will focus on American English, but the equivalent to GA in British English varieties is known as Received Pronunciation (RP). RP is often referred to as the

Table 9.1 **American English consonants**

Manner of articulation	*Place of articulation*								
	Bilabial	**Labiodental**	**Dental**	**Alveolar**	**Post-alveolar**	**Palato-alveolar**	**Palatal**	**Velar**	**Glottal**
Stop	p b			t d				k g	
Fricative		f v	ð θ	s z		ʃ ʒ			h
Affricate						tʃ dʒ			
Nasal	m			n				ŋ	
Lateral				l					
Approximant	w				r		j		

of a group of accents whose speakers inhabit a vast proportion of the United States. However, GA excludes Eastern accents such as the New York City accent and the Southern accent, both of which are considered in chapter 3.

Regardless of a speaker's accent, all vowels are produced with open approximation, and vowels are normally voiced. The production of vowels is a result of tongue position in the mouth, which can vary between high and low, and between front and back placement. Vowel sounds are also affected by varying degrees of lip-rounding or lip-spreading, by how lax or tense the jaw is, and by the amount of time spent maintaining sound production, that is, the length of the vowel. Vowel length, however, is a relative matter. When we say that a vowel is long or short, we are not referring to its duration in milliseconds; rather, we are commenting on its length in relation to other vowels. In addition to describing vowels as tense or long, it is the convention in phonetic transcription to use a colon to specifically indicate vowel length, such as [i:] or [u:].

Phoneticians conventionally represent the vowel space, that is, the area of the mouth where vowels are produced, with a trapezoid, as in figure 9.2.

This trapezoid in turn represents the mouth of a left-facing person, such as the one in figure 9.1, whose nose and lips would be located just outside the upper left acute angle, and whose jawline would then be just outside the lower right corner.

At the center of the vowel space is the neutral position of the tongue: the position in which the tongue lies when we are not speaking. This is where the vowel called 'schwa' is produced. The schwa is the English vowel that appears in unstressed syllables, as in the last two vowel sounds of the first word of *Unbreakable Kimmy Schmidt* (2015–). The schwa is transcribed as [ə].

The front line of figure 9.2 represents vowel articulations in which the body of the tongue is moved forward from the neutral position, while the

---

prestige accent in British society and associated with the speech of the graduates of the English public schools.

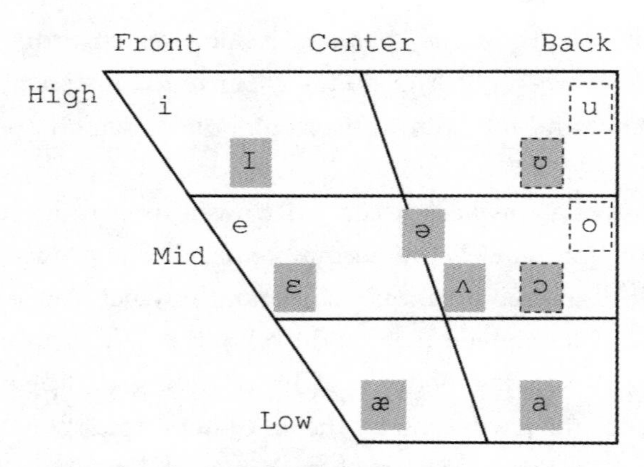

Figure 9.2. American English vowel chart.

back line depicts back vowels, in which the body of the tongue is pulled back from the neutral position.

In addition to specifying the height of a vowel and how front or back it is, phoneticians also indicate whether vowels have rounding of the lips or not, and whether they are lax or tense. Both of these features are indicated in the vowel space in figure 9.2, the former by a dashed line around the vowel, and the latter by shading.

Like consonants, similar vowel sounds tend to be described in terms of groups. However, unlike consonants, vowels are commonly grouped according to the placement of the tongue: high, mid, or low.

High Vowels

High vowels such as [i], [ɪ], [ʊ], and [u] are produced by raising the body of the tongue from the neutral position. The tensed, high, front vowel [i] can be heard in *Freaks and Geeks* (1999–2000), while the lax, high (although slightly lower), front vowel [ɪ] occurs in the first and final words of *King of the Hill* (1997–2010).

Speakers of the General American accent have an [i] in the final, unstressed syllable of words such as *happy*: [hæpi]. This phenomenon, called *happY Tensing* (Wells 1982), reflects a historical change from an [ɪ] vowel to an [i] vowel, said to be more tense than [ɪ], where 'tense' means more on the periphery of the vowel space.

We produce the lax, high, back vowel [ʊ] in the second word of *The Good Wife* (2009–16), and the tense, high, back vowel [u] in both words of *Looney Tunes* (1930–69). A good way to experience the differences between these high vowels is to transition from one sound to another, paying close attention to the tongue and lips. For example, when saying *Just Shoot Me!* (1997–2003), the transition from the vowel of *shoot* to the vowel of *me* allows us to leave our tongue high, while shifting it slightly forward and going from rounded lips to spread lips.

Mid Vowels

The mid, front vowels [e] and [ɛ] can be thought of as the slightly lower counterparts to [i] and [ɪ]; these mid vowel sounds are produced when the tongue is in a lower position, forcing down the jaw and opening the mouth. The tense, mid, front vowel [e] can be heard in *Make It or Break It* (2009–12); the lax, mid, front vowel [ɛ] occurs in the first and last words of *Better Off Ted* (2009–10).

The lax, mid, central vowel sound known as the schwa has already been introduced. The schwa is most likely to occur when a vowel sound does not receive primary stress, as we hear in the last two syllables of the first word in *Unbreakable Kimmy Schmidt*. The vowel [ʌ] has similar properties: it too is lax, mid, and central, but is produced in syllables that receive primary or secondary stress. In the word *unbreakable*, we place primary stress on *break* ([e]), and secondary stress on *un* ([ʌ]); the remaining vowels are not stressed ([ə]).

The mid, back vowels [ɔ] and [o] are both formed with rounded lips, but only [o] is tense. We produce [ɔ] in the first and last words of *Law and Order* (1990–2010), and [o] is produced in words such as *Bones* (2005–).

Low Vowels

As the tongue is lowered from the central, neutral position, the jaw is also lowered and the mouth is opened even more, allowing us to produce the vowel sounds [æ] and [a]. The first of these is lax and front; it can be heard in each of the words in *Last Man Standing* (2011–). The second of these is lax and back; it can be heard in the first word of *Hot in Cleveland* (2010–15).

Tuning in to Vowel Sounds

At this point, we should consider some examples of vowel sound production to understand the essential differences between high, mid, and low vowels, and front, central, and back vowels, and also to consider how orthography can often be the cause of variation in vowel production. We can start with the letter *a*, tuning into *Community* (2009–15), a sitcom starring an ensemble cast playing community college students who form a study group together. In the pilot episode,[14] all of the members of the group are gathered for the first time. The elderly male student, Pierce, assumes responsibility for introducing everyone, and systematically mispronounces each of their names (except for one), including the student Abed, played by Danny Pudi, an actor of Indian descent.

Example 9:

PIERCE: Alright, you already know Brittles.

BRITTA: Britta.

PIERCE: Uh, Ay-bed. Ay-bed the Ay-rab. *(chuckles)* Is that inappropriate?

ABED: Sure.

In actuality, Abed's name is pronounced [abɛd], and not as Pierce says, [ebɛd].[15] Nor is Arab ([ærəb]) conventionally pronounced as [eræb]. Pierce's pronunciations of these words can be considered to mark his perception of Abed as foreign, but the example also illustrates how the letter *a* can be realized as high, front [e], low, front [æ], or low back [a].

We'll continue watching *Community* so as to consider another example of different pronunciations of *a*, this time focusing only on [e] and [æ]. In the episode "Physical Education,"[16] the cast is gathered in their usual study room. Jeff has entered and posed on the study table, spilling a bag of bagels. Britta, entering after Jeff, kneels down to pick up the spill.

14. Written by Dan Harmon.

15. *Community* is available on Netflix; this scene can also be viewed at www.youtube.com/watch?v=uJZEgtifkbU.

16. Written by Jessie Miller.

Example 9:

BRITTA: Oh great. So much for baggels.
JEFF: So much for what?
BRITTA: Baggels. You dropped them on the floor.
TROY: Uh, they're called bagels.
BRITTA: Uh, I lived in New York, Troy. I know what a baggel is.
PIERCE: What the hell is wrong with you?
BRITTA: What?
SHIRLEY: You say bagel wrong.
BRITTA: I say it the same as you.
ANNIE: Say it again.
BRITTA: . . . Baggel.
(all laugh except Britta)

The first three letters of the word *bagel*, *b-a-g*, form a word in their own right, *bag*, which is pronounced with a low, front [æ]. This could be the cause of Britta's mispronunciation.[17] However, in her reply to Troy, Britta does not attend to the difference in pronunciation, but instead confirms that she knows the name of the objects that have spilled. And in her penultimate turn, Britta claims to pronounce *bagel* the same as Shirley does, suggesting that she is unaware of her own mispronunciation with regard to the vowel sounds.

We'll now tune in to *30 Rock*, watching the episode "The Bubble."[18] In this episode the character Kenneth becomes upset while discussing a beloved former coworker. Kenneth comes from rural Georgia, and as this scene reveals, when Kenneth gets emotional, he is unable to suppress his rural accent.

Example 10:

KENNETH: What if it doesn't work? What if he doesn't come back? Oh no! When I get upset my accent come out! And when it gets to comin' out I can't get to talkin', no-oh!

17. This scene can be viewed at www.youtube.com/watch?v=EDQyUqsCLXA.
18. Written by Tina Fey.

When listening to this scene,[19] we notice that Kenneth's accent manifests itself in his pronunciation of the words *get*, *gets*, and *upset*, which are produced with the vowel [ɪ] instead of the vowel [ɛ].

Diphthongs

In the vowels we have considered thus far, the articulators remain more or less in the same position throughout the articulation of the vowel. This means that the vowel quality (the acoustic effect created during the articulation of the vowel) remains more or less constant. This kind of vowel is thus known as a 'monophthong'. However, there are vowel sounds whose production entails some kind of change of position of the articulators, and thus a change in the vowel quality is produced; vowels of this type are called 'diphthongs'. A diphthong is a vowel whose quality changes within a syllable. A diphthong is not simply a sequence of two vowels. For instance, in the title *Being Ian* (2004–8), the vowel sound [i:] is followed by the vowel [ɪ] in the first word and by [ə] in the second: [bi:ɪŋ] and [i:ən]. These sequences are not diphthongs, because the vowels are not in the same syllables: both *being* and *Ian* have two syllables, the first of which ends in [i:] and the second of which begins with [ɪ] and [ə], respectively.

Some diphthongs end in an [ɪ]-like quality. Consider the word-initial syllables of *Friday Night Lights* (2006–11): the vowel begins with an [a]-like quality (low, back) and ends in an [ɪ]-like quality (high, front), resulting in the diphthong [aɪ].

In words such as the final one of *Trailer Park Boys* (2001–16), the vowel begins with an [ɔ]-like quality (mid, back) and ends in an [ɪ]-like quality (high, front): [ɔɪ].

Another diphthong of this type begins with an [e]-like quality (mid, front) and ends in an [ɪ]-like quality (high, front): [eɪ], heard in the final word of *Happy Days* (1974–84). Often the vowel [e] is realized as a diphthong.

19. *30 Rock* is available on Netflix; this scene can also be viewed at www.youtube.com/watch?v=QssII19POFQ.

There are an additional two diphthongs that begin with [a] (low, front) and end in an [ʊ]-like quality (high, back): [aʊ]. This diphthong is found in words such as *House*.

The second of these diphthongs begins with an [o]-like quality (mid, back) and end in an [ʊ]-like quality (high, back): [oʊ]. This diphthong occurs in words such as *Heroes* (2006–10). Often the vowel [o] is realized as a diphthong.

Each of these diphthongs is represented in the vowel space diagram in figure 9.3, showing with which vowel sound the diphthong begins and pointing toward the vowel sound with which it ends.

Before moving on from phonetic descriptions, let's consider some examples of diphthongs on television. In the *Seinfeld* episode "The Letter,"[20] Elaine lies to her boss, Mr. Lippman, claiming she needs to visit her sick father, so as to avoid work and instead attend a baseball game. Her presence at the game is subsequently documented by a picture in the paper, and Mr. Lippman questions Elaine about this.

Example 11:

MR. LIPPMAN: But—but he's feeling better now?

ELAINE: Um, yup. Yes, yes, it just . . . such a miracle, um. My visit must have buoyed *(Elaine says "boyed")* his spirits.

MR. LIPPMAN: *(correcting her)* Boo-eed.

ELAINE: What—what did I say?

MR. LIPPMAN: You said "boyed."

ELAINE: I did?

(Transcript from www.seinfeldscripts.com; used by permission.)

In this example, Elaine pronounces the word *buoyed* with a diphthong, [ɔɪ], when it should be pronounced as two syllables, [bui:d].

A similar example comes from the *Veep* (2012–) episode "Clovis,"[21] which coincidentally features the same actress from example 11, Julia Louis-Dreyfus. In this episode, Louis-Dreyfus plays President Selina

20. Written by Larry David.

21. Written by Kevin Cecil, Roger Drew, and Andy Riley.

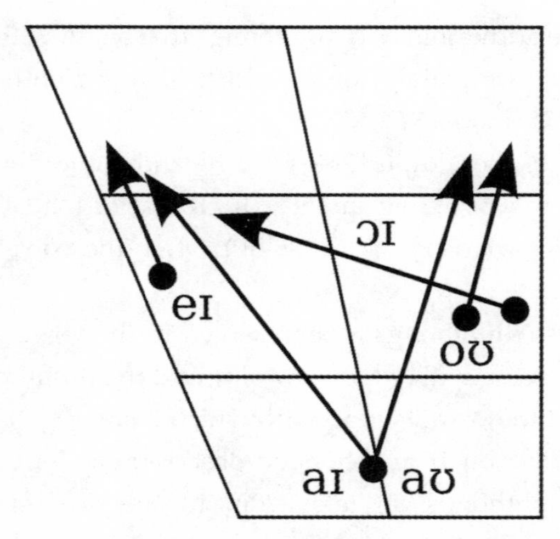

Figure 9.3. American English diphthong movement. Image by Ahls23 via Wikimedia Commons on https://commons.wikimedia.org/wiki/File:Midwestern_American_English_diphthongs_chart.svg#file.

Meyer, on her way to meet an up-and-coming executive named Craig. Selina and her staff are met by an assistant, who draws their attention to the correct pronunciation of Craig's name.

Example 12:

SELINA: Well, I'm *really* looking forward to meeting Craig.
MELISSA: Absolutely, although, um, it is pronounced Cray-ig.
SELINA: Craig.
MELISSA: Yeah, Cray-ig.

This example nicely illustrates how the dual-vowel quality of diphthongs makes them vulnerable to manipulation or mispronunciation. The combination of letters *ai* is normally realized as the diphthong [eɪ].[22] In

22. Compare this example to example 2 presented earlier, which featured diphthongal mispronunciations of Gael.

this example, however, the two vowels in the name Craig are not recognized as a diphthong but instead as two independent vowels, much to the confusion of Selina and her staff.

Phonology: The Phonemic Principle

In order to describe English, we need more than just phonetic description: we need to understand how the sound system of English functions, and this is the domain known as phonology. Central to phonology is the concept of the 'phoneme' (see Carr 2013 and Hyman 1975 for different conceptions of the phoneme). Phonemes are not speech sounds; they are perceptual categories of speech sounds. Let's take the English words *white* and *wide*: using the language of phonetics, we can differentiate between the two by pointing out that *white* ends with a voiceless, alveolar stop, whereas *wide* ends with a voiced, alveolar stop: [waɪt] vs. [waɪd]. The two words differ only with regard to the voicing of the final sounds, but this difference is significant: it is not just phonetic, it also has a semantic function, in that it signals differences in meaning. We know that when we say *white*, it does not convey the same meaning as an utterance of *wide*. A pair of words like this is called a 'minimal pair': two words that differ with respect to only one sound. The difference between [t] and [d] is thus said to be 'phonemic' in English: [t] and [d] are said to be 'phonetic realizations' of distinct phonemes.

We perceive speech via a grid of phonemic categories, so that when we hear *white*, we categorize the final sound as belonging to a different category from the final sound in *wide*. While we transcribe speech sounds using the square phonetic brackets, we transcribe phonemes using the slanted phonemic brackets, to reflect the fact that phonemes are concepts and phones are sounds.

A given phoneme may have more than one realization. For instance, the /w/ phoneme in English is sometimes pronounced as the voiceless labio-velar approximant [ʍ] (which sounds like [hw]) in words spelled with *wh*, such as *when*, *while*, or *wheat*. In many varieties of English this pronunciation has disappeared because of the so-called wine-whine merger, which resulted in a general neutralization of the distinction between the pronunciation of *w* ([w]) and *wh* ([ʍ]). This now allows us to say that the phoneme /w/ has two phonetic realizations, [w] and [ʍ], in words that begin with *wh*. When a phoneme has more than one phonetic realization like these /w/-phones, we call them the 'allophones' of a phoneme.

For example, we have determined that there is a phonemic contrast between the /t/ and /d/ phonemes, because their instances result in different meanings, as illustrated by the words *white* and *wide*. However, there is no such contrast based on the pronunciation of /w/, such that *white* pronounced as [waɪt] or [ʍaɪt] would result in different meanings. It is most commonly considered an affectation, which is illustrated by the British dialect-speaking toddler Stewie from the series *Family Guy* (1999–). In the episode "Barely Legal,"[23] Stewie sits down next to talking-dog Brian, who is eating pie with Cool Whip whipped cream.[24]

Example 13:

STEWIE: Oooh, you got some pie, eh? Can I have a piece?
BRIAN: Uh, sure.
STEWIE: Oooh, let me have some of that Cool h-Whip.
BRIAN: What'd you say?
STEWIE: You can't have a pie without Cool h-Whip.
BRIAN: Cool h-Whip?
STEWIE: Cool h-Whip, yeah.
BRIAN: You mean Cool Whip.
STEWIE: Yeah, Cool h-Whip.
BRIAN: Cool Whip.
STEWIE: Cool h-Whip.
BRIAN: Cool Whip.
STEWIE: Cool h-Whip.
BRIAN: You're saying it weird. Why are you putting so much emphasis on the "h"?
STEWIE: What are you talking about? I'm just saying it, Cool h-Whip.

The character Stewie speaks a British English dialect with a lexical and syntactic level of sophistication that is at odds not only with his

23. Written by Kirker Butler.

24. This scene can be viewed at www.youtube.com/watch?v=7ZmqJQ-nc_s.

toddler status, but also with the General American speaking characters that populate his middle-class American family. Stewie's speech behavior is marked (see chapter 10), thanks to his recurring production of [ʍ],[25] among other affectations. What is important to note here, however, is that [w] and [ʍ] are both allophones of the phoneme /w/. They are two phonetic realizations of a phoneme, the choice of which does not affect meaning. In other words, Stewie's aspiration is not phonemic, because it does not affect the semantics of the word it occurs in.

Discussion

In *Writing Television Sitcoms*, Evan S. Smith (2009, 148) advises potential writers on how to represent pronunciation depending on character type. Smith especially recognizes the importance of mispronunciations in constructing characters who "lack a strong vocabulary" (here, Homer Simpson is given as an example) or who are non-native speakers. In this chapter, we have seen many examples of how mispronunciations that are deliberately integrated into television dialogue succeed in conveying particular emotions, states, or character traits, such as panic, nervousness, illness, ignorance, sophistication, and non-native status (the reader is invited to consider non-native pronunciations in greater depth in the section "Suggestions for Further Viewing and Analysis").

These examples furthermore indicate to us that while standard pronunciation can be expected to constitute the norm of television language so as to ensure comprehension, nonstandard or unusual phonetic and phonological aspects of language are not just observable in television dialogue, but they can also contribute significantly to character and/or plot development. In two of the series considered in more detail in this chapter, the deviant pronunciations constitute recurring jokes or running gags throughout the series: in *Community*, Britta's pronunciation of *bagel*, and in *Family Guy*, Stewie's affected pronunciation of word-initial *wh*. Thus

25. See also "Not All Dogs Go to Heaven," written by Danny Smith, in which Stewie pronounces the name of actor Wil Wheaton. This scene can be viewed at www.youtube.com/watch?v=uqKN8uYLENQ.

the phonetic and phonological levels of language prove to be as integral to analyses of television language as the other disciplines of linguistics addressed in this volume.

In this chapter, we have deviated somewhat from the established practice of this volume by not focusing on one television series to explore linguistic concepts. In doing so, however, we have been able to cover the basics of both phonetics and phonology, although it should be noted that the scope of these fields is actually considerably wider. Nevertheless, our channel surfing has allowed us to take stock of the sounds of General American English by tuning into different programs and, first, using series titles to help us 'hear' the distinct sounds of English, and, second, considering specific episodes to raise our awareness of the differences in sounds and how these sounds are represented within linguistics. This chapter has introduced its readers to the concepts of phonetics and phonology, and has equipped them with the terminology and tools required to analyze the sounds of television dialogue. Readers are more than welcome to continue watching television, but they may now prefer to just listen.

Suggestions for Further Viewing and Analysis

1. Let's return to the featured series of chapter 5, *The Big Bang Theory*, where we can focus on the speech patterns of the main characters, noting the nasalized speech of Leonard and Howard, or the regional accents of Sheldon, who comes from Texas, and Raj, who is Indian. We can also consider some supporting characters, who represent notable pronunciation patterns, for example, Howard's mother, Mrs. Wolowitz, whom we hear but never see; and Barry Kripke, one of Sheldon's many nemeses. In the following episodes, consider what phonetic and phonological features distinguish the speech patterns of these two characters. For Mrs. Wolowitz, see "The Friendship Contraction,"[26] "The Hot Troll Deviation,"[27] and "The Pulled Groin Extrapolation"[28] (in which Bernadette appropriates the speech

26. Written by Bill Prady, Steven Molaro, and Steve Holland.

27. Written by Bill Prady, Lee Aronsohn, and Maria Ferrari.

28. Written by Chuck Lorre, Eric Kaplan, and Jim Reynolds.

patterns of Mrs. Wolowitz). For Barry Kripke, see "The Toast Derivation,"[29] "The Cooper/Kripke Inversion,"[30] and "The Beta Test Initiation."[31]

2. In this chapter, we briefly considered the character of Stewie from *Family Guy*, who speaks a dialect of British English. In chapter 1, we focused on *Sherlock*, which provides other examples of speakers of British English. *The Simpsons*, which is featured in chapter 11, includes a speaker of Scottish English, groundskeeper Willie. In *Orange is the New Black* (2013–), the character Stella Carlin (played by Ruby Rose) speaks Australian English. There are sounds in these dialects that are not represented by the consonants in table 9.1 and the vowels in figure 9.2. Consult additional phonetics sources to determine how the sounds of General American differ from these accents.

3. In television, phonetic and phonological properties of English are often manipulated so as to construct a foreign accent. Smith (2009, 148) advises writers that "characters that speak with an accent" can be created by inserting into their dialogue a "funky mispronunciation every line or so and the reader will remember that the character talks in fractured English." Identify the distinguishing accent features of foreign characters such as Colonel Klink from *Hogan's Heroes* (1965–71), the Swedish Chef from *The Muppets* (1976–81), Latka from *Taxi* (1978–83), Balki from *Perfect Strangers* (1986–93), Antonio from *Wings* (1990–97), Luis from *Suddenly Susan* (1996–2000), Gloria from *Modern Family* (2009–), and Apu from *The Simpsons* (1989–).

References

Carr, Philip. 2013. *English Phonetics and Phonology*. 2nd ed. Oxford, UK: Wiley/Blackwell.

Chion, Michel. 1994. *Audio-Vision: Sound on Screen*. New York: Columbia Univ. Press.

Hyman, Larry M. 1975. *Phonology: Theory and Analysis*. New York: Holt, Rinehart and Winston.

29. Written by Chuck Lorre, Steven Molaro, and Eric Kaplan.

30. Written by Steven Molaro, Jim Reynolds, and Steve Holland.

31. Written by Bill Prady, Dave Goetsch, and Maria Ferrari.

Schaeffer, Pierre. 1968. *Traité des Objets Musicaux*. Paris: Editions du Seuil.

Smith, Evan S. 2009. *Writing Television Sitcoms*. Revised. New York: Penguin.

Wells, John C. 1982. *Accents of English*. 3 vols. Cambridge, UK: Cambridge Univ. Press.

10

Syntax in Seattle

GÜLŞAT AYGEN

To introduce *Frasier*, it is necessary to present its predecessor, the highly successful, half-hour comedy series *Cheers*. Running eleven seasons, 1982–93, *Cheers* was set in a bar of the same name in Boston and featured an array of regular patrons and employees, including bartender Sam, a former professional baseball player and recovering alcoholic, and barmaid Diane, a pretentious pseudo-intellectual. While the early seasons of the series focused on the sexual tension between the two, the third season of *Cheers* introduced a new love interest for Diane: psychiatrist Dr. Frasier Crane. The relationship between Frasier and Diane eventually ends, and ultimately Frasier meets and marries fellow psychiatrist Lilith. By the end of the series *Cheers*, Frasier and Lilith had divorced, and the new series *Frasier* continued the Frasier Crane storyline by having him move to Seattle to reconnect with his brother and ailing father. Hailed as "one of the most successful TV ideas of all time" (Waters 2003), the spin-off *Frasier* aired on NBC for eleven years, 1993–2004.

Cheers was populated primarily by blue-collar or lower-middle-class characters: for example, bartenders, waitresses, a mailman, and an accountant-cum–house painter. Frasier Crane, on the other hand, was introduced in *Cheers* as a Harvard University– and Harvard Medical School–educated, multiple-degree-holding psychiatrist, granting him an upper-class, elite status that both *Cheers* and *Frasier* capitalized on for its stark contrast to the other less educated and less sophisticated characters featured in both series. Although outward appearance helped to distinguish Frasier Crane from the other characters, for example in the form of his coiffed hair and well-fitting suits, his class, erudition, and social standing were conveyed almost entirely by linguistic means. Frasier's enunciation, vocabulary, and even sentence structure contributed significantly to establishing his intellectually superior status.

Frasier's characteristic speech is established in *Cheers* and not only maintained in *Frasier,* but explicitly reinforced by his linguistic double in the form of his brother, Niles Crane, also an Ivy League–educated psychiatrist, who oscillates between being Frasier's ally and his foil. Both Frasier and Niles embody linguistic identities that deviate substantially from the other decidedly less cultured main characters throughout the series' run: their father, Martin Crane, a retired and debilitated police detective; Daphne, Martin's Manchester-born physical therapist; Sherry, Martin's barmaid girlfriend; and Roz, the producer of Frasier's radio program.

The different linguistic styles that can be observed in the various characters of *Frasier* constitute linguistic disparity. In fact, Frasier's sophisticated and elite language use observed in both *Cheers* and *Frasier* was so salient that in linguistics it would be called 'marked'. Markedness refers to the property of language use that stands out as different, unusual, or even deviant in comparison to more common or usual usage that would constitute the unmarked form. This term was originally coined by the Prague school structuralists Roman Jakobson and Nikolai Trubetzkoy (Andersen 1989). Frasier Crane's speech is marked particularly because it is the language of the well-educated elite in society, as well as in the Givônian sense of cognitive complexity, that is, "in terms of attention, mental effort or processing time" (Givôn 1990, 947).

The marked use of language by Frasier and his equally elitist brother Niles is notably different from the speech of many of the other characters (and perhaps of many viewers), resulting in linguistic disparities that are often mined for humor throughout the series. In this chapter, we will look beyond the character conflicts and competitive witticisms that are distinct to *Frasier,* in order to explore the linguistic area of syntax, that is, the branch of linguistics that concerns the structure of sentences, phrases, or clauses as well as word order. The fact that differences in social status, class, education, and even matters of taste and sophistication are reflected in and conveyed not only on the phonetic and lexical levels, but also on the syntactic level makes Frasier particularly interesting to the study of syntax. The application of a linguistic analysis, particularly syntactic analysis, contributes to a better understanding and appreciation of *Frasier,* and, by extension, of television language. A familiarity with the basic syntactic properties of English exemplified by the language of *Frasier* will furthermore illustrate how television language and televisual characters are crafted (Bednarek 2011). This chapter will focus mainly on the episode "The Gift Horse," which is summarized in the next section.

"The Gift Horse"

The theme of "The Gift Horse"[1] is sibling rivalry, which is actually an aspect of the relationship between brothers Frasier and Niles that is often revisited throughout the series. The rivalry between the two brothers has roots not only in childhood issues but also in their educational history and choices they have made in their professional as well as personal lives. Frasier and Niles are both Ivy League–educated psychiatrists, but Frasier attended Harvard and Oxford, while Niles studied at Yale and Cambridge. Niles practices psychiatry the traditional way by serving patients in his private office and publishing research articles. Frasier, on the other hand, puts his psychiatric skills to use by advising people on his own radio show.

The sibling rivalry frequently manifests itself as verbal competition, which is evident at the beginning of "The Gift Horse." Frasier and Niles run into each other at their local coffee shop and discuss their father's upcoming birthday celebration. While Niles searches for an accurate word to describe how out-of-hand their annual contest to buy the most lavish present has become, Frasier suggests *extreme,* which Niles counters with *childish,* and back and forth they volley the words *gaudy, crass, obscene,* and *morose* before Frasier exclaims, "Stop it!" The sibling rivalry and an example of its linguistic manifestation is thus established.

As the episode continues, so does the competition between the siblings, particularly when Martin's girlfriend, Sherry, comes across an old

1. Written by Ron Darion.

picture of Martin in his police uniform atop his service horse, Agides. Niles decides to track down Agides for Martin's birthday present, while Frasier opts to install an absurdly large home-entertainment system.

A Syntactic Overview

This chapter features extracts of dialogue from "The Gift Horse" to illustrate basic syntactic terms and concepts and to explore the relationship between word order and sentence structure, focusing on the fundamentals necessary to conduct simple analyses and to identify phrases and underlying structures. In our approach we adopt the well-established theory of generative syntax proposed by Norm Chomsky as transformational grammar (1957) and later developed into government and binding theory (1981/1993).

Every utterance in any dialogue, including those in "The Gift Horse," is part of a sentence and has a specific structure. Contrary to common belief, a sentence does not consist of simply a chain of words; there is always an underlying structure. Sentences consist of words that are grouped into phrases, among which there is a hierarchical order. Even in a simple greeting such as how Frasier begins the episode with "Oh, good morning, Roz," there is an underlying structure that acknowledges the two words *good* and *morning* as constituting a phrase, which could also be analyzed as a complete sentence, "I wish you a good morning." The conventions for indicating phrases and phrasal structure will be discussed in a later section. First we will consider evidence for underlying sentence structures.

From Boston to Seattle: Long Distance Dependencies

One piece of evidence that indicates that a sentence is more than a string of words is 'long distance dependencies'. Long distance dependencies refer to the fact that different words or phrases in the sentence make sense together even if they do not appear right after each other. Consider the following question, which a child could ask a parent who has just come upstairs for a reading session—but with an unwelcome book: "What did you bring that book that I don't want to be read to out of up for?" (Pinker 1994). This question ends with a series of prepositions and verb particles: *to out of up for.*

If a sentence consisted of strings of words, we would not be able to make sense out of the sequence *to out of up for*. However, we can make sense out of them because each one of these is connected to another word in the sentence, even if these connections are not physically or superficially adjacent: *Bring . . . up, read to . . . out of, what . . . for*. Alternatively, we could have kept the members of these pairs closer to each other and see that they originate from other locations: 'For what did you bring up that book out of which I don't want to be read to'. It is the hierarchical structure of a sentence that allows us to recognize and process such long distance dependencies even when such pairs do not appear next to each other. In similar examples, we observe that the linear order of words in an utterance is a final product; there is an underlying structure in which 'Bring . . . up', 'read to . . . out of', and 'what . . . for' are connected more closely.

Ambiguity

Other evidence for underlying sentence structures can be found in ambiguity. Ambiguity refers to the availability of more than one meaning or interpretation in an utterance. A classic example of syntactic ambiguity is the Groucho Marx line from the film *Animal Crackers* (1930): "One morning I shot an elephant in my pajamas. How he got in my pajamas, I don't know." The phrase 'in my pajamas' can be interpreted as being connected to two grammatical units: to the verb "shot" or to the direct object of the verb, "elephant," which the phrase immediately follows. Groucho Marx exploits this structural ambiguity to humorous advantage, by conjuring up an image of an elephant in pajamas. The fact that we are able to identify two possible interpretations indicates that there is more than the linear order that meets the eye: there must be two different hierarchical structures for two interpretations to be allowed. Therefore, the structure of a sentence is not limited to the linear order of words. The sentence may be disambiguated by beginning the sentence with the phrase "in my pajamas": "In my pajamas, I shot an elephant."

There is a similar syntactic ambiguity in the following example from *Frasier*, but we shall see that the humor is ultimately derived from elsewhere. In the episode "The Gift Horse," Sherry is browsing old photos of Martin in preparation for his birthday party.

Example 1:

MARTIN: Oh, we can't use this photograph, it's too embarrassing.

SHERRY: *(laughs)* That's exactly why we're using it. *(To Niles)* I'm decorating the whole party with old pictures of Marty from the force.

MARTIN: Well, we can't use this one of me at the morgue; it's too disturbing.

(Niles takes a look.)

NILES: You're right. I totally forgot you even had a perm!

(All extracts of "The Gift Horse" from www.kacl780.net/frasier/transcripts/; used by permission. Episode transcribed by Nick Hartley.)

The phrase *at the morgue* in Martin's second turn introduces syntactic ambiguity. On the one hand, it can modify the verb of the sentence *can't use,* meaning where Sherry and Martin can't use the picture. On the other hand, it can modify *me,* meaning a picture of Martin, and specifying where he was when the picture was taken. As is the case with the Groucho Marx example above, there is always a more likely interpretation and a less likely interpretation in ambiguous cases. The more likely interpretation requires *at the morgue* to be modifying the word it is closest to, namely, *me*. Should we go through a similar exercise and place *at the morgue* initially in the sentence ("At the morgue, we can't use this one of me"), we will again see that the sentence is disambiguated, but a possible yet unlikely meaning emerges. In a later section, we will learn more about how going through the exercise of moving parts of sentences in this way can help to determine underlying structure.

Ambiguity can be explained only if we assume a different hierarchical structure for each interpretation. Because the linear order is identical for either interpretation, the difference in structure must lie elsewhere. In the latter interpretation, the prepositional phrase *at the morgue* modifies the verb *use,* and therefore it is directly connected to the verb. In the former and more likely interpretation, *at the morgue* is itself embedded within the prepositional phrase *of me,* thus modifying *me* that precedes it. In other words, the prepositional phrase is embedded within the verb phrase.

The humor of the exchange is derived from Martin's concluding phrase, *it's too disturbing*. As viewers, we are encouraged to assume that "it" refers to the setting at the morgue, given that this context can reasonably be considered "disturbing." Niles's comment, however, shows that the "it" he finds disturbing is in fact Martin's hair, which at the time of the photograph was apparently in a perm. This is an example of lexical ambiguity, which is discussed in chapter 6.

The Good Doctor Prescribes

The examples discussed above suggest that there is an underlying structure to sentences and utterances that makes their interpretation clear. There is some freedom in how words or groups of words can be strung together in speech; however, such options may cause ambiguity. Similar to structural ambiguity, long distance dependencies (such as those illustrated in the section "From Boston to Seattle" above by the question ending with the string of prepositions "to out of up for") impose cognitive demands on the interlocutor. In spoken language, linguistic circumstances such as intonation and focused elements, as well as non-linguistic circumstances such as context, gestures, or prior information about given entities, may help disambiguate or clarify the intended meaning of an utterance. Even if we are able to make ourselves understood to a certain degree with simple words, real communication is possible only if interlocutors follow a shared set of rules. Because written language leaves no room for clarification of an utterance, the educated community requires adherence to strict rules in written language. Such grammar rules for sentence structure contribute to avoiding ambiguities and confusing intricacies. For example, many of us may have been taught not to end sentences with a preposition, but we do so even despite this rule of formal grammar. The concept of using language according to a specific set of rules is known as prescriptive grammar. Because prescriptive grammar is the grammar of the well educated, it is also the prestigious language of the educated elite. This explains why, throughout the series *Frasier*, both Niles and Frasier adhere strictly to prescriptive grammar rules, while other characters flaunt these rules, inviting metalinguistic commentary or admonition, such as in example 2 below. The dialogue occurs during a scene in which Niles is reading over Martin's shoulder as he is writing a letter.

Example 2:

NILES: It's best not to end a sentence with a preposition.

(Martin writes something on a piece of paper and hands it to Niles)

NILES: Not to be technical, but "off" is a preposition too.

(All extracts of "It's Hard to Say Goodbye If You Won't Leave"[2] from www.kacl780.net/frasier/transcripts/; used by permission. Episode transcribed by Iain McCallum.)

Frasier and Niles are both advocates of prescriptively correct grammar, and take it upon themselves to point out incorrect grammar in the speech of others.[3] Most people do not adhere to prescriptive grammar rules when they speak. It is precisely for this reason that Frasier and Niles are able to distinguish themselves as linguistically marked. This markedness creates a disparity that applies not only to their linguistic behavior, but also to their exclusive social and aesthetic standards. For example, in "The Gift Horse," Frasier continuously disapproves of Sherry's and Martin's tastes in dining and entertainment, as the examples in the next sections illustrate.

Word Categories and Parts of Speech

In chapter 8 we learned that morphemes can be categorized as lexical or functional. In this chapter, we recall that categorization and apply it to words, which can also be categorized as either lexical or functional. The *lexical category* contains so-called content words, that is, words that have meaning content and correspond to parts of speech such as nouns, adjectives, and most adverbs and verbs. Nouns are names of people, places, or things. Adjectives are modifiers or qualifiers of nouns or pronouns.

2. Written by Steven Levitan.

3. For an additional example of a similar reaction to exactly this kind of imposed prescriptivism, see *Designing Women,* "A Big Affair," written by Linda Bloodworth-Thomason.

Adverbs are modifiers of adjectives, adverbs, prepositions, or verbs. Verbs in the lexical category of parts of speech denote action or state.

The *functional category* consists of words whose meaning is grammatical and that thus serve specific grammatical functions in sentences; their parts of speech are articles, pronouns, prepositions, and some verbs. Articles precede nouns and include *a, an,* and *the.* Pronouns such as *it* and *them* can substitute for nouns, but other pronouns can be demonstrative, such as *this* or *those*; possessive, such as *my* or *his*; or quantifying, such as *some* or *many.* Prepositions such as *with, off,* or *from* usually precede nouns and pronouns and establish relationships between words. Finally, verbs within the functional category include modal (*will, may, can*) or auxiliary and linking verbs (*be, do, have*).

***Frasier*'s Phrases**

Phrases are words or groups of words, also called constituents, that function together as a single unit in a sentence. There is always one main word or 'head' of a phrase, and thus a phrase may consist of only this one main word, the head, or include other words. The part of speech of the head in any phrase determines the type of the phrase. For example, if the head is a noun, we have a noun phrase; if it is an adjective, we have an adjective phrase, and so forth. In multiword phrases, the words other than the head usually complement or modify the head.

A common convention in linguistics is to put phrases within square brackets and write the abbreviated name of the phrase in upper case subscript. A noun phrase is abbreviated as NP, a verb phrase as VP, an adjective phrase as AdjP, and so on. Depending on the head of the phrase, we may also have adverb phrases, prepositional phrases, and participial or gerundive phrases. A list of syntactic phrase abbreviations is available in the list of abbreviations in the front matter.

The extract in example 3 illustrates many syntactic phrases. In this example from "The Gift Horse," Niles, having just entered Frasier's apartment, discovers the massive entertainment system that Frasier has purchased for Martin and installed in their home.

Example 3:

NILES: I knew how jealous you were, but to go to $[_{AdjP}$ such insane] lengths to top me . . . Frasier, you have lain waste to your apartment with this eyesore!

FRASIER: I disagree! Where you $[_{VP}$ see an eyesore], I see $[_{NP}$ a picture window to a world of art and culture]. Just think how a screen this size will enhance the majesty $[_{PP}$ of the Metropolitan Opera]. Or the $[_{PartP}$ thrilling] artists $[_{PP}$ of the Bolshoi]!

NILES: You're quite $[_{NP}$ a Bolshoi artist] yourself!

FRASIER: Oh, you're right, it's dreadful, isn't it! But you know it's worth it, just to imagine the smile it'll put on dad's face, not to mention the pleasure of $[_{GerP}$ watching you twist and writhe in envy]. *(pauses)* You're not twisting and writhing!

NILES: I'm sorry, my mind wandered. I was remembering Dad $[_{PartP}$ waxing nostalgic] the other day about his beloved old horse, Agides.

FRASIER: Oh, don't try to change the subject, Niles, you've lost, admit it!

NILES: He $[_{AdvP}$ certainly] did love that horse.

In this example, some syntactic phrases are identified. In the following section, we learn how to identify syntactic phrases and their boundaries by applying constituency tests.

Constituency Tests

We can identify the boundaries of phrases by applying some tests to any group of words that might form a phrase, in order to see if the words do indeed function together as constituents. Such tests include the movement test, replacement test, sentence fragment test, coordination test, and ellipsis test. Each of these tests can indicate language usage strategies in action. For example, we can choose to move certain groups of words to the beginning or ends of our utterances for focus and effect; we may answer questions minimally with only a word or short string of words instead of using a complete sentence; or we may replace, coordinate, or omit parts of sentences to avoid repetition.

The 'movement test' refers to moving a group of words that function together to another location in the sentence. If this movement is possible, then the group of words is a phrase. Some phrases, for example prepositional or adverbial phrases, can be moved to various locations in a sentence or utterance. In example 4, Niles has asked Daphne about the food being served at Martin's party.

Example 4:

DAPHNE: With drinks, Sherry is serving cocktail franks.

The serving of cocktail franks is an affront to Niles's sensibilities, which most likely does not escape Daphne. For full effect of this news, Daphne saves it until the end of her utterance. This is in line with the principle of end focus, that is, the placement of the most important information at the end of a sentence, clause, or utterance. Note that having an end focus on *cocktail franks* is enabled by the possibility to begin the sentence with *with drinks*. But how do we know that *with drinks* indeed constitutes a phrase in this sentence? The fact that it can appear in a location other than where we would normally expect to find it is evidence that it is a phrase, because only phrases can be moved in a sentence. We can test this argument by moving only one word or even more than these two words. Note in the examples below that ungrammaticality is marked with a superscript asterisk (*).

First, we will move single words, then a group of words: **drinks, Sherry is serving cocktail franks with; *with, Sherry is serving cocktail franks drinks; *Franks with drinks, Sherry is serving cocktail*. These test sentences help us identify the two-word phrase *with drinks* as a constituent, specifically a prepositional phrase, which can appear at the beginning of a sentence or can be moved to the end. We should remember that phrases may consist of a single word, in which case the word that is moved is considered a phrase.

The 'replacement or substitution test' refers to replacing or substituting a group of words with a single word. If this replacement is possible, then the word or group of words that have been replaced by a(nother) word constitutes a phrase. Noun phrases, prepositional phrases, and even verb phrases, for example, may be substituted by or replaced with pro-forms, such as pronouns. We can see evidence of this substitution in the next example, when Niles gets a first look at the enormous television set that Frasier has bought for their father.

Example 5:

NILES: Oh my God, you didn't?!

FRASIER: Didn't what? You mean buy dad this television set? Of course I did! Ah, it's impressive, isn't it?

In actuality, Frasier is horrified by the television set, but he is trying to convince Niles of its superiority as a birthday present. Niles obliquely refers to and questions Frasier's action with *you didn't,* which Frasier recognizes as needing to be specified, *didn't what?* The use of *what,* a pronoun, is then specified as referring to Frasier's action, the verb phrase *buy dad this television set.* In other words, the dialogue could be expanded such that Niles exclaims, "You didn't ([$_{VP}$ do]/[do it])!" to which Frasier responds, "Didn't do [$_{NP}$ what]? You mean [$_{VP}$ buy dad this television set]? Of course I did ([$_{NP}$ it/that])!" In this expanded version we can clearly see that there are allusions to actions, which could be expressed in verb phrases consisting of only an auxiliary verb *do/did.* The auxiliary verb *do* is a pro-form for verb phrases.

Note furthermore the twice-used pronoun *it* in Frasier's last utterance. How do we know what these instances of *it* refer to? Looking back two utterances, we see the noun phrase [$_{NP}$ this television set]. This entire phrase can be replaced by or substituted with *it,* both in conjunction with the adjective *impressive* ("[$_{NP}$ this television set] is impressive"), and even in the tag question ("isn't [$_{NP}$ this television set]?"). The exact phrase boundaries can be identified by testing for ungrammaticality: **Ah, this it's impressive, isn't it?, *Ah, it set's impressive, isn't it?,* or **Ah, it's impressive, isn't it television set?*

The sentence fragment test refers to identifying parts, or fragments, of sentences that can serve as answers to questions. If the sentence fragment can answer a question, it is a phrase. In the next example, it is the beginning of the episode "The Gift Horse," after Niles and Frasier have been one-upping each other, and Niles is telling Frasier what he got their father for his birthday.

Example 6:

FRASIER: Stop it! So, what did you get him?

NILES: Oh, just some . . . beer.

Instead of answering in a complete sentence, such as "I got him just some beer," Niles is able to reply in a minimal way with a sentence fragment, that is, just a part of a sentence. It is thus clear that *just some beer* is a phrase, and because it answers the question *what?* with the head noun *beer*, it is specifically a noun phrase. Of course, what Niles calls "just some beer" is a monthly delivery of a case from a microbrewery. He tries to make it sound simple so that Frasier does not go ahead and get something better.

Phrases or even complete sentences may be replaced with *so*, as in when Sherry asks Daphne, "Did you get everything, darlin'?" and Daphne answers, "I think so." In this example, *so* serves a pro-form/pronoun function, indicating what Daphne thinks, which corresponds to the sentence "(I think) I got everything," which is similar to "I think [$_{NP}$ that]."

The 'coordination test' is yet another way of determining whether or not a sequence of words is a phrase. This tests works because only constituents of equal structure can be coordinated. In other words, a noun phrase can be coordinated with another noun phrase, a verb phrase with another verb phrase, and so forth. In the next example, it becomes clear to Niles and Frasier that reuniting Martin with his ex–service horse, Agides, did indeed prove to be a successful birthday present. Although Niles is to receive credit for the gift, he decides to share the glory with Frasier.

Example 7:

NILES: Well, I guess this horse wasn't quite the banner gift I thought it would be.

MARTIN: Oh, yes, it was, Niles. I'm feeling a little bit sorry for myself right now, but I'll get over that. But I love this horse, it's the greatest present I've ever gotten.

(Niles notices Frasier beginning to writhe in envy again.)

NILES: Well, I'm glad, dad, but, you know, I think I may have misled you. The horse is from me and from Frasier.

It is Niles's last utterance that illustrates coordination, specifically in the sequence *from me and from Frasier.* The coordinating conjunction *and* joins two phrases of the same kind. In this case, the two phrases are two prepositional phrases [$_{PP}$ from me] and [$_{PP}$ from Frasier]. It is not necessary for coordinated phrases to be equal in length or content. For example, Niles could have said, "from me and from my brother Frasier, who also loves you very much." It would still be a case of two coordinated prepositional phrases.

Yet another alternative way of conveying the same message would be to coordinate only the references to people, that is *from me and Frasier.* In this case, it would be two noun phrases being coordinated.

'Ellipsis' provides yet another test to help us identify a phrase, and refers to any omitted material in a sentence or utterance. Only full phrases can be omitted in a grammatical sentence, and this property allows us to use an ellipsis test to identify phrase boundaries. In the following example, Frasier has learned that his father is embracing his approaching birthday and encouraging his sons to compete in getting him extravagant presents. Frasier thus realizes that he should buy what his father truly desires, but he is reluctant to cohabit with an oversized entertainment system.

Example 8:

DAPHNE: You know, Dr. Crane, the last thing I want to do is encourage more competition between you and your brother. *(goes to him)* But if you really want to make your father happy, maybe the time has come . . .

FRASIER: Oh, don't even say it!

DAPHNE: But it's the only thing he's ever asked for!

FRASIER: No! God, it'll ruin my apartment, my life! I can't, I won't, I mustn't!

DAPHNE: It's over, Dr. Crane.

There are three instances of ellipsis in this utterance. In each case, the verb phrase [$_{VP}$ ruin my apartment, my life] is omitted: "I can't ([$_{VP}$ ruin my apartment, my life])!"; "I won't ([$_{VP}$ ruin my apartment, my life])!"; "I mustn't ([$_{VP}$ ruin my apartment, my life])!" Again, we can test the boundaries by trying sentences such as **I can't ruin* (assuming the verb *to ruin* requires a direct object) or **I won't my apartment,* until we identify the entire phrase. Note that there is implied coordination here between *my apartment* and *my life,* and that the sentence fragment test could also be applied: What can't Frasier do? Ruin his apartment, his life.

Now that we know how to identify phrases, let us move on to considering the linguistic theory behind it all and learn how to analyze the structure of some sentences.

Phrase Structure Rules

'Generative Grammar', particularly as proposed by the pioneering linguist Noam Chomsky, refers to an understanding of syntax in which a set of rules correctly predicts which combinations of phrases would form grammatical sentences. These rules are called 'phrase-structure rules' or 'PS-Rules' for short.

According to Chomsky, grammar is not acquired only from the environment through communication with others. On the contrary, we are born with some linguistic knowledge, and until a certain age, we have access to this knowledge, known as 'Universal Grammar', which represents grammatical structure that underlies all human languages (Chomsky 2007). With this hard-wired knowledge, anyone has the ability to acquire as many languages as he or she is exposed to until a certain age. This linguistic theory of language and language acquisition is called the 'Innateness Hypothesis' (Chomsky 1988). Native speakers of English have an intuition about what is grammatical and what is not, based on this innate knowledge. When generating sentences, they make use of the PS-Rules of English without being conscious of doing so. When they overtly process or analyze sentences, however, they make conscious use of these rules. Adult non-native speakers of English learn these rules rather acquire them.

A complete sentence is generated out of individual lexical items that form phrases, which in turn are formed according to phrase-structure rules (PS-Rules). These PS-Rules can be considered rewrite rules. In other words, phrases are rewritten to reveal their constituent parts, which correspond to functional and lexical categories as well as to parts of speech, such as noun, verb, pronoun, preposition, adjective, and so on. In the following section, we will go through the steps of identifying PS-Rules.

Identifying PS-Rules

To analyze the basic structural knowledge a native speaker of English would make use of to generate a sentence or utterance, let us continue the scene introduced in example 5, when Niles first sees the oversized entertainment system.

Example 9:

NILES: Oh my God, you didn't!

FRASIER: Didn't what? You mean buy dad this television set? Of course I did! Ah, it's impressive, isn't it?

NILES: I knew how jealous you were, but to go to such insane lengths to top me . . . Frasier, *you have lain waste to your apartment with this eyesore*!

FRASIER: I disagree! Where you see an eyesore, I see a picture window to a world of art and culture. Just think how a screen this size will enhance the majesty of the Metropolitan Opera. Or the thrilling artists of the Bolshoi!

NILES: You're quite a Bolshoi artist yourself!

We'll start by looking at the last utterance of Niles's second turn, when he says to Frasier, "[Y]ou have lain waste to your apartment with this eyesore!" but we'll simplify by omitting *Frasier*, and focusing only on the actual sentence, which starts with the subject [you]. For any sentence or utterance, conventionally written as S, there is a phrase-structure rule that assumes a subject (that is, the agent or experiencer) and a predicate (consisting of a verb and providing information about the subject or the object of the verb). The subject is normally in the form of a noun phrase (NP), and the predicate in the form of a verb phrase (VP). Certain verbs sometimes appear in conjunction with other verbs to help express modality, tense, or aspect, or to enable negation or questioning; these are auxiliary (Aux) verbs. As the name suggests, auxiliary verbs fall outside of the boundaries of the verb phrase, as we will see below. Our first phrase-structure rule thus can rewrite any sentence as the following:

S-> NP (Aux) VP

We consider [you] an NP because pronouns can substitute for nouns; as such, they can occur in NPs. We can now rewrite our example sentence in the following way:

S-> [$_{NP}$ You] ($_{AUX}$ have) [$_{VP}$ lain waste to your apartment with this eyesore]

We will continue with our phrase-structure rules, so as to keep rewriting until all constituents of the two phrases in S are accounted for. In other words, we need to specify the noun phrase (NP) and verb phrase (VP) as consisting of their heads and any other optional parts of speech. We'll start simply enough with the subject of the sentence, the noun phrase *you*. This is a personal pronoun, constituting a noun phrase consisting of only the head, a noun:

NP -> Noun

Continuing on to the verb phrase, however, we will see that noun phrases can get more complex. The entire verb phrase consists of the following: [$_{VP}$ lain waste to your apartment with this eyesore]; remember that the auxiliary *have* falls outside the boundaries of the verb phrase. The VP has multiple constituents in it: the noun phrase *waste*, and the prepositional phrases *to your apartment* and *with this eyesore*. In other words: [$_{VP}$ [$_{V}$ [lain] [$_{NP}$ waste] [$_{PP}$ to your apartment] [$_{PP}$ with this eyesore]]. The phrase-structure rule for this complete verb phrase would be the following:

VP -> Verb NP PP PP

In other words, all other constituents than the subject are considered to be part of the VP simply because they together behave as a single unit.

We have a PS-Rule for a one-word noun phrase (NP -> Noun), which can even apply to *waste*, so we will continue with the prepositional phrases. On closer inspection of each of them, we realize they consist of a preposition and a noun phrase. Consider the example, [$_{PP}$ to [$_{NP}$ your apartment]] [$_{PP}$ with [$_{NP}$ this eyesore]]. We can write one PS-Rule for each prepositional phrase in the following way:

PP -> Prep NP

Our current PS-Rule for noun phrases, however, is insufficient and needs to be expanded to include modifying words such as possessive *your* and demonstrative *this*, which we find in the NPs that function as the objects of prepositions. A revised PS-Rule for noun phrases would look like this:

NP -> (Det) Noun

where *Det* stands for determiner, and refers to words such as indefinite and definite articles (*a, the*), demonstratives (*this, those*), possessive pronouns (*my, your*), or quantifiers (*each, many, five*). Although absent from this example, noun phrases can also include adjectives (designated as Adj), that is, descriptive words such as *big, small,* or any in the list of words Niles and Frasier use to describe the nature of their competitiveness: *extreme, childish, gaudy, crass, obscene,* or *morose*. Because all phrases need only consist of their heads, determiners and adjectives are optional in noun phrases, and thus commonly appear in parentheses in PS-Rules:

NP -> (Det) (Adj) Noun

At this point, our example sentence is accounted for from the sentence level, (S), down to the part-of-speech level, via our PS-Rules. It is a common practice in syntax, however, to use so-called syntactic trees to represent sentence structure. Using any sentence, PS-Rules can be represented in a hierarchical structure, which also gives the correct word order, ruling out any implausible or incorrect structures and addressing any structural ambiguities. The syntactic tree for our example sentence would look as shown in figure 10.1.

An infinite number of sentences and utterances can be represented as syntactic trees in this way, and any number of sentences can be subsequently formed by inserting words of the same part of speech into each of the terminal nodes.

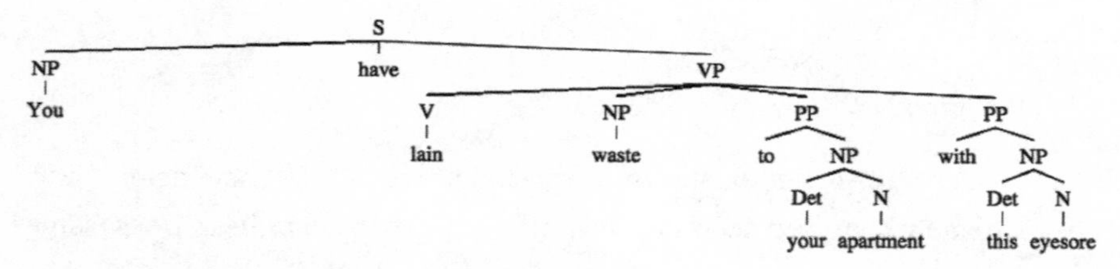

Figure 10.1. Example syntax tree (generated at http://mshang.ca/syntree/).

Interaction between Constituency Tests and PS-Rules

In order to explore further the relationship between phrases, phrase-structure rules, and constituency tests, let us consider yet another example sentence, which we can approach in two steps. First we will identify the phrases; then we will write the PS-Rules based on those phrases. This in turn will allow us to generate a syntactic tree and test hierarchy and word order based on constituency tests. To do this, we will return to example 1, extracting the last utterance of Sherry's turn.

Example 10:

SHERRY: I'm decorating the whole party with old pictures of Marty from the force.

We'll take some liberty with the sentence and rewrite it slightly to introduce objectivity by putting it into the third person, using "Sherry" as the subject and adjusting the verb accordingly: *Sherry is decorating the whole party with old pictures of Marty from the force.* Then, the sentence (S) must be rewritten in terms of a PS-Rule so as to represent the underlying structure of a subject and a predicate. Note, however, that similar to the previous example, there is an auxiliary verb (*is*), which also must be represented:

S -> NP Aux VP

Then we see that the subject is simply a one-word noun phrase $[_{NP}$ Sherry], the PS-Rule for which is the following:

NP -> Noun

Moving on to the verb phase $[_{VP}$ decorating the whole house with pictures of Marty from the force], we see that there is a noun phrase, *the whole house*, and a series of prepositional phrases: *with pictures, of Marty, from the force.* On the surface, this sentence is not very different from our previous example, the predicate of which also consisted of a verb phrase, a noun phrase, and several prepositional phrases. When we construct our syntactic tree, however, we will see that the underlying structure is not at all similar. Let's first identify the constituent phrases of the sentences by asking a few questions based on the example sentence; the answers will reveal phrase boundaries, which we can confirm via constituency tests:

1. Who is decorating (. . .)? => Sherry (NP)
2. What is Sherry decorating? => the whole house (NP)
3. How is Sherry decorating? => with pictures of Marty from the force (PP)

It is unnecessary to test the boundaries of the subject of the sentence; *Sherry* is a noun phrase consisting of only the head. Moving on to the second question and the object of the verb *decorating,* we can use the replacement test to identify the boundaries of the noun phrase *the whole house,* all of which can be replaced by the pronoun *it,* for example, *Sherry is decorating it.* The alternatives are ungrammatical: **the it; *the whole it; *the it house.*

We see that the answer to the third question was the entire prepositional phrase *with pictures of Marty from the force.* This prepositional phrase consists of other prepositional phrases: *of Marty* and *from the force.* In our previous example, the prepositional phrases were on the same level of the syntactic tree, and applying the movement test would reveal that they were independent. For example, we could have reordered the sentence as *With this eyesore, you have lain waste to your apartment* or *To your apartment you have lain waste with this eyesore.* These alternative versions are somewhat awkward, but nonetheless possible. In contrast, we would not be able to move the prepositional phases *of Marty* or *from the force*: **From the force, I'm decorating the whole house with pictures of Marty; *Of Marty, I'm decorating the whole house with pictures from the force; *Of Marty from the force, I'm decorating the whole house with pictures.* This last instance is ungrammatical in terms of modifying *decorating,* but we will see below that while *of Marty from the force* appears to be a constituent phrase, it is in actuality two embedded phrases modifying *pictures,* and thus cannot easily be disconnected from it.

The movement test suggests the boundaries of the prepositional phrase to be demarcated by *with* and *force,* which can be confirmed by the replacement test. Isolating the head of the prepositional phrase, *with,* we see that we can replace the remainder of the phrase with the interrogative pronoun *what* to ask a question and with the plural pronoun *them* to answer it: With *what* is Sherry decorating the whole house? Sherry is decorating the whole house with *them*.

Finally, the sentence fragment test also indicates the same phrase boundaries, in that the question of how Sherry is decorating the house can be answered by the fragment *with pictures of Marty from the force*. Note, however, that this same question could also be answered by *with pictures*, or even *with pictures of Marty*. The sentence fragment test as well as the movement and replacement tests get us closer to realizing that the prepositional phrases *of Marty* and *from the force* are not independent phrases that can easily be replaced or moved, but are rather linked to *pictures*. This subordinate relationship might not be immediately obvious in the PS-Rules, but becomes clear when we generate a syntactic tree (fig. 10.2).

This syntactic tree contrasts with the previous one in that the relationship between *pictures* and both *of Marty* and *from the force* is represented as a subordinate one as opposed to an independent one. In syntactic terms, we would say of the first example that the prepositional phrases *to your apartment* and *with this eyesore* are 'sisters'—they are on the same level and can be moved, replaced, or fragmented in similar ways. They also reflect the same subordinate status within the verb phrase, which is their 'mother'.

On the other hand, in the second example sentence above, the phrases *the whole house* and *with pictures* are sisters within the verb phrase, which

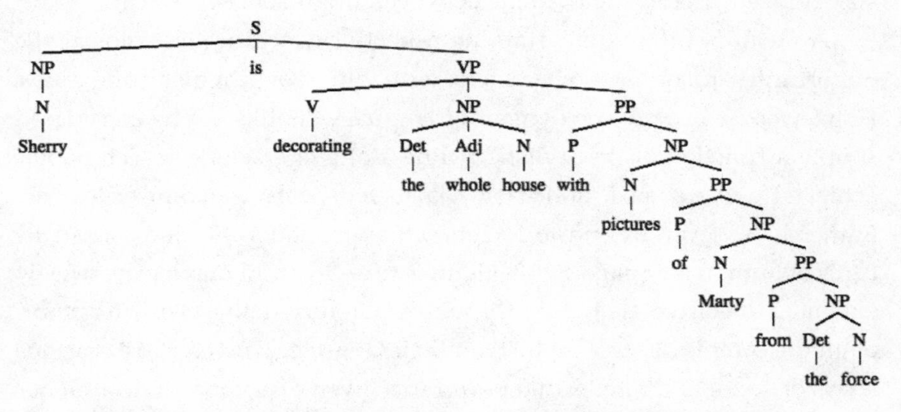

Figure 10.2. Example syntax tree (generated at http://mshang.ca/syntree/).

is their mother, while *with pictures* in turn is the mother of *of Marty*, which, in its turn, is the mother of *from the force*. The syntactic trees thus illustrate underlying structures and subordinate or independent relationships between sentence constituents, indicating that linear order is not sufficient to explain ambiguities in language. Instead, syntactic analysis allows us to look further into sentence structure to identify nonlinear interdependencies.

Discussion

The television series *Frasier* enjoyed prime-time popularity thanks in part to an overt contrast of characters represented by different genders, ages, social statuses, levels of education, and regional backgrounds. It is not the only series to capitalize on character diversity and to explore contrasting lifestyles, ideologies, or attitudes (Feuer 2001), but *Frasier* distinguished itself by featuring an unusual degree of linguistic sophistication and finesse. Indeed, the main premise of the program was to highlight the character Frasier and his brother Niles as upper-class, cultural elitists, similar in how they both differed from their friends, coworkers, and even other members of their own family. Throughout the series, both brothers engaged in marked behavior, that is, actions that deviated noticeably from those of other characters, in particular with regard to language use. Both Frasier and Niles were depicted as distinguished and erudite connoisseurs of the fine arts, but their overall sophistication and (imagined) superiority was, to a great extent, conveyed linguistically.

A meaningful and entertaining aspect of watching television is the opportunity to observe characters with different linguistic identities. As viewers, our active enjoyment of language should not be considered simply a function of the stylistic richness of a character's speech habits, achieved perhaps most noticeably via such aspects as accent or lexicon. Rather it can even extend to include an appreciation of the basic structures of human language. Syntactic structures in particular can be overtly exploited to help create humor through ambiguity, define characters thorough the complexity or simplicity of their language, and establish various levels of social and intellectual power in a given discourse environment.

In this chapter, we focused primarily on the episode "The Gift Horse," which portrayed Frasier and Niles as sibling rivals and showcased the linguistic manifestations of their competitive natures. The episode allows us to consider examples of speech from both Frasier and Niles, as well as other characters such as Daphne, Martin, and Sherry, and through this variety we could explore the fundamentals of syntax. In numerous examples, we saw that long distance dependencies and ambiguity can be successfully processed thanks to recognition of underlying sentence structures with various hierarchical orders, consisting of phrases we can identify through constituency tests and rewrite as phrase-structure rules, which in turn allow us to account for an infinite number of sentences and utterances of never-ending variety. The syntactic analyses presented in this chapter underline the fact that, while Frasier and Niles are indeed distinguished linguistically from the other characters of *Frasier*, this may mostly be owing to their pronunciation, lexicon, or affinity for word play, all of which serve to convey a level of sophistication that often comes across as pretentiousness. In the end, however, both Frasier and Niles operate within the same syntactic system as the other characters of the show (and, in fact, all of the shows considered in this book), and in that respect play by the same rules.

Suggestions for Further Viewing

1. In the *Boston Legal* episode "Word Salad Days,"[4] prosecuting lawyer Alan Shore is addressing the jury during a case on water pollution when his speech quite suddenly becomes nonsensical, confusing the judge and defense attorney as well as others present in the courtroom. Consider the following extract, which begins with the defense attorney's objection to Alan Shore's closing statement:

> ERIC YAVITCH: Objection, Your Honor. Mr. Shore is introducing evidence in his closing that was never presented at trial.

4. Written by Sanford Golden and Karen Wyscarver; transcribed by Imamess for boston-legal.org, http://www.boston-legal.org/script/BL02x21.pdf.

ALAN SHORE: Nonsense, Your Honor. I refer you to plaintiff's exhibit number apple.

ERIC YAVITCH: I beg your pardon?

ALAN SHORE: *Apple trashcan is picked from God.*

ERIC YAVITCH: Huh?

JUDGE BICKEL: Mr. Shore . . .

ALAN SHORE: Not the years sixty when classic electrons are free.

ERIC YAVITCH: Objection! Uh, I think.

JUDGE BICKEL: Mr. Shore, you have a notorious history of courtroom theatrics. If your aim is to force a mistrial, you will be disappointed.

ALAN SHORE: *Pillow pants join forces over embargo pylons.* He is emphatic. You aren't sailing past honor for the liking of a room. These questions are birthday basements. *To end the blue radish is the upside of luxury and sparking a good lizard can only make tears fall in hindsight. Puddles do not ask for why not?* It is cheese! Breath and wind. It is cheese.

(Transcribed by Kristy Beers Fägersten)

Identify the proper phrases in the statements in italics, and determine whether the syntax is viable within an underlying structure corresponding to S -> NP VP. If this is possible, then the nonsense is not syntactic in nature; that is, these statements are syntactically grammatical. In that case, you can conclude that it is most likely owing to semantic incongruities. It is possible to have a syntactically grammatical sentence without a clear meaning.

2. In the *Modern Family* episode "Bringing up Baby,"[5] teenager Haley would like to persuade her mother to allow her boyfriend Dylan to move in with the family. Hayley does not recognize the insincerity of her mother's affirmative response.

HAYLEY: For whatever it's worth, Dylan was very responsible last night. He's a good guy to have around the house.

CLAIRE: Mm. Where we going with this?

5. Written by Paul Corrigan and Brad Walsh.

HAYLEY: Well, since I can't move in with him anymore, he can't afford his apartment. So I was wondering if it would be okay if he could stay with us for a couple weeks?

CLAIRE: Sure. Oh, you know what? Why don't you guys take our room?

(Hayley looks pleased)

ALEX: She's being facetious . . . sarcastic . . . *(Hayley looks perplexed)* Dylan no stay.

HALEY: What?! Oh, come on! He helps out a lot.

(Transcribed by Kristy Beers Fägersten)

In acknowledgment of Hayley's difficulty in understanding both her mother's response and Alex's attempts at explaining them, Alex resorts to the use of basic content words, which serves to convey the message but which distorts the syntax. Alex thus produces an ungrammatical sentence, **Dylan no stay*. This utterance resembles "baby talk," or the use of simplified sentences, the meaning of which is clear but which entails an incomplete phrase structure, rendering utterances ungrammatical. Consider the structure of the simplified and distorted **Dylan no stay* and identify the correct components of the structure.

3. Syntactic ambiguity is made explicit in the "Dead Irish Writers"[6] episode of *The West Wing* (1999–2006), as Press Secretary C.J., White House staffer Amy, and First Lady Abbey Bartlett discuss the fact that Abbey's medical license may be suspended.

AMY: Mrs. Bartlett? I wanted to ask you a question, but I'm not sure how.

ABBEY: What?

AMY: Well if the most they can give you is a year's suspension, is it—

ABBEY: —that big a deal?

AMY: Yes.

ABBEY: Yes. I'm a doctor. It's not like changing your major. You of all people shou— I mean, women talk about their husbands overshadowing their careers. *Mine got eaten.*

6. Written by Aaron Sorkin; transcript from http://communicationsoffice.tripod.com/3-15.txt.

C.J.: Your husband got eaten?

ABBEY: My career.

C.J.: Yeah. Well, I'm on dangling modifier patrol.

(Transcribed by Kristy Beers Fägersten)

We might want to excuse C.J.'s misunderstanding as being an effect of the wine the women have been drinking, but actually she has recognized an underlying structure in conflict with meaning. Assuming an S -> NP VP underlying structure of *their husbands overshadowing their careers*, identify the subject and predicate in terms of NP and VP. Note that the subject and object NPs both include a determiner in the form of a personal pronoun, *their*. For this reason, we might want to consider Abbey's subsequent use of the pronoun *mine* as referring to either "my husband" or "my career." Consider why logic encourages the latter interpretation, while the underlying structure dictates the former.

References

Andersen, Henning. 1989. "Markedness—The First 150 Years." In *Markedness in Synchrony and Diachrony*, edited by Olga Mišeska Tomić, 11–46. Berlin: Mouton de Gruyter.

Bednarek, Monika. 2011. "Expressivity and Televisual Characterization." *Language and Literature* 20(1): 3–21.

Chomsky, Noam. 1957. *Syntactic Structures*. The Hague: Mouton.

———. 1981/1993. *Lectures on Government and Binding: The Pisa Lectures*. Berlin: Mouton de Gruyter.

———. 1988. *Language and the Problems of Knowledge*. Cambridge, MA: MIT Press.

———. 2007. "Approaching UG from Below." *Interfaces + Recursion = Language* 89:1–30.

Feuer, J. 2001. "Situation Comedy, Part 2." In *The Television Genre Book*, edited by Glen Creeber, 81–86. London: British Film Institute.

Givôn, Thomas. 1990. *Syntax: A Functional-Typological Introduction*. Vol. 2. John Benjamins: Amsterdam.

Pinker, Steven. 1994. *The Language Instinct: How the Mind Creates Language*. London: Penguin UK.

Waters, Darren. 2003. "TV's Obsession with Spin-offs." *BBC News*, July 24. Accessed Sept. 19, 2015. http://news.bbc.co.uk/2/hi/entertainment/3089767.stm.

11

I'm Learneding!

First Language Acquisition in The Simpsons

KRISTY BEERS FÄGERSTEN

On December 31, 1999, *Time* magazine published its list of the best TV shows of the twentieth century. *The Simpsons,* winner of twenty-eight Emmys and thirty Annies, was number one. It is the longest-running show in the categories of situation comedy, animation, and prime-time scripted series, with 550 episodes and counting. The Simpson family even has a star on the Hollywood Walk of Fame, a distinction they share with just three other fictional TV characters: *The Muppets'* Kermit and Big Bird, and the *Rugrats* (1990–2006) ensemble.

Of course, most of the shows discussed in this book are hugely successful multiple award winners, but what really sets *The Simpsons* apart is the fact that it is loved by adults, teenagers, and young children alike. At least part of this universal appeal probably lies in the fact that the series' main characters include both adults and children. Homer Simpson is a bumbling, thirty-six-year-old father and employee at a nuclear power plant; Marge Simpson is a caring, raspy-voiced, thirty-four-year-old mother who stays at home but has dabbled in various jobs; Bart Simpson is the mischievous, delinquent, and underachieving ten-year-old son; eight-year-old Lisa Simpson is the family's intellectual and cultural black

I would like to thank Ben Ambridge, reader in psychological sciences at Liverpool University, for his contribution to this chapter and guidance in identifying and explaining key terms and concepts of first language acquisition. Any errors or misrepresentations in this chapter are solely my own.

sheep; and one-year-old Maggie Simpson is known for sucking on her pacifier and being aware of more than she is given credit for. The series is also populated by a myriad of more than two hundred recurring and two thousand guest characters of all ages, including children, adolescents, young and middle-aged adults, and senior citizens. This considerable ensemble is yet another explanation for the universal appeal of the series, in that the various cast members can deliver clever commentary on social and political issues, thereby attracting adult viewers but not affecting the narrative to the extent that younger viewers are alienated.

In this chapter, we will use *The Simpsons* to consider examples of child language in order to explore the field of first language acquisition. However, not all examples of language produced by children illustrate child language. The character of Lisa, for instance, is known for her precocious nature, and her use of language suggests intelligence and linguistic proficiency beyond her eight years; her speech is not representative of language typical for an eight-year-old child. On the other hand, Ralph Wiggum, also eight years old, is portrayed as more age-appropriately immature, and perhaps even a bit dim-witted. He is a more typical example of a child character with a childlike mastery of language. The contrast between these two young characters is evident at the start of the episode "Lisa's Rival."[1] In a schoolroom scene, Lisa and her classmates are taking an exam; Ralph Wiggum is seated in the desk next to Lisa. As the teacher announces that time is running out, Ralph turns to Lisa for help.

Example 1:

TEACHER: 45 seconds 'til pencils down.

RALPH: *(whispering)* Lisa, what's the answer to number seven?

LISA: *(whispering)* Sorry Ralph. That would defeat the purpose of testing as a means of student evaluation.

RALPH: My cat's name is Mittens.

This example effectively represents the two eight-year-old characters' contrasting levels of intellect and maturity via linguistic means. While

1. Written by Mike Skully.

Lisa's turn suggests knowledge, testing ability, integrity, and intellect, Ralph's two turns indicate true childlike ignorance, helplessness, and confusion in the face of mentally demanding tasks, such as taking a test or trying to understand difficult words.

In example 1, both of Ralph's turns are linguistically well formed. Throughout the chapter, however, we will consider additional examples of language produced by Ralph, whose mistakes are characteristic of child language development, and thus can help us to understand the process of first language acquisition.

It should be noted, however, that our use of the phrase 'child language' does not always correspond to language produced by children. Just as we have seen that eight-year-old Lisa's language use is not childlike, we will also discover that her adult father's linguistic production, on the other hand, is in fact comparable to child language.

Series executive producer Al Jean has said that "everyone [in the writing room] loves writing for Homer" (Tanz 2001), which, according to series creator Matt Groening, is because "[w]ith Homer, there's just a wider range of jokes you can do. And there are far more drastic consequences to Homer's stupidity. There's only so far you can go with a juvenile delinquent. We wanted Bart to do anything up to the point of him being tried in court as an adult. But Homer is an adult, and his boneheaded-ness is funnier. . . . Homer is launching himself headfirst into every single impulsive thought that occurs to him" (Snierson 2010). In this quote, Homer is contrasted to Bart specifically as an adult versus a juvenile, but the comparison is enabled by virtue of the implication that Homer's "stupidity," "boneheaded-ness," and "impulsive" nature render him childlike *and* childish. It is not only through behavior that Homer's childish nature is portrayed, but also through linguistic means. Ralph, Homer, and other child or childlike characters therefore make *The Simpsons* an excellent series with which to illustrate the ages, stages, and main phenomena of children's language acquisition.

First Signs of Language Acquisition

Children begin the process of language learning long before they start to speak. In fact, babies just two days old already prefer to listen to their native language rather than a foreign language (for example, Moon,

Cooper, and Fifer 1993), demonstrating that they have come to recognize some of the rhythms and sounds of their language. By the age of four months, babies prefer to listen to child-directed speech—also known as parentese or caregiver speech: the use of short, simple sentences uttered in a characteristic sing-song tone that adults and even older children spontaneously adopt when speaking to infants (Fernald 1985).

Between seven and twelve months, children start babbling, and enter into what D. K. Oller (2000) calls the Canonical Stage. During this period of time, children produce short or even long strings of consonant-vowel combinations. The first such combinations consist of the same syllables repeated again and again, such as *dadadada* or *mama-mama,* and are referred to as reduplicated babbling. Among the consonant sounds produced during the Canonical Stage are /p, b, t, m, d, n, k, g, s, h, w, j/, while the following consonant sounds prove to be infrequent at this stage: /f, v, θ, ð, ʃ, tʃ, dʒ, l, r, ŋ/. This is because a child's acquisition of phonology (which, as explained in chapter 9, refers to the sound system of a language) follows a fairly predictable pattern, believed to be universal for the phonological development of all babbling infants, regardless of native language (O'Grady and Archibald 2000). Incidentally, the reason that the words for mother and father in many languages are similar to *mama, dada,* or *papa* is related to the fact that these are among the earliest strings that children spontaneously produce. In particular, the bilabial nasal [m] and bilabial stop [p] can almost be considered accidental productions, as they can result from infants just vocalizing with closed and opened mouths. Perhaps strings such as [mamamama] or [papapapa] were (and continue to be) among the first produced and as such have been assigned fortuitous meaning.

Reduplicated babbling develops into non-reduplicated or variegated babbling (Oller 1980), referring to non-repeated and varied combinations of consonant and vowels, for instance, [bapabapa] or [dadi:dudi:]. After the babbling stage, children begin to produce their first words.

In the episode "Lisa's First Word,"[2] we discover the first word spoken by each of the Simpson children: *aye carumba* (Bart), *Bart* (Lisa), and *Daddy*

2. Written by Jeff Martin.

(Maggie). *Aye carumba* aside, this is a fairly accurate representation of first words. The names of other family members (and the child's own name) tend to be learned relatively early on, while *Daddy* is actually the most common first word among English-speaking children, slightly edging out *Mommy* (Fenson et al. 1994).

According to the episode "Home Sweet Homediddly-Dum-Doodily,"[3] Maggie's second word is *daddily doodily*. In this episode, a string of unfortunate events leads to Child Services assigning Bart, Lisa, and Maggie to foster care with their neighbors, the Flanders family. Ned, Maude, and sons Rod and Todd Flanders are known for being four enthusiastic Christians, and good-natured, big-hearted Ned is known for his frequent interjections of *diddily* or *doodily* (see Suggestions for Further Viewing, chapter 8). In "Home Sweet Homediddly-Dum-Doodily," Ned and Maude are thrilled to take in the Simpson children, but after being exposed to the antics of Bart and Lisa, they become determined to baptize them as a way of offering them salvation. Riding in the car with Ned and Maude, Bart and Lisa continue to rebel against them, while Maggie, sitting in the front seat between Ned and Maude, seems to have assimilated.

Example 2:

NED: Until this I never thought Homer and Marge were bad parents, but now I know you kids need a less hellbound family!

MAUDE: Just sit back and before you know it you'll be part of the Flanders flock.

BART: Ha ha! You're going to be Lisa Flanders!

LISA: You're going to be Bart Flanders.

(Bart screams)

MAUDE: Oh relax, Bart. Your sister Maggie isn't scared.

BART: That's because she can't talk.

MAGGIE: *(takes out her pacifier and looks at Ned)* Daddily doodily![4]

After this last utterance, Maggie's head appears above the back of the car seat and, smiling, she turns her head to face Bart and Lisa, in a way

3. Written by Jon Vitti.

4. Transcript from http://www.imdb.com/title/tt0701108/quotes.

reminiscent of *The Exorcist*. The joke, of course, is that Maggie's complete acceptance of the Flanders as her new family and Ned Flanders as her "daddily doodily" is expressed in her appropriation of Ned's characteristic way of speaking. The humor is enhanced by the fact that it is unlikely that any child of Maggie's age would produce these types of words until much later in his or her development. While *daddily doodily* looks like Canonical Stage variegated babbling (that is, [daedIli:dudIli]), the scene suggests that Maggie is producing the Ned Flanders–form of *Daddy*, and thus may be further along in her phonological development than a typical child of her age.

Brown's Stages of Development

The child language acquisition analyses presented in this chapter are based on the research of Roger Brown, whose seminal *A First Language: The Early Stages* (1973) has directly contributed to or inspired later seminal studies in child language acquisition and psycholinguistics. Brown's stages describe and document the process of language acquisition and development, and are based on observations of children transitioning from preverbal to verbal stages, in which language is produced intentionally.

Stage I: Semantic Roles and Syntactic Relations

Brown's Stage I is observable in children between approximately one and two years old, or fifteen to thirty months. Most children begin to understand words such as *Mommy, Daddy, hi,* and *bye* at around eight to ten months, and to produce words around the point of their first birthday (Fenson et al. 1994). During Stage I, children's language production reflects an understanding of semantic roles (see chapter 6) in terms of indicating who or what performs and action (for example, *Mommy eat*) and who or what is the receiver of an action (for example, *drink bottle*). Their utterances also indicate an ongoing acquisition of syntactic relations (see chapter 10), using words as subjects, predicates, and objects.

In Stage I, semantic roles and syntactic relations are evident in children's combinations of words to produce two- and three-word utterances, sometimes referred to as telegraphic speech. This term comes from the observation that, like old-fashioned telegrams, children's speech in this stage tends to consist solely of content words, such as nouns, verbs, and adjectives. Few—if any—grammatical function words, such as prepositions, articles, modals, or auxiliary markers of tense and aspect (see chapters 7, 8, and 10) appear in telegraphic speech. This aspect of children's Stage I speech renders it salient as prescriptively ungrammatical, even though the focus on content words means the propositions are usually comprehensible: *that car, more juice, give it*.

An example of Stage I telegraphic speech can be found in "Trilogy of Error."[5] In this episode, Lisa creates a grammar-correcting robot named Linguo for her school science project. We will explore "Trilogy of Error" in fuller detail below, but for now it can be revealed that Linguo meets an early demise, short-circuiting and exploding, causing his head to shoot off into a field where Homer is standing. Cradling Linguo's head, Homer exclaims, "Linguo . . . dead!" With its dying words, the robot corrects Homer's Stage I telegraphic speech with "Linguo *is* dead," inserting the appropriately conjugated copula (namely, the verb *to be*).

A way of identifying a child's progression from one stage to another is by observing errors. One characteristic Stage I error involves pronominal case marking, where the object form of a personal pronoun (for example, *me, us, him*), corresponding to the accusative or dative cases, is used instead of the subject form, or nominative case (*I, we, he*) (Kirjavainen, Theakston, and Lieven 2009; Rispoli 1994). For example, if children are able to produce "I eat" or "I am eating," this may be evidence they have moved beyond Stage I. Typical for this stage, however, is something like "Me eat," which illustrates both telegraphic speech and a pronominal case marking error.

For an example of telegraphic speech and pronominal case marking error, we look to the episode "Burns' Heir,"[6] in which childless Mr. Burns, Homer's infamously wealthy boss at the nuclear power plant, is holding auditions to find an heir. Bart appears before him on a stage and recites a speech that Homer has written for him.

Example 3:

5. Written by Matt Selman.

6. Written by Jace Richdale.

HOMER: OK boy, I wrote down exactly what to say. Just read it and you're a shoo-in!

BART: *(walks onstage, squints at cue cards)* Hello Mr. . . . Kurns. I bad want . . . money now. Me sick.

HOMER: Ooh he card-reads good.

In this example, Bart reads the exact text on the notecards, which remains unseen to the viewer. His need to look more closely at the card to read Mr. Burns's name and the subsequent mispronunciation suggest that the cards were sloppily written; the grammar mistakes suggest the text as well was sloppily composed. This can then be considered either an example of Homer's own childlike grasp of (written) language or his attempt to portray Bart as linguistically younger, helpless, and endearing. Of course, actual ten-year-olds seldom or never make mistakes of this type; Bart's errors are instead typical for a one- or two-year-old Stage I speaker, reflecting both a pronominal case marking error (using object-form *me* instead of subject-form *I* in *me sick*) and telegraphic speech (*I bad want money now*).

Let's now take a closer look at the episode "Trilogy of Error," in which Lisa's school science project, a grammar-correcting robot named Linguo, plays a significant role. In the next example, Lisa is presenting Linguo for Homer.

Example 4:

LISA: Meet Linguo, the grammar robot. I built him all by myself. If you misuse language, he'll correct you.

HOMER: Well, let's put him to the test. *(slowly)* Me love beer.

LINGUO: *I* love beer.

HOMER: Aw, he loves beer. Here, little fellow. *(pours a can of beer in Linguo's mouth)*

LISA: Dad, no!

LINGUO: *(malfunctions)* Error.

In this example, Homer seemingly makes a deliberate pronominal case marking error (*Me like beer*), similar to that of Bart's in the previous example, to test Linguo, who corrects him with the more prescriptively correct form, "*I* like beer." However, Homer fails to recognize Linguo's utterance as a correction of grammatical form, and instead responds to the propositional content, pouring beer in Linguo's mouth and causing sparks—quite literally—to fly.

We'll end this section with one final example of Stage I speech. Taken from the episode, "Lisa on Ice,"[7] this example comes from a scene in which Principal Skinner is announcing at the elementary school assembly that he will be assigning academic alerts to students as soon as their grades start slipping. Ralph Wiggum is the first student to receive such an alert.

Example 5:

SKINNER: First academic alert: Wiggum, Ralph.
RALPH: I won! I won! *(runs up on stage)*
SKINNER: No, no, Ralph, this means you're failing English. *(hands Ralph an academic alert card)*
RALPH: Me fail English? That's unpossible![8]

The first person pronoun *I* is used in only one grammatical context: as a subject. On the other hand, *me* is used in two contexts: as both a direct and an indirect object. For this reason, it is considered the unmarked or default form. As such, *me* would be used in unattached positions (Leech, Deuchar, and Hoogenraad 1982), allowing Ralph to say, "Me? Fail English?" which Knud Lambrecht (1986) refers to as the incredulity construction. Listening carefully to the delivery of this line in the episode, however, one realizes that Ralph is instead committing a Stage I pronominal case marking error. Ralph seems to be processing Principal Skinner's announcement by repeating it, using the object form (accusative case *me*) instead of the subject form (nominative case *I*) of the first person pronoun. His last turn is thus steeped in irony: in very few words he manages to make two salient errors, but at the same time, he both questions and rejects the assessment of his English proficiency. And

7. Written by Mike Scully.
8. Transcript from http://www.imdb.com/character/ch0003015/quotes.

while we now recognize the first utterance, *Me fail English?*, as a Stage I error, his second utterance, *That's unpossible!* is an error of derivational morphology that is not specific to any of Brown's Stages, but can trouble both first and second language speakers alike (see Suggestions for Further Viewing, chapter 8).

Stage II: Modulation of Meaning

At around two years old, children move into Stage II and begin to master not only function words (such as *is, are, from, a*), but also inflectional morphology. Recall from chapter 8 that inflectional morphology in English is represented by eight different suffixes (and some variations of these) for nouns, verbs, and adjectives. Inflectional suffixes for nouns mark plural number or possession with *-s*; verbal inflection includes the present, third person singular *-s*, the past tense *-ed*, the present progressive *-ing*, and the past participle *-en*; and the adjectival inflectional suffixes *-er* and *-est* mark the comparative and superlative forms, respectively.

We can again recognize development according to Brown's Stages by observing children's errors. During Stage II, children typically make three types of characteristic mistake (Ambridge and Lieven 2011); all are illustrated in *The Simpsons*. The first type was presented in the previous section and refers to the omission of free morphemes, such as function words, as illustrated in telegraphic speech. The second type of characteristic mistake is over-applying morphological rules or generalizations to words that are actually exceptions to the rule; in other words, making overgeneralization errors. For example, one particularly well-studied generalization is that English verbs form their past tense by adding *-ed* (for example, *play/played; walk/walked*). Some verbs are exceptions to this generalization (for example, *bleed/bled*), but children often operate under an assumption of regularity and apply the past tense rule anyway. An illustration of this can be found in the episode "The Dad Who Knew Too Little."[9] Having realized he knows very little about Lisa, Homer hires

9. Written by Matt Selman.

private investigator Dexter Colt to gather information about Lisa. At the school, Dexter Colt questions Ralph Wiggum.

Example 6:

RALPH: Lisa Simpson is a girl at my school.

DEXTER: Yes, you said that already. What else do you know?

RALPH: I once picked my nose 'til it bleeded.

DEXTER: No, about Lisa!

RALPH: Lisa Simpson is a girl at my school.

DEXTER: Someone's already worked this guy over.

As we saw in example 1, Ralph has a tendency toward non sequiturs, such as the one constituting his second turn. Despite being off-topic, this turn includes a good example of overgeneralization of an inflectional rule. Why do children make such errors? Although it is tempting to think that they have set up some kind of explicit "add -ed" rule (for example, Pinker 1999), more careful inspection (for example, Marchman 1997; Ambridge and Lieven 2011) suggests that children are misled by analogy with similar-sounding verbs, for example, "If it's *need/needed*, it must be *bleed/bleeded*." Ralph is clearly aware of the use of the inflectional suffix *-ed* to form the past tense, but seems to be ignorant of the fact that *(to) bleed* is an irregular verb generating the irregular past tense form *bled*. This kind of overgeneralization is perhaps the most common error observed among English-speaking children. Any kind of interaction with children will most likely allow for the observation of such ungrammatical forms as *drived, readed, drawed, eated, flied, maked, gived, drinked, runned, throwed, catched, comed*, or *falled*, to mention but a few examples (Maslen, Theaktson, Lieven, and Tomasello 2004).

A more unusual version of this error can be observed in the episode "Bart to the Future."[10] In a glimpse of his possible future, we see Bart as a forty-year-old loser who is living with Ralph Wiggum and in need of money. Bart and Ralph visit Homer and Marge in an attempt to get

10. Written by Dan Greaney.

money from them, but after being rejected, Bart suggests they try Ned Flanders.

Example 7:

BART: *(rings the doorbell)* Flanders is a soft touch. He'll give us the money for sure.

(Ned answers the door. He's wearing dark glasses and has a cane)

NED: Jesus? Is that you?

RALPH: Mr. Flanders, you're blinded-ed!

Forms such as *blindeded* are less common that overgeneralizations such as **goed*, but in example 7, this word effectively conveys that, even thirty years later, Ralph Wiggum remains in the early stages of language acquisition.

Most Stage II errors fall into the categories of inflection omission or overgeneralization. There is, however, a third type of error characteristic of Stage II speech, which involves using the wrong inflectional morpheme. In English, errors of this kind are rare, as there are so few inflectional morphemes to begin with. Such example utterances as **mommy eat* instead of *mommy is eating*, **childs* instead of *children*, **gooder* instead of *better*, or **bleeded* instead of *bled* are more likely evidence of morpheme omission or overgeneralization than the misapplication of a morpheme. Nevertheless, Ralph Wiggum once again provides us with an appropriate example of this phenomenon in the episode "Lisa Gets an A."[11] Lisa cheats on a test and gets such a high score that she manages to raise the grade point average of the entire school. This results in the school being awarded an assistance grant, and money is used to buy an actual computer for the computer room, where, in the scene below, Ralph Wiggum is working while both Lisa and Principal Skinner are touring the school's facilities with Superintendent Chalmers.

Example 8:

SKINNER: And, for the first time ever, our computer lab actually has a computer in it.

11. Written by Mike Scully.

(Ralph is seen working at a computer)

RALPH: Hi Lisa! Hi Super Nintendo Chalmers! *(Ralph types "cat" and the computer emits a "meow" sound)* I'm learneding!

LISA: Aw, way to go Ralph.[12]

In Ralph's last turn, we can observe that there is neither morpheme omission nor overgeneralization, as he instead inserts the past tense inflectional morpheme *-ed* in a context that has no analogical precedent. In other words, it is never the case that two verbal inflectional morphemes can simultaneously be identified on one verb form: we can say *learn, learns, learned,* or *learning,* but not **learnsed, *learnsing,* or **learneding.* Ralph's *learneding* cannot be modeled on any previous construction and can therefore be considered an example of speech occurring in Stage II, in which the ongoing acquisition of the system of inflectional morphology is evident.

Stage III: Simple Sentence Word Order

So far, we have mainly looked at children's learning of individual words and their rudimentary practices of combining them. Eventually children learn how to put words together into complete sentences and utterances, but how do they do this? The instinctive answer as to how children accomplish this is that they simply copy their parents or other linguistic models in their environment. However, a moment's reflection reveals that imitation cannot account for all language acquisition. Consider, for example, the episode "The Frying Game,"[13] in which a new scene begins with television news anchorman Kent Brockman concluding a news story with "And the elephant that couldn't stop laughing was put to death." This is not a sentence that we would expect Brockman to have learned as a whole from a parent or other reliable model of language use. Rather, the young Brockman must have learned from his parents (or other proficient speakers) both the individual words and some kind of abstract rules or sentence patterns (which, as presented in chapter 10, are referred to as

12. Transcript from www.imdb.com/character/ch0003015/quotes.

13. Written by John Swartzwelder.

phrase-structure rules and underlying structure) that allow these words to be put together to convey particular meanings. This collection of rules or sentence patterns is what linguists call grammar or syntax; explaining how children acquire grammar is arguably the key central question in child language research. Two possible answers to this question illustrate a famous debate in child language research: whether children are born with some knowledge of language, corresponding to the Innateness Hypothesis and to Chomsky's Universal Grammar (1957) that is presented in chapter 10, or whether children construct this knowledge gradually on the basis of the language that they hear, known as the constructivist approach (for example, Tomasello 2003).

Given that Universal Grammar is presented in chapter 10, we'll begin here by considering the constructivist approach to the acquisition of grammar before returning to Universal Grammar. Suppose, for example, that a child hears and stores the sentences *I'm eating it, I'm hitting it,* and *I'm kicking it*. The claim is that she then abstracts across these sentences to form a slot-and-frame pattern corresponding to *I'm [ACTION]ing it*. This allows her to produce lots of different sentences, simply by inserting any action word into the slot (for instance, *I'm drinking/throwing/catching/drawing it*). Suppose also that the child hears and stores the sentences *Mommy kissed Daddy, Daddy kissed Mommy,* and *Mommy kissed the baby,* and abstracts across these to form a *[KISSER] kissed [KISSEE]* slot-and-frame pattern. This would allow her to produce *The baby kissed Daddy, Daddy kissed Sue,* and so forth.

At this point, we want to consider how children may construct or acquire knowledge of word order, producing novel sentences according to the underlying structure of English that corresponds to a [SUBJECT][VERB][OBJECT] pattern. In order to arrive at this point, the child needs to notice some similarity between the slot-and-frame patterns that she has stored. But just what is the similarity between, for example, the slot-and-frame patterns *I'm [ACTION]ing it* and *[KISSER] kissed [KISSEE],* which, on the surface, don't seem to have anything common at all? The answer is that the relationship between *I* and *ACTION*—a kind of doer-action relationship—parallels the relationship between *KISSER* and *kiss*. The idea is that this similarity allows children to align and analogize across the two slot-and-frame patterns to form a more general [DOER][ACTION][DONE-TO] pattern that is basically equivalent to a [SUBJECT][VERB][OBJECT] rule. The problem with this account is that no study has yet been conducted that demonstrates that children are able to perform this abstract leap of reasoning. Furthermore, many researchers have claimed that children don't hear enough language to be able to build such an abstract system from scratch in such a short time.

These types of arguments constitute the motivation for the alternative proposal, in which Chomsky (1957) argues that children are born with a Universal Grammar, a set of rules and principles that apply to the grammars of all the languages in the world. Part of this Universal Grammar is the knowledge of an underlying structure that represents word order. A kind of mental switch called a *parameter* (for example, Gibson and Wexler 1994) serves to simplify the language acquisition process in that, rather than abstracting across hundreds or thousands of individual sentences, all children have to do is set the word order parameters for [SUBJECT], [VERB], and [OBJECT]. This is, of course, not a conscious process and it would be wrong to assign too much agency to children. They are neither aware of 'subjects' or 'objects,' nor do they deliberately arrange their words to conform to the SVO structure. According to the Innateness Hypothesis, simple sentence word order will be acquired naturally in children of normal mental development who are exposed to an adequate amount and variety of linguistic models.

The debate between Universal Grammar and Constructivist approaches has been running for more than half a century, and we are certainly not going to resolve it here (see Ambridge and Lieven 2011 for extended discussion). In brief, evidence for the Constructivist approach comes from findings that suggest that most of children's earliest utterances—both in experiments and in more naturalistic settings—look as if they could have been generated using low-level slot-and-frame patterns (for instance, *I'm [ACTION]ing it*; see Tomasello 2000 for a review). Evidence from the nativist approach comes from findings that even very young children (1–2 years) appear to know something general about SVO word order (Gertner, Fisher, and Eisengart 2006; Noble, Rowland, and Pine 2011). For example, if they hear a sentence such as *The duck is glorping the bunny* and are asked to point to the matching video from a choice of two, most correctly choose a video where a duck is doing something to a bunny, rather than one where a bunny is doing something to a duck (note that "glorping" is an invented word for an invented action, in order to prevent children from using their knowledge of familiar verbs to solve the task).

Let's take a look at a contrastive example of word order to get a better understanding of potential differences between languages. In the episode "The Computer Wore Menace Shoes,"[14] Homer is kidnapped, and an imposter takes his place. While physically similar to Homer, the imposter is linguistically different, speaking with a deeper voice and a distinct German accent. In the next example, we can see that he even speaks according to typical German word order.

Example 9:

IMPOSTER: Aren't there any evil movies on? Maybe something about an evil island?

BART: There's something really different about you, Dad.

IMPOSTER: I am a new tie wearing.

BART: Oh, yeah.

The imposter's second turn illustrates a word order that is typical of German, in which main verbs appear last in a sentence when auxiliary verbs are also present—in this case, *am* is the auxiliary verb. This is in contrast to English, where both auxiliary and main verbs are produced as one unit in sentences patterned after the [SUBJECT] [VERB] [OBJECT] word order, which this turn otherwise adheres to.

The successful acquisition of word order is evidenced in Stage III by the production of questions. Questions come in two different flavors, those formed with question words (*who, what, where, when, why, how*) and so-called yes/no questions formed with the auxiliary verbs *do, be,* and *have.* In both processes of question formation, inversion occurs, meaning that the subject and verb change their order.

14. Written by John Swartzwelder.

An example of a yes/no question can be found in "The Springfield Files,"[15] in which *The Simpsons* meets *The X-Files*. In this episode, Homer reports having seen an alien, which brings *The X-Files* characters agents Fox Mulder and Dana Scully to Springfield. Agent Scully interviews Homer, who is monitored by a lie detector.

Example 10:

SCULLY: Now, we're going to run a few tests. This is a simple lie detector. I'll ask you a few yes-or-no questions and you just answer truthfully. Do you understand?

HOMER: Yes.

(The lie-detector explodes)

Agent Scully's yes/no question illustrates inverted word order, as do several examples of wh-questions in the episode "Krusty Gets Busted."[16] This episode opens with a scene from the stage of the "Krusty the Clown Show," in which Krusty is opening the show.

Example 11:

KRUSTY: Hi, kids! Who do you love?

KIDS: Krusty!

KRUSTY: How much do you love me?

BART AND LISA: *(watching the show at home)* With all our heart!

KRUSTY: What would you do if I went off the air?

BART AND LISA: We'd kill ourselves!

Questions are interesting, in that they are one of the few sentence types for which English-speaking children frequently make word-order errors. One particularly common error is putting the wh-word in the wrong place (for example, **How much you do love me?* or **What you would do if I went off the air?*). Bart and Lisa, at ten and eight years old respectively, are too old to make such errors, but if Maggie (ever!) grows up, we would expect to see them right up to age five (for example, Rowland 2007;

15. Written by Reid Harrison.

16. Written by Jay Kogen and Wallace Wolodarsky.

Ambridge and Rowland 2009). But why do children make these errors? As for some of the earlier errors discussed above, imitation of adults seems to be at least part of the story. For example, in "Bart on the Road,"[17] Marge reads aloud the following on a form that Bart brings home from school: "Parent's occupation . . . Please note, 'homemaker' is not allowed, as it is not real work, that's why you don't get paid for it." If a child wanted to ask Marge about this situation, and adopted the strategy of simply repeating her utterance starting with the wh-word, this would yield exactly the type of error shown by real children: "Why you don't get paid for it?"

Let's now revisit example 5, as Principal Skinner gives Ralph an academic alert and says, "You're failing English." Ralph questions this proposition in a declarative SVO statement, "Me fail English?" Aside from not having mastered pronominal case marking, Ralph indicates that he has not yet learned to form questions either, relying instead on intonation. To convince us he has reached Stage III development, he would have had to ask, "Am I failing English?" with the prescriptively correct inverted subject-verb word order. It is fortunate for us that Ralph has not progressed that far in his language development, else we would not have these illustrative examples to consider.

Stages IV and V: Complex Sentences

As children move through Brown's fourth and fifth stages (around three to four years old), they begin to produce and understand not only simple subject-verb-object sentences of the type discussed above, but also more complex constructions. In Stage IV, children begin producing utterances with embedded clauses, and in Stage V, children are able to produce coordinated sentences.

We have already met an example of a sentence with an embedded clause: Kent Brockman's announcement, *And the elephant that couldn't stop laughing was put to death*. In this sentence, the clause *that couldn't stop laughing* is a post-modifier of the subject, *the elephant*. In other words, there is a mini-sentence (a clause), consisting of a subject, the relative pronoun *that*

17. Written by Richard Appel.

which refers back to *elephant*, and a verb phrase, *couldn't stop laughing*, all of which comes after (post) and describes (modifies) the noun phrase subject, *elephant*.

In the episode "This Little Wiggie,"[18] Bart is set up on a play date with Ralph, who shows Bart his toys and where he plays, including a special rock. Ralph tells Bart of the rock, "That's where I saw the leprechaun. He told me to burn things." We might want to consider this sentence as evidence that Ralph may be on the brink of Stage IV. On the one hand, he is able to produce an embedded clause: *That is [where I saw the leprechaun].* On the other hand, he does not take the opportunity to post-modify *the leprechaun* with another embedded clause: *[who told me to burn things].*

Stage V speech would show coordination of simple sentences and propositional relations (Ingram 1989, 50). This means that we would have subject-predicate clauses coordinated with each other, or even phrases coordinated with other phrases of the same kind. Ralph Wiggum provides us with examples of these possibilities in "King-Size Homer."[19] In this episode, Homer is intent on gaining weight so as to be classified as disabled and be allowed to work from home. During his overeating efforts, Homer gorges at restaurants, a fact Ralph delights in recounting for Lisa as they are on the school bus and Homer races by in a hijacked ice-cream truck.

Example 12:

RALPH: I heard your dad went into a restaurant and ate everything in the restaurant and they had to close the restaurant.

LISA: Hey, my dad may have gained a little weight, but he's not some kind of food-crazed maniac.

Ralph's sentence contains an embedded clause, "I heard [your dad went into a restaurant]," and, by a long distance dependency (see chapter 10) and coordination, yet another embedded clause, "and (I heard [your dad] ate everything in the restaurant)." It also includes many examples of coordination, firmly placing Ralph in both Stage IV and Stage V of

18. Written by Dan Greaney.

19. Written by Dan Greaney.

language development. First, there is coordination of two verb phrases "your dad [went into a restaurant] and [ate food in the restaurant]." Then there is coordination of two sentences: "[I heard your dad went into a restaurant and ate all the food in the restaurant] and [they had to close the restaurant]." Even in Lisa's turn, there is coordination of two simple sentences: "[Hey, my dad may have gained a little weight]" but "[he's not some kind of food-crazed maniac]."

What detracts from Ralph's otherwise well-formed sentence in this example is his repetition of *the restaurant*, which renders the entire utterance very childlike and thus befitting of Ralph as a model of child language development.

An additional piece of evidence for successful progression between the Stages IV and V concerns the usage of articles. During Stage IV, children learn to differentiate between the definite and indefinite articles, *the* and *a*, respectively, and to apply them to count and non-count nouns, of which the former can be counted in plural form (for example, *dog-dogs; person-people*) while the latter has no plural form (for example, *milk* (**milks*); *furniture* (**furnitures*)). There are two noteworthy occasions when both Ralph and Homer make mistakes in article usage in combination with count and non-count nouns. In "To Surveil with Love,"[20] Lisa finds out there is a school debate team, the only extracurricular activity that doesn't require equipment. Principal Skinner explains to Lisa that, because of budget cuts, they are forced to improvise, and thus Ralph will act as Lisa's lectern. On hearing this news, Ralph exclaims, "I'm a furniture!"

In "Stop or My Dog Will Shoot,"[21] Homer pretends to be a dog, so convincingly that Marge feels the need to remind him he is not really a dog. Homer reassures her, "Oh, relax, Marge. I'm just messing with you. I know I'm not a dog. I'm a people, like you."

Both Ralph and Homer misuse the indefinite article *a* to refer, in Ralph's case, to a non-count noun and, in Homer's case, to a plural noun—neither of which constitutes something you can have only one of.

20. Written by Michael Nobori.

21. Written by John Frink.

Additional Evidence of Language Development

Throughout each of the stages of language acquisition, children are liable to make errors of overextension (Clark 1973). Particularly in earlier stages, when children have started to produce recognizable words but still have a limited vocabulary, they may use a word they know (for instance, *dog*) to refer to some other object that they do not yet have a name for (such as *goat, cow, sheep*). Examples of overextension can be observed in the speech of Ralph Wiggum in the episodes "This Little Wiggie" and "The Scorpion's Tale."[22]

In "This Little Wiggie," Bart discovers on his play-date with Ralph that Ralph's father, Police Chief Wiggum, has a master key to all the stores in town. Bart and Ralph steal the master key, which then escapes their possession and must be retrieved. Ralph later spots the key, just as a rat absconds with it. Not recognizing the animal or perhaps not knowing the word *rat*, Ralph exclaims, "There's the key! Ah! The pointy kitty took it!" Ralph's modification of *kitty* as *pointy kitty* suggests that he understands the animal is not a standard cat, but for lack of a more accurate term, he overextends a word that he does know to cover this new situation.

"The Scorpion's Tale" opens with various characters complaining about the sun and heat. The viewer sees Ralph standing outside with obvious sweat marks surrounding his underarms, to which he reacts, "I wet my arm-pants." Any loyal viewer of *The Simpsons* knows that Ralph is prone to wetting his pants. The sight of sweat under his arms leads Ralph to draw parallels between sweating and wetting his pants, enabling him to overextend both the verb *(to) wet* and the noun *pants*, which, in Ralph's world, together constitute the collocation *wet my pants*. The use of this phrase would suggest that Ralph does not know the words *sweat* or *shirt*, and thus overextends the verb *wet* and, similar to *pointy kitty*, both modifies and overextends the noun *pants*. Overextension errors persist until the child learns the appropriate word (here *rat*, *sweat*, or *shirt*), which eventually comes to preempt or block the error (though there may be a transition period in which s/he uses both the correct and incorrect terms).

22. Written by Billy Kimball and Ian Maxtone-Graham.

Discussion

This chapter has presented the principles of children's first language development as proposed by Brown (1973) in his stages of grammatical development and illustrated by examples found in the television series *The Simpsons*. We have considered children's first words, telegraphic speech, case marking, inflectional morphology, overgeneralization, simple and complex sentences, and overextension. Our examples have focused on the character of Ralph Wiggum, whose childish nature, diminished intellect, and linguistic struggles provide clear illustrations of the different stages of grammatical development. But we have also considered some examples from Homer, whom we have now come to recognize, at times, as comparable to Ralph in his language use. The overall impression that both Ralph and Homer are childlike is accomplished significantly via linguistic means. Indeed, throughout this book, our interest in analyzing the language of television has provided ample evidence that characters are largely a linguistic construction. In *The Simpsons*, we see that Ralph and Homer are believable as child and childlike adult character, respectively, owing specifically to their use of language that reveals evidence of different stages of first language acquisition, a process unique to children. There is much more to first language acquisition than what we were able to consider in this chapter, but we can rest assured that we are "learneding."

Suggestions for Further Viewing and Analysis

1. Consider additional episodes of *The Simpsons* (1989–), which deal with child development more generally, such as "Girls Just Want to Have Sums"[23] and "Smart and Smarter,"[24] looking for linguistic evidence of child behavior.

2. The series *Scientific American Frontiers* (1990–), hosted by Alan Alda, and *Stephen Fry's Planet Word* (2011) each featured an episode on child language acquisition. In "Born to Talk," Alan Alda is joined by Stephen

23. Written by Matt Selman.
24. Written by Carolyn Omine.

Pinker, whose linguistic experiments with children illustrate spontaneous application of grammar rules. The *Planet Word* episode "Babel"[25] includes interviews with both Steven Pinker and Mike Tomasello, perhaps the leading advocates of the Universal Grammar and Constructivist views of language acquisition respectively. Pinker also outlines his view of language acquisition in this short clip from his Floating University lecture: http://www.youtube.com/watch?v=ir7arILiqxg.

3. Many television series featuring young children mine for humor by capitalizing on the incongruity either of children using mature language or of errors resulting from language development. Consider *Dinosaurs* (1991–94), *Kids Say the Darndest Things* (1998–2000), *Full House* (1987–95), and *Everybody Loves Raymond* (1996–2005) for examples of humorous children's language.

4. *Sesame Street* (1969–) is a children's program that features childlike characters using distinctly childlike language. Consider the speech of Cookie Monster and Elmo as examples.

References

Ambridge, Ben, and Caroline F. Rowland. 2009. "Predicting Children's Errors with Negative Questions: Testing a Schema-Combination Account." *Cognitive Linguistics* 20(2): 225–66.

Ambridge, Ben, and Elena V. M. Lieven. 2011. *Child Language Acquisition: Contrasting Theoretical Approaches*. Cambridge, UK: Cambridge Univ. Press.

Brown, Roger. 1973. *A First Language: The Early Stages*. Cambridge, MA: Harvard Univ. Press.

Chomsky, Norm. 1957. *Syntactic Structures*. The Hague: Mouton.

Clark, E. V. 1973. "What's in a Word? On the Child's Acquisition of Semantics in His First Language." In *Cognitive Development and the Acquisition of Language*, edited by Timothy E. Moore, 65–110. New York: Academic Press.

Fenson, Larry, Philip S. Dale, J. Steven Reznick, Elizabeth Bates, Donna J. Thal, Stephen J. Pethick, Michael Tomasello, Carolyn B. Mervis, and Joan Stiles. 1994. "Variability in Early Communicative Development." *Monographs of the Society for Research in Child Development* 58 (Serial No. 242).

25. Written by Stephen Fry.

Fernald, Anne. 1985. "Four-month-old Infants Prefer to Listen to Motherese." *Infant Behavior and Development* 8:181–95.

Gertner, Yael, Cynthia Fisher, and Julie Eisengart. 2006. "Learning Words and Rules: Abstract Knowledge of Word Order in Early Sentence Comprehension." *Psychological Science* 17(8): 684–91.

Gibson, Edward, and Ken Wexler. 1994. "Triggers." *Linguistic Enquiry* 25:407–54.

Ingram, David. 1989. *First Language Acquisition: Method, Description and Explanation*. Cambridge, UK: Cambridge Univ. Press.

Kirjavainen, Minna, Anna Theakston, and Elena Lieven. 2009. "Can Input Explain Children's Me-For-I Errors?" *Journal of Child Language* 36(5): 1091–1114.

Lambrecht, Knud. 1986. "Pragmatically Motivated Syntax: Presentational Cleft-Constructions in Spoken French." In *Papers from the Parasession on Pragmatics and Grammatical Theory at the 22nd Regional Meeting*, edited by Anne Farley, Peter Farley, and Karl-Erik McCullough, 115–26. Chicago: Chicago Linguistic Society.

Leech, Geoffrey, Margaret Deuchar, and Robert Hoogenraad. 1982. *English Grammar for Today—A New Introduction*. London: MacMillan Education.

Marchman, Virginia A. 1997. "Children's Productivity in the English Past Tense: The Role of Frequency, Phonology, and Neighborhood Structure." *Cognitive Science* 21(3): 283–303.

Maslen, Robert, Anna L. Theakston, Elena VM Lieven, and Michael Tomasello. 2004. "A Dense Corpus Study of Past Tense and Plural Overregularization in English." *Journal of Speech, Language, and Hearing Research* 47(6): 1319–33.

Moon, Christine, Robin Panneton Cooper, and William P. Fifer. 1993. "Two-Day-Olds Prefer Their Native Language." *Infant Behavior and Development* 16(4): 495–500.

Noble, Claire H., Caroline F. Rowland, and Julian M. Pine. 2011. "Comprehension of Argument Structure and Semantic Roles: Evidence from English-Learning Children and the Forced-Choice Pointing Paradigm." *Cognitive Science* 35(5): 963–82.

O'Grady, William, and John Archibald. 2000. *Contemporary Linguistic Analysis*. Toronto: Addison Wesley Longman.

Oller, D. Kimbrough. 1980. "The Emergence of the Sound of Speech in Infancy." In *Child Phonology* 1:93–112

———. 2000. *The Emergence of the Speech Capacity*. Mahwah, NJ: Lawrence Erlbaum Associates.

Pinker, Stephen. 1999. *Words and Rules: The Ingredients of Language*. New York: Basic Books.

Rispoli, Matthew. 1994. "Pronoun Case Overextension and Paradigm Building." *Journal of Child Language* 21:157–72.

Rowland, Caroline F. 2007. "Explaining Errors in Children's Questions." *Cognition* 104(1): 106–34.

Snierson, Dan. 2010. "'The Simpsons': Matt Groening and Dan Castellaneta on EW's Greatest Character, Homer Simpson." *Entertainment Weekly*, June 9. Accessed Nov. 20, 2014. http://popwatch.ew.com/2010/06/09/simpsons-matt-groening-dan-castellaneta-greatest-character-homer-simpson/.

Tanz, Jason. 2001. "The Simpsons Rakes in the D'oh!" *Fortune Magazine*, Oct. 15. Accessed Nov. 20, 2014. http://archive.fortune.com/magazines/fortune/fortune_archive/2001/10/15/311554/index.htm.

Tomasello, Michael. 2000. "First Steps toward a Usage-Based Theory of Language Acquisition." *Cognitive Linguistics* 11(1/2): 61–82.

———. 2003. *Constructing a Language: A Usage-Based Theory of Language Acquisition*. Cambridge, MA: Harvard Univ. Press.

12

Lost and Language Found

KRISTY BEERS FÄGERSTEN AND ILARIA FIORENTINI

Lost aired on ABC for six seasons, 2004 to 2010. Thanks in large part to the compelling and intricate plot, but also to the large ensemble cast and the exotic setting,[1] the series was a favorite among audiences and critics, consistently ranking among the top five series on television throughout its run.[2] It has been nominated for numerous awards and has received such prestigious accolades as an Emmy Award for Outstanding Drama Series in 2005 and a Golden Globe Award for Best Television Drama Series in 2006. It was ranked 27th in the Writers Guild of America list of the "101 Best Written Series of All Time" (Ausiello 2013).

Lost can be summarized as a series about the forty-eight survivors of Oceanic Flight 815, which crashed on an island in the South Pacific while on its way from Sydney to Los Angeles. While the survivors initially take stock of who they are and where they may be, they soon realize that their island surroundings are not as idyllic as they seem, and dangers lurk in the jungle. Throughout the series' six seasons, the survivors band together in different constellations, in an effort to discover more about the island (including the Others, a group of people already inhabiting the island), facilitate their rescue, or engineer ways of escaping.

1. The series was also known for its high production costs (Ryan 2005).
2. See, for example, "Favorites Hold Fast" (2008).

The hallmark of *Lost* is the use of flashbacks, to give the viewer an idea of the characters' backgrounds, how they ended up on Flight 815, and which demons they may need to exorcise during their time on the island. *Lost* is therefore known as a series of adventure and mystery, and its obscure and intricate plot was wildly popular among audiences. The complicated story lines served to instill loyalty in its viewers, who often took to online forums to discuss story developments, background revelations, and potential clues to the mysteries of the island. *Lost* is also known for starring an ensemble cast of characters with a variety of backgrounds, notably including people of varying regional origins, including speakers of both different English dialects and non-English languages, an unusual feature for an American television series. More than a dozen characters revealed themselves to have advanced linguistic skills,[3] such as being bilingual (able to speak two languages) or multilingual (able to speak three or more languages). Throughout the series, the audience members (predominantly American, but *Lost* also enjoyed worldwide popularity) were exposed to foreign language interactions in non-English languages such as Spanish, French, Korean, or Arabic, and they were introduced to characters whose knowledge of languages such as Japanese, Russian, Latin, or Greek was highlighted. Each of the bilingual or multilingual characters had, of course, learned one or more language in addition to their native one. This process is known as second language acquisition.

This chapter will focus on the main terms and concepts regarding second language acquisition, considering in particular two Korean survivors of Oceanic Flight 815, Jin and Sun. The only survivors of the crash who seemingly do not speak English at all, Jin and Sun embark on their post-crash life limited to communicating only with each other. Throughout the series, however, Jin and Sun are shown at various stages of learning and using English as a second language, and by the end of the series, both characters speak English proficiently. In this chapter, we will take a closer look at how their processes of learning English as a second language are represented in *Lost*.

3. For details, see www.lostpedia.wikia.com/wiki/Character_languages.

Jin and Sun: Two Paths to a Second Language

Jin-Soo Kwon and Sun-Hwa Kwon are a married Korean couple featured in each season of *Lost*. Viewers learn through flashbacks the complicated process by which Jin and Sun came to be married. Sun was the privileged but sheltered daughter of a rich and domineering businessman, while Jin was a simple man of modest means. Sun had long wanted to escape the oppression of her father, and proposed that she and Jin elope to America. Jin, however, insisted on taking an honorable path, convincing Sun to stay in Korea and asking her father for permission to marry. Sun's father agreed to the marriage on the condition that Jin would become his employee, but Jin soon found himself performing violent tasks. This put a strain on the marriage, and as Sun once again yearned to escape, she and Jin grew apart. Sun conceived of a plan to leave Jin, secretly taking English lessons from a former lover (and rekindling their old romance) to prepare for a new life in America. At the same time, Jin tried to figure out how to safely terminate his employment with Sun's father. When Jin was assigned to travel to Sydney and Los Angeles to make two deliveries for Sun's father, Sun accompanied him. While Jin was planning on using the trip as a way to escape with Sun to America, Sun had already prepared her escape from Jin. She ultimately rethought her decision, however, and in Sydney she decided to stay with Jin, joining him on the fated crash to Los Angeles.

Once on the island, Sun reveals neither her original plans nor her ability to speak English. Jin speaks no English at all, and under the assumption that Sun does not either, he discourages her from mingling. Eventually Sun is forced to reveal to both Jin and the other survivors that she does, indeed, speak English, so as to save Jin from a misdirected accusation. When Jin discovers his wife's ability to speak English, he refuses to speak to her. The two reconcile prior to Jin's attempt at departure from the island on a raft, and upon his return, Jin agrees to learn English.

Jin's progression in learning English is represented by his first speaking a few words, then seemingly understanding more language than he can actually produce himself, and then engaging in simple interactions until he is conversing with minimal difficulty. For example, at the start of season 3 (in the episode "The Glass Ballerina"[4]), Jin manages only very basic English, but by the end of season 4 ("Ji Yeon"[5]) he can understand it perfectly, and by season 5 he can speak English with little to no difficulty.

Language use by and between these Korean spouses, both before and after the plane crash, shows the different stages in the acquisition of a second language, in two very different ways. In order to understand the two diverse processes, which eventually led them each to acquire fluency in English, we need to consider some basic concepts of second language acquisition.

Basic Concepts of Language Learning

Second language acquisition is defined as the process of learning (or acquiring) a second language (L2), that is, any language one acquires in addition to a first, or native, language (L1). It can also refer to the study of this process. A second language should be distinguished from the concept of a foreign language (FL), in that the former refers to a language learned and used in the context where it is naturally spoken, and the latter to a language that is learned in one setting, but used in another. For example, in the American context, non-native speakers of English would learn and use English in a context where it is naturally spoken, and thus English would represent a second language. Similarly, immigrants to France, Sweden, or Italy would use French, Swedish, or Italian, respectively, as a second language. Regardless how 'foreign' these languages may seem to their new speakers, they remain the language of the surrounding environment and thus become the new speakers' second languages. If, however, one were to study English in Korea, or even French, Swedish, or Italian from outside the environments where they are naturally spoken, these languages would be classified as foreign languages; they are foreign to the native linguistic environment.

The difference between second and foreign languages most often entails distinguishing between acquisition and learning. Acquisition is

4. Written by Jeff Pinkner and Drew Goddard.

5. Written by Edward Kitsis and Adam Horowitz.

the process of acquiring a language (even one's first or native language), without instructions or explicit teaching, usually by living in the second language environment or by exposure to spontaneous, natural communication. This acquisition process is considered to be natural and unconscious. Acquirers tend to be unaware of grammatical rules (similar to the acquisition of one's first language, known as the L1), but instead get a feel for what is correct, common, or appropriate and what is not. Language learning, on the other hand, is conscious and a direct result of teaching and deliberate study. It usually implies attending language classes, receiving direct instructions, and doing vocabulary and grammar exercises. It is not always easy to distinguish between these two processes: acquisition, particularly among adults, may be subject to metalinguistic awareness, while learning does not necessarily entail explicit awareness but can result in naturally internalized abilities.

In order to learn or acquire a language, input is necessary. Input is every linguistic medium one is exposed to in the second or foreign language, whether oral, aural, written, or audiovisual. Input can be provided by people, books, films, television, music, the Internet, or any other platform for linguistic communication. In second language acquisition settings, input tends to be rich and widely available; in foreign language learning settings, input may be deficient, artificial, or not easily accessible.

Ideally, input will be comprehensible, but it is not the case that every linguistic feature of any kind of input is immediately recognized and internalized by the foreign language (FL) or the second language (L2) user. That which a learner or acquirer is able to comprehend from any given input is called *intake*. Everything that is produced by the learner in the second or foreign language, namely the outcome of what she or he has learned, is called *output*.

From One Language to Another via an Interlanguage

Usually (but not exclusively), in the first stages of acquisition or learning, output is in the form of an interlanguage (Selinker 1972), that is, a variety of language that can include features of a speaker's L1 but most often reflects a developing, inaccurate approximation of the L2, characterized by innovation and overgeneralizations of its rules and conventions.

Interlanguages are common to L2 learners, and develop according to several factors, independent of the learner's first language. This means that German, Turkish, or Japanese speakers learning English will experience stages of interlanguage in roughly the same way. Specifically, different stages of interlanguage development can be recognized as the result of transfer and overgeneralization, as well as by strategies of simplification and communication. Erroneous forms are common, and are either eradicated as learners progress toward their target language, or they persist to the point of fossilization. We will now address each of these phenomena.

As the name interlanguage suggests, it is the form of language that is between the learner's L1 and the target language, the L2. L2 learners tend not to completely abandon their first languages, especially in the beginning phase of learning, but rather attempt to transfer the linguistic system of the L1 to the L2. Where the L1 and L2 are similar, positive transfer occurs, which may facilitate learning and result in accurate production and comprehension. Where the two languages differ, negative transfer, or interference, occurs, which may result in inaccurate or nonstandard forms and structures.

Learning or acquiring a second language is not just a matter of discovering and understanding a new vocabulary, but also a new language system, including rules of syntax, morphology, and phonology, among other aspects. Once learners become aware of a rule or pattern, it is common that they overgeneralize it, applying it to similar forms. Overgeneralization occurs even among first language learners, as we saw in chapter 11 with the example of the regular past tense form *-ed*, which learners can overapply to irregular verbs, resulting in overgeneralized forms such as **goed* or **bleeded*.

The process of learning or acquiring a second language can be facilitated by strategies of simplification, such as the omission of phonological, morphological, or grammatical features. Examples include substituting single phones for consonant clusters (for example, saying *tink* instead of *think*), omitting inflectional morphemes (for example, **two cat*, **I am eat my dinner*), or employing a simplified grammar (for example, simplified conjugation: *I go*, **he go*, **she go*, *we go*).

In the interlanguage stages, learners rely on strategies of communication to enable successful interactions. The use of formulaic expressions, or fixed phrases, is one example of communicative strategies. Learners often encounter, memorize, and reproduce such formulae as *how are you* or *see you later.* While expressions of this kind contribute to fluency, they may also be misused or integrated improperly. For example, a learner may produce an utterance such as **Can you tell me, how are you do that?*

Interlanguages generally continue to evolve toward the L2 until fluency and proficiency are achieved. However, remnants of an interlanguage can persist, indicating that a learner has not successfully mastered the L2. The phenomenon of incomplete L2 development is called fossilization (Corder 1981; Selinker 1972), and can apply to phonological, morphological, syntactical, or even pragmatic aspects of development. Some learners are simply unable to progress beyond a particular level, and thus fossilization takes place despite one's best efforts. Other learners may experience that their interlanguage satisfies their communicative needs and goals, and thus fossilization can occur as a result of a deliberate lack of effort toward further development.

Influences on Second Language Learning and Acquisition

Second language learning and acquisition are influenced by both objective and subjective factors. Objective factors include those that the learner cannot control, such as age or first language. Subjective factors, on the other hand, are more related to the learner as a thinking and sentient being, and include such qualities as intelligence, attitude, or personality. One particularly powerful subjective factor is the so-called affective filter, that is, a sort of barrier to the learning or acquisition processes because of anxiety, lack of motivation, low self-confidence, or fear of failing. Another factor that plays a crucial role in acquisition and learning, and that is strongly related to the affective filter, is motivation, which can be either integrative or instrumental. Integrative motivation is based on the desire to become a member of the L2 speaking community; the acquisition or learning of the second language is therefore seen in a positive way, as a means to reach this goal. Instrumental motivation, on the other hand, involves more utilitarian and practical reasons for language learning, and is linked with the use of the L2 as a tool to achieve desired social or professional goals. Both types of motivation are usually connected with successful L2 acquisition, which is expressed in terms of communicative competence.

Communicative Competence

The notion of communicative competence refers to the speaker's knowledge of syntactical, morphological, and phonological rules of a language, as well as the ability to use utterances appropriately and according to context (Hymes 1972). Communicative competence consists of three fundamental components: grammatical competence, sociolinguistic competence, and strategic competence (Canale and Swain 1980). *Grammatical competence* refers to the ability of a speaker to (unconsciously) recognize and reproduce the grammatical rules and structure of a language, including its distinct phonological, morphological, and syntactic forms. *Sociolinguistic competence* denotes the ability to use the L2 in a way appropriate to the context and the circumstances of the interaction, that is, the communicative situation as defined by sociolinguistic variables (see chapter 2). *Strategic competence* refers to the learner's ability to adjust the use of verbal and nonverbal language when lacking the understanding of grammar or the knowledge of social and communicative norms, in order to compensate for communication problems or linguistic deficiencies. Such strategies may involve paraphrase, circumlocution, or direct transfer from the native language of the speaker.

Learning and Acquisition in Action in *Lost*

Now that we have learned the fundamental concepts of foreign language learning and second language acquisition, let's follow Sun and Jin in their experience with English as a second language. In the analyses that follow, we will be reminded that they started with dissimilar motivations and purposes, and that their learning and acquisition processes took place under very different circumstances. Nonetheless, both Sun and Jin prove to be successful users of English, ultimately exhibiting communicative competence.

Sun

As *Lost* begins, the viewer is led to believe that neither Sun nor Jin can speak English. In fact, unbeknown to her husband, Sun can speak English, and in the second part of the pilot episode, the viewer understands as much, when a flicker of understanding shows on Sun's face during an interaction with Michael, another survivor. Sun faces a conundrum: if she continues to pretend that she does not speak English, she can avoid confessing her pre-crash plans to leave Jin, but if she admits her abilities, she can avoid being isolated from the other survivors. By the sixth episode of season 1, however, circumstances force Sun into revealing herself as a competent English speaker. Let's now consider the circumstances that led to this competence.

Foreign Language Learning. Sun was on Oceanic Flight 815 in order to flee to America from Korea, from her criminal father, and from her failing marriage with Jin. She prepared for her escape by secretly taking English lessons in Seoul from her former lover, Jae. Sun's case thus illustrates the concepts of both foreign (vs. second) language and of learning (vs. acquisition). Because English is not the language of the native Korean environment, it has foreign language status. Furthermore, because Sun received direct instruction from Jae, she experienced a process of learning. Example 1 comes from the episode "The Whole Truth,"[6] and illustrates how English is not naturally used in the Korean-language environment, and also indicates how Sun's English lessons transpired. In this example, Sun orders a drink at a local restaurant, whereby Jae encourages her to reformulate her request in English. In all examples, subtitles as they appeared on screen are shown in parentheses below the Korean transcription. All transcripts for the selected dialogue extracts were retrieved from www.lostpedia.wikia.com, and with the exception of the episode "Ji Yeon" are attributed to user Spooky; usage complies with Creative Commons general permission and attribution guidelines.

Example 1:

6. Written by Elizabeth Sarnoff and Christina M. Kim.

SUN: 그냥 아이스티 주세요.

(Just some iced-tea, please.)

JAE: In English.

SUN: *(with difficulty)* I would like iced-tea, please.

JAE: Very good.

SUN: Thank you.

(http://lostpedia.wikia.com/wiki/The_Whole_Truth_transcript)

The fact that Sun struggles to produce the English-language request confirms her beginner status. Note, however, how the use of formulaic expressions, such as *I would like, please,* and *thank you,* suggest a progression toward fluency.

Motivation. We have noted that Sun desperately longed to escape to America. Her desire to learn English was motivated by this goal, and thus we can identify her motivation as instrumental. In other words, Sun was more motivated to learn English so as to have a destination to escape to than to integrate with the native-speaking community. In example 2 (also from "The Whole Truth"), a flashback confirms this motivation, as Sun reveals to Jae her reasons for learning English.

Example 2:

JAE: 우리가 여기서 뭐하는 거죠? (Why are we here?)

SUN: 저한테 영어를 가르쳐 주시고 있잖아요. (Because you're teaching me English.)

JAE: 선 씨는 이미 한달 전부터 영어를 유창하게 하는데요, 왜 영어를 배우려는 거죠? (You've been practically fluent for a month now. Why are you learning English?)

SUN: 저 . . . 미국에 가려고요. (Because I'm moving to America.)

JAE: 진수 씨하고 . . . 헤어질 생각이세요? 난 한 여자 때문에 미국으로 도망갔었어요. 그것이 사랑인줄 알고 . . . 하지만 자기 인생에서 도망갈 순 없죠. (Jin. You're going to leave him. I ran away to America for a woman because I thought I was in love. But you can't run away from your life.)

SUN: 그럼 . . . 그 사람이 제 인생의 전부인가요? 저는요— (And Jin? Is he my life? I should stay because—)

JAE: I'm not saying you should stay for Jin.

While this example does not reveal how Sun is progressing in English, it does make clear that Sun sees a connection between learning English and preparing to move. The process of learning English is thus approached instrumentally, as it will allow Sun not just to move to America, but also to move away from Jin.

Competence. From the very first time she speaks English on the island, in the sixth episode of season 1, Sun shows herself to be a highly proficient speaker of English, as illustrated in example 3. In this example from "House of the Rising Sun,"[7] Jin and another survivor, Michael, had previously had a violent confrontation. In order to help Jin, Sun approaches Michael to explain Jin's actions.

Example 3:

MICHAEL: Oh great, look who came to chat.
SUN: I need to talk to you.
MICHAEL: You speak English?
SUN: Yes.
MICHAEL: What? You speak English? Why didn't you say anything?!
SUN: My husband doesn't know.
MICHAEL: Why would you learn English and not tell your husband?
SUN: He has a bad temper. What my husband did to you today, it was a misunderstanding.
MICHAEL: No. I got it. Loud and clear.
SUN: It was the watch.
MICHAEL: Your husband tried to murder me for a watch?! *(Michael removes the watch)* I found this watch two days ago.
SUN: It belongs to my father. Protecting that watch is a question of honor.
MICHAEL: He calls trying to kill me in front of my kid, honor?!
SUN: You don't know my father. I need your help.
(http://lostpedia.wikia.com/wiki/House_of_the_Rising_Sun_transcript)

7. Written by Javier Grillo-Marxuach.

We may want to consider the possibility that Sun's first use of English on the island was deliberately constructed by the series writers to be somewhat basic; note, for example, the simple sentence structure, the use of simple present and past tenses, the basic vocabulary. Nevertheless, the fact that Sun successfully manages grammatical rules of English and is able to produce phonologically and morphologically accurate utterances indicates grammatical competence. The example also illustrates that Sun has sociolinguistic competence in English, as she uses the language appropriately relative to the communicative situation. At the beginning of example 3, Sun opens the conversation and simultaneously communicates the urgency of her business by using the formulaic expression *I need to talk to you*. Throughout the interaction, Sun not only addresses each of Michael's turns, but also manages to develop the conversation toward her communicative goal, namely, to ask for help.

Sun's use of English throughout the series indicates that the foreign language learning process successfully carried her through and beyond the interlanguage stage to become a communicatively competent speaker. As example 4 (from " . . . In Translation"[8]) illustrates, Sun is also a recognizably proficient bilingual. In this example, she and Jin are involved in a heated discussion, after Jin appears to have been involved in burning up Michael's raft.

Example 4:

SUN: 대답하기 싫어요? 나한테 이러는 이유를 모르겠어. 내가 뭘 잘못했는데? 우리가 언제부터 이렇게 대화가 안 됐어요! (What have I done to deserve this? When did we stop talking?) I was going to leave you! I was going to get away. But you made me change my mind. You made me think that you still loved me. 나 . . . 처음부터 다시 시작하고 싶어. 여보 . . . 우리 새롭게 시작해요, 네? (I . . . want to go back to the beginning. Can't we . . . just start all over?)

(http://lostpedia.wikia.com/wiki/ . . . In_Translation_transcript)

8. Written by Javier Grillo-Marxuach and Leonard Dick.

This example shows Sun making use of each language she has available to her, engaging in code-switching, or the alternate use of two or more languages within one conversation. We might want to interpret Sun's practice of code-switching as an indication of a high level of bilingual language proficiency, allowing her to move effortlessly between English and Korean. Sun's code-switching may also be socially indexical (Heller 1992), signaling to Jin that, as a speaker of English, he and Sun now constitute their own social group as speakers of both English and Korean. Their practice of code-switching not only reflects this status, but, significantly, reminds the viewing audience of their shared background and interpersonal intimacy (Mandala 2008). Code-switching can also serve to create a new social situation for Sun and Jin, who may need to negotiate language choice (Auer 1984).

Jin

Jin is the only survivor on the island who cannot speak English at all. During his courtship with Sun, Jin rejected her proposal of escaping together from Korea and from her father, and he did not initially board Flight 815 with the intention of staying in America. Thus, unlike Sun, Jin did not make any effort to learn English before the journey. Once on the island, he sees no need and expresses no desire to communicate with the other survivors, instructing Sun in the pilot episode to remain by his side, follow him everywhere, not to concern herself with the other survivors, and to focus on staying together. It is most certainly Jin's (and, he assumes, Sun's) inability to speak English that leads him to isolate himself and Sun, believing they have nothing to gain from or contribute to the group. Nonetheless, circumstances eventually impose English upon Jin, and throughout the series he progresses from a Korean monolingual to a competent English speaker. In the following sections, we consider how that happened.

Second Language Acquisition. Jin did not attend English lessons or classes in Korea, and he comes into contact with the language only after surviving the plane crash on the island. There, he is exposed to the language as it is used naturally, and he gradually begins to speak it once his exposure to and interaction with the other, English-speaking survivors increases. While Sun learned English as a result of explicit instruction common to the foreign language environment, Jin's experiences are more typical of second language acquisition: he is in an English-language environment where there is more focus on meaningful interaction than on directed instruction. In example 5 from "Tricia Tanaka Is Dead,"[9] Jin is confronted with a situation that is typical of the acquisition process, namely, immersion in the target language.

Example 5:

> SUN: Will you pass me the box of cereal? *(Jin looks confused)* Will you pass me the box of cereal?
>
> JIN: 무슨 말을 하는지 모르겠어 (I don't know what to say.)
>
> SUN: From now on I will only speak to you in English. It's how you will learn.
>
> (http://lostpedia.wikia.com/wiki/Tricia_Tanaka_Is_Dead_transcript)

In communication with Sun, Jin can at least count on her understanding when he speaks in Korean. With the other survivors, however, there is no such recourse. On the other hand, people often adjust their communication to accommodate those with low proficiency levels, as we see in the next section.

Input. Because the remaining survivors of Flight 815 speak a variety of English dialects, Jin is exposed to a good deal of English, and is therefore in position to receive an abundance of oral input. However, Jin is not always able to comprehend all the available input. In the context of second language acquisition where the target language is used naturally, it is rarely the case that input is difficult to come by. Instead, the challenge for new language users is having access to comprehensible input that allows for meaningful intake and successful acquisition. The following two examples illustrate comprehensible vs. incomprehensible input. First, in example 6 ("Exodus, Part 1"[10]), Michal and Jin are constructing a raft in an attempt to flee the island and seek rescue. Putting on the finishing touches, Jin is about to make a mistake when Michael stops him:

9. Written by Edward Kitsis and Adam Horowitz.

10. Written by Damon Lindelof and Carlton Cuse.

Example 6:

MICHAEL: No, no, no! This one goes here! That one goes there!
JIN: Okay, okay.
(http://lostpedia.wikia.com/wiki/Exodus%2C_Part_1_transcript)

Note that Michael's input is made comprehensible in two distinct ways: by repetition and by deictic, or pointing, expressions. First, there is lexical repetition with a threefold "no" utterance as well as syntactic repetition with the 'X one goes Y' structure. Second, the demonstrative pronouns *this/that* and the adverbials *here/there* are deictic expressions, reflecting objects and locations in relation to the speaker's perspective. If Jin is unfamiliar with these terms, Michael's accompanying physical gestures can make the input more comprehensible by explicitly indicating to Jin which objects and which locations are meant. Jin responds with an early-acquired formulaic expression, *okay*, confirming his intake.[11]

In example 7, it is later in the same episode, as Jin is about to leave the island with Michael on the raft they have been working on. Sun gives him a notebook in which she has written some common English words with Korean phonetic spellings.

Example 7:

SUN: *(handing Jin some papers)* 이거요. (This is for you.)
JIN: *(reading the papers)* Star . . . star board.
SUN: Starboard. 간단한 영어를 발음대로 적었어요. 당신한테 도움이 될 것 같아서 한번 만들어 봤어요. (It's a list of simple English words spelled out phonetically . . . I thought this would help you so I made it for you.)

Sun is perhaps empathetic to Jin's struggles with learning English and tries to support him, not only by helping him with his production but also by preparing him for comprehensible input.

11. Some viewers may recognize this scene as an homage to *Star Wars: A New Hope*, as it mirrors an interaction between Han Solo and his partner, Chewbacca, who can understand English but not speak it.

Other survivors are supportive of Jin's undertaking as well. In example 8 ("Tricia Tanaka Is Dead"), Sawyer initiates an instruction session, engaging Jin in a repeat-after-me routine that is commonly used with novices of any activity.

Example 8:

SAWYER: Beer.

JIN: Beer.

SAWYER: Bingo. Beautiful. *(tapping the van)* Car.

JIN: Car.

The scene is continued at a later point in the same episode, and thanks to Sawyer's coaching, Jin has graduated to longer phrases.

Example 9:

SAWYER: I'm sorry.

JIN: I'm sorry.

SAWYER: Okay, nice. Keep it coming.

JIN: You were right.

SAWYER: Okay. That's two. Hit me.

JIN: Those pants don't make you look fat.

SAWYER: Now you got it—only three things a woman needs to hear.

The viewer is not sure how much Jin understands of what he is saying, but Sawyer seems to think he is providing Jin with valuable instruction. Indeed, the phrases are grammatically correct, formulaic expressions, which may even increase Jin's sociolinguistic, and thereby communicative, competence.

Should example 9 suggest to the viewer that Jin is a more competent language user than is actually the case, example 10 shows that not all input is comprehensible for Jin. Previously in the same episode, the survivor Hurley has discovered an abandoned vehicle in the jungle, and he has rushed back to camp to share the news, meeting survivors Nikki, Paulo, Charlie, and Jin along the way. It is this vehicle that Sawyer uses to teach Jin the word "car" in example 8.

Example 10:

HURLEY: *(triumphantly)* Car! I found a car tipped over in the jungle.

NIKKI: You found a car?

HURLEY: And we could totally fix it and get it going again. It's not far, come on.

PAULO: Why do we need to start a car?

HURLEY: Because it'll be fun. We could all use some fun. I mean, after everything's that happened we need it. Especially you, dude. So who's with me?

PAULO: Well, I've got to cut some bananas. Sorry.

CHARLIE: I don't think so, Hurley.

HURLEY: Come on. Anyone. We're going to drive it! Who's coming?

(Everyone walks away except Jin. Hurley walks over and puts a hand on his shoulder.)

HURLEY: Thanks, dude. *(Hurley laughs)* You have no idea what you volunteered for, do you? *(Jin laughs)* Come on.

In this exchange, there are no physical cues to help Jin understand what Hurley is talking about. For this reason, he cannot understand why the others, one by one, reject Hurley's idea and walk away. This lack of understanding prevents Jin from being able to decide if he, too, should walk away, and so he is left alone with Hurley, which Hurley decides to interpret as agreement and approval, albeit acknowledging that Jin has not understood.

Output. Though Jin seems gradually to understand more and more of the linguistic input that surrounds him, his own output, as one might expect, is limited. Example 11, which comes from the third-season episode "The Glass Ballerina," shows that at that point, Jin's spontaneous production has not progressed beyond single words or short phrases.

Example 11:

SAYID: Let's bring the boat in. We'll tie it to the dock and build a fire on the beach. The visibility's excellent. Jack will be able to see us for miles around.

JIN: Safe?

SAYID: Yes, Jin. Of course it's safe.

(http://lostpedia.wikia.com/wiki/The_Glass_Ballerina_transcript)

As time passes, however, Jin's interlanguage develops. During season 4, we can see that although his English is still characterized by simple syntactic structures and basic morphology, Jin has clearly emerged from the previous one-word stage. In example 12, from "Ji Yeon,"[12] Jin and fellow survivor Jack are eating breakfast on the beach.

Example 12:

> JIN: Uh, can you pass, uh, the cereal?
> *(Jack passes the cereal.)*
> JACK: Pretty good English, Jin.
> JIN: Thank you. I . . . understand better than I, uh, speak.
> JACK: Has Sun been teaching you, or are you just picking it up?
> JIN: Uh, Sun teach me . . . Uh, Sawyer, too. Sun, is . . . better.
> JACK: I bet.
> (http://lostpedia.wikia.com/wiki/Ji_Yeon_transcript)

Jin's interlanguage is evolving toward the L2 as his linguistic skills improve. At this point, the lack of inflectional morpheme for third person present tense on "teach" may be a sign of Jin's approaching an acquisition stage (see chapter 11), or it may be owing to negative transfer from Korean. In other words, because verbs are not inflected for person or number in Korean, this is not a feature that Jin would naturally include. Should this error persist, it would be a case of fossilization. This exchange between Jin and Jack is a case of satisfying continuity, as example 10 invites us to recall example 5, where Sun provided Jin with similar input, and suggests that Jin is following in her footsteps to communicative competence.

Motivation. After the crash, Jin is uninterested in interacting with the other survivors, and discourages Sun from communicating with them, particularly with Michael. Jin of course does not know that Sun understands English, and that she is certainly interested in knowing what the other survivors have to say. When Sun's abilities in English are revealed, Jin is shocked and humiliated. The fact that his wife has mastered a language that he himself does not know puts him at a disadvantage, and

12. Written by Edward Kitsis and Adam Horowitz.

raises his affective filter. Nonetheless, Jin has no other way to communicate with the other survivors but to use English. His primary motivation is thus likely instrumental, because he needs English to survive on the island. It can be said to become integrative as well, as learning English allows Jin, as it did Sun, to become part of the group.

Competence. In comparison to his wife, Sun, Jin's grammatical competence is poor and characterized by simple structures, basic vocabulary, and a general lack of inflectional morphology. His strategic competence is also very limited; basically, when he does not know an English word, he gestures in order to fill his linguistic gaps. In example 13 (from "Tricia Tanaka Is Dead"), Jin is helping Hurley with the vehicle that was discovered in the jungle, but Jin does not yet have the skills to express his ideas in English.

Example 13:

JIN: *(gesturing at the van)* 시체 꺼내자. (Let's pull out the corpse)
HURLEY: I suck at charades. You want to what?
JIN: *(gesturing)* 아냐, 아냐. (No, no)
HURLEY: Oh, you want to take Roger out? *(Jin continues gesturing)* And turn it over. *(yelling to Jin)* I understand!

Jin behaves as a typical language learner, employing gesture as a communicative strategy when his skills are insufficient. Note that this behavior benefits Jin as a learner, because it causes his interlocutor to speak, providing Jin with input that in this immediate, tangible context is most likely comprehensible.

Finally, as Jin becomes more fluent in English, his sociolinguistic competence improves. In our final example, Jin and Hurley are working on recovering the found vehicle when Sawyer, who had been captured by the Others and believed to be dead, suddenly and unexpectedly appears. Both Hurley and Jin are elated to see Sawyer and make a spontaneous show of emotion. (Note that this interaction also occurred in the third season episode "Tricia Tanaka Is Dead," but after the interaction featured in example 10, and prior to that featured in examples 8, 9, and 13.)

Example 14:

HURLEY: Dude! You're alive!! You're alive.

SAWYER: *(chuckling)* Yeah, yeah, Snuffy. Good to see you, too. I'll be damned. You all found yourselves a hippy car.

HURLEY: Pretty cool, huh?

JIN: *(reaching for a hug)* Sawyer.

SAWYER: Jin-bo. How are you doing?

JING: Good . . . to see . . . you.

SAWYER: Well, look at that. Somebody's hooked on phonics.

Jin's awareness of how to act and what to say in this reunion context indicates that he is not just acquiring a language, but also absorbing contextual features and appropriating cultural practices, allowing him to interact appropriately in a variety of situations.

Discussion

In addition to its compelling plot, ensemble cast, and alluring production, *Lost* also stands out for including non-English-speaking characters and for devoting part of its story line to showing their realistic linguistic development. Sun and Jin must therefore also be recognized as noteworthy characters for unconventionally challenging English-language viewing audiences.[13]

In order to fully appreciate the efforts required not only of Sun and Jin to learn and acquire English as a foreign or second language, but of the writers and producers of *Lost* to portray these processes accurately and believably, let us consider the following quote:

> In the United States . . . knowing more than one language is often considered a sign of intelligence, diligence, and a privileged education—but only if the possessor of this skill is a native speaker of English. Some of the same people who admire an English speaker for knowing other languages are conspicuously unimpressed by reciprocal skills in a non-native speaker of English, on the apparent assumption that speaking English is just normal. (Thomason 2001, 43)

13. The characters of *Firefly* (2002–3) are also notable for their linguistic unconventionality, consisting of frequent code-switches to Chinese; see Mandala 2008).

It is worth pointing out that *Lost* was produced by an American television company and targeted, presumably, at a primarily American audience, yet included not only non-American dialects, but also non-English speakers. The series therefore enriches the linguistic landscape of television by including diversity in the form of other varieties of English, and languages other than English. Although fluency in English is presented as an obvious goal, the usual English-only triumphalism of Hollywood (Bleichenbacher 2012) is significantly tempered in *Lost*, which ultimately illustrates that one's inability to speak English is not equivalent to having no linguistic ability at all. The series can be lauded for demonstrating that language learning requires considerable effort.

Whether or not viewers of *Lost* have had their own experiences with a second or foreign language, they can still be expected to entertain the idea that, even today, and even on a planeload of people traveling from Sydney to Los Angeles, not everyone speaks English. Viewers can also be assumed to expect that any non-English-speaking characters stranded on an island for an indefinite amount of time with English speakers will necessarily have to go through a language learning process before they are able to communicate with some proficiency. It is therefore vital to the narrative that Sun and Jin, as speakers of another language than English, engage in realistic and meaningful communication not only with each other, but with the other English-speaking characters as well, and that their own linguistic evolution into bilinguals is accounted for and realistically portrayed. Both Sun and Jin illustrate that, despite different learning conditions, their ultimate success in learning a foreign language and acquiring a second language, respectively, was a function of motivation, comprehensible input, and meaningful interaction. Sun and Jin may have been lost, but language was found.

Suggestions for Further Viewing and Analysis

1. In the *My Name is Earl* (2005–9) episode "Teacher Earl,"[14] Earl becomes a teacher of English as a second language in order to make amends

14. Written by Victor Fresco.

for the fact that he has "made fun of people with accents." One of his students receives additional instruction by Earl's ex-wife, Joy. While Earl devotes his first lesson to teaching his students his name, Joy's goal is to sabotage her own student's competing manicure business. Earl's students learn how to say "My name is Earl," while Joy's student practices saying, "I give you big infection." Consider how the episode illustrates unsuccessful language acquisition because of a lack of comprehensible input provided through meaningful interaction.

2. In the first season of *Game of Thrones* (2011–), Daenerys Targaryen is sold for marriage to Khal Drogo. She is a native speaker of the language of Valyria, while her husband is a Dothraki speaker. In the beginning, she cannot speak Dothraki and is helped by the first knight of her Queensguard, Ser Jorah. Then, after her handmaiden Irri teaches her to speak the Dothraki language, Daenerys grows confident and begins to take part in the responsibilities of her reign, eventually winning the love of her husband and the Dothraki people. Consider the case of Daenerys as an example of foreign language learning vs. second language acquisition, and instrumental vs. integrative motivation.

3. In *The Simpsons* (1989–) episode "The Crepes of Wrath,"[15] Bart is punished for in-school delinquency by being forced to participate in a foreign exchange program. He is sent to France, where he is received by two winemakers, César and Ugolin, who host Bart in their Château Maison, which is, in spite of its name, a decaying farmhouse on a squalid vineyard. Bart's hosts treat him like a slave, forcing him to labor long hours and sleep on the floor. When Bart is sent to Paris by his tormentors, he tries to ask a gendarme for help, but his inability to speak French prevents him from explaining his predicament. While walking away, Bart admonishes himself aloud, suddenly realizing he is actually speaking French:

> BART: I'm so stupid. Anybody could've learned this dumb language by now. Here I've listened to nothing but French for the past deux mois, et je ne sais pas un mot. Eh! Mais je parle Français maintenant!

15. Written by George Meyer, Sam Simon, John Swartzwelder, and Jon Vitti.

Incroyable! (Two months, and I haven't learned a word. Wait! I'm speaking French now! That's incredible!)

(Transcribed by Kristy Beers Fägersten)

Compare Bart's experience with that of Sun, Jin, and Daenerys, considering whether Bart's ability in French is an example of learning or acquisition, and how his progression toward communicative competence may have been a function of motivation, exposure to input, and lack of directed instruction.

4. The series *Modern Family* (2009–) features an American extended family whose paterfamilias, Jay, is living with his second wife, a beautiful Columbian woman named Gloria, and her twelve-year-old son, Manny. Because Gloria was born and raised in Columbia, she is a native speaker of Spanish and a second language speaker of English. In the episode "Halloween,"[16] Jay points out Gloria's production errors, including her pronunciation of *gargoyle* as *gargle*.

JAY: Did you pick up my gargle costume too?

GLORIA: Are you making fun of me?

JAY: No.

GLORIA: First Manny correcting me and now you? If I have a problem I want to know Jay.

JAY: Honey, look, English is your second language. You're doing great.

GLORIA: Yeah you're not helping by protecting my feelings. I want you to be honest with me.

JAY: Okay well I may have noticed some tiny, little mistakes you might want to take a look at.

GLORIA: Like what?

JAY: Just little mispronunciations. Like, for example, last night you said we live in a doggy-dog world.

GLORIA: So?

JAY: Well it's dog-eat-dog world.

16. Written by Jeffrey Richman.

GLORIA: Yeah but, that doesn't make any sense. Who wants to live in a world where dogs eat each other? A doggy-dog world is a beautiful world full of little puppies!

(Transcribed by Kristy Beers Fägersten)

From this extract it is clear that both Gloria's husband and son notice her language mistakes and occasionally call her attention to them, either overtly or covertly. While Gloria seems eager to understand and correct her mistakes, her persistent mispronunciations and her dissatisfaction with the expression dog-eat-dog world suggests that she may not be willing to speak correctly all the time. In light of this, what can we say about the risk of Gloria's inaccurate forms becoming fossilized?

References

Auer, Peter. 1984. *Bilingual Conversation*. Amsterdam: John Benjamins.

Ausiello, Michael. 2013. "Writers Guild Names 101 Best-Written Shows Ever: What Made the List? What Got Snubbed?" *TV Line*, June 3. Accessed Sept. 20, 2015. http://tvline.com/2013/06/03/100-best-written-tv-shows-ever-the-sopranos/.

Bleichenbacher, Lukas. 2012. "Linguicism in Hollywood Movies? Representations of and Audience Reactions to Multilingualism in Mainstream Movie Dialogues." *Multilingua* 31:155–76.

Canale, Michael, and Merrill Swain. 1980. "Theoretical Bases of Communicative Approaches to Second Language Teaching and Testing." *Applied Linguistics* 1:1–47.

Corder, Stephen Pit. 1981. *Error Analysis and Interlanguage*. Oxford, UK: Oxford Univ. Press.

"Favorites Hold Fast." 2008. *TV Week*, July 6. Accessed Sept. 20, 2015. http://www.tvweek.com/news/2008/07/favorites_hold_fast.php.

Heller, Monica. "The Politics of Codeswitching and Language Choice." 1992. *Journal of Multilingual and Multicultural Development* 13(1–2): 123–42.

Hymes, Dell H. 1972. "On Communicative Competence." In *Sociolinguistics: Selected Readings*, edited by Dell H. Hymes, John B. Pride, and Janet Holmes, 269–93. Harmondsworth, UK: Penguin.

Mandala, Susan. 2008. "Representing the Future: Chinese and Codeswitching in *Firefly*." In *Investigating* Firefly *and* Serenity*: Science Fiction on the Frontier*, edited by Rhonda V. Wilcox and Tanya R. Cochran, 31–40. London: I. B. Tauris.

Ryan, Tim. 2005. "'Lost' Opportunity? High Filming Costs Force ABC Network Executives to Consider Relocating." *Star Bulletin*, Jan. 26. Accessed Sept. 20, 2015. http://archives.starbulletin.com/2005/01/26/news/story2.html.

Selinker, Larry. 1972. "Interlanguage." *International Review of Applied Linguistics* 10:209–41.

Thomason, Sarah G. 2001. *Language Contact*. Edinburgh: Edinburgh Univ. Press.

13

The One Based on 738,032 Words

Language Use in the Friends-*corpus*

PAULO QUAGLIO

The American sitcom *Friends* (1994–2004) was one of the most successful shows produced by the network NBC. During its ten-year run, it received numerous awards and nominations, and was considered one of the most popular sitcoms all over the world. The show is about a group of three single males and three single females, all in their twenties when the series begins. These friends share their life experiences (and, in some cases, apartments) with each other, as each attempts to find success and happiness on professional and personal levels. Most of the friends' interactions take place either at their homes or at Central Perk, a coffee house in New York City. The situations experienced by the characters in the show do not occur in a social vacuum; rather, the plots incorporate a series of relevant social topics, such as same-sex marriage, artificial insemination, surrogate mothers, age difference in romantic relationships, loyalty among friends, and, simply, friendship.

The popularity of the show secured its status as a popular cultural artifact, and as such has been the object of academic research (for example, Quaglio 2009; Tagliamonte and Roberts 2005). In a previous study (2009), I concluded that the language of *Friends* shares most of the core linguistic features of natural conversation and can thus be used as a fairly accurate representation of natural conversation. In fact, video clips of the show with transcribed dialogues have even been part of several ESL/EFL

(English as a Second/Foreign Language) courses in the United States and abroad. As Jennifer Rey (2001) states, the language of television dialogue is a representation of the perception that scriptwriters have of actual conversation, and this may have been one of the factors contributing to the success of the show.

This chapter introduces corpus linguistics, a fascinating field of study within applied linguistics. We will learn about the techniques used by corpus linguists in the investigation of language use and will learn how to create our own corpus (the data used in corpus linguistics) and do our own investigations. In this chapter, all of the examples of television dialogue come from the sitcom *Friends*, and the analyses are based on a corpus of all of the dialogue from the series' ten seasons: a total of 738,032 words.

Corpus: Definition and Collection

Lynne Bowker and Jennifer Pearson (2002) define a corpus as "a large collection of authentic texts that have been gathered in electronic form according to a specific set of criteria" (9). When it comes to creating corpora (plural of corpus) based on television series, we're in luck: there are many websites dedicated to providing episode transcripts, such as those referred to in many of the chapter examples throughout this volume. If no episode transcriptions of the target series are available online, then the corpus building process would start with careful listening and transcribing. The transcriptions, whether copied from a website or self-created, would then need to be saved into a specially created folder on the computer. The corpus compiler decides how much material to include from a television series, but however targeted the corpus is, it could be a good idea to save individual episodes in separate files, grouped by seasons (if relevant), which would allow for easy comparisons of episodes or seasons, in turn allowing for a diachronic study (see, for example, Bednarek [2011a; 2011b], in which the author compiled and compared seasonal corpora of *Gilmore Girls*).

It is important to mention that the collection of data available online, especially transcriptions of spoken language, must be checked for accuracy. In other words, the data must be 'cleaned' before analyses are conducted. For example, once the *Friends*-corpus was collected from a fan website in my 2009 study, the transcripts were compared against the show videos. Typos and transcription inaccuracies were fixed, and scene descriptions provided by the transcribers (for example, *The intercom buzzes*) were eliminated.

Does Size Matter?

Corpora today typically have several million words (such as the American National Corpus (ANC), the British National Corpus (BNC), and the Corpus of Contemporary American English (COCA)). The need for large corpora will depend on the research question. For example, if we want to find information on the frequency and use of a particular word such as *unlike* (which can be an adjective, a preposition, or a conjunction), a corpus of several million words may be required as *unlike* is not, relatively speaking, a frequent word in conversational language (it is used only three times in *Friends*). However, getting information on the frequency and use of articles in English (that is, *the, a, an*), requires a much smaller corpus, as these words are extremely common in any text type. The need for larger corpora is related to the ability to generalize our findings. For example, if we were to use a *Friends*-corpus containing only a few episodes of the show, we would not be able to generalize our findings to 'the language of the sitcom *Friends*'. Instead, the findings would be restricted to those few episodes, which might or might not be representative of the language used in *Friends* in general.

Characteristics of Corpus-Based Analysis

Douglas Biber, Susan Conrad, and Randi Reppen (1998) explain that corpus-based analysis is empirical, uses a principled collection of natural texts, makes extensive use of computers, and combines quantitative and qualitative techniques. In other words, the purpose of corpus-based analysis is to investigate how *real language* is used in different text types. Examples of text types are: face-to-face conversation, general fiction, academic language, product manuals, advertisements, or television shows. With spoken texts, transcripts are used as the basis for analysis. Whatever the text type, the analysis is empirical, that is, the findings are based on hard data and not on one's own intuition.

In order to make sense, the data (the corpus of texts) needs to be principled, or guided by rules of practice. For example, to investigate the language of news editorials in American national newspapers, we should not include in our corpus British newspapers or even local American newspapers. Corpus-based analysis relies not only on quantitative analysis, or computer-generated frequency counts of words, phrases, or grammatical features, but also on qualitative analysis, or more in-depth investigations of specific instances. Initial frequency counts may lead to the investigation of particular features of the data in a more in-depth fashion by means of reading it closely with the aim of interpreting it functionally. For example, as will be shown in the section "Corpus Tools in the Analysis of Discourse" below, the high frequency and co-occurrence of certain linguistic features led to the conclusion that the dialogues in the *Friends*-corpus are emotionally loaded.

Tagged Corpora

A 'tagged corpus' is one that has been annotated for grammatical, semantic, or phonological features. For illustrative purposes, this chapter will focus on grammatically and semantically tagged corpora. Let's consider an example from the *Friends* episode "The One After Ross Says Rachel,"[1] in which Ross, at his second wedding, called his fiancée by the wrong name. In all examples, transcripts come from the author's previous work (Quaglio 2009).

Example 1:

MINISTER: You may kiss the bride.
MRS. GELLER: This is worse than when he married the lesbian.

If the dialogue lines from *Friends* in example 1, above, were to be manually tagged for parts of speech (nouns, pronouns, adjectives, verbs, adverbs, prepositions, and so forth), we would place 'tags' (or labels) after each word based on context. For example, NN1 could stand for singular nouns, JJ could stand for adjectives. It is not hard to imagine how time-consuming it would be to do this for a whole page of text, not to mention a million-word corpus. That would obviously be unmanageable. Thanks to the advances in computer science, we now have programs called 'taggers',

1. Written by Seth Kurland.

Table 13.1 **POS-tagged and semantically tagged utterance (*WMatrix*)**

Word	*POS*	*Sem. Field*	*Word*	*POS*	*Sem. Field*
You	PPY	Z8mf	worse	JJR	A5.1
may	VM	A7+	than	CSN	Z5
kiss	VVI	S3.2	when	CS	Z5
the	AT	Z5	he	PPHS1	Z8m
bride	NN1	S4f	married	VVD	S4 A2.2
This	DD1	Z8 M6 Z5	the	AT	Z5
is	VBZ	A3+ Z5	lesbian	NN1	S3.2/S2.1f

which, by means of a complex system of probability calculations, can perform this task automatically with a high degree of accuracy. The Biber Tagger, developed by Douglas Biber from Northern Arizona University, has been independently tested and found to be more than 95 percent accurate depending on the text type. With more formal text types, such as academic writing, the accuracy rate of taggers can reach 97 percent. With texts such as natural conversation, the accuracy rate is a little lower, as natural dialogues tend to be full of false starts, repetition, and interruptions. Table 13.1 shows the results of the tagging for POS (parts of speech) and semantic fields, using Wmatrix,[2] a software tool for corpus analysis and comparison (Rayson 2009). For example, it shows that *bride* was labeled as a 'singular noun' (NN1) for part of speech and as 'kin' (feminine) for semantic field (S4f); *married* was tagged as 'past tense of lexical verb' (VVD) and as 'kin' and/or 'affect cause/connected' as a semantic field. Appendices A and B provide the description of all of the parts of speech and semantic fields WMatrix is capable of tagging.

Concordancing Methodology and Corpus Linguistic Concepts

Now that we know what a corpus is, how to collect one, and that corpora can be untagged (without any additional annotation, just plain text) or

2. Information on Wmatrix can be found at http://ucrel.lancs.ac.uk/wmatrix/. Free tagging is available for texts up to 100,000 words at http://ucrel.lancs.ac.uk/claws/trial.html (POS) and http://ucrel.lancs.ac.uk/usas/tagger.html (Semantic).

tagged (for example, with grammatical annotation), the question is: How can such collections of texts be used to carry out linguistic analyses? One of the most important tools used in corpus linguistics is a software program called a 'concordancer'. The following sections will focus on how this software program is used to conduct analyses in untagged and tagged corpora. The findings of such analyses can be of interest to language teachers, language learners, those seeking to understand the language of particular disciplines (such as history, biology, mathematics) or text types (for example, advertisements, product manuals, letters of recommendation, television shows), or anyone who wants to investigate language use in general.

In this chapter, an excellent free concordancer, called AntConc, which was developed by Laurence Anthony (2007), will be used.[3] As the features of this concordancer (namely, what it can do and the information it provides) are explored, some important corpus linguistic concepts, such as 'frequency lists', 'type-token ratios', 'collocations', and 'lexical bundles' will be presented, explained, and illustrated.

Frequency Lists

Once the corpus of the text type the researcher wants to investigate has been collected and *AntConc* has been installed on the computer, the first step in compiling a frequency list is to load the corpus into the program. The concordancer will automatically count all of the words and will output a list of words with their rank and frequency. Figure 13.1 shows a snapshot of AntConc displaying such a frequency list for *Friends*, which indicates that the first-person pronoun *I* and second-person pronoun *you* are the most frequent words in the series dialogue, with 34,116 and 28,087 occurrences, respectively.

Notice that the box for "Treat all data as lowercase" is checked. This way, the same word written in uppercase and lowercase is not counted as two different words (for example, *Guess* and *guess*). After the names of the

3. *AntConc* can be downloaded at http://www.laurenceanthony.net/antconc_index.html. PC, Mac, and Linux versions are available.

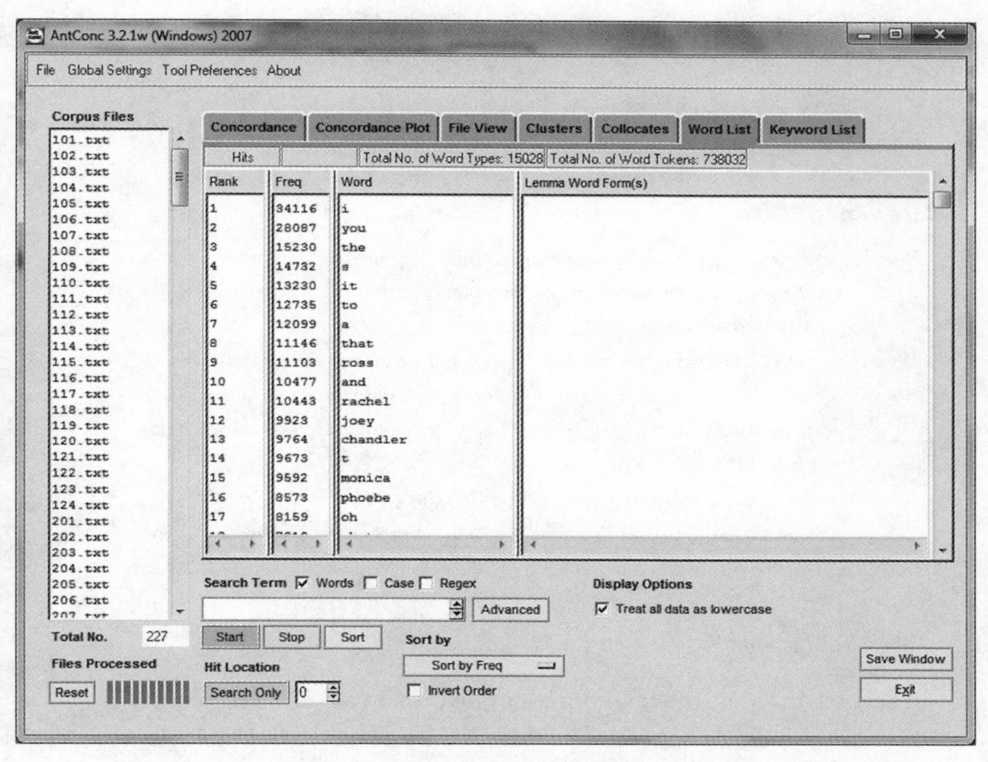

Figure 13.1. *Friends*-corpus: AntConc frequency list (Word List tab).

show's characters (Rachel, Joey, Chandler, and so on) are discarded, the following are the top twenty words in *Friends*, shown in table 13.2.

A simple analysis of the top twenty words in the *Friends*-corpus can provide us with interesting information. Corpus-based research has shown that personal pronouns *I*, *you*, *me*, and *it*, the demonstrative pronouns *this* and *that*, *be* as main verb, contractions in general, and general emphatics, such as *so* or *just*, are associated with interactive discourse and informality. High frequencies of the discourse marker *oh* and the general emphatic *just* are two of the linguistic features that have been associated with emotional language. Even though this is just an initial analysis based on the frequency of merely a few words, some insight into the characteristics of the language of *Friends* can be gained.

Table 13.2 **Top twenty words in the *Friends*-corpus**

I	to[2]	oh	we
you	a	what	m[5]
the	that[3]	know	this
s[1]	and	no	me
it	t[4]	is	just

[1] "s" = *'s*, mostly contraction of third-person singular pronoun and verb *be* (e.g., *he's*); contraction of third-person pronouns and auxiliary *has* (present perfect, e.g., she*'s* been) or genitive (e.g., Monica*'s* orders).

[2] to = verb infinitive marker (as in *to* go); or preposition (e.g., *to* me).

[3] that = demonstrative determiner (e.g., *that* guy) or pronoun (e.g., *that*'s right); relative pronoun (e.g., the girl *that* I'm seeing); or verb complementizer (e.g., I think *that* a person should...).

[4] t = cases of negative contractions (e.g., *can't, don't, isn't*).

[5] m = contraction of first-person personal pronoun *I* and *am* (e.g., *I'm*).

Types, Tokens, and Type-Token Ratio

In corpus analysis, the total number of words in a corpus is referred to as the total number of 'tokens'. The *Friends*-corpus has 738,032 tokens, as figure 13.1 shows. The number of 'types' refers to uniqueness of occurrence of a word (not its overall frequency) and is thus counted as one only the first time it appears in the corpus, regardless of its frequency. Let's explore the difference between these two concepts by considering another example from the series. In example 2, from the episode "The One Where Ross Finds Out,"[4] Rachel is talking to Ross, trying to remember her drunken actions from the night before.

Example 2:

RACHEL: I feel like I had a dream about you last night, but I don't remember.

In this example, there are fifteen tokens (counting the contraction of do + not as one word), but only thirteen types. The personal pronoun *I*

4. Written by Michael Burkow.

occurs three times and thus counts as three tokens and one type. In other words, there are thirteen original words (types) and fifteen total words (tokens).

The type-token ratio is a measure of vocabulary variation. The more unique (that is, not repeated) the vocabulary, the more variety a text displays. Even writers who have never heard of type-token ratios show awareness of this concept every time they think something along the lines of "I used this word five times already; I need to use a synonym instead." The attempt not to be overly repetitive indicates a desire for the type-token ratio to be as close as possible to 100 percent.

The type-token ratio is calculated by dividing the total number of types by the number of tokens and multiplying the result by 100 to indicate percentage. In the hypothetical (if not impossible) example of a 120-word paragraph in which no word is repeated, the number of tokens would be 120 and the number of types would also be 120. The type-token ratio would then be 120/120 x 100 = 100%. Therefore, the less a word is repeated, the closer to 100 percent variety the text will display. Research has shown that higher percentages of type-token ratio (that is, higher variety) are associated with informational discourse (for example, academic writing). The more interactive or conversational the text type is, the lower the type-token percentage (that is, the lower the degree of variety).

Large Corpora and the 'Artificial' Type-Token Ratio

The type-token ratio becomes less accurate with large corpora. The number of types does not increase proportionally to the number of tokens. Just to mention one example, the presence of articles (*a*, *an*, *the*) is ubiquitous in any corpus. Their occurrences will keep being added to the total number of tokens but not to the number of types, as they have already been counted. As such, in the type-token ratio calculation, the denominator (number by which the number of types is divided) will increase at a much higher rate than the nominator (number that is being divided). As a result, even though samples of the same text type are being added to the corpus, the degree of variation will be artificially reduced proportionally to the increase of the corpus size. For example, if a sub-corpus of a particular text type containing one hundred thousand words shows a type-token ratio of 65 percent, the same corpus of one million words will display less variety, which is just not true.

To solve this problem, researchers often write simple computer programs that calculate the type-token ratio of every *n* words (for example, every one thousand words), and then calculate the average of all of these results to obtain a more precise ratio. For example, when the overall type-token ratio of *Friends* seasons 1 through 4 is calculated (9,800 types and 295,658 tokens), the result is a meager 3 percent. When the same ratio is calculated every 1,000 words, the result is 48 percent, which is a much more accurate degree of vocabulary variety.

Word and Phrase Searches

This section focuses on how searches for words are done with a concordancer. The word we search for is referred to as a KWIC (key word in context). This section will also show how these searches can reveal specific ways in which certain words 'behave' and how they can be indicators of specific discourse characteristics. The different meanings of a word in context, collocations, lexical bundles, and grammatical patterns are topics that will be addressed as well.

Individual Words: Discovering Their Meanings. A search for *totally* in the *Friends*-corpus will yield 271 instances of the word. As an adverbial intensifier, *totally* is one of the features associated with emotional language in *Friends*. In its most common use, *totally* modifies an adjective and its meaning is interchangeable with *completely*, expressing a sense of completeness or totality. We can find this use of totally in example 3, from the episode "The One Where Heckles Dies."[5] In this example, Monica is comforting Chandler, who has concluded that he is no different than the guys his female friends complain about.

Example 3:

MONICA: Wait a minute, wait a minute. Yes, he is. You are *totally* different.

In example 4, however, *totally* is not interchangeable with *completely*; it has the meaning of *for sure* or *definitely*. Here, Chandler is working up the

5. Written by Michael Curtis and Gregory S. Malins.

nerve to ask someone out on a date in the episode "The One Where the Stripper Cries."[6]

Example 4:

CHANDLER: I know it. You know, I'm *totally* gonna ask her out.

Finally, in example 5, *totally* is not modifying a verb or an adjective; it is part of a non-clausal unit. In this scene, from "The One with Ross's Denial,"[7] Monica and Chandler are discussing how best to use the extra room in their apartment. Monica's use of *totally* expresses emphatic agreement.

Example 5:

CHANDLER: That's a great idea! We can easily think of a way for us both to enjoy the room.
MONICA: *Totally*!

The search for the word *totally* is an example of how quantitative and qualitative analyses are combined. The high frequency of *totally* encouraged a closer examination of all of its instances. The result was a functional interpretation of the word, which, in this particular case, revealed three different meanings and uses.

Collocations. Very often, when non-native English speakers use a combination of words that is understandable but that does not exactly sound right, it may be because those words are not collocations; in other words, those words do not tend to co-occur. Biber, Conrad, and Reppen (1998) analyzed the use of *small* versus *little*, which are often defined as synonyms in dictionaries. The analysis showed that *small* tends to co-occur with nouns indicating quantities, amounts, and proportions. For this reason, the phrase *small amount* sounds right and familiar, while *little amount* does not.

Biber, Conrad, and Leech (2002) define collocation as "the relationship between two or more independent words which commonly appear

6. Written by Marta Kauffman and David Crane.

7. Written by Seth Kurland.

together (or co-occur)" (18). An interesting way of finding potential collocations using a concordancer is to search for frequent words and then examine the words that follow or precede them. A word that follows the searched term with a high frequency is called its *right collocate*; a word that precedes it with a high frequency is called its *left collocate*. Very often, collocations involve the co-occurrence of nouns, adjectives, verbs, and adverbs. In Biber and colleagues' example above, the adjective *small* and the noun *amount* are collocates; *small* is the left collocate of *amount*.

A very interesting feature that concordancers offer is *sorting*. Once a search is done, it is possible to alphabetically sort the words that follow or precede the KWIC within a window established by the user (for instance, first or second or third word to the right or to the left). This way, the invisible becomes visible. Figure 13.2 shows the results of a search for the adjective *great* in *Friends*, with the words that precede it alphabetically sorted. Each of the lines in which *great* appears is called a concordance line. The adjective *great* is relatively frequent in *Friends*; it occurs sixty-five times in the corpus. It often co-occurs with the adverbial intensifier *really*. We can thus say that the phrase *really great* is a collocation. If a non-native speaker of English says "completely great," the connotation may be understood but the phrase will sound odd because *completely great* is not a collocation.

This 'visual' way of finding collocations is referred to as "collocation-via-concordance" by Tony McEnery and Andrew Hardie (2012). A more complex way of finding collocations, referred to as "collocation-via-significance" by the same authors, is based on statistical measures. AntConc has two available measures: MI (Mutual Information) and the t-score. For a discussion and interpretation of these statistical measures in the analysis of collocations, see McEnery and Hardie (2012) and Cheng (2012).

Lexical Bundles. Biber, Conrad, and Leech (2002) refer to lexical bundles as the building blocks of discourse. These frequently occurring sequences of three or more words are, in a sense, 'extended collocations'. Researchers often prefer to focus on four-word bundles because three-word bundles are often contained in four-word bundles. Examples of frequent lexical bundles in conversation are *I don't know what, are you going to, I don't know*

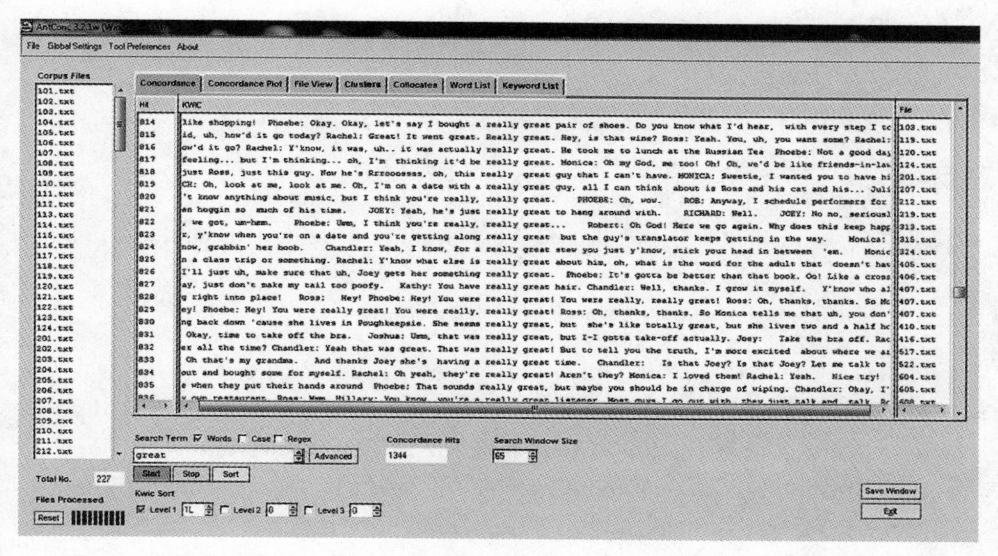

Figure 13.2. Search for *great* in *Friends*-corpus (the words to its left are sorted alphabetically).

if, and *you want me to.* These formulaic expressions are also referred to as clusters or n-grams.

AntConc has a feature called *clusters,* which enables the user to determine the size and minimum frequency of the bundle. Some of the most frequent four-word bundles that AntConc revealed in the *Friends*-corpus are: *I don't want to, I don't know what, I can't believe you, you don't have to, I can't believe this, I don't think so,* and *what are you doing.* Notice that all of these bundles have first- or second-person pronouns, which are features associated with interactive discourse. The following dialogue extract from the episode "The One with the Birth Mother"[8] has three of these bundles. In this scene, Monica and Chandler have met Erica, who is seeking adoptive parents for her unborn baby. Erica, however, has received incorrect information about Monica and Chandler, neither of whom immediately pointed this out, because the false information painted them in a better light.

8. Written by Seth Kurland.

Example 6:

ERICA: *I can't believe this.*

MONICA: But we were hoping that since we told you the truth that you still might consider . . .

ERICA: Giving you my baby? You think I'd give you my child after this?

MONICA: Well, *you don't have to* decide right now, but if you could just look at our file . . .

ERICA: *I don't want to* look at your file! This is over.

Along with other data, the frequency of lexical bundles can be used to analyze the discourse characteristics of a particular corpus or compare different corpora. For example, Monika Bednarek (2011a) included such clusters in her analysis of the series *Gilmore Girls*. Using key words and trigrams (three-word bundles), the author then extended the scope of her analysis to seven fictional series, concluding that "the expression of emotion is a key defining feature of the language of television, cutting across individual series and different televisual genres" (Bednarek 2012, 35).

The Grammar of a Word: Discovering Grammatical Patterns. A search for the verb *agree* (including *agrees*, *agreed*) in the *Friends*-corpus yielded forty-four hits. Once the resulting concordance lines are alphabetically sorted according to the first word to the right of the verb, the grammatical patterns in which the verb *agree* can occur becomes clearly visible. The following is a selection of concordance lines, appearing as they do in the AntConc concordancing tool (that is, in truncated form) but with repeated patterns removed.

1. . . . and Rachel: Oh yeah, I totally *agree.* Monica: I think he deserves a Nobel Prize.
2. . . . was somebody else so she would *agree to work* with you, so 'cause you figure
3. . . . a minute, all jokes aside? I didn't *agree to* that! Monica: Do you really see this
4. . . . system. I mean, before, I didn't *agree with* you, but at least I respected you.
5. . . . Julia? Carol: Julia . . . Susan: We *agreed on* Minnie. Ross: It's funny,
6. . . . I gonna do, I mean we-we both *agreed that* it was gonna be a two-week thing

This simple snapshot of the verb *agree* shows that it can be used intransitively (that is, with no immediate object) as in line 1. Line 2 shows the verb + infinitive marker + verb pattern. Lines 3, 4, and 5 show that it can be used with three different prepositions in specific semantic environments. Notice that the prepositions are not interchangeable. One *agrees with* a person, *to* something, and *on* a topic (in this case, the name of a baby). The last line shows that *agree* can also be followed by a *that*-complement clause.

Using Grammatically Tagged Corpora

As described in the section "Tagged Corpora" above, corpora can be untagged (just text without any type of annotation) or tagged (for example, with grammatical or semantic annotations). This section focuses on the kind of data that can be automatically generated by a concordancer with a corpus that has been annotated for parts of speech (POS).

The *Friends*-corpus was tagged for parts of speech using WMatrix. Appendix A shows all of the POS that WMatrix is capable of tagging. Instead of searching for words or phrases, we can search for a specific part of speech (such as noun, adjective). For example, a search for *JJ* (the general adjective tag in WMatrix) will output all of the words that have been tagged as general adjectives in context (that is, each in its respective concordance line). With this procedure, the total frequencies of nouns, adjectives, lexical verbs, and so on can be determined, which would be impossible to do with an untagged corpus. In the *Friends*-corpus, the top ten adjectives are: *good, sorry, great, big, little, fine, right, sure, okay*, and *new.*

It is also possible to search for a combination of tags or a combination of words and tags. For example, a search for the adjective tag followed by the noun tag will output adjectives in attributive position (that is, adjectives that precede nouns). A search for a particular adjective (for example, *great*) followed by the noun tag will reveal all of the instances in which *great* is used in attribute position, as in example 7. This scene is from "The One Where Ross Moves In,"[9] and features Monica making small talk to a fellow party guest.

9. Written by Perry Rein and Gigi McCreery.

Example 7:

MONICA: Oh, it's a *great* party! *Great* food. Y'know, most parties it's all chips and salsa, chips and salsa.

In other instances, as in example 8, the adjective *great* appears in predicative position. In the scene depicted here, from "The One with the Boob Job,"[10] Ross is talking to Phoebe, who is considering moving in with her boyfriend.

Example 8:

ROSS: But come on! I mean living together will be *great*! I mean you guys have so much fun . . . and you love Mike.

Using Semantically Tagged Corpora

WMatrix also tags corpora for semantic fields. Appendix B lists all of the semantic fields WMatrix is capable of tagging. This software program tags words with the most likely semantic field to which they belong. To explore semantic tagging, let's return to the dialog presented in example 1:

Example 1:

MINISTER: You may *kiss* the bride.

MRS. GELLER: This is *worse* than when he *married* the lesbian.

In this dialogue extract, the word *kiss* was tagged as S3.2, which corresponds to the field *Relationship: Intimate/sexual*; the tag A5.1, *Evaluation: Good/bad*, was assigned to the word *worse*, and *married* was tagged as *kin* and/or *affect cause/connected*, tag S4 A2.2. A corpus that is semantically tagged in this way can reveal interesting information about the nature of the data. For example, a frequency list of semantic fields can be generated. The most frequent fields will point to possible topics, themes, and even attitudes commonly found in the corpus. Some of the most frequent fields in *Friends* are listed below. Each field is followed by examples of words that have been tagged as belonging to that field.

10. Written by Mark Kunerth.

- A5.1+Evaluation: Good/bad (e.g., *bad, best, fine, good, great, wonderful*)
- M6Location and direction (e.g., *anywhere, around, here, there*)
- M1Moving, coming, and going (e.g., *chase, come, go, leave, move*)
- A13.3Degree: Boosters (e.g., *really, very, so, damn*)
- A14Exclusivizers/particularizers (e.g., *alone, especially, just, only*)
- X2.1 Thought, belief (e.g., *believe, consider, feel, feelings, guess, think, wonder*)
- Q2.2 Speech acts (e.g., *admit, advice, answer, apologize, protest*)
- B1 Anatomy and physiology (e.g., *arm, ass, beard, butt, chest, head, pregnant, pee*)
- F1Food (*breakfast, cheese, cook, eat, feed, hungry, starving*)
- S4Kin (e.g., *divorce, marriage, married, relatives, wedding, ex-wife*)
- X3.4Sensory: sight (e.g., *blind, eye, look, see, stare, watch*)

Not surprisingly, aspects of the nature of the *Friends*-corpus can be gleaned from the list of semantic fields above. *Friends* is a show that involves friendship and relationships (kin); the casual dialogues that characterize the show express high emotional content (degree: boosters and exclusivizer/particularizers), attitudes (evaluation: good/bad), and opinions (thought, belief).

Also useful in understanding the nature of a series is the possibility of searching for a particular semantic field using a concordancer. The output will be all of the words that have been tagged as part of that field in context. For example, a search for the field *E* (Emotional Actions, States, and Processes) in *Friends* has generated among other words the ones in table 13.3. These words can then be grouped as nouns, adjectives, adverbs, and so forth.

Comparing Different Corpora

In addition to the analysis of individual corpora, it is also possible to make comparisons across corpora. Frequencies of individual features, such as nouns, adjectives, verbs, and adverbs, can be compared. The issue that researchers often face is the difference in the size of different corpora. This section will explain how this problem can be solved.

Norming of Counts. Suppose that it has been found that a particular corpus (corpus A) has 8,532 adjectives and another (corpus B) has 5,763

Table 13.3 **Some of the words that have received the tag *E* (Emotional Actions, States, and Processes)**

abrasive	afraid	amusing	angry	animal	annoying
appreciate	beating	bothering	brave	bumming	bums
calm	care	celebrate	clowns	crazy	creeps
creepy	cried	depressed	ecstasy	embarrassment	emotion
Emotional	emotions	enjoy	favorite	feel	fool
freak	fun	funny	glad	good	happiness
Happy	hate	horror	jealous	joke	joy
joyous	kick	knock	laugh	laugh	laughing
laughing	laughing	like	liked	live	love
mad	Merry	messing	party	please	pleasure
pleasure	pleasure	proud	punching	relaxes	relaxing
rest	sad	satisfied	scare	scary	shock
shy	slap	slap	smile	smiling	smiling
suffered	teasing	tenderness	tormenting	trouble	upset

adjectives. Can we say that corpus A has a higher frequency of adjectives than corpus B? The answer depends on the size of the two corpora. In this hypothetical example, let's assume that corpus A has 1,300,000 words, and corpus B has 850,000 words. In order to compare the frequency of features between these two corpora, the counts need to be normed (or normalized) to a specific numerical basis first. Corpus-based studies often report the counts of features normed to a basis of one million words. This allows for comparisons with other studies, regardless of the size of the corpora.

The norming process is very simple, and uses the following formula: the number of instances of a feature divided by the total number of words in the corpus multiplied by a numerical basis. In our hypothetical example, we will norm the raw counts of adjectives to a basis of one million words. The result will be expressed in frequency per million words. These figures are referred to as 'normed counts' (as opposed to raw counts).

- Corpus A: (8,532 / 1,300,000) x 1,000,000 = 6,563 adjectives per million words
- Corpus B: (5,763 / 850,000) x 1,000,000 = 6,780 adjectives per million words

The normed counts of adjectives show that, in fact, Corpus B has a slightly higher frequency of adjectives, contrary to what the comparison initially suggested. The assumption is that if the corpus is representative of its text type, the addition of more texts to it will not alter its linguistic characteristics.

The same procedure is used to compare particular words in two or more corpora. For example, the adjective *cool,* the vocative or noun *dude,* the adverb *totally* (see previous analysis), and the phrasal verb *hang out* are associated with informal language, so it would be interesting to see if they are represented in the spoken language of television sitcoms. We can compare the frequency of these four items in the *Friends*-corpus with another corpus, such as one compiled from the dialogues of *How I Met Your Mother,* another American sitcom about single, white males and females in their twenties living in New York City (see chapter 7). In order to perform the comparison, we need the raw counts of these words in both corpora, and we need to know the size of each corpus. The ten-season *Friends*-corpus has a total of 738,032 words; a sub-corpus (seasons 2–6) of *How I Met Your Mother* totals 328,103 words. Table 13.4 shows that *cool, dude, totally,* and *hang out* are all more frequent in *How I Met Your Mother. Dude,* for example, is used more than three times as much, occurring 679 times per million words in *How I Met Your Mother* and 200 times per million words in *Friends.* This initial quantitative analysis may encourage the researcher to further investigate the contexts of each of these words. Doing so may reveal, as it did earlier with the qualitative analysis of *totally,* that each of the words has different meanings and/or functions in different contexts.

Keyness: Finding Significant Differences between Corpora. In simple terms, when the difference between two numbers (for example, numbers of adjectives in two different corpora) is said to be statistically significant, it means that such a difference is not due to chance. The results of statistical measures are expressed in critical values, which indicate the degree of confidence we can have that the difference is not due to chance. For example, when using log-likelihood statistics (see below), a critical value of 3.84 indicates a degree of confidence of 95 percent; 99 percent of confidence is indicated by a critical value of 6.63; 99.9 percent and 99.99 percent of confidence are expressed by values of 10.83 and 15.1 respectively. The

Table 13.4 **Frequency of *Cool, Dude, Hang out,* and *Totally* in *Friends* vs. *How I Met Your Mother***

	Friends		*How I Met Your Mother*	
Word	**Raw Counts**	**Normed Counts**[1]	**Raw Counts**	**Normed Counts**[1]
Cool	245	**331**	143	**435**
Dude	148	**200**	223	**679**
Totally	271	**367**	158	**481**
Hang out (including inflections)	92	**124**	52	**158**

[1] Counts were normed to a basis of one million words.

higher the critical value, the more confident we can be that the result is not due to chance.

When the difference between the frequencies of a particular word in two different corpora (taking into account the size of the two corpora) is statistically significant, this word is referred to as a keyword. The section "Frequency Lists" above showed that concordancers can generate frequency lists using a corpus. Two different corpora can be loaded into a concordancer, and a keyword list can be generated. This list will show the words that are significantly more frequent in one of the corpora from a statistical point of view. This measure of comparison is called 'keyness'. As Paul Baker (2006, 125) explains, "[a] keyword list . . . gives a measure of *saliency*, whereas a simple word list only provides *frequency*." In other words, a keyword list shows what differentiates one corpus from the other, such as words that are significantly overused and underused in one corpus in relation to another. The analysis of such a list can point to themes or situations that are more common, or salient, in one of the corpora. Using the log-likelihood statistics, table 13.5 shows the top ten keywords (overused items) in the *Friends*-corpus in relation to the *How I Met Your Mother*-corpus, indicating their rank, frequency, and keyness. The higher the keyness value, the stronger the saliency of the word. As explained above, a value of 3.84 or higher is considered statistically significant.

Table 13.5 **Keywords in *Friends* vs. *How I Met Your Mother***

Friends				*How I Met Your Mother*			
Rank	**Frequency**	**Keyness**	**Keyword**	**Rank**	**Frequency**	**Keyness**	**Keyword**
1	8159	1014.013	**oh**	1	3429	311.692	**of**
2	4222	644.188	**hey**	2	8615	311.624	**the**
3	4843	630.425	**okay**	3	2866	293.902	**not**
4	5048	575.712	**yeah**	4	184	255.619	**bar**
5	2605	508.327	**uh**	5	149	242.993	**awesome**
6	7023	485.487	**know**	6	6696	202.172	**a**
7	9673	449.191	**t**[1]	7	752	180.721	**will**
8	4184	440.047	**well**	8	80	159.334	**bro**
9	2831	381.128	**gonna**	9	71	157.538	**architect**
10	1431	336.848	**hi**	10	113	156.849	**super**

[1] Denotes negative contractions (e.g., can't, doesn't, didn't).

Table 13.5 provides two types of information. The keywords in *Friends* are the words that are *overused* in *Friends* and *underused* in *How I Met Your Mother* and vice versa. Most of the words that are overused in *Friends* suggest a high frequency of greetings (*hey, hi*) and dialogue features (hesitator *uh,* discourse marker *well,* emotionally loaded interjection *oh,* reduced form *gonna*). The underused items (which are overused in *How I Met Your Mother*) are surprising. This keyword list has the preposition *of* and the articles *the* and *a,* which are features usually associated with written text types. In addition, a higher frequency of articles suggests a higher frequency of nouns, which is also typical of written texts, especially informational text types. The presence of *bar* refers to the place where the characters often meet to drink, and *architect* is the profession of one of the main characters. The presence of *awesome, bro,* and *super* may be related to terms that characterize the speech of individual characters; this is confirmed in chapter 7. Again, such frequency information may lead the researcher to carry out qualitative analyses using concordancing lines to further investigate the contexts in which these items occur. Examples 9 and 10 show instances of some of the overused words (marked in italics) in their context in *Friends*. In Example 9 ("The One in Barbados,

Part 1"[11]), the friends have traveled to Barbados, where Phoebe's former boyfriend, David, makes a surprise appearance to propose to her.

Example 9:

DAVID: Mike is your ex . . . *uh* . . . boyfriend!

PHOEBE: That's right! Oh, yeah . . . Well, I've totally forgotten about him!

In the next example, Phoebe makes what appears to be an innocent announcement about her immediate plans, when really she is trying to sneak a dog out in her bag ("The One Where Chandler Doesn't Like Dogs"[12]).

Example 10:

PHOEBE: *Hey* you guys, I'm *gonna* go out and take a walk.

ROSS: Phoebe, why is your bag moving?

PHOEBE: *Oh*, it's not!

It should be noted that a lack of consistency in the transcriptions of spoken data may interfere with the result of the analysis. For example, *gonna* may be recorded as *going to* by different transcribers (as noted in Bednarek 2011b, 191). When the analysis involves such items, an accuracy check (such as comparing the actual audio with the transcription) is necessary.

In addition to the analysis of keyword lists of words, an analysis of keyword lists of tags can be done. For example, using grammatically tagged corpora, a particular corpus can be compared with a corpus of general English. The overused grammatical features in this particular corpus will grammatically characterize it. This is a very useful tool in the grammatical analysis of any text type. An interesting exercise that can be done with the results of such an analysis is the creation of sample texts that are representative of the text type, which, ultimately, provide a 'grammatical snapshot' of the corpus.

11. Written by Shana Goldberg-Meehan and Scott Silveri.

12. Written by Patty Lin.

Corpus Tools in the Analysis of Discourse

This section presents a brief summary of a study based on frequencies of linguistic features and their functional interpretation with regard to the *Friends*-corpus. In Quaglio (2009), I compared the language of *Friends* with natural conversation, using the American English conversation subcorpus of the *Longman Grammar Corpus*. The first part of the study used multidimensional analysis (Biber 1988), which is a technique that allows researchers to find and interpret the co-occurrence of linguistic features in a particular corpus (see chapter 4 of Quaglio [2009] for an explanation of the procedure). Briefly, this first part of the analysis concluded that the language of *Friends* has the core linguistic characteristics found in natural conversation.

The second part of the study took a closer look at the grammatical features that have been associated with face-to-face conversation (more than one hundred features) and compared their frequency in *Friends* and in natural conversation using keyness analysis. After the keyness analysis was conducted, features that were significantly more frequent in either corpus were grouped together. Thereafter, a functional analysis was carried out, during which some discourse-related patterns emerged. In summary, the study revealed that the language of *Friends* is more emotional and informal than natural conversation. Natural conversation, on the other hand, has a much higher frequency of features associated with vague language (for example, hedges, such as *kind of* and *sort of* [see chapter 4]; vague coordination tags, such as *or something* and *and stuff*; discourse markers, such as *probably*; and modal verbs such as *might*).

To illustrate again how an initial frequency analysis can point to broader discourse characteristics, we will consider examples of some of the emotionally loaded features that were identified in the keyness analysis of *Friends*: adverbial intensifiers (such as *really*), emphatic *do*, and expletives (such as *bitch*). Example 11 comes from "The One with Phoebe's Rats,"[13] in

13. Written by Brian Buckner and Sebastian Jones.

which Rachel, after offering an apology for previous mistreatment toward a coworker, expresses how she feels about moving forward.

Example 11:

RACHEL: But you know what, hey, new day, new leaf. I am just really, really happy . . .

Illustrating the use of emphatic *do*, example 12 comes from the episode "The One with Phoebe's Dad,"[14] in which Ross encourages Rachel to list his unattractive qualities, to make up for Ross having made a similar list about Rachel. Rachel is at first reluctant to do so, but ultimately does as Ross suggests, easily providing a long list.

Example 12:

ROSS: See there, you uh, alright, ya, you did what I said.

RACHEL: Yeah, and you know what? You're right. I *do* feel better, thank you, Ross.

Finally, example 13 comes from the episode "The One with Rachel's Other Sister,"[15] in which Rachel's sister, Amy, comes to visit her. Amy's visit culminates in a fight after she makes disparaging comments about Ross and Rachel's apartment, and gets upset when she finds out she has not been chosen to care for their baby if something should happen to Ross and Rachel. To make matters worse, Amy discovers that Rachel has not been sharing her retail discount, which Amy thought was 30 percent but, as Rachel informs her, is actually 45 percent.

Example 13:

AMY: You *bitch*. You just think you're so perfect. With your new baby and your, your small apartment.

Discussion

Corpus linguistics can contribute much to our understanding of language use in general, and television language specifically. Because of the

14. Written by Jeff Astroff and Mike Sikowitz.

15. Written by Shana Goldberg-Meehan.

great amount of data targeted, corpus analyses can make salient features that we might otherwise not notice via incidental television viewing. This chapter showed us how to build a television series corpus and do searches using a concordancer. Through the use of concordance methodology, several concepts were examined: frequency lists, collocations, lexical bundles, and how to investigate the grammar of a particular word by analyzing its grammatical patterns. Tagged corpora can provide important information, such as frequency of specific grammatical or semantic features, which would be impossible to determine with a non-annotated corpus. In addition to investigating an individual corpus, this chapter even showed how to compare different corpora and determine significant differences between them through keyness analyses. Finally, it is important to point out that corpus-based analysis is not restricted to frequency. Functional analysis can be performed at word, phrase, and discourse levels.

At just over 700,000 words, the *Friends*-corpus includes all 236 episodes that comprise the series' ten seasons. The six lead actors appeared on every single one of these episodes, and thus the corpus not only represents rather equally the speech of each of their television personas, but is also a reliable representation of the series' characteristic language. The corpus analyses presented in this chapter were indeed able to reveal salient and noteworthy linguistic characteristics of *Friends*. While the *Friends*-corpus confirms what we would have suspected, that is, that the dialogue of *Friends* is both interactive and informal, it is important to point out that the corpus analyses have revealed the specific ways informality and interactivity were achieved. These ways may not be immediately identifiable by watching one or two episodes, or even by considering one or two seasons. However, because the *Friends*-corpus includes the dialogue from 236 episodes over a span of ten seasons, it is able to reveal the distinct patterns and characteristic aspects of language use that were presented in this chapter.

By way of concluding the volume, we can reflect on the fact that the methods and analyses presented here can be repeated using corpora from any of the featured television series. The amount of work required to compile a series corpus depends on the availability of digital transcripts.

Once a series corpus is compiled, however, the results can be used to learn about various aspects, such as a series' overall patterns of language use, the linguistic identity of specific characters, the evolution of a series' language use over time, or the difference in language use between various series, either of the same type (comparing sitcoms) or of different types (comparing sitcoms and dramas). This information raises our awareness not only about how language is used, but also about how people, such as television writers, think language is used. As such, corpus data would even be ideal for guiding television writing practices.

Suggestions for Further Viewing and Analysis

It is not necessary to compile a corpus of hundreds of thousands of words to uncover interesting patterns and phenomena in the language of television. Basic corpus exploration can require little more than accessing an online transcript and using the browser's search function. However, you are encouraged to try compiling a large corpus and using a variety of corpus tools to explore it, using the following suggestions to guide you.

1. The sitcom *Seinfeld* (see chapter 8) often features repetition in the dialogue, such that one word or phrase is repeatedly uttered by several characters, as in the following example from the episode "The Pitch."[16] Jerry and George are in their usual diner, making simple conversation.

GEORGE: Why don't they have salsa on the table?
JERRY: What do you need salsa for?
GEORGE: Salsa is now the number one condiment in America.
JERRY: You know why? Because people like to say "salsa." "Excuse me, do you have salsa?" "We need more salsa." "Where is the salsa? No salsa?"
GEORGE: You know it must be impossible for a Spanish person to order seltzer and not get salsa. *(Angry)* "I wanted seltzer, not salsa."
JERRY: "Don't you know the difference between seltzer and salsa? You have the seltzer after the salsa!"

(Transcript from www.seinfeldscripts.com; used by permission.)

16. Written by Larry David.

Should a *Seinfeld*-corpus be compiled, the word *salsa* (and perhaps even *seltzer*) might be identified as a frequently used word or even a keyword, even though it is not used frequently throughout the series, only in this one episode. Similar examples are the repetition of *merlot* ("The Yada Yada"[17]) and *coincidence* ("The Statue"[18]). Consider how a corpus study of television language may have to account for distribution of word frequencies across episodes and seasons.

2. Chapter 4 features an analysis of *Sex and the City*, a sitcom that features voice-over narration in every episode. The narrator is Carrie, a journalist who writes a newspaper column about sex. The narration is guided by Carrie's inquisitiveness, which she often expresses in terms of wondering, particularly in the phrase "I couldn't help but wonder . . .". A corpus analysis of this series would identify the phrase as a lexical bundle, but a concordance analysis would also neatly present the syntactic patterns of Carrie's wondering, showing, for example, whether she wonders if, why, how, what, and so forth. A similar pattern can be explored in *MacGyver* (1985–92) with the phrase "I knew that . . ." in which he introduces a summary of the circumstances surrounding the episode's featured problem.

3. Most television dramas follow a strict structure of four to five acts. Genre dramas such as medical series also tend to include profession-specific practices that are associated with particular language usage. For example, in a medical drama, a patient is usually introduced in every episode, the ailment is discussed, possible diagnoses are presented, and finally there is a resolution. A corpus study of such series as *St. Elsewhere* (1982–88), *Chicago Hope* (1994–2000), *ER* (1994–2009), and *House* (2004–12) can help reveal if certain words are associated with specific acts in the narrative structure and, if so, whether these associations apply across genre-specific series.

References

Anthony, Laurence. 2007. AntConc (Version 3.21w) [Computer software]. Tokyo, Japan: Waseda Univ. Available from http://www.laurenceanthony.net.

17. Written by Peter Mehlman and Jill Franklyn.

18. Written by Larry Charles.

Baker, Paul. 2006. *Using Corpora in Discourse Analysis*. London: Continuum.

Bednarek, Monika. 2011a. "The Language of Fictional Television: A Case Study of the 'Dramedy' *Gilmore Girls*." *English Text Construction* 4(1): 54–83.

———. 2011b. "The Stability of the Televisual Character: A Corpus Stylistic Case Study." In *Telecinematic Discourse: Approaches to the Language of Film and Television Series*, edited by Roberta Piazza, Monika Bednarek, and Fabio Rossi, 185–204. Amsterdam: John Benjamins.

———. 2012. "'Get Us the Hell Out': Key Words and Trigrams in Fictional Series." *International Journal of Corpus Linguistics* 17(1): 35–63.

Biber, Douglas. 1988. *Variation Across Speech and Writing*. Cambridge, UK: Cambridge Univ. Press.

Biber, Douglas, Susan Conrad, and Geoffrey Leech. 2002. *A Student Grammar of Spoken and Written English*. London: Longman.

Biber, Douglas, Susan Conrad, and Randi Reppen. 1998. *Corpus Linguistics: Investigating Language Structure and Use*. Cambridge, UK: Cambridge Univ. Press.

Bowker, Lynne, and Jennifer Pearson. 2002. *Working with Specialized Language: A Practical Guide to Using Corpora*. London: Routledge.

Cheng, Winnie. 2012. *Exploring Corpus Linguistics: Language in Action*. London: Routledge.

McEnery, Tony, and Andrew Hardie. 2012. *Corpus Linguistics*. Cambridge, UK: Cambridge Univ. Press.

Quaglio, Paulo. 2009. *Television Dialogue: The Sitcom* Friends *vs. Natural Conversation*. Amsterdam: John Benjamins.

Rayson, Paul. 2009. *Wmatrix: A Web-Based Corpus Processing Environment*. Lancaster, UK: Computing Department, Lancaster Univ. http://ucrel.lanc.ac.uk/wmatrix.

Rey, Jennifer M. 2001. "Changing Gender Roles in Popular Culture: Dialogue in *Star Trek* Episodes from 1966 to 1993." In *Variation in English: Multidimensional Studies*, edited by Susan Conrad and Douglas Biber, 138–55. London: Longman.

Tagliamonte, Sali, and Chris Roberts. 2005. "So Weird; So Cool; So Innovative: The Use of Intensifiers in the Television Series *Friends*." *American Speech* 80:280–300.

Appendixes |

Glossary |

Contributors |

Index |

APPENDIX A

WMatrix Grammatical Tags

APPGE	possessive determiner (e.g., my, your, our)
AT	article (e.g., the, no)
AT1	singular article (e.g., a, an, every)
BCL	before-clause marker (e.g., in order (that), in order (to))
CC	coordinating conjunction (e.g., and, or)
CCB	adversative coordinating conjunction (but)
CS	subordinating conjunction (e.g., if, because, unless, so, for)
CSA	as (as conjunction)
CSN	than (as conjunction)
CST	that (as conjunction)
CSW	whether (as conjunction)
DA	after-determiner or post-determiner capable of pronominal function (e.g., such, former, same)
DA1	singular after-determiner (e.g., little, much)
DA2	plural after-determiner (e.g., few, several, many)
DAR	comparative after-determiner (e.g., more, less, fewer)
DAT	superlative after-determiner (e.g., most, least, fewest)
DB	before determiner or pre-determiner capable of pronominal function (all, half)
DB2	plural before-determiner (both)
DD	determiner (capable of pronominal function) (e.g., any, some)
DD1	singular determiner (e.g., this, that, another)
DD2	plural determiner (these, those)
DDQ	wh-determiner (which, what)
DDQGE	wh-determiner, genitive (whose)
DDQV	wh-ever determiner, (whichever, whatever)
EX	existential there
FO	formula

FU	unclassified word
FW	foreign word
GE	Germanic genitive marker - (' or 's)
IF	for (as preposition)
II	general preposition
IO	of (as preposition)
IW	with, without (as prepositions)
JJ	general adjective
JJR	general comparative adjective (e.g., older, better, stronger)
JJT	general superlative adjective (e.g., oldest, best, strongest)
JK	catenative adjective (able in, be able to, willing in, be willing to)
MC	cardinal number, neutral for number (two, three . . .)
MC1	singular cardinal number (one)
MC2	plural cardinal number (e.g., sixes, sevens)
MCGE	genitive cardinal number, neutral for number (two's, 100's)
MCMC	hyphenated number (40-50, 1770-1827)
MD	ordinal number (e.g., first, second, next, last)
MF	fraction, neutral for number (e.g., quarters, two-thirds)
ND1	singular noun of direction (e.g., north, southeast)
NN	common noun, neutral for number (e.g., sheep, cod, headquarters)
NN1	singular common noun (e.g., book, girl)
NN2	plural common noun (e.g., books, girls)
NNA	following noun of title (e.g., M.A.)
NNB	preceding noun of title (e.g., Mr., Prof.)
NNL1	singular locative noun (e.g., Island, Street)
NNL2	plural locative noun (e.g., Islands, Streets)
NNO	numeral noun, neutral for number (e.g., dozen, hundred)
NNO2	numeral noun, plural (e.g., hundreds, thousands)
NNT1	temporal noun, singular (e.g., day, week, year)
NNT2	temporal noun, plural (e.g., days, weeks, years)
NNU	unit of measurement, neutral for number (e.g., in, cc)
NNU1	singular unit of measurement (e.g., inch, centimeter)
NNU2	plural unit of measurement (e.g., ins., feet)
NP	proper noun, neutral for number (e.g., IBM, Andes)
NP1	singular proper noun (e.g., London, Jane, Frederick)
NP2	plural proper noun (e.g., Browns, Reagans, Koreas)
NPD1	singular weekday noun (e.g., Sunday)

NPD2	plural weekday noun (e.g., Sundays)
NPM1	singular month noun (e.g., October)
NPM2	plural month noun (e.g., Octobers)
PN	indefinite pronoun, neutral for number (none)
PN1	indefinite pronoun, singular (e.g., anyone, everything, nobody, one)
PNQO	objective wh-pronoun (whom)
PNQS	subjective wh-pronoun (who)
PNQV	wh-ever pronoun (whoever)
PNX1	reflexive indefinite pronoun (oneself)
PPGE	nominal possessive personal pronoun (e.g., mine, yours)
PPH1	3rd person sing. neuter personal pronoun (it)
PPHO1	3rd person sing. objective personal pronoun (him, her)
PPHO2	3rd person plural objective personal pronoun (them)
PPHS1	3rd person sing. subjective personal pronoun (he, she)
PPHS2	3rd person plural subjective personal pronoun (they)
PPIO1	1st person sing. objective personal pronoun (me)
PPIO2	1st person plural objective personal pronoun (us)
PPIS1	1st person sing. subjective personal pronoun (I)
PPIS2	1st person plural subjective personal pronoun (we)
PPX1	singular reflexive personal pronoun (e.g., yourself, itself)
PPX2	plural reflexive personal pronoun (e.g., yourselves, themselves)
PPY	2nd person personal pronoun (you)
RA	adverb, after nominal head (e.g., else, galore)
REX	adverb introducing appositional constructions (namely, e.g.)
RG	degree adverb (very, so, too)
RGQ	wh- degree adverb (how)
RGQV	wh-ever degree adverb (however)
RGR	comparative degree adverb (more, less)
RGT	superlative degree adverb (most, least)
RL	locative adverb (e.g., alongside, forward)
RP	prep. adverb, particle (e.g., about, in)
RPK	prep. adv., catenative (about in be about to)
RR	general adverb
RRQ	wh- general adverb (where, when, why, how)
RRQV	wh-ever general adverb (wherever, whenever)
RRR	comparative general adverb (e.g., better, longer
RRT	superlative general adverb (e.g., best, longest)

RT	quasi-nominal adverb of time (e.g., now, tomorrow)
TO	infinitive marker (to)
UH	interjection (e.g., oh, yes, um)
VB0	be, base form (finite i.e., imperative, subjunctive)
VBDR	were
VBDZ	was
VBG	being
VBI	be, infinitive (To be or not . . . It will be . . .)
VBM	am
VBN	been
VBR	are
VBZ	is
VD0	do, base form (finite)
VDD	did
VDG	doing
VDI	do, infinitive (I may do . . . To do . . .)
VDN	done
VDZ	does
VH0	have, base form (finite)
VHD	had (past tense)
VHG	having
VHI	have, infinitive
VHN	had (past participle)
VHZ	has
VM	modal auxiliary (can, will, would, etc.)
VMK	modal catenative (ought, used)
VV0	base form of lexical verb (e.g., give, work)
VVD	past tense of lexical verb (e.g. gave, worked)
VVG	-ing participle of lexical verb (e.g., giving, working)
VVGK	-ing participle catenative (going in be going to)
VVI	infinitive (e.g. to give . . . It will work . . .)
VVN	past participle of lexical verb (e.g., given, worked)
VVNK	past participle catenative (e.g., bound in be bound to)
VVZ	-s form of lexical verb (e.g., gives, works)
XX	not, n't
ZZ1	singular letter of the alphabet (e.g., A, b)
ZZ2	plural letter of the alphabet (e.g., A's, b's)

APPENDIX B

WMatrix Semantic Tags

A. General and Abstract Terms

A1	General
A1.1.1	General action, making, etc.
A1.1.2	Damaging and destroying
A1.2	Suitability
A1.3	Caution
A1.4	Chance, luck
A1.5	Use
A1.5.1	Using
A1.5.2	Usefulness
A1.6	Physical/mental
A1.7	Constraint
A1.8	Inclusion/Exclusion
A1.9	Avoiding
A2	Affect
A2.1	Affect: Cause/Connected
A3	Being
A4	Classification
A4.1	Generally kinds, groups, examples
A4.2	Particular/general; detail
A5	Evaluation
A5.1	Evaluation: Good/bad
A5.2	Evaluation: True/false
A5.3	Evaluation: Accuracy
A5.4	Evaluation: Authenticity
A6	Comparing
A6.1	Comparing: Similar/different
A6.2	Comparing: Usual/unusual
A6.3	Comparing: Variety
A7	Definite (+ modals)
A8	Seem
A9	Getting and giving; possession
A10	Open/closed; Hiding/Hidden; Finding; Showing
A11	Importance
A11.1	Importance: Important
A11.2	Importance: Noticeability
A12	Easy/difficult
A13	Degree
A13.1	Degree: Non-specific
A13.2	Degree: Maximizers
A13.3	Degree: Boosters
A13.4	Degree: Approximators
A13.5	Degree: Compromisers
A13.6	Degree: Diminishers
A13.7	Degree: Minimizers
A14	Exclusivizers/particularizers
A15	Safety/Danger

B. The Body and the Individual

B1	Anatomy and physiology
B2	Health and disease

B3	Medicines and medical treatment
B4	Cleaning and personal care
B5	Clothes and personal belongings

C. Arts and Crafts

C1	Arts and crafts

E. Emotional Actions, States and Processes

E1	General
E2	Liking
E3	Calm/Violent/Angry
E4	Happy/sad
E4.1	Happy/sad: Happy
E4.2	Happy/sad: Contentment
E5	Fear/bravery/shock
E6	Worry, concern, confident

F. Food and Farming

F1	Food
F2	Drinks
F3	Cigarettes and drugs
F4	Farming & Horticulture

G. Government and the Public Domain

G1	Government, Politics, & elections
G1.1	Government, etc.
G1.2	Politics
G2	Crime, law and order
G2.1	Crime, law and order: Law & order
G2.2	General ethics
G3	Warfare, defense and the army, Weapons

H. Architecture, Buildings, Houses, and the Home

H1	Architecture
H2	Parts of buildings
H3	Areas around or near houses
H4	Residence
H5	Furniture and household fittings

I. Money and Commerce

I1	Money generally
I1.1	Money: Affluence
I1.2	Money: Debts
I1.3	Money: Price
I2	Business
I2.1	Business: Generally
I2.2	Business: Selling
I3	Work and employment
I3.1	Work and employment: Generally
I3.2	Work and employment: Professionalism
I4	Industry

K. Entertainment, Sports, and Games

K1	Entertainment generally
K2	Music and related activities
K3	Recorded sound, etc.
K4	Drama, the theater, & show business
K5	Sports and games generally
K5.1	Sports
K5.2	Games
K6	Children's games and toys

L. Life and Living Things

L1	Life and living things

L2 Living creatures generally
L3 Plants

M. Movement, Location, Travel, and Transport

M1 Moving, coming and going
M2 Putting, taking, pulling, pushing, transporting, etc.
M3 Movement/transportation: land
M4 Movement/transportation: water
M5 Movement/transportation: air
M6 Location and direction
M7 Places
M8 Remaining/stationary

N. Numbers and Measurement

N1 Numbers
N2 Mathematics
N3 Measurement
N3.1 Measurement: General
N3.2 Measurement: Size
N3.3 Measurement: Distance
N3.4 Measurement: Volume
N3.5 Measurement: Weight
N3.6 Measurement: Area
N3.7 Measurement: Length & height
N3.8 Measurement: Speed
N4 Linear order
N5 Quantities
N5.1 Entirety: maximum
N5.2 Exceeding: waste
N6 Frequency, etc.

O. Substances, Materials, Objects, and Equipment

O1 Substances and materials generally
O1.1 Substances and materials generally: Solid
O1.2 Substances and materials generally: Liquid
O1.3 Substances and materials generally: Gas
O2 Objects generally
O3 Electricity and electrical equipment
O4 Physical attributes
O4.1 General appearance and physical properties
O4.2 Judgment of appearance (pretty, etc.)
O4.3 Color and color patterns
O4.4 Shape
O4.5 Texture
O4.6 Temperature

P. Education

P1 Education in general

Q. Linguistic Actions, States, and Processes

Q1 Communication
Q1.1 Communication in general
Q1.2 Paper documents and writing
Q1.3 Telecommunications
Q2 Speech acts
Q2.1 Speech etc: Communicative
Q2.2 Speech acts
Q3 Language, speech, and grammar

Q4	The Media
Q4.1	The Media: Books
Q4.2	The Media: Newspapers, etc.
Q4.3	The Media: TV, Radio, & Cinema

S. Social Actions, States, and Processes

S1	Social actions, states, & processes
S1.1	Social actions, states, & processes
S1.1.1	General
S1.1.2	Reciprocity
S1.1.3	Participation
S1.1.4	Deserve, etc.
S1.2	Personality traits
S1.2.1	Approachability and Friendliness
S1.2.2	Avarice
S1.2.3	Egoism
S1.2.4	Politeness
S1.2.5	Toughness; strong/weak
S1.2.6	Sensible
S2	People
S2.1	People: Female
S2.2	People: Male
S3	Relationship
S3.1	Relationship: General
S3.2	Relationship: Intimate/ sexual
S4	Kin
S5	Groups and affiliation
S6	Obligation and necessity
S7	Power relationship
S7.1	Power, organizing
S7.2	Respect
S7.3	Competition
S7.4	Permission
S8	Helping/hindering
S9	Religion and the supernatural

T. Time

T1	Time
T1.1	Time: General
T1.1.1	Time: General: Past
T1.1.2	Time: General: Present; simultaneous
T1.1.3	Time: General: Future
T1.2	Time: Momentary
T1.3	Time: Period
T2	Time: Beginning and ending
T3	Time: Old, new, and young; age
T4	Time: Early/late

W. The World and Our Environment

W1	The universe
W2	Light
W3	Geographical terms
W4	Weather
W5	Green issues

X. Psychological Actions, States, and Processes

X1	General
X2	Mental actions and processes
X2.1	Thought, belief
X2.2	Knowledge
X2.3	Learn
X2.4	Investigate, examine, test, search
X2.5	Understand

X2.6	Expect
X3	Sensory
X3.1	Sensory: Taste
X3.2	Sensory: Sound
X3.3	Sensory: Touch
X3.4	Sensory: Sight
X3.5	Sensory: Smell
X4	Mental object
X5	Attention
X5.1	Attention
X5.2	Interest/boredom/excited/ energetic
X6	Deciding
X7	Wanting; planning; choosing
X8	Trying
X9	Ability
X9.1	Ability: Ability, intelligence
X9.2	Ability: Success and failure

Y. Science and Technology

Y1	Science and technology in general
Y2	Information technology and computing

Z. Names and Grammatical Words

Z0	Unmatched proper noun
Z1	Personal names
Z2	Geographical names
Z3	Other proper names
Z4	Discourse bin
Z5	Grammatical bin
Z6	Negative
Z7	If
Z8	Pronouns, etc.
Z9	Trash can
Z99	Unmatched

Glossary

ablaut: A vowel change in related word forms

accent: Distinct variations in pronunciation associated with a geographical region or social class

accommodation: Shifting or adjusting speaking style to accentuate social similarities or differences with regard to other interactional participants

acronym: The combination of the first letters of a string of words, pronounceable as a new word

adjacency pair: Pairs of related utterances, such as question-answer or greeting-greeting

affective filter: A barrier to the learning or acquisition processes owing to anxiety, lack of motivation, low self-confidence, or fear of failing

affixation: The process of attaching a morpheme to a root or stem

affricate: A consonant sound produced via complete closure followed by a fricative release

allomorph: Variant forms of morphemes that have the same function, but apply in different environments

allophone: One of two or more phonetic realizations of a phoneme

ambiguity: The availability of more than one meaning or interpretation of an utterance

approximant: Consonant sound produced with the least degree of airstream constriction; also called frictionless continuant

asymmetry: An inequality in gender-marked terms, such that there are noticeably more or fewer terms for one gender than the other

babbling: Short or even long strings of consonant-vowel combinations; **reduplicated babbling** is in the form of repeated combinations (such as [bababa]) while **variegated babbling** refers to nonrepeated and varied combinations (such as [dadi:dudi:])

back-channeling: The use of minimal responses, such as *mm-hmm* or *yeah*, to signal attention to the speaker

back-formation: The shortening of a word that results in a new meaning and a new part of speech

bidialectalism: The ability to speak two or more dialects of the same language

bilingual: Able to speak two languages

bilingualism: The state of having competence in two (or more) languages

blend: A new word resulting from combining parts of two words

borrowing: The use of a linguistic form from one language in another language

bound morpheme: A morpheme, such as a prefix or suffix, that must be attached to another morpheme or word

bystander: One who is present but excluded from the speech event and whose access to the occasion is recognized by the participants

child-directed speech: The language adults and even older children spontaneously adopt when speaking to infants, characterized by short, simple sentences uttered in a characteristic sing-song tone; also called **parentese** or **caregiver speech**

clipping: A shortened version of a longer word

closed word class: Functional word class that is closed to receiving new members

co-text: The textual cues surrounding an interaction

code-switching: The alternate use of two or more languages within one conversation

collocation: Words that tend to co-occur

communicative competence: A speaker's knowledge of syntactical, morphological, and phonological rules of a language, as well as the ability to use utterances appropriately and according to context

compound: A new lexeme formed by the combination of two, free lexical morphemes

concordancer: A software tool or program used to engage with and analyze corpora

consonant: A speech sound produced when air is obstructed before or while being released

constituent: Word or group of words that function together as a single unit in a sentence

constructivist approach: The idea that first-language learners construct knowledge about a language gradually, based on the language they are exposed to

context: The situation in which an interaction occurs

conversation analysis: An approach to language as a form of human social behavior that is essentially orderly

conversational implicature: An underlying message conveyed by the flouting of a maxim

conversion: The process of forming new words by assigning new parts of speech to existing words

cooperative principle: The overall tendency of interlocutors to make an effort to cooperate with each other when communicating

covert prestige: The prestige awarded a speaker who uses explicitly nonstandard or stigmatized forms

deficit theory: The theory that women's perceived social subordination to men is evident in their language use, which is similarly viewed as unequal, or deficient

derivational morpheme: Affixes that produce, or derive, new words

dialect: Language variety that can be identified by distinguishing features of pronunciation, grammar, and vocabulary

difference theory: The theory that proposes a different-but-equal perspective on language use, such that men and women constitute two different cultures, each with their own communicative styles, one neither inferior nor subordinate to the other

diphthong: A vowel sound whose quality changes within a syllable owing to a change of position of the articulators

direct speech act: A speech act in which the sentence meaning equals the utterance meaning

dominance theory: The theory that interaction participants co-construct a pattern of male dominance and female submission

empirical research: Studies based on data and not on intuition

ethnography of communication: The study of the use of language in particular social communities; also called **ethnography of speaking**

extension: The emergence of a new meaning when a word is used in new contexts

face: A speaker's self-image; **positive face** refers to the desire to be acknowledged, while **negative face** is the desire to be free from imposition

facework: Impression management

felicity conditions: Factors that guarantee the ultimate success of a speech act

flouting: Violating a maxim

folk linguistics: The beliefs, opinions, perceptions, and evaluations of language by non-linguists

footing: Different alignments that participants can have to the talk they are producing and receiving

foreign language: A language learned in one setting, but used in another

fossilization: The persistence of interlanguage forms, owing to incomplete L2 development

fragment: A part of a sentence separate from the main clause

free morpheme: A morpheme that can stand alone, such as a word

fricative: A consonant sound produced when two parts of the vocal apparatus are brought very close together, causing audible friction

functional category: A closed word-class category consisting of functional words

functional morpheme: A free morpheme such as an article, pronoun, or preposition

genderlect: The style of speech associated with women

grammar: Collection of rules or sentence patterns

grammatical competence: The ability of a speaker to unconsciously recognize and reproduce the grammatical rules and structure of a language, including its distinct phonological, morphological, and syntactic forms

grammaticalization: The process whereby a semantically blank word fulfills a grammatical or discourse function, no longer holding the semantic properties of the core definition

hegemonic discourse: The dominant, and often blindly accepted, way of thinking and talking about a subject

homonym: One word with different meanings

homophony: Words that have the same sounds but different spellings and meanings

hypocorism: A clipping in combination with an affixation of the suffix [-i], a diminutive morpheme commonly spelled as *-y* or *-ie*

idiolect: Speech habits particular to an individual

illocution: The intent of an utterance

indirect speech act: A speech act in which the sentence meaning does not equal the utterance meaning

inference: Interpretation beyond the literal meaning of an utterance

inflection: A word change or affixation indicating grammatical meaning or syntactic function

inflectional morpheme: A morpheme that only carries grammatical meaning and serves syntactic functions; all English inflectional morphemes are suffixes

initialism: The combination of first, or initial, letters to produce a word that must be pronounced as the string of letters

innateness hypothesis: The idea that everyone is born with some linguistic knowledge, making possible language acquisition

input: Every linguistic medium one is exposed to in the second or foreign language, whether oral, aural, written, or audiovisual

instrumental motivation: The desire to learn a language for utilitarian and practical reasons, such as to attain social or professional goals

intake: That which a learner or acquirer is able to comprehend from any given input

integrative motivation: The desire to learn another language so as to become a member of the L2 speaking community

interactionist theories: Theories based on language use in conversation or other interactional forms of communication

interlanguage: A variety of language that can include features of a speaker's L1, but most often reflects a developing, inaccurate approximation of the L2, characterized by innovation and overgeneralizations of its rules and conventions

intersectionality: That state of additional factors such as interlocutors' class, age, ethnicity, or even social positions and relationships interacting with their gender

isogloss: Geographic boundary of a dialectal feature

jargon: A specific lexicon associated with a particular profession or social group

keyword: A word whose different frequencies in two corpora are statistically significant

KWIC: Key word in context; refers to the search term of a corpus

L1: First, or native, language

L2: Second (or additional) language

language acquisition: The process of acquiring a language (even one's first or native language), without instructions or explicit teaching, usually by living in the second language environment or by exposure to spontaneous, natural communication

language learning: A conscious process and a direct result of teaching and deliberate study

lateral: A consonant sound produced via closure between the blade of the tongue and the alveolar ridge, such that the air escapes over the sides of the tongue

lexical ambiguity: Lexemes (or lexical words) sharing a common linguistic form but having distinct semantic content

lexical bundle: A frequently occurring sequence of three or more words, such that it constitutes an extended collocation; also known as **cluster** or **n-gram**

lexical category: An open word-class category consisting of content words
lexical morpheme: A free morpheme such as a noun, verb, or adverb
locution: The form of an utterance
long distance dependencies: Different words or phrases in a sentence that make sense together even if they do not appear right after each other
manner of articulation: The degree of air constriction in the production of a speech sound
markedness: The property of language use that stands out as different, unusual, or even deviant in comparison to more common or usual usage
maxim: A general truth; the Gricean maxims are often misinterpreted as rules
minimal pair: Two words of distinct meanings differing with regard to only one phonetic feature
monophthong: A vowel sound produced with articulators remaining in the same position
morpheme: The smallest meaningful unit of language
morphology: The study of words or morphemes
multidimensional analysis: A technique that allows researchers to find and interpret the co-occurrence of linguistic features in a particular corpus
multilingual: Able to speak three or more languages
nasal: A consonant sound produced with air flowing freely out through the nose
negative transfer: The production of inaccurate or nonstandard forms and structures owing to differences between the L1 and the L2; also known as interference
normalization: The re-expression of corpus frequencies (raw counts) according to a specific numerical basis (normed counts), to allow for inter-corpus comparison
open class of words: Lexical word classes that are open to receiving new members
output: Everything that is produced by a learner in the second or foreign language, i.e., the outcome of what has been learned
overextension: The use (or extension) of a known word to refer to something unknown, for example, a child's use of the word *dog* to signify unknown animals such as *goat* or *bear.*
overgeneralization: The application of rules or generalizations to words that are exceptions to the rule, for example, the application of the past tense inflection -ed to irregular verbs such as **goed* or **bleeded*
overhearer: One who is present but excluded from the speech event and whose access is not acknowledged

overt prestige: The positive prestige associated with the use of dialects that are established as being representative of the standard or most correct usages of the language

part of speech: Category of a word corresponding to its syntactic function

participation framework: An underlying system for analyzing interactional roles

perlocution: The effect of an utterance on the hearer

phoneme: A perceptual category of a speech sound

phonetics: The study of human speech sounds

phonology: The study of human language systems

phrase structure rules: Rules predicting which combinations of phrases would form grammatical sentences

place of articulation: The placement of the tongue in relation to the oral cavity, teeth, or lips in the production of a speech sound

polysemy: A single word with multiple meanings

positive transfer: The facilitation of L2-learning or acquisition owing to similarities between the L1 and the L2

prefix: A bound morpheme added to the beginning of a word

pronominal case marking error: The use of a personal pronoun to function in a way that does not correspond to its case, for example, **me speak English* or **I see she*

prototype: A typical member of a category, possessing all of the semantic features associated with the concept

qualitative research: Studies based on in-depth, detail-oriented investigations

quantitative research: Studies based on large amounts of data, the analysis of which, such as frequencies and statistics, provide generalizable results

ratified hearer: An interactional participant understood to be giving some attention to a speaker

regional variation: Differences in language use as a function of geographical influences

register: A variety of language associated with a particular purpose or social context

repair: A response to an indication that something disorderly has happened

schema: A cluster of properties that readers, listeners, and audiences already know about generic situations, entities, and events

second language acquisition: The process of learning a language in addition to one's first, or native, language; also refers to the study of this process

second language: A language learned and used in the context where it is naturally spoken

semantic bleaching: A shift to a meaning increasingly void of its original semantic content; also called **desemanticization**

semantic feature analysis: The definition of a set of necessary and sufficient conditions to determine membership in a category

semantic role: In a proposition or utterance, the relationship between a participant and the predicate

side sequence: An embedded adjacency pair

social constructivism: The theory that language usage is not so much an inherent function of gender as it is a social construction reflecting outside influences

social network: The system of connections within or the structure of a speech community

sociolinguistic competence: The ability to use the L2 in a way appropriate to the context and the circumstances of the interaction

sociolinguistics: The study of the relationship between language use and social factors

SPEAKING: A mnemonic device for differentiating contextual variables; stands for Setting, Participants, Ends, Act sequence, Key, Instrumentalities, Norms, Genres

speech act: An utterance designed to cause another to perform an action

speech community: A group of people who typically interact with each other through some common activity, often sharing specific forums for communicating with each other; also called **discourse community**

stance: Evaluative position of a speaker in relation to the interaction

Standard English: The variety of English widely considered as the most correct

stem (root) morpheme: The primary, base, or central lexical unit of a word

stop (plosive): A consonant sound produced via complete airstream obstruction, followed by release

strategic competence: The ability to adjust the use of verbal and nonverbal language when lacking the understanding of grammar or the knowledge of social and communicative norms, in order to compensate for communication problems or linguistic deficiencies

style-shifting: Blending or switching between features of formal and informal styles

style: The ways in which a speaker can vary an utterance in terms of formality

suffix: A bound morpheme added to the end of a word

tag question: An utterance-final question, such as *isn't it?*, asked in order to receive confirmation of a statement

tag: An annotation of a grammatical, semantic, or phonological feature

telegraphic speech: A stage in children's speech characterized by the use of content words, such as nouns, verbs, and adjectives

token: A distinct word contributing to the total word count of a corpus

transfer: The process of applying the L1 linguistic system to the L2

troubles talk: The sharing of problems, worries, or concerns

turn: The contribution of a single interaction participant

type-token ratio: A measure of vocabulary variation

type: The unique occurrence of a word, not its overall frequency; a corpus consists of generally more tokens than types, because only first occurrences of types are counted

universal Grammar: Grammatical structure that underlies all human languages

vernacular: A casual style of language that is distinguished from the standard

voicing: The engaging of vocal cords while producing a speech sound

vowel: A speech sound produced with no airstream obstruction

zero morpheme: An allomorph that produces no change in word form

Contributors

Jean Ann is a professor in the Linguistics and TESOL programs at the State University of New York at Oswego. Much of her work concerns sign languages of Deaf communities, and she is the author of *Frequency of Occurrence and Ease of Articulation in Sign Language Handshapes: The Taiwanese Example* (2006). Her other areas include immigrant languages and linguistics in schools.

Gülşat Aygen is a professor of linguistics at Northern Illinois University. Her areas of specialization include syntactic theory, morphology-syntax interface, and brain and language, as well as heritage languages, second language pedagogy, and sociolinguistics. Her most recent publications include *English Grammar: A Descriptive Linguistic Approach*, *Zazaki Grammar*, *Kurmancki Grammar*, and "The Languages of Kapalicarsi/Grand Bazaar."

Kristy Beers Fägersten is a professor of English linguistics at Södertörn University, Sweden. Her areas of specialization include sociolinguistics, discourse analysis, and conversation analysis, and her research has covered computer-mediated communication, language and the media, comic strip language, and native vs. non-native swearing. She is the author of *Who's Swearing Now? The Social Aspects of Conversational Swearing* (2012).

Matthias Eitelmann is a lecturer at Johannes Gutenberg-University, Mainz, Germany. He received his doctorate from Mannheim University for a thesis that explores the concept of cultural memory in the context of the Old English heroic poem *Beowulf*. His research interests include grammatical variation in English and its determining factors, language and the media, and cultural linguistics as well as theoretical aspects of language change.

Ilaria Fiorentini is a postdoctoral researcher at Insubria University, Italy. Her areas of specialization are discourse markers and language contact situations. She has published articles in Italian and international journals. Her main research interests include sociolinguistics, language acquisition, minority languages, and computer-mediated communication.

Michael Percillier is a postdoctoral researcher at the University of Mannheim, Germany. His areas of specialization include corpus linguistics, World Englishes, literary linguistics, and historical linguistics. His research has covered the comparative study of institutionalized and learner varieties of English in Southeast Asia, the representation of non-standardized varieties of English in literary texts, and the contact effects of Old French on Middle English in the medieval period.

Paulo Quaglio is an associate professor of applied linguistics and TESOL at the State University of New York at Cortland. His research interests include corpus-based text type analysis in general and television dialogue in particular. He is the author of *Television Dialogue: The Sitcom* Friends *vs. Natural Conversation* (2009).

Kay Richardson is professor of communication and media at the University of Liverpool, UK. She has written extensively on television discourse, from the shopping channel to current affairs, documentary, and television drama. With colleagues she has produced books on the history of *World in Action*, a long-running British current affairs series, and on mediated politics beyond the news. She is the author of *Television Dramatic Dialogue: A Sociolinguistic Study* (2010).

Jessie Sams is an associate professor of linguistics at Stephen F. Austin State University in Nacogdoches, Texas. Her primary research interests include the intersection of syntax and semantics, genre studies based on linguistic features, written English quotatives, and constructed languages (conlangs).

Ulrike Stange holds a PhD in English linguistics and is a research assistant at the Department of English and Linguistics at Johannes Gutenberg-University, Mainz, Germany. Her research interests include emotive interjections, translation studies, and dialectal variation in British English. She is the author of *Emotive Interjections in British English: A Corpus-based Study on Variation in Acquisition, Function and Usage* (2016).

Hanna Sveen is an assistant professor of English linguistics at Södertörn University, Sweden. Her research interests include language and gender, corpus linguistics, and stylistics, and she has published several articles on academic writing in relation to supervision and independence. In her current research project she explores the concept of menstruation from a linguistic perspective.

Joe Trotta is an associate professor of English linguistics at the Department of Languages and Literatures, University of Gothenburg, Sweden. His research is best characterized as an interdisciplinary combination of sociolinguistic and grammar theories with elements of media studies and cultural studies. He is also the founder and main coordinator of GotPop, the Popular Culture research profile at the Department of Languages and Literatures, University of Gothenburg.

Index

Italic page number denotes illustration.